CBEST®
Second Edition

CBEST®

Second Edition

Allan Mundsack with Charlotte Doctor

PUBLISHING

New York

This publication is designed to provide accurate and authoritative information in regard to the subject matter covered. It is sold with the understanding that the publisher is not engaged in rendering legal, accounting, or other professional service. If legal advice or other expert assistance is required, the services of a competent professional should be sought.

Editorial Director: Jennifer Farthing
Senior Editor: Ruth Baygell
Production Editor: Samantha Raue
Production Artist: Virginia Byrne
Cover Designer: Carly Schnur

Published by Kaplan Publishing, a division of Kaplan, Inc.
1 Liberty Plaza, 24th floor,
New York, NY 10006

Printed in the United States of America

December 2006
10 9 8 7 6 5 4 3 2

ISBN 13: 978-1-4195-4225-1

Library of Congress Cataloging-in-Publication Data
Mundsack, Allan.
 Kaplan CBEST : California Basic Educational Skills Test / by Allan Mundsack with Charlotte Doctor. -- 2nd ed.
   p. cm.
 Rev. ed. of: CBEST, c2004.
 ISBN-13: 978-1-4195-4225-1
 ISBN-10: 1-4195-4225-7
 1. California Basic Educational Skills Test--Study guides. I. Doctor, Charlotte. II. Mundsack, Allan. CBEST. III. Kaplan, Inc. IV. Title.
 LB3060.33.C34M86 2006
 370.'76--dc22   2006029782

Kaplan Publishing books are available at special quantity discounts to use for sales promotions, employee premiums, or educational purposes. Please email our Special Sales Department to order or for more information at kaplanpublishing@kaplan.com, or write to Kaplan Publishing, 1 Liberty Plaza, 24th floor, New York, NY 10006.

Contents

Section Five: Practice Tests

Section Six: CBEST Resources

About the Authors

Allan Mundsack graduated with the Highest Honors from Wisconsin State University, La Crosse. Since then, he has taught for over 30 years in nine different schools. He has been recognized by *Who's Who Among America's Teachers*, and has contributed his mathematical knowledge to several education books. He currently resides in California.

Charlotte Doctor earned her undergraduate degree from San Diego State University and later received her Masters in English from the University of Kentucky. She is currently teaching at Los Angeles Pierce College, where she has served as Director of the Honors Program and of the PACE program. She lives in California.

Available Online

FOR ANY TEST CHANGES OR LATE-BREAKING DEVELOPMENTS

kaptest.com/publishing

The material in this book is up-to-date at the time of publication. However, the California Commission on Teacher Credentialing may have instituted changes in the test or test-registration process after this book was published. Be sure to carefully read the materials you receive when you register for the test. If there are any important late-breaking developments—or any changes or corrections to the Kaplan test preparation materials in this book—we will post that information online at **kaptest.com/publishing**.

FEEDBACK AND COMMENTS

kaplansurveys.com/books

We'd love to hear your comments and suggestions about this book. We invite you to fill out our online survey form at **kaplansurveys.com/books**. Your feedback is extremely helpful as we continue to develop high-quality resources to meet your needs.

How to Use this Book

Just as you need a plan of attack before starting the test, you need a plan of attack before starting this book. All of the sections in this book are important to your success on the CBEST. The first section contains the basic details of the CBEST and strategies to help you work through the test and to manage stress. This chapter also contains a diagnostic test.

DIAGNOSTIC TEST

The diagnostic test should be taken before you move on to any of the subject sections. A passing score on each of the Mathematics and Reading sections is 13 or more correct. If your score on either section (or both) is lower than 13, you should plan to do the review sections in detail. If you scored reasonably well on the diagnostic test, you can maximize your overall CBEST score by studying the review sections in detail, as well. However, if time is short, choose the sections of the Mathematics and Reading reviews that correspond to the topics you struggled with, and concentrate on those sections.

READING, MATHEMATICS, AND WRITING SECTIONS

The middle three sections are for each of the subjects tested on the CBEST; they are designed to give you a broad review of the different question types and content.

In the Mathematics section, you should read with a pencil in your hand, work through the many examples, do all the practice exercises, and check your solutions against those given. Likewise, in the Reading section, you should practice all of the suggested techniques for improvement in all of your reading skills. The last chapter in this section is a practice set for you to try out your skills. Don't skip this section. The more practice the better. The Writing section offers you plenty review and insight into what the essay graders will be looking for. Be sure to try all of the essay topics at the end, and review the sample essays provided.

It is helpful to establish a timeline to accomplish the review you need so that you have ample time to do the practice CBEST tests in this book. A month of daily two- or three-hour study sessions should be enough time to devote to this task. Be careful that you don't work yourself into a frenzy. The day before the actual CBEST should be free of study. It should be a relaxing, restful day so that you can go to the test site able to do your best work.

PRACTICE TESTS

There are three practice tests in the final section of this book. When it is time to take the first test, find four hours of uninterrupted time so you can work. Set up actual test-taking conditions as closely as possible—no TV, no radio, and no CDs—and try to complete the test in one sitting. Use a timer. Don't forget to use the strategies in chapter 2, and be sure to answer every question. Lucky guesses count as correct answers.

After completing the first practice test, check your answers, and read the answer explanations. In the explanations you will find many hints and suggestions for arriving at the correct answers in the most efficient way, so don't skip them.

Although the actual CBEST is scaled according to difficulty with a total score of 123 as passing, you should consider that a score higher than 50% on each section is passing for the tests in this book (26 or more correct on both the Mathematics and Reading sections). You can use the information in chapter 12 to score your essay. Be fair. It might be helpful to have a friend score the essay for you. After you have scored your Practice Test and read the answer explanations, go back to the review sections to help you understand where mistakes were made.

On another day, repeat the test-taking conditions, and do Practice Test Two. Grade it, and analyze the results as you did for Practice Test One. You should see an improvement, but there will be room to enhance your score. Study the mistakes and explanations, and on another day (several days before the actual test), do Practice Test Three. Do any extra reviewing in the last few days before the test, but don't overdo it.

CBEST RESOURCES

At the back of this book, you will find two resources to assist your preparation for the test: word roots and vocabulary words. We suggest you try to build these resources into your study plan whenever possible to further improve your score.

With the preparation outlined in this book, you should achieve your optimum score on the CBEST.

Let's get started!

| SECTION ONE |

Introduction

Chapter One: **Overview of the Test**

WHAT IS THE CBEST?

To give prospective teachers an opportunity to demonstrate basic skills in reading, writing, and mathematics, the state of California developed the California Basic Educational Skills Test (CBEST). It is required in both California and Oregon but may be used in other locations. Applicants should contact the state's credentialing office to determine whether or not they are required to pass the CBEST. The CBEST tests only basic skills and not the ability to teach these subjects or any subject. Passing the CBEST does not take the place of any other requirement for a credential.

The CBEST is administered six times a year (every other month starting in February), and it may be retaken as many times as necessary in order to pass. There is a $41 fee required each time the test is taken. The three separate parts of the test may be taken individually or together. If you pass only one portion of the test and not the other two, you may choose to take only the two failed parts at the next attempt, or you may decide to take the entire test again in order to boost your overall score on the test. Once all sections have been passed, the top scores, regardless of when they were taken, will be added together for your total score. The test is always scheduled for a four-hour period, during which time you may work on any or all of the sections of the test. Individual sections, reading, math, and writing, are not timed separately.

A passing score on the CBEST is 123 points. The passing score for each section is 41 points. The points are scaled for each test to reflect varying levels of difficulty so that the passing score is always 41. It is possible to pass the CBEST with a section score as low as 37 as long as the total for all three parts is 123 or more. However, scoring less than 37 on any section means failing the CBEST as a whole, no matter how high the total score is. If you repeat the test, the highest score for any repeated part is always the one that is counted.

Applicants can view, print, or request a *Registration Bulletin* at the CBEST website: cbest.nesinc.com. When you receive the Bulletin, READ IT. The Bulletin will contain specific up-to-date information that you will need for registration.

After you have read and studied this book and taken and scored the practice tests, you will be ready to do well on the CBEST.

FORMAT

The CBEST is made up of three sections. Both the Reading and Mathematics sections are made up entirely of multiple-choice questions. There are 50 questions in each section.

The Reading section assesses your ability to understand concepts and content necessary for educating students and to use basic reading skills to communicate information. The questions will be drawn from different subject areas, including the arts, social sciences, physical science, and humanities. No outside knowledge will be required because all of the questions will be accompanied by a passage with the necessary information needed to answer the question.

The Mathematics section will test your skills in basic math concepts including estimation and measurement, statistical principles, computation, and graphical relationships. You will be asked to solve equations, most of which will be in the form of a word problem. You should be familiar with the basic mathematical elements of operations and terms.

The Writing section requires you to write two essays. These essays will be used to test your knowledge of grammar, sentence structure and organization, and your ability to write about a specific topic. One of the essays will direct you to analyze a given scenario or statement, and the other essay will direct you to write about a personal experience. Your essays will be scored and given a diagnostic evaluation to help you develop your writing skills in the event you fail this section.

SCORING

All of the sections will be scored using a raw score and a scaled score. For the Reading and Mathematics sections, the number of correct answers will equal your raw score. There is no penalty for incorrect answers. The raw scores are then converted into scaled scores ranging from 20 to 80 for each section.

The essays for the Writing section are scored by trained educators in the California or Oregon area. Two scorers are assigned to each essay and will assign a score from 1 to 4. The four scores are then added together to give a raw score of 4 to 16. That raw score is what will be converted into the scaled score of 20 to 80 that will make up your total with the scores from the other two sections. You need a total score of 123 to pass the CBEST.

Now that you know about the fundamentals of the test, move on to chapter 2 where you will learn strategies for the test and for managing stress.

Chapter Two: **Strategies to Prepare for the Test**

Many successful test-takers often consider test taking a game or competition. Their attitude is not fearful or timid. They ask themselves, "Can I beat the test?" or "How well can I do?" not "Will I pass?" When they enter the testing room, they feel in charge, capable, and up to the challenge.

The secret to success on any test is preparation. Knowing what to expect on a test not only allows the test taker to better prepare for topics and skills that need improvement, but it also eases the severe anxiety that is experienced by too many people. The following 10 specific strategies will help you maximize your score on the CBEST, which will give you the confidence you need when you walk into the testing room. We also provide tips to help you manage your stress in the days before and during the test.

KAPLAN'S TOP 10 TEST-TAKING STRATEGIES

Strategies 1–3: Stress Management Techniques for Before the Test

Strategy 1. Familiarize Yourself with the Test

It is a big mistake to go into any exam cold. Most exams produce anxiety, but because the CBEST has a direct bearing on your future employment, it probably produces more anxiety than other tests. If you do not prepare for the CBEST in advance, your anxiety level will be much higher than necessary, and your performance will not be as good as it could be.

The basic skills tested by the CBEST are well known. Each test covers the same material, but each test has different questions. The purpose of this book is to review the basic skills needed to perform well on the test and to present sample questions in a test-like format so that test takers can be as comfortable as possible on test day. There are special techniques that will help you to answer some questions efficiently; it is better to practice these techniques in advance to have the best possible chance of performing well.

Spending time with this book will also give you an idea of what topics you will need to review and the topics that will not appear on the test and do not have to be reviewed. Begin about a month before the test date, and allot about two hours each day for test preparation. A schedule such as this should allow enough time for you to review and practice adequately for the test. The more you feel prepared, the lower your anxiety level will be.

Strategy 2. Practice

Reading about Olympic swimmers does not make a person a swimmer. Reading books about baseball does not mean you can play baseball. Studying the acoustics of the violin does not make one a concert violinist. Each of these skills requires practice, practice, and more practice. To begin any skill, there are sets of basic fundamentals that must be accomplished at some level. Baseball requires the basic skills of running, throwing, catching, and hitting. After you have a certain level of ability in each of these skills, then you can play baseball— at an amateur level. Even after a lot of practice, most people don't play baseball at or near the collegiate or professional level. The same generalization can be made about swimmers and violinists. Test taking is another skill that requires practice to do well. The lesson is to practice the skills presented in this book so that you can do your best on the CBEST.

The best way to use this book is to review all of the preliminary material first until you feel comfortable with each topic. Remember the CBEST covers *basic* skills—skills that you certainly have studied in some math or English class but perhaps don't remember adequately. This book is not meant to be a textbook but, rather, a review aid. The topics included in this book are for review only, and the diagnostic test will help you determine the topics that need your further attention or particular concentration.

After you have satisfied yourself that you understand the basics, try one of the practice CBEST tests. Try to give yourself actual test-like conditions as much as possible. For instance:

- Time yourself.
- Do an entire test in one sitting (with maybe one or two bathroom breaks).
- Don't even look at the questions until you are ready to begin the practice test.
- Check your answers with the answer keys, and read all of the solutions, even for the questions you answered correctly. Many hints for answering the questions efficiently are given in the solutions.

Because the practice tests in this book were not scaled for difficulty, you may assume 26 or more correct answers to be a passing score on the reading and mathematics sections.

Strategy 3. The Days Before the Test

Be sure that you know where the test site is. You may want to make a test run a day or two early to be sure you can find it easily and to check out parking. Remember that traffic may be slower on the day of your test.

The best plan is that all of your practice activities will be completed so that the evening before the test is free for relaxation. Treat yourself well, watch a good movie, read a good book, go for a short walk, but don't study for the CBEST. Last minute study—cramming—is counterproductive. It creates anxiety and makes it difficult to sleep as well as you should. Get a good night's sleep by going to bed at approximately the usual time, and use an alarm to get up in plenty of time to eat your usual breakfast. (If you are in the habit of not eating breakfast, this one time you must eat something. Four hours of testing requires energy.) Take care of the usual bodily functions. If you are not a coffee drinker, don't drink coffee. If you are a coffee drinker, don't overdo it. Excessive trips to the bathroom during the test waste a lot of time, and too much caffeine will make you jumpy.

Dress comfortably with layers that can accommodate various temperatures that may occur in the testing room. Pack some hard candy or other snacks for emergencies, but it is important to be careful not to disrupt other test takers with noisy wrappers or cracking candy. If you are easily distracted, consider packing some earplugs.

During the evening before the test, assemble the items to take with you, including:

- Admission ticket
- Photo ID
- Second ID if required
- Several No. 2 pencils. The answer forms require No. 2 pencils.
- Twist pencil sharpener. Not all test rooms have a pencil sharpener, and the usual crank sharpener is noisy and disruptive.
- Good eraser. If mistakes on the answer form are not erased cleanly, the grading machine may read them incorrectly.
- A watch without a calculator or an alarm or buzzer of any kind.

You will not be allowed to use a calculator, a cell phone, or any other communication device, books, notes, or scratch paper. Any calculation or other scratch work can be done in the test booklet.

Strategies 4–10: During the Test

Strategy 4. Pace Yourself

Test-takers usually begin at the beginning and plow on through a test, but it is better to have a strategy. If you know that your strength is mathematics, for example, do that section first.

Keep an eye on the time so that at least one hour and twenty minutes is allotted to the writing portion. If you find a particularly difficult or time-consuming question, don't become frustrated. Frustration only serves to increase anxiety, and it decreases the ability to think clearly. It is better to either temporarily skip the question or to guess and move on. Often an answer will come to you easily on the second reading—your brain may have been at work on the question subconsciously while you worked on other questions.

No one expects a perfect score on the CBEST, but you can maximize you score by answering all of the easy questions first. One of the unstated goals of the CBEST is to reward those who can stay composed under pressure. Don't get flustered. Work at a steady pace, but don't rush. Use your watch to check the time occasionally. As you do the practice tests, use these techniques so that they will be second nature during the actual CBEST.

Strategy 5. Prioritize the Questions

As we said earlier, if you know your strong suit is mathematics, do that part of the test first. If reading is easier than math, then do the reading part first. Doing the easier questions first will give you an opportunity to feel comfortable with the test, and because you will undoubtedly answer the easier questions in less time than the others, you will gain time to spend on the more difficult (for you) part of the test.

KAPLAN

As you read a question, decide in a flash whether you can answer the question or not. If you understand it and think you can answer it easily, do it. If it looks like it will slow you down, circle the question number in your booklet and on your answer sheet and move on. You can come back later to the circled question numbers. If a circled question seems impossible for you, try to eliminate unlikely answers, and guess. Don't waste time struggling with an impossible task. If you believe that you can answer a question but think it will take too much time, you might consider another approach to the solution. For example, if you have a fraction that requires multiplication in the numerator and denominator, try to cancel out common factors instead of performing all of the operations. It might only save you a few moments, but those are moments you can put to good use.

None of the problems on the CBEST are designed to take a lot of time. If you believe you can answer one later, put a check beside the circle and leave it for the end. If you don't find the time to return to such a problem, don't forget to guess before you hand in the answer sheet. Every question should have an answer, even if you have to guess. Don't leave blanks!

The purpose of prioritizing questions is to maximize your use of time. Remember that the easy questions count the same as the hard questions, and you don't get extra points for a struggle. Do all of the easy questions first.

Strategy 6. Read and Think

Although you are trying to move through the test at an efficient and measured pace, you will do better if you read each question carefully and then see if you know the answer or speculate on what the answer might be before you look at the choices. You may profit by reading the stem a second time to make certain you haven't misread a word or misunderstood what is being asked. It is easier to spot the correct answer if you have some idea of what you are looking for. If your answer is found among the choices, mark your answer sheet and move on.

Strategy 7. Consider All Options

On many questions, there will be more than one attractive answer, but you are looking for the best answer. You must read all of the choices before choosing your answer. Although the first response may be correct, the third response may be the *best* choice.

However, be careful not to read too much into the question. Determine the answer from the question stem and nothing else.

Strategy 8. Eliminate Obviously Wrong Answers

Sometimes the correct answer doesn't leap out at you on the first reading of a question. In that case, circle the number and move on. Then come back later and confront the question for a second time. If you are able to eliminate one or two answers as impossible or very unlikely, you can greatly improve your chances of guessing the answer successfully. If you can narrow the choices to two reasonable answers, read the question again. There may be a key word or other hint that will allow you to choose the correct answer. Underlining key words and phrases, drawing a line through the eliminated choices, and writing anything in the test booklet is permitted and recommended.

Strategy 9. Answer Every Question

There is no penalty for wrong answers. On some tests, a fraction of the number of incorrect answers is subtracted from the number of correct answers; in that case, it is possible to end up with a negative score. The CBEST is not like that. There is no penalty for incorrect answers. Thus, it is foolish not to answer every question, even if you guess. Lucky guesses are counted as correct answers.

Strategy 10. Be Careful Marking Your Answer Sheet

You could have the clearest insight into a question, with carefully reasoned logic, and still not get credit for a correct answer if you mark the answer in the wrong place on the answer sheet. To minimize the possibility of marking answers incorrectly, we suggest not marking the answer sheet after every question. Mark answers in the test booklet, and transfer them to the answer sheet in groups of five. This technique will diminish the chance of marking the answers in the wrong spaces. If time is running out, you may not have time to mark a whole group of answers. If there are only a few minutes left, mark answers one-by-one.

Carefully and completely fill in the circle or oval on the answer sheet that corresponds to the answer for each question. If you skip a question, circle it in your booklet and on your answer sheet. This is where the marking errors typically occur. Be sure to erase completely any stray marks after you answer the questions. The scoring machine may misinterpret marks that are not completely erased. If you change an answer, be extra careful to erase the old answer. Incompletely erased marks are troublesome for scoring machines.

STRESS MANAGEMENT

So you've done everything we suggested to prepare for the CBEST, and as the big day approaches, you still find yourself overwhelmed by stress. You can't sleep; your last lunch sits like a rock in your stomach; you can't concentrate. What to do?

Don't panic. If you freak out, all is lost. We have some suggestions to control the last minute urge to scream. As we've said before, it's the sense of not being in control that leads to feelings of helplessness and despair. Having some concrete things to take control will help to reduce your stress. In this chapter, we show you how to reduce stress to a manageable level in the days leading up to the test as well as on test day. Don't misunderstand; some stress is a good thing. It gives you the motivation and adrenaline to perform at a high level of ability. Athletes depend on the adrenaline rush to push their bodies to excel. Too much stress causes headaches, stomachaches, and a lack of concentration, and the body reacts by shutting down, but some stress is actually helpful. So the title of this section is not *Stress Elimination* but rather *Stress Management.*

Quick Tips for the Days Just Before the CBEST

As test day approaches, you may find your anxiety on the rise. Don't worry. If you have followed our advice so far, you are in good shape to take the CBEST and do well. The following suggestions will help to calm the pretest jitters.

- The best test takers do less and less preparation as the test approaches. Everything you need to know is in your memory, and you just need to fine-tune your test-taking skills. It is best to feel relaxed and ready on the day of the test. So taper off; reward yourself for a job well done. During the day before test, put this book away so you can enjoy a relaxing evening after having assembled all of the materials you need to take with you to the test.

- Work on training yourself to think positively. Replace worrisome thoughts like, "I wonder if I'll pass" with, "I can do this." Replace "They're forcing me to take this test" with "This will be an opportunity to show that I have the skills." Replace "I'm scared" with "I'm eager to show what I can do." Working on positive visualizations can create a positive reality. It's a skill worth practicing.

- Have your act together well in advance of test day. Know what you will wear (remember layers of clothing); have the admission ticket, ID, pencils, eraser, and some candy (quiet wrappers, please). Don't take things that you know are not allowed. Know where the test will be held, the easiest and quickest way to get there, where to park, and how to enter the building. Mismanaging details can derail your day. Is there gas in the car? Do I know the directions to the site?

- Go to the testing room a few days early. Sit in the room for a while. Bring some practice material with you, and do it as you sit there. In this case, familiarity doesn't breed contempt; it generates comfort and confidence.

- Don't do any practice on the day before the test. Use the day to treat your physical body well. Don't dwell on the upcoming test—put it out of your mind. Go to a movie, take an easy and pleasant hike, or just relax. Don't eat a lot of junk food or sugar, and, of course, get a good night's sleep. Don't go to bed too early. It's hard to fall asleep earlier than usual, and you don't want to lie awake staring at the ceiling and worrying about the test.

Coping with Stress During the Test

The instant of greatest stress will be the moment the proctor hands you the test. Fear not—you're ready. But just in case, we have some methods to cope with stress during the test.

- Do the part of the test in which you have greatest confidence first. Don't let yourself get bogged down. The goal is not perfection; just the best possible score. Keep moving. The best test takers skip difficult questions and mark them to return later. This strategy buys time and builds confidence to handle the more difficult questions later.

- Don't be distracted if other people seem to be working faster or at a feverish pace. CBEST does not give extra points for appearing to be busy or finishing early. You have your game plan. Remember the 10 strategy points. Spend your time reading the questions, thinking through your answers, and being careful with the answer sheet. Steadiness will lead to better results.

- *Keep breathing.* Anxious people tend to hold their breath without realizing it. Make a conscious effort to pause regularly to breath deeply. Improper breathing can cause anxiety, headaches, and a lack of concentration.

- If you find your concentration waning, some isometric exercises may help. Try this: Put your palms together and press firmly for a few seconds. Feel the tension in your muscles through your palms, wrists, forearms, and into your biceps and shoulders. Quickly release the pressure. You can feel the tension leave as you let the muscles relax. Now get back to work.

- Another relaxation technique is to slowly rotate your head from side to side, turning your head and eyes to look as far over your shoulder as you can. Feel the muscles contract on one side and relax on the other side as you rotate your head. Repeat this five times in each direction.

- When you first receive the test, take several slow, deep breaths, exhaling slowly while visualizing yourself doing well on the test. Do not be alarmed by a little anxiety—it's normal. Try to remain calm during the test. Stop periodically; breathe deeply to help you relax. This is the day you've been preparing for. Follow your test plan, and do the best you can.

With what you will learn in this book, you will be well prepared for the CBEST. You have reviewed the pertinent information needed to answer the questions. You have a plan to get you to the test site prepared and on time. You have planned a test-taking strategy that will allow you to move confidently through the questions. You have some methods to alleviate the stress that besets all of us under conditions like this. You are going to get a great score.

Chapter Three: **Diagnostic Test**

Questions 1–3

When movie theater admissions decline, film executives seek a cause. _____ some analysts think the fare offered does not attract the infrequent moviegoer, causing ticket sales to drop off, _____ suggest that the increased use of cell phones and the Internet, which amplify the effects of word of mouth opinions about how good a movie is, are responsible. Word of mouth, however, can also work in favor of a good film, increasing its audience.

A third possibility that entertainment executives do not always mention is the increase in ticket prices as a possible contributor to declining ticket sales.

1. The selection above implies that the cause of declining movie attendance may be due to

    (A) increases in ticket prices

    (B) increased use of cell phone and the Internet

    (C) several factors

    (D) older people do not attend many movies

    (E) the choice of films being shown

2. The word *fare* as used in this selection means

    (A) equal selection

    (B) money paid for admission

    (C) result

    (D) selection of films presented

    (E) impartial

3. Which words or phrases, if inserted *in order* into the blanks in the passage, would help the reader understand the sequence of the writer's ideas?

    (A) Although; As a result

    (B) While; Others

    (C) Because; Meanwhile

    (D) Not only; But also

    (E) Since; Finally

Questions 4–6

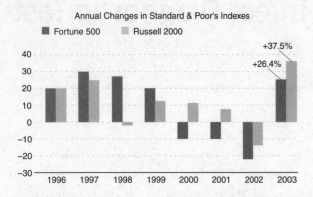

Annual Changes in Standard & Poor's Indexes

The graph represents the comparative performance of stocks of Fortune 500 companies (large companies) and Russell 2000 (small) companies over 8 years.

4. The graph shows that the best performance of stocks in Fortune 500 companies was in

    (A) 2003
    (B) 1997
    (C) 2002
    (D) 1998
    (E) 1996

5. The best performance of Fortune 500 companies over the performance of Russell 2000 companies was in

    (A) 2002
    (B) 1997
    (C) 1999
    (D) 1998
    (E) 2003

6. The investor who wishes to make the most profit should have bought

    (A) the small company index in 2002
    (B) the large company index in 1996
    (C) the small company index in 1998
    (D) the Fortune 500 index in 2002
    (E) the Fortune 500 index in 1997

Questions 7–9

Teaching requires more than knowing subject matter. The difference in children's learning styles have been discussed in education for many years. One theory divides learning styles into visual, auditory, and kinesthetic. ___

_____

_____.

Teachers also learn best according to their preferred styles. In order to be most effective, teachers must take into account mastery of the subject matter and an understanding of the unique learning styles of their students and then plan lessons and teaching strategies that take those and other factors into account.

7. The author's main point is that in teaching

    (A) knowing subject matter is not enough
    (B) there are three different learning styles
    (C) each student is unique
    (D) effectiveness requires knowledge and mastery of diverse and sometimes complex factors
    (E) teachers have different learning styles

8. The term *kinesthetic* refers to learning by

    (A) reading and looking at pictures
    (B) using energy resulting from bodily motion
    (C) perceiving through nerve end organs in muscles, tendons, and joints
    (D) listening carefully and paying attention
    (E) participating in games

9. Which of the following sentences would fit best in place of the blank lines?

    (A) There is more to being a good teacher than simply knowing subject matter.
    (B) Many teachers don't understand how they, themselves, learn.
    (C) Teaching strategies are a way to incorporate activities that will help students learn, regardless of their learning styles.
    (D) Students, however, are not familiar with learning styles.
    (E) History, math, English, and geography all require special study approaches.

Questions 10–12

Most sites that evidence early habitation by humans in the Americas date from approximately 12,000 to 15,000 years ago. A recent find in Siberia dates to 30,000 years ago and indicates that tool-using humans lived in the Arctic much earlier than had been previously thought. Scientists speculate that this may indicate that early man crossed the Bering bridge to the Americas significantly earlier than had been previously postulated. Tools at the site are similar to those discovered near Clovis, New Mexico, but made 15,000 years earlier. Some scientists think the Siberians were ancestors of the Clovis people. Other experts believe the Siberian tools are quite different from those of the Clovis people. Still others think the design of tools could change immeasurably over 15,000 years.

10. The writer uses which of the following rhetorical modes in this selection?

    (A) definition

    (B) division and classification

    (C) analogy

    (D) comparison and contrast

    (E) cause and effect

11. The article demonstrates clearly that

    (A) early man lived in the Americas 30,000 years ago

    (B) the Clovis people made the same tools as early Siberian man

    (C) scientists disagree as to the lineage of the Clovis people based on this find

    (D) the tools of early Siberian and Clovis people were identical

    (E) it is impossible to know whether ancestors of Clovis people lived in Siberia

12. As used in the selection, the term *postulate* means

    (A) the way things stand

    (B) postglacial

    (C) arising after one's death

    (D) to assign a later date than the current date

    (E) to assume without proof to be true

Questions 13–15

[1]The long war against smoking is still being waged in America. [2]More than 10 years ago restrictions on smoking in public began to be passed across the country in cities like Los Angeles and San Francisco and states like Vermont, Maryland, and Washington. [3]Now even those old bastions of individualism and liberty, New York City and Washington, D.C., are falling under the onslaught of legislation that purports to be for our own protection. [4]Have our legislators gone overboard? [5]In 1950, we could ride in cars without seatbelts or infant seats, and motorcyclists were not required to wear helmets. [6]Today, even three year olds on tricycles wear helmets, skateboarders and cyclists are required to wear helmets, and we are told where and when we can and can't smoke. [7]Man has a right to live a free and unfettered life, even if it kills him. [8]Trying to legislate behavior, whether it is sexual behavior in the privacy of your own home or prohibition against purchasing and consuming alcohol, has not been successful in America, much to the disappointment of any remaining Puritans or members of the WCTU. [9]It is time to relax all these restrictive laws. [10]People should have a right to certain liberties and to live a life that is free and unfettered by unreasonable laws. [11]Let us smoke where we want to, drive without seat belts, and bike without helmets. [12]After all, we live in a nation that believes in liberty for all.

13. Which of the numbered sentences best expresses an opinion rather than a fact?

    (A) 2

    (B) 5

    (C) 6

    (D) 7

    (E) 8

14. This passage is primarily an argument

    (A) against wearing seat belts and helmets

    (B) for smoking anywhere one wishes

    (C) against certain social restrictions

    (D) for doing away with laws that restrict certain behaviors

    (E) for individual liberty

15. The most effective argument in opposition to this passage would include

    (A) individual examples

    (B) statistics on death rates of smokers and unprotected riders and drivers

    (C) interviews with physicians and celebrities

    (D) statistics on the decline of smoking among teenagers

    (E) opinions of famous people

Questions 16–18

The following graph shows membership in a health club that substantially raised membership fees in 1992. Fees were lowered substantially in 2 of the following 10 years.

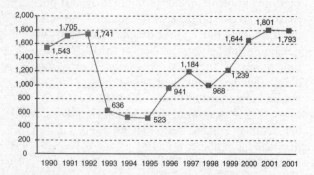

16. The recovery in membership numbers indicates that the largest drop in fees probably occurred in

    (A) 1993

    (B) 1994

    (C) 1995

    (D) 1996

    (E) 1997

17. Because membership had still not recovered in 1997, fees were lowered again. The chart suggests that fees were lowered again in

    (A) 1997

    (B) 1998

    (C) 1999

    (D) 2000

    (E) 2001

18. How many years did it take for membership levels to be recovered?

    (A) 3 years

    (B) 5 years

    (C) 7 years

    (D) 9 years

    (E) 10 years

Questions 19–21

People who behave as other people do are called conformists. Teenagers are often good examples of conformists. They want to belong to a group, and so they dress in a way that will help them fit in. They listen to the same music and use the same slang as their friends. Even if they are trying to rebel against authority, they are also conforming. Sometimes conformity is good and wise, like getting in at the end of the line at the grocery store rather than crowding or cutting in line or like wearing seat belts when we drive to protect ourselves in case of an accident. These choices to conform help keep us out of trouble. _____

_____

_____

Some people, however, never think they have a choice. They conform mindlessly, sleepwalking through life. In contrast to the conformist who decides whether to conform or not, these people usually go along with the crowd rather than draw attention to themselves. They are the sheep in our society, easily herded. They are often shy or lazy, and when asked about their conformity will say, "I just don't want to make waves."

19. The author of this passage is contrasting

    (A) teenagers and ordinary conformists

    (B) people who conform by choice or mindlessly

    (C) lazy conformists and wise conformists

    (D) nonconformists and conformists

    (E) conformists and rebels

20. Which of the following sentences would fit best in place of the blank lines?

    (A) Not everyone thinks to make these choices.

    (B) They are wise choices because they protect us from possible danger and other people's wrath.

    (C) Children need to be taught to make these choices for their own protection.

    (D) The difference between adults and children lies in an ability to choose wisely.

    (E) Daredevils, like Evil Knievel, can make a career out of taunting consequences.

21. The author's reference to sheep is

    (A) an opinion

    (B) an example

    (C) a simile

    (D) a personification

    (E) a metaphor

22. The topic sentences of the two paragraphs are

    (A) 3 and 4

    (B) 3 and 5

    (C) 2 and 6

    (D) 1 and 4

    (E) 1 and 5

23. The best title for this passage might be

    (A) "Shoes and Spaghetti"

    (B) "How to Do a How-To Speech"

    (C) "Steps to a Good Demonstration Speech"

    (D) "First Things First"

    (E) "Demonstration Speeches for Beginners"

24. The purpose of this selection is to

    (A) compare an unfamiliar with a familiar thing

    (B) explain a process

    (C) define a concept

    (D) identify causes of a good speech

    (E) describe a good speech

25. According to the author, the second step in preparing a demonstration speech is

    (A) choosing a good topic

    (B) choosing something simple

    (C) make a list

    (D) don't leave anything out

    (E) practice several times

Questions 22–25

[1]When preparing a demonstration speech, first choose a topic. [2]"How to tie your shoes" or "How to make spaghetti" are good topics. [3]You should choose something simple to demonstrate because you must break the instructions down into individual steps. [4]A topic that is too complex will take too long and may become confusing.

[5]Once you have chosen your topic, you should make a list of each step you are going to explain in order. [6]Be sure you don't leave anything out. [7]Sometimes, as in tying your shoes, you will have to practice each step several times in order to write down every single detail of the process. [8]That can be very time consuming.

Math Section

Directions: Each of the questions in this test is followed by five suggested answers. Select the one that is best in each case.

26. The home center has a roll of fencing with 200 feet on the roll. The garden department wants to set aside a rectangular area that is 4 feet 8 inches by 10 feet 2 inches. How many feet of fencing are left on the roll after the garden area is fenced?

    (A) 29 feet 8 inches

    (B) 140 feet 8 inches

    (C) 170 feet 4 inches

    (D) 185 feet 2 inches

    (E) 229 feet 8 inches

27. Which of the following numbers is **NOT** between 0.24 and 0.31?

    (A) 29%

    (B) 0.23

    (C) $\frac{1}{4}$

    (D) $\frac{3}{10}$

    (E) $\frac{13}{50}$

28. Ricardo's scores on the first three exams in his algebra class were 81, 75, and 78. What is the minimum score on the fourth exam so that his mean score for the four exams is 80 or more?

    (A) 80

    (B) 78

    (C) 100

    (D) 86

    (E) The mean of the four scores could not be 80 or more.

29. The distances above or below sea level of five locations in the Caribbean Sea are recorded to the nearest foot.

Location	V	W	X	Y	Z
Distance above sea level	215	319	−52	5	−37

    What is the vertical distance in feet between locations V and X?

    (A) 267

    (B) −267

    (C) 15

    (D) 163

    (E) −163

30. Mrs. Sanchez's class has G girls and B boys. What is the ratio of girls to the total number of students in her class?

    (A) $\frac{G}{B}$

    (B) $\frac{B}{G}$

    (C) $\frac{B+G}{G}$

    (D) $\frac{G}{B+G}$

    (E) $\frac{G-B}{G+B}$

31. What is the value of $x^2 - xy$ when $x = -2$ and $y = -3$?

    (A) −1

    (B) 10

    (C) −10

    (D) 2

    (E) −2

32. A contractor wants to order concrete for a wall that is 24 feet long, 10 feet high, and 9 inches thick. How many cubic yards of concrete should she order?

    (A) $26\frac{2}{3}$

    (B) $6\frac{2}{3}$

    (C) 180

    (D) 240

    (E) 2,160

33. The shadow of a tree that is standing vertically is 60 feet long. At the same time and at the same location a 5-foot stick held vertically on the ground casts a shadow that is 4 feet long. What is the height of the tree?

    (A) 15 feet

    (B) 48 feet

    (C) 60 feet

    (D) 75 feet

    (E) 300 feet

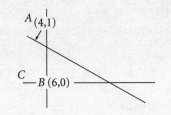

34. Line $\overleftrightarrow{AB}$ passes through B (6,0) and A (4,1). What is the area in square units of $\triangle ABC$?

    (A) 9

    (B) 18

    (C) 24

    (D) 12

    (E) The area cannot be determined from the information given.

35. In Mrs. Sturm's class there are 12 boys and 15 girls. If one student is chosen from this class at random, what is the probability that the selected student is a girl?

    (A) $\frac{1}{5}$

    (B) $\frac{4}{9}$

    (C) $\frac{5}{9}$

    (D) $\frac{4}{5}$

    (E) $\frac{9}{5}$

36. The scores and percentile ranks of four students are recorded for a standardized test.

Student	Score	Percentile rank
Corey	60	83
Theo	52	78
Elizabeth	75	92
Lucy	62	85

    Which of the following statements can you conclude to be true regarding these students?

    (A) Eighty-three students who took the test scored lower than Corey.

    (B) Theo got 78% of the questions correct on the test.

    (C) Elizabeth's score, 75, is better than 92% of the students who took the test.

    (D) Lucy got 2% more of the questions on the test correct than Corey did.

    (E) No one got all of the questions on the test correct.

37. Which of the following numbers is (are) prime?

    I. 7
    II. 73
    III. 123
    IV. 51

    (A) All of these numbers are prime.

    (B) Only I.

    (C) Only II.

    (D) I, II, and IV.

    (E) Only I and II.

38. What number is the square of 25?

    (A) 5 and –5

    (B) 5 only

    (C) 50

    (D) 625

    (E) 100

39. What is the solution set of the following equation?

    $7 - (3x - 2) = 12$

    (A) $\{1\}$

    (B) $\{-1\}$

    (C) $\{7\}$

    (D) $\{-7\}$

    (E) $\left\{\dfrac{-7}{3}\right\}$

40. To prepare for the beginning of the semester, Sara bought the following items:

    | 1 English anthology | $45.25 |
    | 1 Math textbook | $78.40 |
    | 3 Notebooks | $4.10 each |
    | 2 Highlighters | $1.50 each |
    | 5 Pens | $2.10 each |

    How much change should Sara get if she pays with two hundred-dollar bills? Disregard any sales tax.

    (A) $50.55

    (B) $149.45

    (C) $131.35

    (D) $68.65

    (E) None of these.

41. While on a diet to lose weight, Stan's weight went from 180 to 162 pounds. What is the percent decrease in Stan's weight?

    (A) 90%

    (B) 10%

    (C) 18%

    (D) 110%

    (E) $1\dfrac{1}{9}\%$

42. The statement "Not all prime numbers are odd" means the same as which of the following statements?

    (A) The number 2 is not an odd number.

    (B) The number 2 is an even number.

    (C) More than one prime number is even.

    (D) At least one prime number is not odd.

    (E) There may be a very large even prime number.

43. The San Diego Zoo has 4,235 mammal specimens, and the Los Angeles Zoo has 3,310 mammal specimens. Approximately how many more mammal specimens are in the San Diego Zoo than in the Los Angeles Zoo?

    (A) 200
    (B) 7,545
    (C) 8,000
    (D) 2,000
    (E) 1,000

44. One worker can assemble three desks for display in 3 hours and 45 minutes. At this rate, how long would it take this worker to assemble five desks?

    (A) 1 hour 15 minutes
    (B) 8 hours 45 minutes
    (C) 6 hours 15 minutes
    (D) 18 hours 45 minutes
    (E) 4 hours

45. On the first five algebra tests Kevin's scores are 94, 80, 78, 83, and 90. What is his median score?

    (A) 85
    (B) 78
    (C) 83
    (D) 80
    (E) None of these.

46. Which of the following equations may be used to solve this problem?

    One more than twice a certain number is the same as five less than three times the same number. Find the number.

    (A) $2x + 1 = 3x - 5$
    (B) $2(x + 1) = 3(x - 5)$
    (C) $1 + 2x = 5 - 3x$
    (D) $2x - 5 = 3x + 1$
    (E) $5 - 2x = 1 + 3x$

47. How many different amounts of money can be formed by choosing at least one coin from among one penny, one nickel, and one dime?

    (A) 3
    (B) 4
    (C) 5
    (D) 6
    (E) 7

48. Which of the following is equal to $(3x - 5)(2x + 1)$?

    (A) $6x^2 - 7x - 5$
    (B) $6x^2 + 7x - 5$
    (C) $6x^2 - 10x - 5$
    (D) $6x^2 - 5$
    (E) $6x^2 + 5$

49. Which of the following sets of three numbers could not be the measures of the three sides of a triangle?

    (A) $\{1, 2, 2\}$
    (B) $\{2, 5, 10\}$
    (C) $\{\frac{1}{2}, \frac{1}{3}, \frac{1}{5}\}$
    (D) $\{3, 4, 5\}$
    (E) $\{1, 3, 3\}$

50. What additional information would allow you to solve the following problem?

    A square of largest possible area is cut from a piece of cardboard in the shape of a rectangle whose length is more than its width. What is the area of the square?

        I. The thickness of the cardboard
        II. The length of the rectangle
        III. The width of the rectangle

    (A) I only
    (B) II only
    (C) I and II only
    (D) III only
    (E) None of these.

Writing Section

Directions: The Writing section contains an essay topic. Be sure you write about the given topic. Essays on topics of your choosing will not be acceptable. Your written responses must be your work, must be in your own words, and must not be plagiarized from some other work.

This topic is designed to give you an opportunity to demonstrate your skills in writing effectively. Spend some time considering the topic and organizing your ideas before you start. For the essay, be sure to address all parts of the topic, support generalizations with examples, and use multiple paragraphs.

You may use any space provided in the test booklet to write notes or to prepare an outline or rough draft. However, your score will be based solely on the version written in the space provided in your answer document. Please write as neatly and legibly as possible. To ensure that you have enough space for your essay, do not skip lines, write in large print, or leave large margins.

TOPIC

In a letter to John Adams, Thomas Jefferson wrote, "When we have lived our generation out, we should not wish to encroach on another. I like the dreams of the future better than the history of the past." Do you agree with Jefferson's conclusion, or disagree? Support your opinion with one or more specific examples.

_____

_____

_____

_____

_____

_____

_____

_____

_____

_____

_____

Diagnostic Test: **Answer Key**

READING SECTION	MATH SECTION	WRITING SECTION
1. C	26. C	See Sample Essay on page 33.
2. D	27. B	
3. B	28. D	
4. B	29. A	
5. D	30. D	
6. A	31. E	
7. D	32. B	
8. C	33. D	
9. C	34. E	
10. D	35. C	
11. C	36. C	
12. E	37. E	
13. D	38. D	
14. E	39. B	
15. B	40. A	
16. C	41. B	
17. B	42. D	
18. D	43. E	
19. B	44. C	
20. B	45. C	
21. E	46. A	
22. E	47. E	
23. B	48. A	
24. B	49. B	
25. C	50. D	

Answers and Explanations

READING SECTION

1. C

The selection offers three possible causes, any or all of which could be possibly true. There may be other causes that are not mentioned. You are asked to choose one answer. (C) is the only inclusive choice and is therefore correct. (A), (B), (D), and (E) all single out one possible explanation as correct, and reject the others without justification from the passage. Moreover, (D) is not an appropriate choice because older people are not even mentioned in the passage.

2. D

The word fare *as it is used* in the selection, i.e., *fare offered*, means the menu of film attractions. The words *as it is used* provide the critical information you need. Replacing the word *fare* in the passage with the meanings provided makes it easy to find the correct answer. (A) improperly combines two words, *fare* meaning *available selection* and *fair* meaning *equal,* in a way that simply does not make sense in the passage. (B) is incorrect because the use of the word *fare* meaning *price* is generally restricted to the price one pays to ride a moving vehicle (bus or taxi). (C) is incorrect because it wouldn't make sense and because *result* and *fare* are not synonyms. (E) is incorrect because impartial is a synonym for *fair* not *fare*.

3. B

Only (B) (While; Others) makes sense if you read the first and second sentences sequentially. None of the other possibilities include a noun/subject as the second choice. (A) at first may appear to be correct, but if you insert *as a result* in the sentence, the sentence doesn't make sense. (C) may also appear at first to be correct, but *meanwhile* does not help the sentence make sense. (D) is incorrect because *Not only; but also* is used in comparisons. This

sentence demonstrates contrast, not comparison in the passage. (E) looks like a possibility at first, but the insertion of *finally* is confusing. It does not follow logically.

4. B

Fortune 500 companies are the dark bars as shown by the key. Looking across the chart, one finds that the return of slightly over 30% in 1997 is the best performance. The performance in 2003 (A) is marked at 26.4%. In 1997 (B), the performance was slightly over 30%. Choice (C) was the poorest performance year, down more than 20%. Choice (D) (1998) was higher than choice (A) but lower than choice (B). Choice (E), (1996) while not the worst, is clearly not the best.

5. D

To answer this question, you need to compare performance of both indexes; you are looking for the *broadest spread* of difference. (A) is incorrect because in 2002 both indexes were down, although the Russell 2000 index was down less than the Fortune 500 index. (B) is wrong because the spread of difference is only 5%–6%. (C) is incorrect because the spread of difference is only 8%–9%. (E) is incorrect because the difference is only 9%. The spread of difference in 1998 (D) was more than 20%.

6. A

Here, you are looking for the broadest spread within one index between the lowest year and the highest following year. In this case (A), the spread is more than 50%. (B) might appear to be correct because both indexes were even in 1996, but it is not because a larger spread shows up further on in the chart. (C) is also incorrect because the upside difference is only 12% or 14%. (D) is incorrect because the spread of difference is below 50%. (E) is incorrect because the index lost money between those two years, so there was no profit.

7. D

You are looking for the best answer. (A) is an acceptable answer but too general; (D) is the best answer because it is more complete and specific. (B) and (E) are subpoints of the main point, so not acceptable. (C) is incorrect because the passage does not actually say that. Rather, it discusses differences in learning style not individual differences.

8. C

You need to know vocabulary definitions in order to answer correctly and not confuse (C) with (B), which refers to kinetic energy. (A) is incorrect because it describes visual learning. (D) describes auditory learning and is also incorrect. (E) is too general to be an acceptable answer because there are many different kinds of games, not only physical games.

9. C

First read the sentences to determine which one makes the most sense. Sentence (C) is a good transition between the sentence before and the sentence that follows it. (A) is incorrect because it simply states the first sentence. (B) is probably a valid point, but it is not relevant to the meaning of the paragraph. (D) is incorrect because the paragraph is about teachers, not students. (E) is not a valid choice because subject matter and study approaches are not the subject of the passage. Only choice (C) makes good sense.

10. D

The writer compares the tools of the Clovis people with those of the people living in Siberia. He contrasts the opinions of experts. He does not use any of the other choices. (A) is not an acceptable answer because he does not describe specific characteristics of the tools. (B) is not a good choice because he does not break the content into types. (C) is not a good choice either because analogy draws attention to the sameness of two items that ordinarily goes unrecognized. (E) is also a poor choice because there is no clear connection between a cause and an effect signaled by words such as *therefore* and *as a result*.

11. C

If you missed this, reread the passage. Then eliminate all of the choices that could possibly be correct but aren't quite on target. This is an example of a passage that could confuse you if you only skim it. (C) is the only viable choice. Three differing scientific opinions are presented in the last half of the paragraph. (A) is incorrect because the passage specifically indicates that early man lived in the Siberian Arctic 30,000 years ago. (B) and (D) are also incorrect because the passage indicates that the tools were *similar* not *the same* or *identical* and that some scientists see them as quite different. (E) is not a good choice

because the passage does not draw a conclusion. Further scientific study might be conclusive, and then scientific opinions could change and come into agreement.

12. E

This answer requires thinking about how the word is used in the sentence. You can get the meaning from the context of the sentence. Try replacing *postulated* with the other choices to determine whether or not they make sense. Only *assume* works. (A) is incorrect because the phrase *the way things stand* cannot be fitted in place of the one word and make sense. (B) is incorrect for the same reason but could mislead you because of the association of glacial with the Arctic. (C) is also an inadequate choice because it doesn't fit into the sentence but could confuse you because of its association with early man. (D) is incorrect because it doesn't fit the sentence at all but could be confusing because of your associating it with dating ancient artifacts.

13. D

This sentence follows a string of factual statements that can be verified from published sources. By contrast, sentence number 7 has a sarcastic tone and is clearly the opinion of the author. It obviously is in disagreement with the factual statements preceding it. Choices (A), (B), (C), and (E) are all sentences that include facts.

14. E

Here is a case where a more general answer is the best of the possible choices. (A) and (B) are too specific. (C) and (D) are too vague. Sentences 7 and 10 are statements in favor of individual liberty.

15. B

Statistics on death rates are accurate and difficult to misuse. The other choices might be used in an argument in opposition to the passage but are not as convincing. (A) is a poor choice because examples like testimonials are not considered reliable data. (C) and (E) offer opinions, which are also not considered reliable data. (D) is a poor choice because statistics on smoking alone are not broad enough to defeat the argument.

16. C

1995 is when membership increased most substantially after the big decline. (A) is incorrect because it is near the bottom of the decline. (B) is even closer to the bottom of the decline and is also incorrect. (D) is incorrect because by 1993, membership had increased from the bottom of 523. (E) is incorrect because in 1997 membership had begun to drop again.

17. B

1998 was the next year that membership began to climb following the lowering of fees. (A) is incorrect because membership dropped in 1997. (C), (D), and (E) are incorrect because membership was obviously recovering in 1999 and continued to recover until 2001.

18. D

Counting from the first decline in 1993, (D) is correct. (A), (B), and (C) are not good choices because membership levels were struggling upward, but full recovery had not been attained. (E) is incorrect because membership had started to decline in 2002.

19. B

Careful reading will lead you to choose (B). Skimming might cause you to choose a different answer. The third sentence in the second paragraph gives the answer. (A) is incorrect because these two populations are not contrasted. (C) is incorrect. It is part of the last sentence of the second paragraph but not contrasted with another type. (D) and (E) are incorrect because this passage is about types of conformists, not a contrast between conformists and nonconformists or conformists and rebels.

20. B

(B) is the best answer in that it explains and expands on the foregoing paragraph. (A) is not good because it is an ineffective conclusion to the paragraph. (C), (D), and (E) are also poor choices because they each introduce new ideas into the passage—ideas that disrupt paragraph unity.

21. E

The best answer is (E) because *sheep* represents *people who are easily herded to an opinion or destination*. A *simile* (C) would include the words *like* or *as*, i.e. people are like sheep. The author is not giving sheep human qualities, as would be the case with *personification* (D). (A) and (B) are inadequate because they are comments, not opinions.

22. E

Careful reading reveals that all sentences in the paragraphs develop the ideas in 1 and 5. Topic sentences are often the first sentence in a paragraph. (A) and (D) are incorrect because they are both in the first paragraph. (B) is incorrect because sentence 3 develops the topic sentence 1. (C) is incorrect because both sentences are subordinate ideas to the topic sentence.

23. B

While choices (C) and (D) do address the purpose of the paragraphs, (B) is a more interesting title because of the use of brief but rhythmic words. (A) and (E) are poorer choices because they do not address the topic.

24. B

(B) is the most specifically appropriate answer of all the choices given. (A), (C), (D), and (E) are incorrect because the passage does not define, describe, or identify causes or compare two things. Using a process of elimination, you get to the right answer.

25. C

(A) is incorrect because it is the first step. Sentences 2–4 develop the first step. Therefore, (B) is incorrect. A clue to your correct choice is the phrase, *Once you have chosen your topic*. (D) and (E) are incorrect because they are sub points of the second step.

MATHEMATICS SECTION

26. C

Subtract the perimeter of the rectangle from the length of the roll.

$200\ ft - 2(4\ ft\ 8\ in + 10\ ft\ 2\ in)$

$= 200\ ft - 2(14\ ft\ 10\ in)$

$= 200\ ft - (28\ ft\ 20\ in)$

$= 200\ ft - (29\ ft\ 8\ in)$

$= (199\ ft\ 12\ in) - (29\ ft\ 8\ in)$

$= 170\ ft\ 4\ in$

Choice (A) is the perimeter of the rectangle, not the amount left on the roll. You would answer (B) if you multiplied the sum of the length and width by four instead of two, as the formula for perimeter of a rectangle indicates. If your answer is (D), you did not multiply the sum of length and width by the required two. Choice (E) is the answer you would get if you added the perimeter to the roll instead of subtracting.

27. B

Only 0.23 is not between 0.24 and 0.31.

(A) $29\% = 0.29$

(C) $\frac{1}{4} = 0.25$

(D) $\frac{3}{10} = 0.30$

(E) $\frac{13}{50} = \frac{26}{100} = 0.26$, all four of which are between 0.23 and 0.31.

28. D

Set up and solve an inequality:

$\frac{81 + 75 + 78 + x}{4} \geq 80$

$\frac{234 + x}{4} \geq 80$ Multiply both sides by 4.

$234 + x \geq 320$ Subtract 234 from both sides.

$x \geq 86$

If the fourth exam is 80 (A) or more, the average will be only 78.5 or more. A fourth exam 78 (B) or more yields an average of 78 or more. Choice (C), 100 on the fourth exam gives an average of 83.5 or more. Choice (E) is negated by (D).

29. A

To find vertical distance, subtract the lower elevation from the upper elevation:

$215 - (-52) = 215 + 52 = 267$

Choices (B) and (E) are eliminated because distance is *positive* only. If your choice is (C), you subtracted the two negative values, not what the question specified. If you responded (D), you added instead of subtracting.

30. D

The phrase *ratio of A to B* is translated as the fraction $\frac{A}{B}$. This problem asks for the ratio of girls, G, to the total, $B + G$: $\frac{G}{B + G}$. (A) is the ratio of girls to boys. (B) is the ratio of boys to girls. (C) is the ratio of total number of students to girls. (E) is the ratio of the difference between boys and girls to the total of boys and girls.

31. E

Substitute and follow the order of operations rules:

$x^2 - xy = (-2)^2 - (-2)(-3)$

$= 4 - (-2)(-3)$ Exponents before multiplication.

$= 4 - 6$ Multiplication before subtraction.

$= 4 + (-6)$ Rule for subtraction.

$= -2$

If you responded (A), perhaps you added −2 and −3 incorrectly instead of multiplying. Choice (B) indicates that you probably multiplied −2 and −3 incorrectly. Choice (C) indicates that you squared −2 incorrectly. (D) indicates that you subtracted incorrectly at the last step.

32. B

Because there are 27 cubic feet in a cubic yard, find the volume of the wall in cubic feet, and divide by 27.

$(24)(10)\left(\frac{9}{12}\right) = 180$ Number of cubic feet.

$\frac{180}{27} = 6\frac{2}{3}$ Number of cubic yards.

Choice (A) indicates that you calculated the volume incorrectly. Choice (C) is the volume in cubic feet, not what the question specified. If you responded (D), you probably multiplied length by width by height, as if they were all in feet, and then divided by 9. All of this is wrong. You would obtain (E) if you multiplied all three numbers as if they were all in feet and ignored the requirement that the answer be in cubic yards.

33. D

This is a direct proportion problem:

$$\frac{\text{Length of tree's shadow}}{\text{Height of tree}} = \frac{\text{Length of stick's shadow}}{\text{Height of stick}}$$

$\frac{60}{x} = \frac{4}{5}$ Cross multiply.

$4x = 300$ Divide both sides by 4.

$x = 75$

For choice (A), you merely divided 60 by 4; for (E), you multiplied 60 times. Neither of these approaches makes any sense. If your choice was (B), you established an incorrect proportion and solved it correctly. (C) is a non-sensical answer. How could the tree and its shadow be the same length in this circumstance?

34. E

The correct answer is choice (E). Without any way of knowing the coordinates of point C, the area cannot be determined.

35. C

Probability in this situation is given by the formula

$$P(A) = \frac{\text{number in event } A}{\text{total number of possibilities}}$$

$P(\text{girl}) = \frac{15}{15 + 12} = \frac{15}{27} = \frac{5}{9}$

Choice (A) indicates that you did $\frac{\text{girls} - \text{boys}}{\text{girls}} = \frac{3}{15} = \frac{1}{5}$.

Choice (B) indicates $\frac{\text{boys}}{\text{boys} + \text{girls}} = \frac{12}{27} = \frac{4}{9}$. (D) is the ratio of boys to girls. No probability can be greater than one, so (E) is not a reasonable choice.

36. C

If the raw score x is at the nth percentile, then $n\%$ of the raw scores are less than x. So Elizabeth's score, 75, is better than 92% of all scores. (A) 83 *percent* scored lower than Corey. (B) Theo's score is better than 78% of the students who took the test. (D) Two percent of the students who took the test scored between Lucy and Corey. (E) We have no idea whether or not anyone got all of the questions correct. There is not enough information given in the table.

37. E

A whole number is prime if it has exactly two factors. The prime numbers are 2, 3, 5, 7, …, 73,… . Factors of 123 are 1, 3, 41, and 123, so it is not prime. Factors of 51 are 1, 3, 17, and 51.

38. D

The square of a number (not the square root) is found by multiplying the number by itself. $25^2 = 25 \times 25 = 625$

(A)   5 and −5 are the *square roots* of 25.

(B)   5 is the *principle square root* of 25.

(C) $50 = 2 \times 25$ This has nothing to do with squaring.

(E)   100 is the square of 10, not 25.

39. B

Solve the equation:

$7 - (3x - 2) = 12$ Use the distributive property.

$7 - 3x + 2 = 12$ Combine similar terms.

$9 - 3x = 12$ Subtract 9 from both sides.

$-3x = 3$ Divide both sides by −3.

$x = -1$

(A) showed a sign error at the last step. (C) not only added 9 incorrectly, but also made a sign error. (D) added 9 instead of subtracting. (E) made a sign error in using the distributive property at the beginning.

40. A

Total all costs and subtract from $200:

$200 - [45.25 + 78.40 + 3(4.10) + 2(1.50) + 5(2.10)]$

$= 200 - [45.25 + 78.40 + 12.30 + 3.00 + 10.50]$

$= 200 - 149.45 = 50.55$

Choice (B) is the cost of the material, not the change. Choice (C) is the total of the second column of the table. It doesn't account for the 3 notebooks, 2 highlighters, and the 5 pens. (D) is the change you get if (C) were the cost of the items.

41. B

Stan lost 18 pounds, so the question becomes

18 is what percent of 180? This question translates to the proportion

$\dfrac{18}{180} = \dfrac{P}{100}$ Cross multiply.

$180P = 1,800$ Divide by 180

$P = 10$ Stan lost 10% of his weight.

(A) Stan now weighs 90% of his former weight, but that is not the question. (C) Stan lost 18 pounds but that is not the percent of his decrease in weight. (D) A change of 110% would indicate an *increase* in weight. (E) One and one-ninth percent of 180 is two pounds, not 18 pounds.

42. D

The phrase *Not all...* means *At least one is not....* (A) and (B) The given statement says nothing about any specific number. (C) *Not all...* does not mean *More than one is not....* (E) It says nothing about size of numbers.

43. E

The word *approximately* indicates rounding. The San Diego Zoo has approximately 4,000 mammal species, and the Los Angeles Zoo has approximately 3,000. So San Diego has approximately 1,000 more. Choice (B) is the sum of the given numbers. *How many more...* suggests subtraction. Choice (C) is the result of rounding off choice (B). Choice (D) probably results from incorrect rounding.

44. C

This is a direct proportion problem.

$\dfrac{3}{3\frac{3}{4}} = \dfrac{5}{x}$ Cross multiply.

$3x = (5)\left(3\dfrac{3}{4}\right)$

$3x = (5)\left(\dfrac{15}{4}\right)$

$3x = \dfrac{75}{4}$ Divide by 3.

$x = \dfrac{25}{4} = 6\dfrac{1}{4} = 6$ hours 15 minutes

Choice (A) is the time required to assemble one desk. In choice (B), it is nonsense to add 5 desks and 3 hours. Choice (D) ignores the fact that three desks are assembled in the given time. Eighteen hours and 45 minutes is the product of 3 hours 45 minutes times five. Choice (E) is the result of setting up an incorrect proportion.

45. C

The median is the middle of the ranked scores. If you rank the scores from smallest to largest,

   (78, 80, 83, 90, 94)

you see that the median is 83.

(A) In a data set with an odd number of items of data, the median will be one of the numbers in the data set. (B) If the data are not ranked from smallest to largest, this is the number that would most likely be incorrectly chosen as the median. (D) Perhaps the data was ordered incorrectly.

46. A

Equation (A) is almost a word-for-word translation of the word problem.

The following are the translations of the given choices.

(B) Two times the sum of one more than a certain number is the same as three times the difference of five less than the same number.

(C) One more than twice a certain number is the same as five less three times the same number.

(D) Five less than twice a certain number is the same as one more than three times the same number.

(E) Five less twice a certain number is the same as one more than three times the same number.

47. E

It is easiest to list the different sums of money.

   Choosing 1 coin: 1, 5, 10

   Choosing 2 coins: 6, 11, 15

   Choosing 3 coins: 16

There are seven different sums of money.

If the choice is (A), you misread the problem as *choosing*

one coin… Choices (B) and (C) indicate a miscounting of amounts of money. If the choice is (D), you forgot to choose all three coins.

48. A

Use the FOIL procedure:

First terms: $6x^2$

Outer terms: $3x$

Inner terms: $-10x$

Last terms: -5

Combine the outer and inner to get $6x^2 - 7x - 5$.

(B) The sign of the outer and inner combination is wrong. (C) leaves out the outer step. (D) and (E) Unless the terms of the binomials are identical except for sign, the product will always be a trinomial.

49. B

One property of any triangle is that the sum of any two sides must be greater than the third side. A triangle could not have sides 2, 5, and 10. For all of (A), (C), (D), and (E), the sum of any two sides is greater than the third side.

50. D

You would need to know only the width of the rectangle to find the area of the square.

(A) The thickness of the rectangle has nothing to do with the area of its surface. (B) The length of the rectangle is not necessary to find the area of the square.

WRITING SECTION

Topic

4 Essay

Jefferson was wrong, at least this once. The past and the future are inseparable: the present is the only brief moment that distinguishes them. Because the future is continually a direct result of the past, you cannot *look to the future* without considering that past events are creating that future.

The scientific process is an excellent example of how future events must grow directly from past experiences. Each proposed theory did not pop into existence out of thin air; rather, scientists developed them over long periods of time based on the findings of their predecessors and on their own past work. Einstein developed his theory of special relativity after years of work studying inconsistencies in Newton's laws of motion. Later, he built upon his own work to develop his general theory. These great theories of how light, space, and motion operate did not suddenly occur to Einstein as he lay daydreaming in a hammock on a warm summer day. They resulted from his careful examination of the past. Other great discoveries in the field, such as super string theory and Hawking's theories of space and time, have similarly been theories built on the foundations of past scientists' work.

Individual choices also must result from past experiences. A continuous stream of experiences that alter self-perception and determine our understanding of the world shapes each individual. Regardless of where you might stand on the nature versus nurture debate, both your genetic make-up and your life experiences are past influences that influence your values, your thoughts, and your actions in the future. Even your choices add to the past's influence on your future experiences.

History books are filled with examples of how similar situations result in similar outcomes: Groups with superior weaponry and technology—or with more virulent diseases—conquer or dominate groups that do not have these advantages. Without proper planning, people will starve after long periods of draught. Expect conflict if one group attempts to forcefully change the values of another. There are countless patterns like these throughout history. It is impossible to accurately predict future outcomes of current events, because of the complexity of social situations and the unique experiences of the individuals involved. However, to effectively dream of the future, it is essential to recognize that the past is its immediate predecessor.

Grader's Comments

This essay effectively and completely addresses the topic. The author's position is clearly defined, well developed, and supported by several detailed examples, each of which is solidly connected to the clear thesis statement.

The author planned the essay well and logically: each paragraph serves a clear purpose and does not contain any extraneous information. The examples are well thought-out and appropriate to the author's point. The author also uses transition words well to clarify meaning.

The author demonstrates language facility and an engaging style, with varied sentence structure unmarred by errors in spelling, grammar, and diction.

2 Essay

It is wise to learn from the past and from the future, because those who cannot remember the past are condened to repeat it. This is what George Santayana said in the life of reason. I think that it's true especially for things like wars and other violence too. There have been wars for hundreds and hundreds and hundreds of years, but no one seems to understand anything with all of the mistakes. There was a war in Troy where there was a lot of bloodshed and death, but just look at now. There have been wars today because we did not learn that war can cause a lot of really nasty problems like death. There have been lots of wars in between too like World War I and II and Vietnam. No one learned from those wars either. Maybe it is because there is enough time that passes in between each of the wars for people to not remember the war since they were not born yet and only older people know about the war but they can't they hear stories their parents, but that is not enough to convince everyone that war is terible and could happen again. Thomas Jeferson in the quote is wrong because we should learn from our grandpas if everyone only took a little bit of time each and every

day listening to their grandpa, then we wouldn't need to have war ever again in this world today. These quotes make me think of war because that is something when I ever saw it that we would not want it to happen again. If you talk to your grandpa you will see easy that war is such a big mistake. Not only do people die fighting but also their family members suffer because of all of the people which died.

Grader's Comments

This essay only partially addresses the topic. At the beginning, the writer seems to be trying to use war as an example of why people should learn from the past, but the connection is not clearly made. The author quickly digresses and does not sufficiently connect his or her supporting ideas to the original topic. The author writes at length about learning from the wars of the past, but the examples do not logically support the author's position, and many of the statements are incomplete or unreasonable (like the author's claim that *no one learned from those wars either*). As the essay progresses, the author's supporting statements drift further and further from the original thesis.

The essay isn't organized. The author copied part of the first quote word-for-word to use as his or her thesis. While this establishes a clear point of view, it shows little thought, and the lack of coherence quickly clouds the essay's meaning. Many of the ideas are repetitive, and throughout much of the essay the author appears to be merely rambling to fill up space. Clearly, the author did not spend much time—if any—planning.

The essay is riddled with grammatical and spelling errors. Some of the spelling errors, missing words, and run-on sentences are obvious mistakes that could have been easily corrected by proofreading. Other common problems include wordiness, pronoun agreement, and the incorrect use of relative pronouns.

Reading

Chapter Four: **Reading Section Overview**

The reading section of the CBEST is designed to test your ability to understand information presented in written passages, reference materials, and graphs. The selections will be of varying degrees of difficulty and are drawn from many areas of study, such as consumer studies, health, the humanities, and social sciences. All questions will test only the information provided in the presented material. You will not be required to use knowledge from outside sources.

The passages can range in length from one or two sentences to more than 200 words. The reading section of the CBEST is divided into three general categories: critical analysis and evaluation, reading comprehension, and research skills. In the following chapters, we will discuss each question category and provide examples of test questions and strategies to ace them.

GENERAL SKILL BUILDING

Careful reading of the passage and the multiple-choice answers is the first key to success. How do you build those skills? Here are a few helpful hints:

- Practice reading articles in novels, textbooks, magazines, and newspapers to get as much information as possible from a selection. Choose these sources carefully to be sure you are being exposed to a college-level vocabulary.

- Pay attention to graphs, charts, and maps that you find in magazines and newspapers.

- Review basic English grammar and usage rules. There are many general grammar reference books available for this purpose.

- Try developing your own questions about a passage or graph you have read.

- Keep a notebook specifically designed to keep track of the skills you have mastered and the ones you still need to work on.

- Review the words and word roots in Resources One and Two, and make note of any words you are unfamiliar with.

The key to all of the above activities is to be engaged in the test preparation. It is essential that you learn to manage your time during the test. Managing your time is doable with practice. Time yourself as you take the practice exams, and note whether you exaggerate or underestimate the time available. You can learn to establish an efficient working pace so that you do not feel panicked on test day.

READING COMPREHENSION QUESTIONS

In chapter 5, we will address the three question types in this section, the first of which is Reading Comprehension. The Reading Comprehension skills required are specific and include identifying facts and details, recognizing paraphrases or summaries of ideas in a passage, and recognizing the main or general idea and arranging it and the subordinate ideas into an outline. Similar skills will help you to determine the sequence of events of a passage and to identify the relationships between the general and specific ideas presented.

One way you can learn to recognize paraphrases is to practice writing them yourself. You can use your notebook for developing this skill. Identify the main idea of a story or article you have read, and write down as many ways as you can think of to restate it.

Other questions will require you to recognize the main idea in a reading passage or to draw conclusions or make generalizations based on material presented in a passage. Similar skills are necessary to make inferences from or recognize implications of information in a passage. Other questions may test your ability to recognize relationships between people, ideas, or events in a given reading selection.

Some questions will focus on language. They will ask you about vocabulary and will require you to use context clues, syntax, or sentence structure. You may also be asked to discover a word's meaning through word roots, affixes, or prefixes. Other questions that focus on language might ask for an interpretation of figurative or colloquial language in a reading selection. Figurative language is used to give imaginative description. Colloquial language is used in informal conversation but not in proper writing.

There are also questions that will ask you to identify different interpretations that can be made using the same word, sentence, paragraph, or reading selection and to recognize how a word's meaning or the meaning of a sentence or paragraph is affected by the context in which it is used.

Finally, you need to have an understanding of transition indicators in a reading selection such as *however, moreover, by contrast, on the other hand*, or *in conclusion*.

Feeling overwhelmed? No need to worry. By the time your finished with this book, you'll be feeling confident with each question type in the Reading Comprehension section.

RESEARCH SKILLS QUESTIONS

Research skills include being able to use a table of contents or an index to find information, locate information in selected reference materials, understand how a paragraph or passage is organized, and develop logical conclusions.

You can practice using a table of contents and index by going to the reference room of a library and looking for information. If you have difficulty, you can ask the librarian for help. You can become quite proficient using these reference tools with practice.

All of these tasks may seem daunting. However, the strategies for building these skills in the next chapter will help you to do just what you need to do—pass the test. Some suggestions have been included in this chapter, but they will be more developed in chapter 5.

CRITICAL ANALYSIS AND EVALUATION QUESTIONS

For this question type, you should be prepared to identify reasons, examples, and facts that support an author's main idea and determine whether they are relevant and strengthen or weaken an argument in a reading passage. You will need to distinguish between facts and opinions in an article and recognize inconsistencies within or between two or more selections. Having the skill to compare and contrast ideas is important here. You should also be able to identify logical assumptions made by the author and challenge the statements and opinions presented. You may also be asked to expand on the attitude expressed by the author toward the topic of the passage.

Other important skills that will be tested are your ability to recognize the intended audience for a specific reading selection and determine whether the language is inappropriate or inconsistent for that given audience.

You can begin to build the skills you need well in advance of the test by reading short articles from magazines, recording the main idea of a selection in a notebook, and noting in outline form the supporting points. As you read, ask yourself, "Is this a reason, an example, or a fact?" Then consider whether or not it supports the main idea. Does each point strengthen or weaken the argument? Is it relevant?

WHAT YOU CAN DO

As we suggested earlier, in the months before the exam, keep an ongoing record of each practice selection you read, whether it is a textbook, magazine, newspaper article, short story, or novel.

Start this way:

1. Write down the title of the selection.
2. As you read, mark any words you don't know. At the end of the passage, write them in your journal. Set aside time at the end of your reading to look up definitions. Write them down and practice using them in sentences to enhance your understanding.
3. After you have finished, summarize what you have read.
4. Write down the following things:
   - what you think the author's purpose is
   - what tone the author takes
   - what type of writing it is (i.e., informative, persuasive, etc.)
   - You may use a series of pluses and minuses to quickly identify whether a sentence is supportive of the main idea or not.

Your note page may look something like the following:

I.   (Main idea or Topic Sentence) or (Author's premise or Assumption)

    A. (supporting statement)
       1. (fact)
       2. (reason)
       3. (example)
       4. (fact)

    B. (supporting statement)

If comparable or contrasting ideas are presented, you can record them in two columns entitled *pro* and *con*. Likewise, if the author's argument may be refuted, you may note contrasting arguments on your notebook page.

In your notes, you should also include the assumptions that you believe the author holds. Ask yourself what premise the author is building his argument on. Then write it down. The best approach is to take charge of the text you are reading and own it.

These are simple ways to start a journal or a reading record. In the following chapters, we will explore all of these preparation techniques more fully.

As you read through this preparatory text, highlight or otherwise identify points you want to remember. You may be aware of certain skills you need to work on more than others. Going back to review approaches to building those skills will help you stay focused in your efforts.

ONE LAST THING

Before you proceed, it would be a good idea to review the diagnostic test and note your errors. Do you see a pattern of errors? What kinds of questions did you miss? Did you miss questions because you read the passages too fast? Were there words that were unfamiliar to you? Use the answer key to discover which answer is correct, and then analyze why it is the best answer. You may discover that you really knew it but read the question too quickly or misread it. Did an unfamiliar word throw you off? This is an activity that will help you know yourself better as a test taker. You can adjust your test preparation strategies according to what you discover.

Chapter Five: **Reading Section Strategies**

In this chapter, we will discuss strategies for the three question topics that make up the Reading Section of the CBEST. Read this chapter carefully, and be sure to follow the preparation tools provided. A practice set in the following chapter will help you practice what you've learned.

The three topics covered in the Reading Section are:
- Reading Comprehension
- Research Skills
- Critical Analysis and Evaluation

Each of these topics tests different skills and concepts required to be an effective Reading teacher. Some of the tested concepts are similar between the topics, but don't skip any part of this chapter, even if you think you know it already. It never hurts to be overly prepared. The rest of this chapter will break down each topic and the concepts and skills covered in them.

READING COMPREHENSION QUESTIONS

The three key skills covered in this question type are:
- Building Your Vocabulary
- Reading for the Main Idea
- Drawing Inferences

Building Your Vocabulary

Developing a strong vocabulary is the best preparation you can make to have success on any college or professional test.

One effective way to build your vocabulary is to write down every word you come across in general reading (newspapers, magazines, and textbooks) that you don't recognize or understand. Your focused attention is required. The human brain tends to skip over unknown or unrecognized words. Students sometimes complain that they can read a passage and not know what they have just read when they are finished. If there are enough unknown words in the passage, the brain doesn't register them, and the meaning is lost.

Keep a small notebook with you wherever you go. It will be your vocabulary journal. Jot down any new or unfamiliar word and the sentence in which it is used. Take a few minutes every day to look up the meanings of the words you didn't know. Write down the meanings, and then practice using the words in sentences.

Some people prefer to use flashcards to learn vocabulary. Write the word you want to learn on one side and the definition and one or two sample sentences on the other. Flashcards can be helpful because you can have a friend test you every so often to be sure you have not forgotten what you have learned.

"Word-a-Day" vocabulary builders are available in many formats such as calendars, items in daily newspapers, via certain reference websites, or relevant e-mail lists. Learning specialists know that 15-minute segments of study are very effective in learning new information, so short, frequent reviews of vocabulary are best. The other component to continual review is to lay down a pattern of memory in your brain.

Also, review the vocabulary words in Resource Two. The words from this list can be incorporated into the vocabulary-building techniques mentioned above.

Practice, Practice, Practice

Over several days, practice using each new word in written sentences and in conversation until it becomes part of your personal lexicon.

Get acquainted with a thesaurus. Once you learn a dictionary definition of a word, a thesaurus will show you other words that are closely related in meaning. Using a dictionary and thesaurus together, you can begin to refine your vocabulary so it becomes more specific and nuanced.

Another good strategy is to review word roots. Resource One provides a comprehensive list of word roots. If you memorize those roots, you can decipher unfamiliar words by a combination of your knowledge of the word root and the context in which the word is used.

Discerning Meanings of Unfamiliar Words

Questions that ask you to discern meanings of unfamiliar words from their context or by analyzing their syntax or structure take the following forms:

- "The word_____ as it is used in the second paragraph means…"
- "Which of the following is the best meaning of the word _____ as it is used in the passage?"
- "The word _____ as used in the selection means…"

The best preparation for encountering this type of question is vocabulary study, especially studying prefixes and suffixes. This type of review can be done for a brief time each day. Beginning your preparation weeks before the test will give you ample time to build your vocabulary.

Using Context Clues to Find Meaning

Context is the sentence or paragraph an unfamiliar word is used in. It can help you figure out the meaning of a word and answer a vocabulary question successfully. It is important not to panic when you are confronted with an unfamiliar word on one of the questions. Breathe, relax, and reread the passage. Then look at the answer choices again. You can probably figure out the correct answer from the context. Eliminate the choices that you know are wrong, and then look for clues, such as similarity of grammatical form (verbs, nouns, or adjectives) or usage to choose the best answer.

This skill is one you can practice frequently well in advance of the exam. Simply look for contextual understanding in your everyday reading. Practice is a matter of exercising your mind in this way.

Reading for the Main Idea

Some of the questions you encounter will ask you to find the main idea of a passage. Those questions may be structured in the following way:

- "The main idea of the passage may be best expressed as…"
- "Which of the following best states the theme of the passage?"
- "This selection illustrates…"
- "The title that best expresses the ideas in the passage is…"

Your goal on a main idea question is to find an answer that incorporates the ideas of all of the sentences in the passage. If you have a passage of two or more paragraphs, look for an answer that includes the ideas in both or all of the paragraphs. It is often that the main idea can be found in the opening paragraph.

First, look for the topic sentence in the first paragraph. If you can't find it, ask yourself what the paragraph is about or what important idea is being set forth. You may need to reread the paragraph. Remember, it is acceptable to make notes in the margins of the test booklet. Jot down words or ideas that recur or have similar meanings. They can be clues to the topic or main idea. Underline or circle significant elements.

To practice, read the following paragraph and identify the main idea:

> Some people have a gift for success in whatever they undertake. My aunt Jennifer has become a successful photographer after living in Europe with a good job and then moving to California where she established a multimillion-dollar home health care business. It seems success has followed her doggedly, just as failure haunts the lives of others. I have often wondered what her secret is in addition to good looks and an engaging personality. Could it be her willingness to work hard?

Main idea _____.

If you chose the first sentence, you are correct. All of the sentences in the paragraph expand upon the first sentence. They make up one long example.

Now try to identify the main idea in this paragraph:

> A new school in New Mexico has turned around the lives of many students. In an area that had 65 percent dropouts, the South Valley Academy has had only one dropout after having been in existence for two years. Many people credit the work of an outstanding teacher who did everything from planting trees and pouring concrete to transforming what had been a small farm into a fine school. She also coordinated the bilingual program and developed a unique grading system for both skills and habits, such as cooperation and perseverance. Her caring and perseverance helped to make the dream of a fine school a reality. This is an example of how one person can make a difference in students' lives and in a community.

Main idea _____.

In this case, choosing the last sentence would be the correct response. The first sentence may at first seem to be correct, but as you read through the paragraph, you quickly see that the sentences lead up to a conclusion that states the main point.

Every sentence in a paragraph should relate to the main idea, including selections with multiple paragraphs. The easiest way to identify the main idea of a passage is to be able to identify the topic sentence. The topic sentence can appear anywhere in the paragraph, but it is usually at the beginning or the end.

Other ways to find the main idea are:

- Think of a good title for the selection, one that is specific but inclusive.
- Determine generally what the selection is about: a person, idea, place, process, or thing. Then look at the answer choices for the second time, and choose the best one.
- Ask yourself what the author is saying about the subject. Often, that information is at the end of the selection.

Example

> Community gardens have long offered low-income residents the opportunity to grow fresh food at little cost, to provide a safe place for their children, and to teach their children where food comes from and how it is grown. These gardens are like oases in the city, offering hope, a healthy lifestyle, and a green space in an area that is usually drab, run down, and depressing.
>
> The main idea of this passage can best be expressed as:
>
> (A) Community gardens have been around for many years.
> (B) Community gardens are like oases.
> (C) Community gardens are good for children.
> (D) Community gardens are valuable assets.
> (E) Community gardens offer important benefits to low-income families.

The best answer is (E). It is the most inclusive of the points brought forth in the passage. Whereas the idea is not stated in one sentence in the passage, it brings together nearly all of the supporting points.

Try to apply the ideas discussed in the previous examples to locate the main idea in this next passage:

> Scientists at two drug companies are working on a vaccine that might halt or reverse symptoms of Alzheimer's disease. This is a much-needed drug that could help stem the tide of new Alzheimer's cases. In 1995, there were 377,000 new cases. It is estimated that there will be 454,000 new cases each year by 2010. Approximately 4.5 million Americans currently suffer from the disease.
>
> Unfortunately, early trials resulted in some life-threatening side effects, but research has continued, and a new drug may be released for testing soon. Not all scientists support this line of research. They feel it is too risky. In the first trials, no one was cured, but 20% of subjects made slight improvements. Nevertheless, brain shrinkage increased, which suggested that mental acuity would diminish.

1. Possible title: _____

2. What is the passage generally about? _____

3. What is the author saying about the subject? _____

Drawing Inferences

On the CBEST, you will also see Reading Comprehension questions that ask you to draw conclusions, or inferences, based on the language and tone the author uses to convey key points and ideas in the passage. Here are some examples of how these questions may be asked:

- "It may be inferred from the paragraph that…"
- "The authors' intention in this passage is…"
- "It is unlikely that the author feels…"
- "One may not conclude from this passage that…"

Your task is to choose the answer that is inferred by the author, or not specifically stated, in the passage. For inference questions, your ability to read closely and logically will be tested. Again, this skill is easily practiced by reading newspapers and magazine articles with the specific goal of finding the author's inference use in mind and noting your conclusion and the information from which you drew it in your journal.

When you are reading practice articles, ask yourself as you near the conclusion, "What may I infer from this information?" or "Logically, what should come next?" This kind of detail-oriented thinking is what helps you anticipate the punch line of a joke a fraction of a second before it is spoken. You can apply that same skill of focused engagement to anything you read.

Other Key Aspects of Reading Comprehension Passages

As you read, be aware of the writer's tone and the type of passage you are reading. For instance, is it humorous, factual, emotional, sarcastic, gloomy, or melodramatic? Speculate on the audience for whom the author is writing; is the language general or specific in context for small factions of society, such as students, experts, popular readers, children, or others? Is the tone consistent with what the audience will expect? Jot down that information at the end of your brief outline of the article's content.

Ask yourself whether the author is trying to persuade you to a certain viewpoint. If so, the passage can be identified as persuasive or argumentative. Does the passage tell a story? If so, it's a narrative.

Is the selection enriched by adjectives and adverbs, painting a picture of a place or a person? If so, it's descriptive.

Does it tell how two things, places, or ideas are the same, similar, or different? If so, it's using comparison and contrast.

Does it report information factually and in a straightforward manner to explain an idea? If so, it's expository.

Knowing the differences between these categories of text will help you identify with the author's purpose for writing the passage and make finding the main idea and making the appropriate inference a breeze.

RESEARCH SKILLS QUESTIONS

The CBEST test will present a certain number of Research Skills questions that will test your ability to use a table of contents, an index, and other various reference materials to find specific information. In answering these types of questions, your skills in organizing information and locating a specific topic or idea based on clue words or phrases will be tested. The following question is an example of one way that Research Skills questions are formatted.

Example

Long-term care insurance	105,218,140–142,306
benefits and costs of	140–141
buying of	142
for single people	306
Managed care plans	30,83–86,143
employee assistance	11
programs, and	166
HMOs	27,141,183,201–202

If you wish to compare coverage and premium charges for eldercare insurance, on which pages would you look?

(A) 142

(B) 83–86

(C) 201–202

(D) 105

(E) 140–141

The best answer is (E). Eldercare and long-term care insurance mean the same thing. Thus, you can focus your attention on the topic *Long-term care insurance* and its subtopics. The question asks you where the appropriate information would be to compare coverage and charges of this type of insurance. Coverage and charges are another way of saying benefits and costs; thus, your best option is to look in those pages, 140–141, for the appropriate information, making (E) the correct choice.

Some Research Skills questions will also ask about your ability to locate specific information in a selected reading excerpt based on the organization of the paragraphs and information. Answering this type of question may call on you to use the inference skills you learned in the Reading Comprehension discussion earlier in this chapter. Below is an example of this type of question.

Example

Students in community colleges who wish to go into business can usually benefit from courses in etiquette that are offered at some colleges. These help students learn table manners and how to order from a menu so they can feel comfortable at business lunches.

Some of the tips they get are:

1. Only butter the piece of bread you are going to eat in one bite.

2. If you're the host, take care of payment away from guests.

3. If you're the guest, never order the most expensive item on the menu.

4. Wait for the host to unfold his napkin and place it in his lap before you do the same.

5. Leave cell phones in the car so there are no interruptions.

The overriding rule of etiquette is to think of the other person before you think of yourself, and make that person feel comfortable.

Learning good manners and being able to use them comfortably takes time and practice. CEOs sometimes hire etiquette consultants to spruce up their social skills. Students who can learn these skills in college will have a leg up in their careers, and as they practice good manners, they should become even more successful.

Which of the following best organizes the main topics addressed in this passage?

(A) the need for etiquette training among college students/the benefits of learning etiquette

(B) good manners are important for success in business/CEOs and college students need etiquette training

(C) lots of table manner tips can help you in business/good manners training can jumpstart your career.

(D) etiquette training is important in order to be comfortable and successful in business/CEOs and college students can both benefit from etiquette training

(E) self-improvement in many areas is worthwhile/self-improvement should continue throughout a business career

The best answer is (D). You can find both statements directly in the question. (A) is too general. (B) does not really address the topics with specificity. (C) is a poor choice because it picks out minor points. (E) has to do with self-improvement in general, not etiquette itself.

You can see by this example just how Research Skills questions differ from Reading Comprehension questions. The practice questions in chapter 6 will help you become more familiar with more types of Research Skills questions.

CRITICAL ANALYSIS AND EVALUATION QUESTIONS

Critical Analysis and Evaluation questions require the application of more sophisticated reading and thinking skills than those described in the previous two question types. Attacking these questions requires flexibility in applying analytical skills. Different types of questions require different types of reading skills. If you learn and practice the following approaches, you will have a better chance for success with each question you encounter.

You will be asked to compare or contrast information from the given reading selection. This requires the skill of seeing similarities and differences in the examples the author has used, a skill that can be fine-tuned over time as you practice engaged reading skills. What we mean by engaged reading is reading with a careful eye or paying close attention to the author's main point and the intended audience of the piece you are reading. In anything you read, whether it is for work or pleasure, training your mind to focus on critical aspects of the text, such as paragraph structure, supporting evidence or examples, and author tone, will help you feel confident about using these skills when it counts on test day.

Another helpful activity will be to practice writing comparison and contrasting pieces in your notebook. This is a way that writing practice can help your conscious reading skills.

Easy and entertaining topics to practice with are to compare and contrast drivers you have seen on freeways or city streets, celebrity images, or popular films. More sophisticated topics might include history, such as comparing or contrasting government policies between or among governments at a certain time in history, or topics from natural science.

The purpose of these exercises is to make you aware of comparison and contrast techniques so that you recognize them quickly during an exam.

Identifying Reasoning, Details, Facts, and Examples in a Passage

This skill requires an opposite technique or approach than what you learned about identifying the main idea in Reading Comprehension questions. Rather than looking for the main idea by seeing how all the sentences relate to it, find the main idea first, and then detail the supporting information. You will need to be able to discern differences among facts, reasons, opinions, examples, and details.

Questions of this type will take the following form:

- "Which of the following numbered sentences in the paragraph best expresses an opinion rather than a fact?"
- "How does the author support his views …"
- "Give an example of the author's idea of …"

Example

[1]In 1982, a study of graduating high school seniors found that 71% planned to get a college degree. [2]Ten years later that percentage had increased to 84%. [3]The intentions of people do not always match up with the later reality of their lives. [4]As the years go by, complications can interfere with a person's achievement goals. [5]Generally, however, fewer than 50% of those who enter college actually achieve a degree within 10 years.

Which sentences include facts rather than opinion?

(A) 1,3,5

(B) 1,2,4

(C) 2,3,5

(D) 1,2,5

(E) 1,3,4

The best answer is (D). Both dates and percentages are factual. Sentences 3 and 4 are opinions, even though they may be based on information. (C) and (E) are incorrect because sentence 3 does not include a fact. (A) and (B) are also incorrect.

Recognizing an Author's Attitude or Opinion

Some questions ask you to recognize an attitude, opinion, or viewpoint expressed by the author about the subject. Look for clue words to help you decipher what the author's feelings are. For example, "I hope," "It would be best if," and "Another problem is" all suggest an attitude or viewpoint of the author. Emotionally charged words will help to guide you to the overall attitude of the selection. Read for the tone to help discern the author's opinion. Good practice sources for developing this skill are editorial and opinion pages of newspapers because writers of the articles on those pages always have a position they are arguing for or against. Online newspapers of conservative or liberal bent can also be useful sources, especially in identifying emotionally charged or inflammatory language. Much of what passes for legitimate discourse today is really quite slanted in point of view.

As usual, keep a record in your reading notebook of what you discover.

Example

[1]Atrazine, a chemical product manufactured by a Swiss company, has been shown to cause organ defects in frogs. [2]It has also been linked to such diverse diseases as infertility, heart disease, and muscular degeneration. [3]Banned by the European Union last year, it is still being used heavily in the United States. [4]It is important for the Food and Drug Administration to take a stand on this chemical to protect Americans. [5]Heart disease and infertility are major concerns to most Americans. [6]Health concerns preoccupy much of television advertising, but little is said about chemical products that can damage health.

Which of the following numbered sentences best expresses an opinion rather than a fact?

(A) 1
(B) 2
(C) 3
(D) 4
(E) 6

The best choice is (D). (E) may look like a good choice, but it would be a generally accepted fact to anyone watching television advertising. The other choices are all facts that are verifiable from research data.

Determining Between Strong and Weak Arguments

These questions especially challenge your critical thinking skills and ability to analyze the elements of a good argument. If you have completed a California college freshman composition course or composition and critical thinking course, you would be wise to review the text from either or both of those courses because they all address argument and critical thinking issues.

Once again, the editorial and opinion pages will be most helpful. Here is where you need to take an aggressive approach in reading. Ask yourself as you read whether a statement actually strengthens or weakens the argument.

Imagine yourself debating the author. Can you poke holes in his or her argument? How would you argue against the author?

Questions that measure these skills may take the following forms:

- "Which of the following numbered sentences is least relevant to the main idea of the paragraph?"
- "Which words or phrases if inserted *in order* in the blanks would help the reader understand the sequence of the author's argument?"

Example

[1]Smart vacationers go to nature areas in the off-season, even to Yellowstone National Park, cold as it is in the winter. [2]The benefits are that there are fewer travelers, so it is less crowded, and there can be many encounters with wildlife. [3]Although the bears are hibernating, visitors can see bison and elk and a wolf now and then. [4]Also, the thermal geysers are spectacular amidst the snow. [5]Other destinations can be as appealing in the off-season. [6]October is actually a good month to travel to many places.

Which of the following numbered sentences is least relevant to the paragraph?

(A) 1
(B) 2
(C) 3
(D) 4
(E) 6

The best answer is (E). It is irrelevant to the rest of the paragraph because the paragraph is not about times to travel as much as it is about the benefits of going places during the off-season. Choices (A), (B), (C), and (D) are all examples of why Yellowstone in winter is a good vacation destination.

Recognizing Persuasive Techniques

Persuasive techniques may include appeals to emotion, challenging assumptions, appeals to authority, or using significant statistical data. The author may use examples and evidence to back up his opinion or main idea in a persuasive passage. The important thing to remember when encountered with a persuasive passage is to decide which side the author is on, and look for clues that support that side.

Example

> The concern over global warming may be an overreaction to a
> natural phenomenon. The twentieth century was probably colder
> than the Medieval Warm Period when olive trees grew as far north
> as Germany in Northern Europe, but a new meta-study reviewing
> more than 100 studies of coral, glacial ice cores, tree rings, and
> other historical climate indicators concluded that the twentieth cen-
> tury was not unusually warm by historical standards.

> The passage best illustrates the use of what persuasive
> techniques?

> (A) challenging assumptions

> (B) appealing to emotion

> (C) appealing to authority

> (D) using significant examples

> (E) identifying with readers

(A) is the best choice. The writer is challenging popular assumptions using data. The other choices
are not accurate. There are no examples used. There is no appeal to emotion or identification with
readers.

Challenging Statements Presented in the Reading Passage

In your reading notebook, make two columns on a page and write down the arguments *for* a
position in an article you are reading in the first column. Then, rate them by strength (1, 2, or 3).
In the second column, enter the arguments you can discover *against* that position. You will be
strengthening your analytical skills as you practice. Soon, you will automatically look at how an
argument is constructed as you read it. When you are in the testing room, these questions will
not seem too difficult because you will have practiced sufficiently.

Questions that test this skill may take the following form:

- "Which of the following choices would be the strongest argument against the author's
  position?"

Identifying Inconsistencies or Differing Points of View

Another skill that will be tested is that of identifying inconsistencies or differences in points of
view within an argument or between two separate passages. This is a skill you can develop by
making use of the same sources (editorial and opinion pages of the newspaper) and your reading notebook. Very skilled writers who appear in these pages may not evidence inconsistencies in
their own writing, but they will certainly point out inconsistencies in the thinking of others. Less
skilled writers will often have flaws in their own logic that you can identify.

Recognizing the Intended Audience

You will also be asked to recognize the audience to which a selection is addressed in some questions. Most often the audience will fit into a category of readers, such as readers of certain newspapers, journals, or magazines, users of certain products, or specialists in a certain field.

This is a situation where the tone the author takes will be revealing. Is it formal, informal, colloquial? Does it seem scientific or highly formal? Is it most likely from a professional journal? Is it from a popular magazine?

The choice of language and sentence structure or syntax will be revealing clues in helping you answer these questions. As you practice for this type of question, you will also be preparing for another type of skill, which is to recognize language that creates an inappropriate tone in light of the intended audience.

Now that we've shown you the three types of questions you'll encounter on the CBEST, it is time for you to learn our top strategy for acing these questions. Read through the method carefully, and be sure to use it as you work through the questions in chapter 6.

KAPLAN'S FIVE-STEP METHOD FOR READING QUESTIONS

Once you've read a passage strategically, you're ready to attack the questions. Here's Kaplan's Five-Step Method for Reading questions.

    Step 1. Read the question stem.
    Step 2. Locate the material you need.
    Step 3. Predict the answer.
    Step 4. Scan the answer choices.
    Step 5. Select your answer.

Step 1. Read the Question Stem

This is the place to really read carefully. Make sure you understand exactly what the question is asking. Is it a vocabulary question? Are you looking for an overall main idea or a specific piece of information? Are you trying to infer the author's attitude or the meaning of a particular phrase?

Step 2. Locate the Material You Need

If you are given a vocabulary question, read the material surrounding the word in question. It will clarify exactly what the question is asking and provide you with the context you need to answer the question correctly. If you are looking for supportive information for the author's argument, scan the passage for clue words or phrases that relate to the main idea.

Step 3. Predict the Answer

Don't spend time making up a precise answer. You need only a general sense of what you're after so you can recognize the correct answer quickly when you read the choices.

Step 4. Scan the Answer Choices

Scan the choices, looking for one that fits your idea of the right answer. If you don't find an ideal answer, quickly eliminate wrong choices by checking back to the passage. Rule out choices that are too extreme or go against common sense. Get rid of answers that sound reasonable but don't make sense in the context of the passage or the question. Don't pick farfetched inferences, and make sure there is evidence for your inference in the passage.

Step 5. Select Your Answer

You've eliminated the obvious wrong answers. One of the remaining should fit your ideal. If you're left with more than one contender, consider the passage's main idea, and make an educated guess.

Using Kaplan's Five-Step Method

Read the following passage, and use Kaplan's Five-Step Method to answer the question that follows.

The Cradle of Humankind, a newly designated UNESCO World Heritage site, spreads over 183 square miles near Johannesburg, South Africa. The ground is littered with fossils only a half-hour drive from civilization. Though not as famous as the Leakey site in East Africa, this site is a veritable trove of anthropological artifacts. Forty percent of the evidence of early human evolution is here, partly because of the geological history of the area. One of the largest meteorites ever to hit the earth landed near where Johannesburg is now, covering the dolomite that was left from the earth's cooling period. Caves were formed by underground streams, and animals and hominids were sucked into them through shafts after rainfalls. It was a unique area for preservation of physical remains, just as the La Brea Tar Pits in Los Angeles were.

Excavations have to be done slowly and painstakingly, so many years will pass before the area has been completely mined of all of its archeological and anthropological evidence.

Step 1. Read the Question Stem

The location of the World Heritage site is

(A) near the Leakey site

(B) East Africa

(C) South Africa

(D) Johannesburg

(E) Los Angeles

Step 2. Locate the Material You Need

The Cradle of Humankind, *a newly designated UNESCO World Heritage site, spreads over 183 square miles near Johannesburg, South Africa.* The ground is littered with fossils only a half-hour drive from civilization. Though not as famous as the Leakey site in East Africa, this site is a veritable trove of anthropological artifacts. Forty percent of the evidence of early human evolution is here, partly because of the geological history of the area. One of the largest meteorites ever to hit the earth landed near where Johannesburg is now, covering the dolomite that was left from the earth's cooling period. Caves were formed by underground streams and animals and hominids were sucked into them through shafts after rainfalls. It was a unique area for preservation of physical remains, just as the La Brea Tar Pits in Los Angeles were.

Excavations have to be done slowly and painstakingly, so many years will pass before the area has been completely mined of all of its archeological and anthropological evidence.

Step 3. Predict the Answer

The text states that the new site for the World Heritage is *near Johannesburg, South Africa,* but it does not give a specific location. So, you will be looking for an answer that mentions either South Africa or an area near Johannesburg.

Step 4. Scan the Answer Choices

The location of the World Heritage site is

(A) near the Leakey site

(B) East Africa

(C) South Africa

(D) Johannesburg

(E) Los Angeles

Step 5. Select Your Answers

From the choices given, there are two answers that seem to fit your prediction—choices (C) and (D). But look carefully at the text and the answers. Choice (D) just has Johannesburg as your choice, but the text states that the site is near Johannesburg, not in it, so (D) can be ruled out, leaving you with (C), South Africa.

Were you able to follow? Let's try another question using the same passage.

Step 1. Read the Question Stem

The author uses the word *veritable* to

(A) show it is old

(B) emphasize a fact he believes to be true

(C) contrast the Leakey site

(D) add action

(E) argue a point

Step 2. Locate the Material You Need

The Cradle of Humankind, a newly designated UNESCO World Heritage site, spreads over 183 square miles near Johannesburg, South Africa. The ground is littered with fossils only a half-hour drive from civilization. Though not as famous as the Leakey site in East Africa, this site is a *veritable* trove of anthropological artifacts. Forty percent of the evidence of early human evolution is here, partly because of the geological history of the area. One of the largest meteorites ever to hit the earth landed near where Johannesburg is now, covering the dolomite that was left from the earth's cooling period. Caves were formed by underground streams and animals and hominids were sucked into them through shafts after rainfalls. It was a unique area for preservation of physical remains, just as the La Brea Tar Pits in Los Angeles were.

Excavations have to be done slowly and painstakingly, so many years will pass before the area has been completely mined of all of its archeological and anthropological evidence.

Step 3. Predict the Answer

The question asks you to interpret the usage of the word *veritable* from the context of the sentence. You don't need to re-read the entire selection, but you should read the sentences surrounding the one containing the word in question. In this context, *veritable* is an adjective modifying the noun *trove*. Adjectives are used to add expression, indicate a special quality, or add distinction to the noun that it is modifying. Thus, the answer you are looking for will show how *veritable* is used in one of these three ways.

Step 4. Scan the Answer Choices

The author uses the word *veritable* to

(A) show it is old
(B) emphasize a fact he believes to be true
(C) contrast the Leakey site
(D) add action
(E) argue a point

Step 5. Select Your Answer

The correct answer is (B). It is used to emphasize the statement, or add expression, that this is a *trove* rich with artifacts. (A) is a poor choice because you cannot tell what *it* refers to. *It* is vague. (C) is a poor choice because the author is trying to draw a parallel between this trove and the Leakey site. (D) and (E) do not make sense in the context of the passage.

Remember to use this method on the practice questions in chapter 6. If you find you are struggling with a specific skill or question type, refer back to this chapter, and review the skills that will be tested and the strategies to build those skills.

Chapter Six: **Reading Practice Set**

This chapter contains a random assortment of practice questions covering the three question types discussed in chapter 5. Be sure to use the Five-Step Method you learned when answering these questions. Complete answers and explanations follow the question set. Read the explanations for all questions, even the questions you answered correctly. A little extra review never hurts. If after you're finished checking the results you still don't feel comfortable about one or more question types, go back and review the strategies before going on to the practice tests. Review and practice are the most important elements of preparation for the CBEST. Good luck!

PRACTICE

Questions 1–2

Politics in America have changed immeasurably since the time of the Founding Fathers, at least in terms of money. At first, political jobs didn't pay much, so candidates were usually wealthy gentlemen of respectable reputation. At that time, women and black Americans did not have the vote.

At some point, however, candidates began campaigning very publicly and had to raise money for advertising pamphlets, buttons, and ribbons. It wasn't long before they sought donations from wealthy individuals and corporations to cover those expenses.

1. The author's main point seems to be

    (A) candidates in early America were usually gentlemen

    (B) American politics have changed a lot in terms of money

    (C) candidates originally campaigned at their private clubs and at exclusive dinners

    (D) soon candidates sought money from wealthy friends

    (E) early political jobs didn't pay much

2. Which of the following is implied in the first sentence of the second paragraph?

    (A) Candidates campaigned privately for years, which cost little money.

    (B) Going to individuals to raise money was required by changes in campaign tactics.

    (C) Candidates did not campaign for office for the first 100 years of the republic.

    (D) For years candidates were able to give speeches and engage in debates that cost little.

    (E) Candidates today need to raise a lot of money.

KAPLAN

Question 3–4

Use the excerpt below from a table of contents to answer the two questions that follow.

Contents

3. In which section would the reader find an explanation of the significance of this book about the United States Civil War?

    (A) Editor's Introduction

    (B) Prologue: From the Halls of Montezuma

    (C) The United States at Mid-century

    (D) The Counterrevolution of 1861

    (E) Amateurs Go To War

4. In which chapter would the reader most likely find a discussion of the political attitudes of working people?

    (A) An Empire for Slavery

    (B) Mexico Will Poison Us

    (C) The Crime Against Kansas

    (D) Mudsills and Greasy Mechanics for A. Lincoln

    (E) Facing Both Ways: The Upper South's Dilemma

Questions 5–6

A recent California report on air quality and transportation planning indicates air pollution costs $10 billion a year in health costs, which is $1,500 per household, from pollution-related illnesses. These costs are not paid for by the individual driver or shippers. Neither are they provided from gas taxes. _____
_____.
The health costs are absorbed by our private health insurance plans. Other costs are the damages to trees and global warming.

The report, which looks to the future, did not consider public transit, telecommuting, or "self-supporting" motoring (where drivers and shippers pay the full cost of using roads) as possible solutions. If it had, the future might look brighter than it does. As things stand now, we're facing more gridlock over larger geographical areas and worse air pollution in the future.

5. Choose the best sentence to place in the blank space.

    (A) Shippers and drivers should pay all the costs of driving.

    (B) Gas taxes go to repairing roads and freeways and providing lighting.

    (C) Taxes could be increased but drivers would revolt.

    (D) All of us are happy to have a free ride, but it's not fair.

    (E) Most people don't have any idea of the true costs of freeway drivers.

6. Locate the main idea of the passage.

    (A) at the beginning of the first paragraph

    (B) at the end of the first paragraph

    (C) in the middle of the first paragraph

    (D) in the middle of the second paragraph

    (E) at the end of the second paragraph

Questions 7–9

Use the bar graph below to answer the three questions that follow.

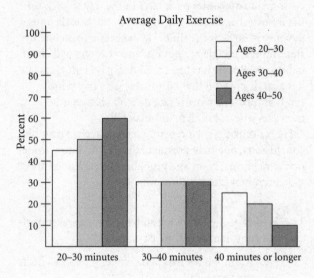

Average Daily Exercise

8. Which of the following statements is best supported by information in the graph?

    (A) Only serious athletes exercise for longer than 40 minutes.

    (B) People ages 40–50 need to exercise longer than 20 minutes.

    (C) The same percentage of age groups exercises for 30–40 minutes.

    (D) Exercising for longer periods has a positive effect on one's health.

    (E) Most people are only able to exercise for no longer than 30 minutes.

9. Which of the following is another way that the information above could be presented?

    (A) illustration

    (B) line graph

    (C) timeline

    (D) preface

    (E) index

7. Which of the following statements is best supported by information in the graph above?

    (A) The length of exercise decreases as one gets older.

    (B) As a group, people ages 30–40 exercise the longest.

    (C) Thirty minutes of exercise helps maintain optimum health.

    (D) The majority of people exercise longer than 30 minutes a day.

    (E) People ages 40–50 prefer to exercise about 40 minutes everyday.

Questions 10–11

A change is occurring in America's food tastes. The move is toward sustainable agriculture, whether it is the production of vegetables, fruits, or beef. Chefs are looking for locally grown food, preferably organic, from farmers who practice *sustainable agriculture*, and in their restaurants, they serve seasonal vegetables and fruits. In many cities and towns, residents plant gardens or shop at farmers' markets. The result of all of this is lower fossil fuel costs for transportation of food and less pollution. Organic produce also means less pesticide use. The organic industry has expanded by more than 20% each year since 1990.

10. *Sustainable agriculture* most likely means

   (A) agricultural practices that can be continued

   (B) agricultural practices that enrich rather than deplete the needs of the planet

   (C) agricultural practices that sustain animal life

   (D) agricultural practices that mass produce products

   (E) using every part of an agricultural product

11. If the organic food industry has grown by more than 20% annually for ten years, one may logically predict

   (A) very little

   (B) the growth may continue unabated

   (C) a shift away from this pattern

   (D) it can't go on forever

   (E) a major shift in Americans' eating habits is underway

Questions 12–14

Are people basically honest? One man started a bagel delivery business in which he leaves a moneybox for customers and comes back later in the day to pick up the leftover bagels and any money in the box. People pay nearly 90% of the time. He has come to a conclusion: honest people are honest, and cheaters will cheat habitually. But he has been studying payment rates and has also discovered that customers who pay poorly rarely improve. Payment rate doesn't change if he increases prices, but demand may fall.

He is doing his own research using bagels. From his conclusions, one may postulate that if you know someone who cheats, he or she probably won't change and, *moreover*, may cheat indiscriminately.

12. Which of the following statements is an appropriate continuation of the passage?

   (A) Although a small percentage of people cheat, they are consistent.

   (B) If 90% of people are honest, that's not so bad.

   (C) It may behoove you to observe your friends carefully and not be too idealistic.

   (D) Chronic cheaters apparently make up 10% of the population.

   (E) All cheaters will eventually be caught.

13. The author draws a conclusion based on the conclusions of the experimenter. What does the author conclude?

   (A) Most people are honest.

   (B) People will not buy bagels if the price goes up.

   (C) Cheaters seem to prosper.

   (D) Cheaters make up a small percentage of people.

   (E) People who cheat in one situation will continue to cheat in nearly all situations.

14. The use of the word *moreover* signals

    (A) a further conclusion to the preceding one

    (B) over time, a cheater will get worse

    (C) more importantly

    (D) better than

    (E) the only option in a sentence

Questions 15–16

Use the excerpt below from an index to answer the two questions that follow.

The Gap	49, 108, 123, 184, 201, 214
gas stations	127–128, 136
gastrointestinal remedies	209
gender differences	96–97, 98–128
in affinity for shopping	98–99, 113, 114,116
car dealerships and	126–127
consumer electronics and	123–126
fast-food restaurants and	119
gender upheaval and	121–128
in information gathering	99, 101–102, 105, 124–125
in looking at price tags	99–100
in movement through store	99
in paying	101
in supermarket shopping	100–101
in technology use	124
in trying on clothing	107
see also men; women	
General Mills	144–145, 163–164
generic brands	21
gift-wrapping	198
Gillette	111, 175

15. On which page should one look to find information about the differences in the way men and women make decisions about clothing purchases?

    (A) 21

    (B) 101

    (C) 107

    (D) 124

    (E) 214

16. On which pages has the author most likely described the way in which men and women approach shopping?

    (A) 96–97

    (B) 98–102

    (C) 127–128

    (D) 144–145

    (E) 163–164

Question 17

Use the table below to answer the question that follows.

Amount You Save Each Week Earning 7%

	$1	$5	$10	$15	$20
5 years	$319	$1,597	$3,194	$4,791	$6,388
10 years	$796	$3,979	$7,957	$11,936	$15,914
20 years	$2,566	$12,828	$25,655	$38,483	$51,310
25 years	$4,146	$20,728	$41,455	$62,183	$82,910
30 years	$6,502	$32,509	$65,091	$97,528	$130,037
40 years	$15,257	$76,285	$152,570	$228,855	$305,140
50 years	$34,730	$173,649	$347,299	$520,948	$694,598

17. Which statement is best supported by the information in the chart above?

    (A) Compounding interest is the slowest way to make money.

    (B) Saving $10 per week is the fastest way to reach $10,000.

    (C) The money you save actually decreases between 10 years and 20 years.

    (D) One can easily double their money by saving a few dollars every week.

    (E) Seven percent interest represents the best interest rate for making money.

Questions 18–20

Use the excerpt below from a table of contents to answer the three questions that follow.

Contents

18. Which of the following best describes the organizational pattern used in this book?

    (A) by animal species
    (B) by regions of the United States
    (C) by publication date
    (D) by theme
    (E) by alphabetical order

19. In which year was the author probably more interested in marine life?

    (A) 1979
    (B) 1980
    (C) 1982
    (D) 1984
    (E) 1985

20. In which of the following would you most likely find the author's views on storytelling?

    (A) Gone Back into the Earth
    (B) Landscape and Narrative
    (C) Searching for Ancestors
    (D) Children in the Woods
    (E) A Reflection on White Geese

Questions 21–23

Scholars, journalists, and theologians have studied Disney films for years to identify what values they teach to young people who watch them. Some researchers call the films "The Gospel According to Walt." Today, when small children watch Disney videos and DVDs over and over, the questions become more significant than in the days when children saw a Disney film once or twice in their lives in a movie theater. The films actually teach acceptable human behavior and relationships; they present problems, dilemmas, failures, and triumphs of the characters in the stories. Overall, the films portray the values of hard work, the triumph of good over evil, and faith in yourself and in a higher power, especially if it seems the odds are stacked against you. In other words, "Be a good person and you will be happy!"

21. The author's attitude toward the subject seems to be

    (A) favorable to Disney films because they teach core values
    (B) detached from any judgment about the films
    (C) unfavorable to Disney films because of their sophomoric approach to real life problems
    (D) unappreciative of what Disney films offer to children
    (E) disgusted with the offerings of Disney films

22. What would be the most effective method to challenge the author's statements?

    (A) discuss other animated films that do not fit the formula

    (B) bring up an example of a Disney film that does not fit this formula

    (C) present data about the uselessness of propagandizing children

    (D) disagree with the author as forcefully as possible

    (E) quote a researcher who disagrees with the author

23. This passage is probably written for an audience of

    (A) film buffs

    (B) students in a film class

    (C) students in a sociology class

    (D) filmmakers

    (E) general readers

Questions 24–25

Use the table below to answer the two questions that follow.

Top Retirement Communities

City	Population	Average Monthly Rent	Average Cost
Prescott, Ariz.	28,211	$800	115,000
Fairhope, Ala.	9,000	$400–$600	80,000
Mount Dora, Fla.	7,500	$400–$600	65,000–70,000
Las Vegas, Nev.	920,000	$875–$1,150	110,000–115,000
Chapel Hill, N.C.	41,524	$800–$900	100,000–180,000
Naples, Fla.	19,505	$1,100	80,000 (condo)
Sedona, Ariz.	7,898	$1,150–$1,350	150,000–200,000
Palm Springs, Calif.	41,674	$850–$900	96,000 (condo)
Aiken, S.C.	20,534	$400–$850	40,000–85,000
Fayetteville, Ark.	42,962	$500	60,000

24. Which of the following statements is best supported by information in the chart above?

    (A) Mount Dora, Fla. represents the lowest average cost of retirement housing.

    (B) Of communities of comparable size, Las Vegas, Nev. is the most expensive.

    (C) Of communities of comparable size, Fayetteville, Ark. is the most affordable.

    (D) Condos are the only available housing in Naples, Fla. and Palm Springs, Calif.

    (E) Average rents in Fairhope, Ala. and Aiken, S.C. have increased in the last five years.

25. Which of the following statements is best supported by information in the chart above?

    (A) Retirement communities are important industry in Florida.

    (B) Retirement communities are made up mostly of condominiums.

    (C) Retirement communities have lower rents than other communities.

    (D) Retirement communities are only found in small population centers.

    (E) Retirement communities are found mostly in the southern United States.

Questions 26–28

Have American politics stooped to a new low? The phrase "May the richest and most vicious man win" seems to be standard in most of today's candidate campaigns. Presidential candidates spend millions of dollars and use slanderous statements to garner votes now. Years ago, George Washington and Thomas Jefferson seldom campaigned and didn't publicly *disparage* their opponents. Maybe they felt that using such methods to win an election signaled corruption. Today, the American population may just want to be entertained with interesting and fun politics.

26. The best title for this passage would be

    (A) How to Run a Fun Campaign

    (B) How to Vote for a Good Leader

    (C) Is Corruption Taking Over Politics?

    (D) An American Dilemma

    (E) Only the Rich Can Win an Election

27. The word *disparage* as used in this passage means

    (A) to lessen in value

    (B) to make a joke of

    (C) to discredit

    (D) to make fun of

    (E) to praise

28. The passage is intended to say that

    (A) American politics have changed throughout the years.

    (B) Are American politics corrupt?

    (C) Only rich candidates can be president.

    (D) George Washington was a better president.

    (E) Corruption begins with the campaign and gets worse once a candidate is elected.

Questions 29–31

Use the table of contents below to answer the three questions that follow.

Contents

29. Which of the following best describes the organizational pattern of the book on women's law?

    (A) by general subject

    (B) by order of importance

    (C) by author's state of origin

    (D) by alphabetical order of author

    (E) by alphabetical order of subject

30. In which chapter would one most likely find answers to copyright issues regarding a magazine article on handicapped athletes?

    (A) Chapter 4

    (B) Chapter 5

    (C) Chapter 6

    (D) Chapter 7

    (E) Chapter 8

31. Who would be the best author to consult regarding selecting the best representation in a property dispute involving a business?

    (A) Judith A. Ginsberg

    (B) Laura Shonenweis

    (C) Andy Wilhite

    (D) Sharon Tillman

    (E) Lewis Nimerov

Questions 32–33

What is sportsmanship? The 2004 Olympic games in Athens, Greece sparked much interest and publicity with regard to this issue. Many of the events had the audience booing or cheering. In some events, there was controversy among the judges. And, most of the winners exhibited overwhelming joy at their success. A sportsman can be defined as someone who can take a loss or defeat without complaint or a victory without *gloating*, and someone who treats his opponents with fairness, *generosity*, and courtesy.

32. As it is used here, the meaning of the word *gloating* is

    (A) jumping up and down

    (B) grinning scornfully

    (C) hugging your friends and relatives

    (D) yelling and screaming

    (E) clapping and waving your hands

33. The word *generosity* has many different meanings. As it is used in this passage, the best meaning would be

    (A) rich and full-flavored

    (B) magnanimous

    (C) willing to give or share

    (D) liberal

    (E) large

Questions 34–35

Use the chart below to answer the two questions that follow.

The Seven Wonders of the Ancient World

2560 BC	Pyramids of Giza built
600 BC	Hanging Gardens of Semiramis built
550 BC	The Temple of Artemis built
435 BC	The Statue of Zeus built
356 BC	The Temple of Artemis destroyed
353 BC	Tomb of Mausolus built
280 BC	The Pharos of Alexandria built
280 BC	The Colossus of Rhodes built
220 BC	The Colossus of Rhodes destroyed
462 AD	The Statue of Zeus destroyed
796 AD	The Pharos of Alexandria destroyed
1522 AD	Tomb of Mausolus destroyed

34. Which of the following is best supported by the information in the timeline above?

   (A) Of the Seven Wonders, the Statue of Zeus took the longest to build.

   (B) One could see most of the Wonders of the Ancient World in the year 250 BC.

   (C) The Temple of Artemis had the shortest lifespan of the other ancient wonders.

   (D) Most of the Seven Wonders of the Ancient World were destroyed by earthquakes.

   (E) The year 350 BC saw most of the Wonders of the Ancient World built.

35. Which date saw the most construction of new Wonders of the Ancient World?

   (A) 435 BC

   (B) 356 BC

   (C) 280 BC

   (D) 462 AD

   (E) 796 AD

Questions 36–39

Many employers now require pre-employment drug testing. Is this an attempt to make the workplace safe and efficient, or does this costly practice contribute to lowering the morale of the workers?

Eighty-one percent of large employers now require drug testing according to governmental statistics. The drug most likely to be detected—marijuana—is also the most *innocuous*. Heroin and cocaine are generally undetectable three days after use, and alcohol, the drug most available, is not even tested for.

Employers tend to hold the belief that drugs are illegal and cause workers to lose days of work with related illnesses. They feel they have a right to hire healthy and reliable workers because they lose income when employees are out sick.

However, opponents to drug testing say it is a huge waste of time and money. It costs thousands of dollars to hire drug-testing companies, when the most dangerous drugs can't even be detected. Some argue that the number of days off caused by alcohol-related illness far out way any other drug, which is contradictory to the philosophy behind drug testing because alcohol is not included in the testing.

36. What are the most important reasons for drug testing?

   (A) Alcohol and heroin cause workers to lose days of work due to illness and cost employers money.

   (B) Healthy employees make better workers.

   (C) The work place is safer and more efficient when workers are drug free.

   (D) Marijuana cannot be detected, but since cocaine and heroin can be detected and are the most dangerous, it is a valid test.

   (E) Workers feel good when they know that their co-workers are drug free.

37. When you compare the two opinions, what are the most significant differences?

   (A) waste of time versus a safe environment

   (B) lowering the morale versus saving money

   (C) employee illness versus efficiency

   (D) friendly work environment versus hostile employers

   (E) safety and efficiency versus loss of money and ineffective testing methods

38. In this passage, what does the word *innocuous* mean?

   (A) harmless

   (B) dangerous

   (C) harmful

   (D) illness causing

   (E) effective

39. Most of the passage is stating the pros and cons of drug testing. What is the only fact presented?

   (A) Alcohol is the drug of choice for most people.

   (B) Heroin and cocaine cannot be detected in drug testing.

   (C) Marijuana is not harmful.

   (D) Eighty-one percent of large company employers require drug testing.

   (E) Drug testing lowers morale at work.

Questions 40–42

Use the excerpt below from an index of a book on oceans to answer the three questions that follow.

Water motion	78–113
coastal upwelling and,	86–88
as conveyor belt,	94–96
Coriolis effect and,	82–85
deep-sea circulation and,	90–94
Gulf Stream and,	96–100
measurement of,	93–94
in regional seas,	96
sunlight and,	78–81
tides and,	109–113
waves and,	100–109
winds and,	81–88
Water strider,	77
Wave-cut terraces,	139
Waves,	100–109
rogue,	108–109
Wegener, Alfred,	142–144
Whales,	49–50, 232–236
Whittington, Harry,	26
Wilson, J. Tuzo,	147–148
Wind,	81–88
coastal upwelling and,	86–88
convection and,	81
Coriolis effect and,	82–85
over land,	81–82
over water,	85–86
sediment transported by,	166
sun and,	78, 80
waves and,	102
Woods Hole Oceanographic Institution,	70

40. On which pages would one most likely encounter mathematical formulas?

   (A) 49–50

   (B) 86–88

   (C) 93–94

   (D) 100–109

   (E) 147–148

41. On which page would one most likely find a description of geographic features created by water?

    (A) 26

    (B) 70

    (C) 96

    (D) 139

    (E) 166

42. In which pages would you mostly likely find information about important contributors to the study of oceans?

    (A) 86–88

    (B) 78–113

    (C) 93–94

    (D) 142–148

    (E) 232–236

Questions 43–44

Vigilantes were an accepted part of frontier justice in the old west in America but only recently has vigilantism been important in Mexico, where people have tolerated an inefficient and corrupt police force for many generations. Now, when a shop owner in Mexico calls for help, the townspeople rush to catch the thief. Someone will ring the church bell to signal an emergency, and what had been a small group becomes an angry mob. In one town, the suspected thief was tied to a flagpole, beaten, and insulted until the police arrived. Some townsfolk are so fed up with assaults and vandalism that they will take action in a bid to show criminals and potential criminals what the consequences of crime are. Vigilantism is rising across Mexico in villages and towns.

43. Identify the words or phrases that are inconsistent in tone with the rest of the passage.

    (A) rush to catch

    (B) fed up, in a bid

    (C) consequences, vigilantism

    (D) inefficient and corrupt

    (E) signal an emergency

44. Which of the following sentences or clauses is most relevant to the author's argument?

    (A) but only recently has vigilantism been important in Mexico

    (B) In one town, the suspected thief was tied to a flagpole, beaten, and insulted until the police arrived.

    (C) what had been a small group becomes an angry mob

    (D) Vigilantism is rising across Mexico in villages and towns.

    (E) Now...townspeople rush to catch a thief.

Question 45

Use the chart below to answer the question that follows.

Who Visits the United States

45. Which of the following is best supported by information in the chart above?

    (A) To an extent, proximity determines who visits the United States.

    (B) The United States does not appeal to people who live in Africa.

    (C) Europeans visit the United State more than any other nationality.

    (D) Few visitors to the United States speak English as a first language.

    (E) Canadians tend to stay longer during their visits to the United States.

Questions 46–48

Use the excerpt from the index below to answer the three questions that follow.

46. On which page would one most likely begin to find a discussion of how urban legends are retold?

    (A) 13
    (B) 53
    (C) 96
    (D) 144
    (E) 312

47. On which page would one most likely find an urban legend involving air travel?

    (A) 101
    (B) 120
    (C) 167
    (D) 287
    (E) 312

48. On which page would one mostly likely find a citation of another book on urban legends?

    (A) 214
    (B) 264
    (C) 297
    (D) 312
    (E) 315

Questions 49–50

High school students who want to be successful in the college admissions process should begin their research as early as the ninth grade. First, you will need to make some decisions about who you are, what you like and don't like, and most importantly, how you learn the best. You are in control of how well you do academically and how much you learn.

Grades and test scores are naturally important in achieving admission, but other factors are just as important. Location of a campus can be important; you need to consider how far away from home you can be and still feel comfortable. Weather and climate can be important to some. If you hate 100-degree heat or can't stand to be cold, or if the mountains make you happy or you love the smell and sound of the ocean, use this information when making your campus selections.

Also important is the classroom setting. Do you like knowing all the students in your class, saying "hi" in the hallways, being engaged in every classroom discussion, forming study groups, and talking with your teachers? You might decide that a small campus would be best for you. Or, would you rather sit in the back of a large lecture hall taking notes, studying alone, not interacting with your teachers, and not being in small discussion groups? You might do very well on a large campus with big lecture sections.

Once you know your learning style and what you like about a particular location, you should consider what majors are offered on each campus. You don't want to be a business major on a campus that doesn't offer business as a major.

Now, you are ready to make a list. Start with the most difficult campuses to get into. End your list with several schools that are "safety" or "for sure" schools where you will most likely be admitted.

You will be successful in the admission process if you know who you are, know what makes you happy, how you learn the best, and have researched what it takes to be admitted academically. Start early, visit campuses, and get your list started. Most students who follow these steps will find success and be happy at the best college for them.

49. Which of the following statements best exemplifies a logical assumption of the author?

(A) All high school students will go to college.

(B) Students who have poor grades and test scores cannot go to college.

(C) There is a perfect college campus for every student, but the student must do his or her research.

(D) College campuses in the mountains are too cold for most students.

(E) Learning style is the most important element in selecting a college.

50. The author uses the following persuasive technique in this passage

(A) appeal to authority

(B) emotional language

(C) statistics

(D) logic and reasoning

(E) evidence

ANSWERS AND EXPLANATIONS

1. B

The correct answer is (B). It includes information from both paragraphs. (A) is actually a sub point of the main point. (C) is incorrect because it may be implied, but it isn't directly stated. (D) is incorrect because it is a sub point in the second paragraph. (E) is also a sub point, but in the first paragraph.

2. A

The best answer is (A). (B) is incorrect because it presents the information in reverse order. Campaign tactics changed, which required raising money. (C) is incorrect because the sentence says or implies nothing about the first 100 years. (D) is a second best choice, but giving speeches and engaging in debates are too specific to be implied. (E) is incorrect because the sentence does not refer to today.

3. A

The editor's introduction most likely introduces the work that follows. That is why (A) is the correct answer. The other answer choices are incorrect because the chapters probably do not comment on the significance of the work of which they are a part.

4. D

The working classes and presidential politics are implied in the chapter "Mudsills and Greasy Mechanics for A. Lincoln." That is why (D) is the correct answer. Nothing in the titles in the other choices suggests or mentions working people or politics.

5. B

In this case, you need to determine the answer by the context, just as you would a word meaning. Read up to the sentence before the blank and then the sentences after it. Notice style and tone. The best answer is (B). (A) is not a good choice because the author's voice is interjected with "should." (D) and (E) similarly are poor choices. They are comments by the author that intrude into the straightforward expository style. (C) is a possibility but interjects the idea of driver revolt, which does not lead into the next sentence.

6. E

(E) is the best choice. All of the information leads to that end. The conclusion states the main idea.

7. A

The chart shows that fewer people ages 40–50 exercise for longer than 40 minutes, whereas a larger percentage of people ages 20–30 exercise for the same period of time. That is why (A) is the correct answer. Choice (B) is incorrect because more people ages 20–30 exercise longer. Choice (C) is incorrect because nothing in the chart mentions how to maintain optimum health. Choice (D) is incorrect because the information in the chart does not support this statement. Choice (E) is incorrect because the information in the chart does not specifically mention preferences.

8. C

The chart shows that 30 percent of each group exercises for longer than 30 minutes. That is why (C) is the correct answer. Choice (A) is incorrect because athletes are not mentioned in the chart. Choice (B) is incorrect because the chart does not make recommendations about how long people should exercise. Choice (D) is incorrect because the chart does not make a correlation between one's health and the length of exercise. Choice (E) is incorrect because the chart does not mention people's abilities to exercise.

9. B

A line graph could use three different lines to represent the ages, and one axis could represent exercise time in minutes. That is why (B) is the correct answer. Choices (A), (D), and (E) are incorrect because they are features in books and are not used to graphically represent information. Choice (C) is incorrect because a timeline only shows when something happened.

10. B

(B) is the best answer. In this case, the interpretation of meaning comes from the overall thrust of the article. (A) is not correct, although a dictionary definition might make it look like a good choice. (C), (D), and (E) are poor choices because there is nothing in the passage to suggest any of those answers.

11. E

(E) is the best choice. It is actually stated in the first sentence and reinforced in the last sentence. (A), (B), (C), and (D) are all opinions but not specifically supported in the passage.

12. A

(A) is the best answer because it carries the most recent thought somewhat further. (B) is a comment that is not in the style of the passage and is therefore not as good. (C) is a possibility but injects the second person into the passage and so is not consistent in style. (D) is a conclusion based on earlier information, so it is not a good sequence. (E) does not follow logically from the passage.

13. E

(E) is the best answer. Reread the last sentence. (A) is possible but not well stated. It doesn't follow logically. (B) is not mentioned at the end of the piece, so it would not be a good conclusion. (C) is not stated at all. (D) is stated much earlier in the passage.

14. A

(A) is the best answer because *moreover* means "in addition to what has been said" and is used to signal an additional statement. (B) is not appropriate because it is not a structural signal. (C) is not correct because the question does not ask for a definition. (D) is not a good choice because it also would be a definition. (E) is incorrect because it doesn't make sense in terms of the sentence and the question.

15. C

The best place to find information about the differences in the way men and women make decisions about clothing purchases would probably involve trying on clothing on page 107. That is why (C) is the correct answer. Choices (A) and (E) are incorrect because these pages do not appear under the heading "gender differences." Choice (B) is incorrect because it is unclear if topics on that page involve clothing. Choice (D) is incorrect because the page discusses gender differences in using technology and not necessarily in purchasing clothing.

16. B

Several subjects that appear under the subheading "gender differences," involve things that people normally do when they shop. That is why (B) is the correct answer. Choice (A) is incorrect because it is unclear exactly what gender differences the author discusses on these pages. Choices (C), (D), and (E) are incorrect because it does not appear under the heading of gender differences.

17. D

The table shows that a person who saves can double their money over time. That is why (D) is the correct answer. Choices (A), (B), (C), and (E) are incorrect because they are not supported by information in the table.

18. C

The book is organized by the publication dates, which appear in parentheses. That is why (C) is the correct answer. Choice (A) is incorrect because the titles include animal names but the book is not organized by animal species. Choice (B) is incorrect because it is not supported by information in the table of contents. Choice (D) is incorrect because one cannot tell by the table of contents if the book is organized by theme. Choice (E) is incorrect because the titles are not arranged in alphabetical order.

19. D

In 1984, the author published two essays with whales and seals in the titles. That is why (D) is the correct answer. Choices (A), (B), (C), and (E) are incorrect because there is no mention of marine life in the titles of the essays published during those years.

20. B

Narrative is another word for story. That is why (B) is the correct answer. Choices (A), (C), (D), and (E) are incorrect because there is no mention of stories or storytelling in the titles of the essays.

21. A

The best answer is (A). While the author's attitude is not expressly stated, you can infer it because the other choices, (B) *detached*, (C) *unfavorable*, (D) *unappreciative*, and (E) *disgusted* are not expressed at all in the selection.

22. B

(B) is the best answer. It may be hard work to find a film that doesn't fit the formula, but that would be the best answer. (A) is not good because it refers to animated films in general, not Disney films. (C) is also not acceptable because it may be hard to find that sort of data. (D) is not a good choice because to disagree forcefully is general and ineffective as an argument. (E) might be a possibility if you could find a researcher who disagrees because an expert opinion can be reliable information, but (B) shows a flow in the writer's general reasoning process and is still the best answer.

23. C

(C) is the best answer because sociology is a subject that studies culture. (A) is not as good because film buffs are people who enjoy watching films but they don't necessarily read about them. (B) is not as good a choice because students in a film class would probably be studying more than general values taught in films. Their interest is more technical than cultural, and (D), *filmmakers*, would definitely be studying technical information. (E) is not as good an answer because whereas the style is fine for general readers, the topic may not be of general interest.

24. C

Fayetteville, Ark., Chapel Hill, N.C., and Palm Springs, Calif. have about the same population. Of those three communities, Fayetteville, Ark. has the cheapest rent. That is why (C) is the correct answer. Choice (A) is not supported by information in the table. Choices (B), (D), and (E) are incorrect because the table does not provide sufficient information to support the statements.

25. E

All of the cities in the table are located in the southern United States. That is why (E) is correct. Choices (B) and (D) are not supported by information in the table. Choices (A) and (C) are incorrect because the table does not provide sufficient information to support the statements.

26. D

The correct answer is (D). The passage compares the past to the present, thus suggesting a dilemma between what is right in politics and what is wrong. (A) and (B) are wrong because it is not a "How to" passage. (C) is wrong

because there is nothing about corruption in the passage, and (E) is too specific because the passage also mentions using slander to get votes.

27. C

(C) is the correct answer. (A) implies something of material value, and (B) and (D) are not specific enough. (E) has the opposite meaning because *dis* is a negative prefix.

28. A

(A) is the correct answer. (C), (D), and (E) are too specific and do not cover the broader perspective presented. (B) is incorrect because the passage is not asking a question; it is just making a statement.

29. A

The subjects in this table of contents appear in boldface. That is why (A) is the correct answer. Choice (B) is incorrect because nothing in the table of contents indicates that the chapters are arranged in order of importance. Choice (C) is incorrect because the author's place of origin does appear in the table of contents, but the table of contents is not organized according to state of origin. Choices (D) and (E) are not supported by information in the table of contents.

30. E

Questions about copyright would be included under intellectual property. That is why (E) is the correct answer. Choice (A) is incorrect because a chapter that deals with child adoption would not cover copyright issues. Choice (B) is incorrect because a chapter that deals with sports would not cover copyright issues. Choice (C) is incorrect because a chapter that deals with disabilities would not cover copyright issues. Choice (D) is incorrect because a chapter that deals with starting a business would not cover copyright issues.

31. C

Andy Wilhite has written the article on how to select a lawyer. That is why (C) is the correct answer. Choice (A) is incorrect because Ginsburg is an authority on consumer rights and insurance. Choice (B) is incorrect because whereas Shonenweis is an authority on real estate, she may not be the best to give advice about selecting a lawyer. Choice (D) is incorrect because whereas Tillman is an authority on starting a business, she may not be the best to give advice about selecting a lawyer. Choice (E) is incorrect because Nimerov is an authority on intellectual property law.

32. B

(B) can be implied from the context of the proposed definition of *gloating*. The clue in this answer is the word *scornful*; (A), (C), (D), and (E) all show happiness towards winning and not scorn towards the other competitors.

33. B

The correct answer is (B). As an athlete, overlooking injury or insult and rising above pettiness or meanness are elements of being *magnanimous*. (A) would be best used in describing wine, (C) would mean giving something material, as in money, (D) could mean tolerant of others views and broadminded and is not specific to athletics, and (E) could mean ample or big.

34. B

More of the seven wonders existed in the year 250 BC than at any other time. That is why (B) is the correct answer. Choices (A) and (D) are incorrect because the timeline does not give sufficient support for these statements. Choices (C) and (E) are incorrect because they are not supported by information in the timeline.

35. C

Construction of the Pharos or Alexandria and The Colossus of Rhodes started around the year 280 BC. That is why (C) is the correct answer. Choice (A) is incorrect because only the Statue of Zeus was built in 435 BC. Choices (B), (D), and (E) are incorrect because there were no wonders constructed during these periods.

36. C

The answer is (C). You can find evidence for this answer in the first paragraph. (A) is an incorrect statement because alcohol is not even included in the drug test. (B) is generally a correct statement but not the best answer. (D) is an incorrect statement because marijuana can be detected, and (E) is a false statement because it is also argued that workers feel morale is lowered by drug testing.

37. E

(E) is correct. (A) is incorrect because waste of time is not the most important issue. (B) and (C) do not cover enough of the issues presented, and (D) is wrong because a friendly work environment is not mentioned in the passage.

38. A

The author seems to say that marijuana is a less dangerous, or *harmless*, drug with the best chance of being detected. The author believes that heroin and cocaine are much more dangerous drugs. (B), *dangerous*, does not fit in this context. (C) and (D) are negative effects, and the author wants to point out how contradictory drug testing is, and (E) is in direct opposition to the author's meaning.

39. D

Eighty-one percent is the only fact presented, so the answer is (D). (A), (B), (C), and (E) are just statements presented by the author.

40. C

Pages 93–94 contain information about the measurement of wave motion, which means that some formulas for measuring wave motion could be included. That is why (C) is the correct answer. Choice (A) is incorrect because those pages contain information about whales and probably would not contain mathematical formulas. Choice (B) is incorrect because those pages contain information about coastal upwelling and probably would not contain mathematical formulas. Choice (D) is incorrect because those pages contain information about waves and wave motion and probably would not contain mathematical formulas. Choice (E) is incorrect because those pages contain information about Wilson J. Tuzo and probably would not contain mathematical formulas.

41. D

Page 139 contains information about wave-cut terraces. That is why (D) is correct. Choice (A) is incorrect because this page contains information about Harry Whittington. Choice (B) is incorrect because this page contains information about Woods Hole Oceanographic Institution. Choice (C) is incorrect because this page contains information about wave motion in regional seas. Choice (E) is incorrect because this page contains information about sediment transported by wind.

42. D

The pages 142–148 contain information about Alfred Wegener and Wilson J. Tuzo, who are both significant enough to be mentioned in a book about the oceans. That is why (D) is the correct answer. Choice (A) is incorrect because these pages contain information about coastal upwelling. Choice (B) is incorrect because these pages contain information about water motion. Choice (C) is incorrect because these pages contain information about measurement of wave motion. Choice (E) is incorrect because these pages contain information about whales.

43. B

The best answer is (B). *Fed up* and *in a bid* are phrases using informal language. (A) and (E) are incorrect because they each offer only one phrase, and the question asks for more than one. It is plural. (C) and (D) are incorrect because although each offers two choices, the language is more formal than the phrase in (B) and is consistent with the tone of the passage.

44. B

(B) is the best answer. It is stated as a fact. (A) is incorrect because it is part of the argument and not necessarily relevant to it. (C) and (E) are not the best choices because they are incomplete ideas. They do help develop the arguments but are not the most relevant. (D) is a poor choice because it is actually a statement of the argument.

45. A

Almost half of the visitors to the United States come from neighboring Mexico and Canada. That is why (A) is the correct answer. Choice (B), (D), and (E) are incorrect because the chart does not contain sufficient information to support these statements. Choice (C) is incorrect because it is not supported by information in the chart.

46. B

Page 53 contains information about computer bulletin board dissemination of urban legends. That is why (B) is the correct answer. Choice (A) is incorrect because this page contains information about city life reflected in urban legends. Choice (C) is incorrect because this page contains information about antecedents of urban legends. Choice (D) is incorrect because this page contains information

about imitating urban legends. Choice (E) is incorrect because this page contains information about a book on urban legends.

47. C

Airlines are not mentioned under the subheading *urban legends*, so United Airlines would be the next best place to look for an urban legend involving air travel. That is why (C) is the correct answer. Choice (A) is incorrect because this page contains information about the debunking of urban legends. Choice (B) is incorrect because this page contains information about city life reflected in urban legends. Choice (D) is incorrect because this page contains information about the dying out of urban legends. Choice (E) is incorrect because this page contains information about a book about urban legends.

48. D

The italics indicate that a book is discussed on page 312. That is why (D) is the correct answer. Choices (A), (B), (C), and (E) are incorrect because there is nothing to indicate a book reference on any of these pages.

49. C

(E), although very important, is just one of the elements discussed by the author. (A) is never mentioned, and (B) is a false statement according to this author, as is (D). (C) is the correct answer because the author does believe there is a perfect college for every student who does the research on both themselves and the campuses.

50. D

The answer is (D). This author uses logic and reasoning to persuade the reader to organize their college search early. The author does not appeal to any authority as in "one college president states…," so (A) in incorrect. There is no emotional language used, so (B) is incorrect, and there are no statistics presented or evidence sighted, so (C) and (E) would be incorrect.

Mathematics

Chapter Seven: **Mathematics Section Overview**

The CBEST covers only basic mathematical skills of arithmetic, algebra, geometry, and statistics. No advanced concepts or theorems are found on the test. In this section, the important mathematical ideas found on the CBEST will be reviewed. The application of some rules and formulas requires a logical sequence of steps, and these will be explained and reaffirmed with examples, but this is not a textbook.

THREE TYPES OF QUESTIONS

The questions on the CBEST can be grouped into three types.

Question Type 1

Some questions are about the *process* required to answer problems of various kinds:

Examples

A. Do you see that division is needed to answer this question?

What is the width of the rectangular floor of a room that is 8 feet long and is tiled with 56 1-foot square tiles?

The area of a rectangle is length times width. The width of the room is 8 feet. Since the room is tiled with 56 tiles that are each a square with an area of 1 square foot, the area of the floor is 56 square feet. thus, the width is 8 feet and the area is 56 square feet. Since, for a rectangle area = length × width, length = $\frac{\text{area}}{\text{width}}$. So the length of the floor is $\frac{56 \text{ square feet}}{8 \text{ feet}}$, which is 7 feet.

B. Can you identify the correct equation or algebraic expression as the interpretation of a word problem?

Can you pick out the expression that is the algebraic interpretation of the phrase: Five less than twice a certain number, x.

    A. $5 - 2x$

    B. $2x - 5$

    C. $2(x - 5)$

    D. $5 + 2x$

    E. $2(5 - x)$

The correct answer is choice B.

C. Do you understand important definitions?

For example, which of the following is (are) prime?

    A. 0

    B. 13

    C. 57

    D. 97

The correct answer is B and D.

D. Do you know, and can you apply, important rules such as the Order of Operations?

Perform the indicated operations:

$3(7 - 5) + 8^2 \div 2$

The correct answer is 38.

Question Type 2

Some questions ask you to solve various types of mathematical word problems. These problems may be from arithmetic, algebra, or geometry and include applications such as, but not limited to, direct and inverse proportions, percent, area, perimeter, weight, time, and other measurements from the U.S. measurement system, and statistical concepts such as average, stanine, percentile, and probability. You will not be expected to have complicated formulas memorized, but you should know some basic, familiar formulas such as the following:

$P = 2w + 2l$	Perimeter of a rectangle
$A = lw$	Area of a rectangle
$d = rt$	Distance, rate, time (Uniform motion)
$i = prt$	Simple interest
$a^2 + b^2 = c^2$	Pythagorean theorem (pertains to right triangles)
$A = \frac{1}{2}bh$	Area of a triangle
$A = \pi r^2$	Area of a circle

$C = \pi d = 2\pi r$ Circumference of a circle

$V = lwh$ Volume of a rectangular solid

The average (mean) is the sum of n numbers divided by n.

Examples

A. You should know that the formula $d = rt$ applies to this problem. Can you solve it?

Eugene started jogging at the rate of 4 miles per hour. One hour later, Clarice started on the same route at the rate of 6 miles per hour. If Eugene started at 7:00 A.M., at what time will Clarice overtake him?

Let x be the time Eugene spent jogging. The following equation may be used to answer the question.

$$4x = 6(x - 1)$$

The solution set for this equation is {3}. This means that he jogged for 3 hours, and Clarice overtakes him at 10:00 A.M.

B. Here is a direct proportion problem. Can you solve it?

Carol travels 150 miles in 4 hours. At the same speed, how long will it take her to travel 90 more miles?

Set up and solve the proportion:

$\dfrac{4}{x} = \dfrac{150}{90}$ The solution is $\left\{2\dfrac{2}{5}\right\}$.

Carol can travel 90 miles in 2 hours and 24 minutes.

C. A rectangle has a semicircle attached, as shown. What is the perimeter of the figure?

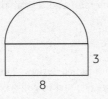

The perimeter is the sum of 3, 8, 3, and $\dfrac{1}{2}$ of a circle of radius 4. The semicircle has length $\dfrac{1}{2}(2\pi(4)) = 4\pi$. The answer is $14 + 4\pi$.

Question Type 3

There may be some questions to determine your conceptual understanding of mathematical relationships.

Examples

A. Which of the following sets of numbers could be the lengths of the sides of a right triangle?

    I. {1, 2, 3}

    II. {3, 4, 5}

    III. {2, $\sqrt{5}$, 3}

Determine which of these sets of numbers satisfies the Pythagorean theorem. The answer is only II and III. $3^2 + 4^2 = 5^2$ and $2^2 + (\sqrt{5})^2 = 3^2$.

B. What is the probability of drawing an ace from a well-shuffled deck of cards?

The answer is $\dfrac{4}{52} = \dfrac{1}{13}$. There are 52 cards in the deck, and 4 of them are aces.

There are no questions on the CBEST that merely ask you to calculate equations such as 236×23, or $5\dfrac{2}{5} - 1\dfrac{3}{4}$. But, of course, there may be some calculations that are required to find the correct answer. In any case, if a problem requires you to multiply and divide, it is usually better to leave the actual calculation until the very end so that you can take advantage of the possibility of cancellation. Consider this calculation:

$\dfrac{50 \times 18 \times 7}{42}$ Cancel 7 in the numerator and denominator.

$\dfrac{50 \times 18 \times 1}{6}$ Cancel 6 in the numerator and denominator.

$\dfrac{50 \times 3 \times 1}{1} = 150$

Review the material in this section with a pencil in hand. Do all of the examples. Be involved with the reading. Use the results of the diagnostic test to guide you. When you have mastered the basics in this book, then do the practice tests. Study the explanations, especially for those questions you got wrong. If you do all of these things, you will be well prepared for the CBEST.

Chapter Eight: **Computation and Problem Solving**

We will assume in this book that you are familiar with basic operations of arithmetic—addition, subtraction, multiplication, and division of whole numbers. The remainder of basic mathematics will be briefly reviewed. All of the material you will find here was part of some course in your academic history, and you need only to be reminded about how to perform certain mathematical tasks and how to apply them to problems of various types.

Our intention is to present each topic in as clear and concise a manner as we can without sacrificing accuracy. We are not going to go into detail about the various memory aids that many use, such as PEMDAS, in our review. Rather, the emphasis is on following rules to get correct answers.

HELPFUL HINT: PEMDAS

When performing multiple operations, remember to perform them in the right order: PEMDAS, which means Parentheses first, then Exponents, then Multiplication and Division (left to right), and last Addition and Subtraction (left to right). In the expression $9 - 2 \times (5 - 3)^2 + 6 \div 3$, begin with the parentheses: $(5 - 3) = 2$. Then do the exponent: $2^2 = 4$. Now the expression is: $9 - 2 \times 4 + 6 \div 3$. Next do the multiplication and division to get: $9 - 8 + 2$, which equals 3. If you have difficulty remembering PEMDAS, use this sentence to recall it: Please Excuse My Dear Aunt Sally.

FACTORS, DIVISORS, AND MULTIPLES

For the purposes of this section only, we are restricting the discussion to **whole numbers**. Notice that 0 is whole number, but fractions, decimals, and negative numbers are not.

If there are three whole numbers that are related by the equation $a \times c = b$, such as $5 \times 3 = 15$, then:

a **divides** b	5 divides 15
a **is a factor of** b	5 is a factor of 15
b **is a multiple of** a	15 is a multiple of 5
b **is divisible by** a	15 is divisible by 5

The list of all *factors* of 20 is 1, 2, 4, 5, 10, and 20. These numbers are also the *divisors* of 20. However, the list of *multiples* of 20 is 0, 20, 40, 60,.... These are also the numbers that are *divisible by* 20. The set of factors of a given whole number is always a finite set, whereas the set of multiples is an infinite set.

PRIME AND COMPOSITE NUMBERS

A **prime number** is a whole number that has exactly two factors. A **composite number** is a whole number greater than one that is not prime. Determining the factors of the whole numbers will allow us to categorize them as either prime or composite.

Whole Number	Factors	Prime or Composite
0	0, 1, 2, 3, …	Neither
1	1	Neither
2	1, 2	Prime
3	1, 3	Prime
4	1, 2, 4	Composite
5	1, 5	Prime
6	1, 2, 3, 6	Composite
7	1, 7	Prime

The first few prime numbers should be memorized: 2, 3, 5, 7, 11, 13, 17, 19, and so on. Notice that the factors of the prime numbers are always 1 and the number itself. To determine whether a larger number is prime or composite, test for divisibility by the numbers you know to be prime, in order, up to the point where the quotient is smaller than the divisor. If you find another factor other than 1 and the number itself, the number is composite. If there is no other factor, the number is prime.

For example, let's determine whether 51 is prime. We know that 1 and 51 are factors. The number 2 is not a factor, but 3 is a factor (as well as 17). The whole number 51 is composite.

Let's do the same for 61. We know that 1 and 61 are factors.

$61 \div 2 = 30 \ r1$ 2 is not a factor
$61 \div 3 = 20 \ r1$ 3 is not a factor
$61 \div 5 = 12 \ r1$ 5 is not a factor
$61 \div 7 = 8 \ r5$ 7 is not a factor
$61 \div 11 = 5 \ r6$ 11 is not a factor

This last division shows that the quotient is smaller than the divisor—our signal to stop. We conclude that 61 is prime.

Periodically, throughout this section, you will find small sets of practice exercises to solidify the ideas just presented. These practice sets are not presented in CBEST format but rather as you might have encountered them in your classes. Do not look at the answers until you have finished the exercises.

Practice Exercises

True or false.

1. 9 is a factor of 117.

2. 143 is a multiple of 11.

3. 7 divides 163.

4. 6 is a prime factor of 42.

5. There are no even prime numbers.

6. 87 is not divisible by 3.

Determine whether these numbers are prime or composite.

7. 31

8. 119

9. 4,785

10. 131

Solutions to Practice Exercises

1. True. Do the division $117 \div 9 = 13$ r0. Therefore, $9 \times 13 = 117$.

2. True. $11 \times 13 = 143$.

3. False. There is no whole number, c, such that $7 \times c = 163$.

4. False. Although 6 is a factor of 42, it is not a prime number.

5. False. The number 2 is the only even prime number.

6. False. 87 is divisible by 3. $3 \times 29 = 87$.

7. Prime

8. Composite. $7 \times 17 = 119$.

9. Composite. Any number ending in a 0 or a 5 is divisible by 5, so 4,785 is divisible by 5.

10. Prime

LOWEST (LEAST) COMMON MULTIPLE AND GREATEST COMMON FACTOR

It is important to be able to find the **prime factorization** of any composite number, that is, we want to write a composite number as a product of its prime factors. For example, $12 = 2 \times 2 \times 3$. A factor tree is one way to do this. To demonstrate this procedure, we'll factor 72 using a factor tree. First, find any two numbers that you can multiply and get 72, say 9 and 8. Then look for factors of both 9 and 8, and continue until the numbers at the bottom of each branch are prime. The prime factorization consists of all the numbers at the bottom of the branches.

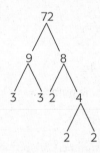

The prime factorization is $72 = 2 \times 2 \times 2 \times 3 \times 3$.

We can use prime factorization to help find the **lowest common multiple** (LCM) and the **greatest common factor** (GCF) of two or more numbers. Both the LCM and GCF are particularly useful in the operations with fractions.

To find the LCM of 48 and 72, first find their prime factorizations.

$48 = 2 \times 2 \times 2 \times 2 \times 3$

$72 = 2 \times 2 \times 2 \times 3 \times 3$

The rule then is to set up a multiplication equation using each prime factor the number of times it appears most in each factorization. In this example, the prime number 2 appears four times in the first factorization and three times in the second; therefore, we should use 2 four times. Three appears once in the first and twice in the second, so we will use 3 twice. The LCM of 48 and 72 is $2 \times 2 \times 2 \times 2 \times 3 \times 3 = 144$.

To find the GCF of 54 and 60, first find their prime factorizations.

$54 = 2 \times 3 \times 3 \times 3$

$60 = 2 \times 2 \times 3 \times 5$

The rule for GCF is to multiply the common prime factors, or those that appear in both (or all) factorizations. In this case, one 2 and one 3 are common to both lists. The GCF of 54 and 60 is $2 \times 3 = 6$.

Let's find both the LCM and GCF of 30, 36, and 48. Find their prime factorizations.

$30 = 2 \times 3 \times 5$
$36 = 2 \times 2 \times 3 \times 3$
$48 = 2 \times 2 \times 2 \times 2 \times 3$

For the LCM, we should use four 2s, two 3s, and one 5.

$2 \times 2 \times 2 \times 2 \times 3 \times 3 \times 5 = 720$

For the GCF, we should use one 2 and one 3.

$2 \times 3 = 6$

Practice Exercises

1. Find the prime factorization of 120.
2. Find the prime factorization of 143.
3. Find the prime factorization of 80.
4. Find the prime factorization of 41.
5. Find the LCM of 28 and 35.
6. Find the LCM of 42 and 66.
7. Find the LCM of 8, 14, and 24.
8. Find the GCF of 84 and 96.
9. Find the GCF of 48 and 52.
10. Find the GCF of 48, 60, and 84.

Solutions to Practice Exercises

1. $120 = 2 \times 2 \times 2 \times 3 \times 5$

2. $143 = 11 \times 13$

3. $80 = 2 \times 2 \times 2 \times 2 \times 5$

4. Because 41 is a prime number, there is no prime factorization. Prime factorization applies only to composite numbers. The answer is *not* 1×41.

5. $28 = 2 \times 2 \times 7$
$35 = 5 \times 7$ So the LCM is $2 \times 2 \times 5 \times 7 = 140$.

6. $42 = 2 \times 3 \times 7$
$66 = 2 \times 3 \times 11$ So the LCM is $2 \times 3 \times 7 \times 11 = 462$.

KAPLAN

7. $8 = 2 \times 2 \times 2$

$14 = 2 \times 7$

$24 = 2 \times 2 \times 3$ So the LCM is $2 \times 2 \times 2 \times 3 \times 7 = 168$.

8. $84 = 2 \times 2 \times 3 \times 7$

$96 = 2 \times 2 \times 2 \times 2 \times 2 \times 3$ So the GCF is $2 \times 2 \times 3 = 12$.

9. $48 = 2 \times 2 \times 2 \times 2 \times 3$

$52 = 2 \times 2 \times 13$ So the GCF is $2 \times 2 = 4$.

10. $48 = 2 \times 2 \times 2 \times 2 \times 3$

$60 = 2 \times 2 \times 3 \times 5$

$84 = 2 \times 2 \times 3 \times 7$ So the GCF is $2 \times 2 \times 3 = 12$.

FRACTIONS

A **fraction** is any expression of the type $\frac{a}{b}$ in which the number on top, the **numerator**, may be any number, and the number on the bottom, the **denominator**, may be any number except 0. If the numerator of a fraction is less than the denominator, the fraction is **proper**; otherwise, it is **improper**. A **mixed number** is a special form that represents the sum of a whole number and a fraction, such as $5\frac{7}{8} = 5 + \frac{7}{8}$.

Equivalent fractions are two or more fractions that represent the same number. Equivalent fractions are formed by any application of the Fundamental Principle of Fractions. This rule states that you can form equivalent fractions by multiplying or dividing the numerator and denominator by the same nonzero number.

$\frac{a}{b} = \frac{a \times k}{b \times k}$ as long as b and k are not equal to 0.

The fractions $\frac{2}{3}$ and $\frac{8}{12}$ are equivalent. The second fraction can be **reduced** to the first by dividing both the numerator and denominator by 4. Notice that 4 is the GCF of the numerator and denominator of $\frac{8}{12}$. If the numerator and denominator have no other common factors (other than 1), we say that the fraction is reduced to lowest terms.

Another application of the Fundamental Principle of Fractions is to rewrite a given fraction so that it has a specific denominator. Suppose you want to find a fraction equivalent to $\frac{3}{5}$ that has denominator 20. To accomplish this, multiply the numerator and denominator of the original fraction by 4: $\frac{3}{5} = \frac{3 \times 4}{5 \times 4} = \frac{12}{20}$.

Practice Exercises

Reduce each fraction to lowest terms.

1. $\dfrac{9}{12}$

2. $\dfrac{20}{15}$

3. $\dfrac{21}{35}$

4. $\dfrac{48}{72}$

5. $\dfrac{91}{104}$

Find the new numerator so that the new fraction is equivalent to the given fraction.

6. $\dfrac{2}{9} = \dfrac{?}{27}$

7. $\dfrac{3}{4} = \dfrac{?}{36}$

8. $\dfrac{5}{8} = \dfrac{?}{72}$

9. $\dfrac{11}{24} = \dfrac{?}{96}$

10. $\dfrac{17}{14} = \dfrac{?}{70}$

Solutions to Practice Exercises

1. $\dfrac{9}{12} = \dfrac{3}{4}$ — Divide the numerator and denominator by 3.

2. $\dfrac{20}{15} = \dfrac{4}{3}$ — Divide by 5.

3. $\dfrac{21}{35} = \dfrac{3}{5}$ — Divide by 7.

4. $\dfrac{48}{72} = \dfrac{24}{36} = \dfrac{2}{3}$ — Reducing can be done in stages. First, divide by 2 and then by 12.

5. $\dfrac{91}{104} = \dfrac{7}{8}$ — When in doubt, factor the numerator and denominator: $91 = 7 \times 13$ and $104 = 8 \times 13$. Divide by 13.

6. $\dfrac{2}{9} = \dfrac{6}{27}$ — Multiply the numerator and denominator by 3.

7. $\dfrac{3}{4} = \dfrac{27}{36}$ — Multiply by 9.

8. $\dfrac{5}{8} = \dfrac{45}{72}$ — Multiply by 9.

9. $\dfrac{11}{24} = \dfrac{44}{96}$ — Divide 24 into 96. Multiply the top and bottom by the quotient 4.

10. $\dfrac{17}{14} = \dfrac{85}{70}$ — Multiply by 5.

MIXED NUMBERS

You often need to change an improper fraction to a mixed number and vice versa. To convert an improper fraction to a mixed number, divide the denominator into the numerator. The quotient is the whole number part of the mixed number, and the remainder is the numerator of the fraction part of the mixed number. The denominator of the fraction part is the same as the denominator of the original improper fraction. For example, to convert $\frac{8}{5}$ to a mixed number, divide 5 into 8. The quotient is 1, and the remainder is 3, so the mixed number is $1\frac{3}{5}$.

To convert a mixed number to an improper fraction, multiply the denominator times the whole number part of the mixed number part. Add the numerator of the fraction part to the product. Place that number over the denominator of the fraction part. For example, to convert $2\frac{3}{4}$ to an improper fraction, multiply 2 times 4 and add 3. The result, 11, is placed over the original denominator. The improper fraction is $\frac{11}{4}$.

Practice Exercises

Convert each improper fraction to a mixed number in simplest form.

1. $\frac{10}{3}$ 3. $\frac{24}{8}$

2. $\frac{17}{5}$ 4. $\frac{30}{12}$

Convert each mixed number to an improper fraction.

5. $3\frac{5}{8}$ 7. $12\frac{1}{2}$

6. $1\frac{7}{9}$ 8. $8\frac{3}{5}$

Solutions to Practice Exercises

1. $3\frac{1}{3}$

2. $3\frac{2}{5}$

3. 3   This is not a mixed number.

4. $2\frac{6}{12} = 2\frac{1}{2}$ Simplest form means reduce fractions to lowest terms.

5. $\frac{29}{8}$

6. $\dfrac{16}{9}$

7. $\dfrac{25}{2}$

8. $\dfrac{43}{5}$

MULTIPLICATION AND DIVISION OF FRACTIONS

To **multiply** two or more **fractions**, multiply the numerators and the denominators, respectively.

$$\frac{a}{b} \times \frac{c}{d} = \frac{ac}{bd}, b \text{ and } d \text{ cannot be 0.}$$

Of course, the answer should be written in reduced form. Any reduction is normally performed before actually multiplying by a process called **cancellation**. Before multiplying, look for any common factors in the numerators and denominators. Cancel from any numerator together with any denominator.

$$\frac{2}{3} \times \frac{5}{8} = \frac{\overset{1}{\cancel{2}}}{3} \times \frac{5}{\underset{4}{\cancel{8}}} = \frac{5}{12} \text{ Cancel 2 and multiply.}$$

All mixed numbers must first be written as improper fractions before multiplication.

$$\left(2\frac{1}{3}\right)\left(7\frac{1}{2}\right) = \left(\frac{7}{3}\right)\left(\frac{15}{2}\right) = \left(\frac{7}{\underset{1}{\cancel{3}}}\right)\left(\frac{\overset{5}{\cancel{15}}}{2}\right) = \frac{35}{2} = 17\frac{1}{2}$$

The rule for division is to replace the second fraction by its reciprocal and change the operation to multiplication. Then follow the rule for multiplication. The reciprocal of any fraction is found by interchanging the numerator and denominator (turn the fraction over).

$$\frac{a}{b} \div \frac{c}{d} = \frac{a}{b} \times \frac{d}{c} \quad b, c, \text{ and } d \text{ cannot be 0.}$$

$$3\frac{3}{4} \div 1\frac{1}{2} = \frac{15}{4} \div \frac{3}{2} = \frac{15}{4} \times \frac{2}{3} = \frac{\overset{5}{\cancel{15}}}{\underset{2}{\cancel{4}}} \times \frac{\overset{1}{\cancel{2}}}{\underset{1}{\cancel{3}}} = \frac{5}{2} = 2\frac{1}{2}$$

Practice Exercises

Find the reciprocal of each number.

1. $\dfrac{5}{8}$

2. $1\dfrac{3}{4}$

3. 8

4. 0

Perform the indicated operations.

5. $\left(3\dfrac{1}{3}\right) \times \left(1\dfrac{3}{5}\right)$

6. $15 \times \dfrac{1}{6}$

7. $\dfrac{2}{3} \div 1\dfrac{3}{5}$

8. $\dfrac{7}{12} \div \dfrac{2}{3}$

9. $24 \div \dfrac{3}{8}$

10. $2\dfrac{2}{5} \div \dfrac{9}{10}$

Solutions to Practice Exercises

1. The reciprocal is $\frac{8}{5} = 1\frac{3}{5}$.

2. $1\frac{3}{4} = \frac{7}{4}$ The reciprocal of $\frac{7}{4}$ is $\frac{4}{7}$.

3. $8 = \frac{8}{1}$ The reciprocal of $\frac{8}{1}$ is $\frac{1}{8}$.

4. 0 is the only number that has no reciprocal.

5. $\left(3\frac{1}{3}\right)\left(1\frac{3}{5}\right) = \left(\frac{10}{3}\right)\left(\frac{8}{5}\right) = \left(\frac{\overset{2}{\cancel{10}}}{3}\right)\left(\frac{8}{\underset{1}{\cancel{5}}}\right) = \frac{16}{3} = 5\frac{1}{3}$

6. $15 \times \frac{1}{6} = \frac{15}{1} \times \frac{1}{6} = \frac{\overset{5}{\cancel{15}}}{1} \times \frac{1}{\underset{2}{\cancel{6}}} = \frac{5}{2} = 2\frac{1}{2}$

7. $\frac{2}{3} \div 1\frac{3}{5} = \frac{2}{3} \div \frac{8}{5} = \frac{2}{3} \times \frac{5}{8} = \frac{2}{3} \times \frac{5}{\underset{4}{\cancel{8}}} = \frac{5}{12}$

8. $\frac{7}{12} \div \frac{2}{3} = \frac{7}{12} \times \frac{3}{2} = \frac{7}{\underset{4}{\cancel{12}}} \times \frac{\overset{1}{\cancel{3}}}{2} = \frac{7}{8}$

9. $24 \div \frac{3}{8} = \frac{24}{1} \times \frac{8}{3} = \frac{\overset{8}{\cancel{24}}}{1} \times \frac{8}{\underset{1}{\cancel{3}}} = \frac{64}{1} = 64$

10. $2\frac{2}{5} \div \frac{9}{10} = \frac{12}{5} \div \frac{9}{10} = \frac{12}{5} \times \frac{10}{9} = \frac{\overset{4}{\cancel{12}}}{\underset{1}{\cancel{5}}} \times \frac{\overset{2}{\cancel{10}}}{\underset{3}{\cancel{9}}} = \frac{8}{3} = 2\frac{2}{3}$

Addition and Subtraction of Fractions

The rules for **addition** and **subtraction** seem deceptively easy to apply. When the denominators are the same, add or subtract the numerators, and keep the same denominator.

$$\frac{a}{b} + \frac{c}{b} = \frac{a+c}{b} \quad \text{and} \quad \frac{a}{b} - \frac{c}{b} = \frac{a-c}{b}, \text{ if } b \text{ is not 0.}$$

The problem becomes more difficult when the denominators are not the same. In that instance, you must first determine the lowest common denominator (LCD; the lowest common multiple of the denominators), rewrite each fraction so that it has that denominator, and follow the rule above. You should work through each of the following examples.

Example 1: $\frac{7}{8} + \frac{5}{8} = \frac{12}{8} = 1\frac{4}{8} = 1\frac{1}{2}$

Example 2: $\frac{2}{3} - \frac{1}{4}$ You must first find the LCD: 12

$\qquad = \frac{8}{12} - \frac{3}{12} \qquad \frac{2}{3} = \frac{?}{12}$ and $\frac{1}{4} = \frac{?}{12}$ as before.

$\qquad = \frac{5}{12}$

Example 3: $\dfrac{7}{18} + \dfrac{11}{15}$ The LCM of 18 and 15 is 90.

$\dfrac{?}{90} + \dfrac{?}{90}$

$= \dfrac{35}{90} + \dfrac{66}{90}$

$= \dfrac{101}{90} = 1\dfrac{11}{90}$

Example 4: $2\dfrac{3}{4} + 5\dfrac{1}{2}$ For mixed number addition, you have the choice of adding the improper fractions or adding the fraction parts and whole number parts separately.

$= \dfrac{11}{4} + \dfrac{11}{2}$

$= \dfrac{11}{4} + \dfrac{22}{4}$

$= \dfrac{33}{4} = 8\dfrac{1}{4}$

Or do this: $2\dfrac{3}{4} + 5\dfrac{1}{2}$

$= 2\dfrac{3}{4} + 5\dfrac{2}{4}$

$= 7\dfrac{5}{4} = 7 + 1\dfrac{1}{4} = 8\dfrac{1}{4}$

Example 5: $7\dfrac{1}{3} - 2\dfrac{4}{5}$

$= 7\dfrac{5}{15} - 2\dfrac{12}{15}$ In order to subtract, you must borrow 1 part from 7, which is equivalent to $\dfrac{15}{15}$ and add it to the fraction $\dfrac{5}{15}$ to get $\dfrac{20}{15}$.

$= 6\dfrac{20}{15} - 2\dfrac{12}{15} = 4\dfrac{8}{15}$

Practice Exercises

Perform the indicated operations.

1. $\dfrac{11}{9} - \dfrac{8}{9}$
2. $\dfrac{3}{8} + \dfrac{5}{6}$
3. $10 - 1\dfrac{1}{2}$
4. $\dfrac{23}{60} - \dfrac{9}{40}$

5. $7\dfrac{7}{8} - 2$
6. $14\dfrac{4}{5} - 7\dfrac{5}{8}$
7. $11\dfrac{1}{5} - 3\dfrac{3}{8}$
8. $5\dfrac{5}{8} + 9\dfrac{2}{3}$

Solutions to Practice Exercises

1. $\dfrac{11}{9} - \dfrac{8}{9} = \dfrac{3}{9} = \dfrac{1}{3}$

2. $\dfrac{3}{8} + \dfrac{5}{6} = \dfrac{?}{24} + \dfrac{?}{24} = \dfrac{9}{24} + \dfrac{20}{24} = \dfrac{29}{24} = 1\dfrac{5}{24}$

3. $10 - 1\dfrac{1}{2} = 9\dfrac{2}{2} - 1\dfrac{1}{2} = 8\dfrac{1}{2}$

4. $\dfrac{23}{60} - \dfrac{9}{40} = \dfrac{?}{120} - \dfrac{?}{120} = \dfrac{46}{120} - \dfrac{27}{120} = \dfrac{19}{120}$

5. $7\dfrac{7}{8} - 2 = 5\dfrac{7}{8}$

6. $14\dfrac{4}{5} - 7\dfrac{5}{8} = 14\dfrac{?}{40} - 7\dfrac{?}{40} = 14\dfrac{32}{40} - 7\dfrac{25}{40} = 7\dfrac{7}{40}$

7. $11\dfrac{1}{5} - 3\dfrac{3}{8} = 11\dfrac{8}{40} - 3\dfrac{15}{40} = 10\dfrac{48}{40} - 3\dfrac{15}{40} = 7\dfrac{33}{40}$

8. $5\dfrac{5}{8} + 9\dfrac{2}{3} = 5\dfrac{15}{24} + 9\dfrac{16}{24} = 14\dfrac{31}{24} = 14 + 1\dfrac{7}{24} = 15\dfrac{7}{24}$

RATIO AND PROPORTION

A **ratio** is just another name for a fraction. The phrase "the ratio of a to b" is translated to the fraction $\dfrac{a}{b}$. If Mr. Sturm's class contains 12 boys and 15 girls, there are several ratios that might be written with this information.

The ratio of boys to girls: $\dfrac{12}{15} = \dfrac{4}{5}$

The ratio of girls to boys: $\dfrac{15}{12} = \dfrac{5}{4}$

The ratio of girls to total number in class: $\dfrac{15}{27} = \dfrac{5}{9}$

A **proportion** is an equation that states that two ratios are equal. The proportion $\dfrac{2}{3} = \dfrac{12}{18}$ may be read *two is to three as twelve is to eighteen*. All proportions have the property that the equation obtained by cross-multiplication is also true.

If $\dfrac{a}{b} = \dfrac{c}{d}$, then $ad = bc$.

The variables a, b, c, and d in this equation are called the terms of the proportion; b and c are called the **means**, and a and d are called the **extremes**. So the rule above can be stated, "The product of the means equals the product of the extremes." If any three terms of a proportion are known, this rule can be used to find the fourth term. For example, solve the next proportion for the unknown term.

$\dfrac{n}{10} = \dfrac{18}{4}$ Cross multiply.

$4n = 180$ Divide both sides by 4.

$n = 45$

Solve this proportion for the unknown term.

$\dfrac{7}{11} = \dfrac{2}{n}$ Cross multiply.

$7n = 22$ Divide by 7.

$n = \dfrac{22}{7} = 3\dfrac{1}{7}$

Practice Exercises

Solve each proportion for the unknown term.

1. $\dfrac{16}{12} = \dfrac{24}{x}$ 3. $\dfrac{z}{13} = \dfrac{2}{9}$

2. $\dfrac{7}{y} = \dfrac{1}{2}$ 4. $\dfrac{\left(\dfrac{5}{4}\right)}{\left(\dfrac{5}{8}\right)} = \dfrac{\left(\dfrac{3}{2}\right)}{w}$

Solutions to Practice Exercises

1. $\dfrac{16}{12} = \dfrac{24}{x}$ Cross multiply.

$16x = 24 \times 12$ Divide by 16.

$x = \dfrac{24 \times 12}{16} = \dfrac{\overset{3}{\cancel{24}} \times 12}{\underset{2}{\cancel{16}}} = \dfrac{3 \times \overset{6}{\cancel{12}}}{\underset{1}{\cancel{2}}} = \dfrac{18}{1} = 18$ It's easier to cancel than to actually multiply and divide.

2. $\dfrac{7}{y} = \dfrac{1}{2}$

$y = 14$

3. $\dfrac{z}{13} = \dfrac{2}{9}$

$9z = 26$

$z = \dfrac{26}{9} = 2\dfrac{8}{9}$

4. $\dfrac{\left(\dfrac{5}{4}\right)}{\left(\dfrac{5}{8}\right)} = \dfrac{\left(\dfrac{3}{2}\right)}{w}$

$\dfrac{5}{4}w = \dfrac{5}{8} \times \dfrac{3}{2} = \dfrac{15}{16}$

$w = \dfrac{15}{16} \div \dfrac{5}{4} = \dfrac{15}{16} \times \dfrac{4}{5} = \dfrac{\overset{3}{\cancel{15}}}{\underset{4}{\cancel{16}}} \times \dfrac{\overset{1}{\cancel{4}}}{\underset{1}{\cancel{5}}} = \dfrac{3}{4}$

APPLICATIONS OF PROPORTIONS

Many practical problems can be solved using proportions. These problems can be grouped into two basic types: **direct** proportion and **indirect** proportions. Indirect proportions are also called inverse proportions. Sometimes the word **variations** is used instead of proportions.

In every application problem, there will be two quantities that change such as hours and miles, weight and amount of medicine, tickets and money, square feet in a house and selling price, inches on a map and miles, number of workers and time to do a job, area of the walls in a room and amount of paint, and so on. In some problems, both quantities will increase together; for example, inches on a map increase and miles increase. This type of problem is a direct proportion.

In other problems, one quantity will decrease while the other increases; for example, if you increase the number of people working on a job, the time it takes to do the work decreases. This type is called an inverse or indirect proportion.

To solve either type, we begin by establishing two ratios. In one of the ratios we put the numbers associated with one of the quantities, and in the other ratio we put the numbers associated with the other quantity. It is important to place corresponding values in the top of both ratios. It is best explained in the following example.

> The distance between two towns on a map is three inches. These towns are actually 50 miles apart. What is the distance between two cities that are five inches apart on the same map?

Set up two ratios: one with inches in the top and bottom, the other with miles top and bottom. Be sure that corresponding values appear on top in both. By reading the problem we see that 3 inches corresponds to 50 miles, so place these numbers in the top of their respective ratios.

$\dfrac{3}{5}$ (inches top and bottom) $\dfrac{50}{x}$ (miles top and bottom)

As the number of inches increases, so does the number of miles. This is a direct proportion. Write the proportion by setting the two ratios equal to each other. Solve the proportion.

$\dfrac{3}{5} = \dfrac{50}{x}$

$3x = 250$

$x = 83\dfrac{1}{3}$ The cities are $83\dfrac{1}{3}$ miles apart.

> It takes a crew of 5 people 8 hours to clean up a stadium after a concert. How long would it take a crew of 7 people to clean the stadium?

Set up two ratios.

$\dfrac{5}{7}$ (people) $\dfrac{8}{n}$ (hours)

In this situation, as the number of people increases, the time to do the work decreases. This is an indirect or inverse proportion. Write the proportion by inverting one of the ratios. Solve the proportion.

$\dfrac{5}{7} = \dfrac{n}{8}$

$7n = 40$

$n = 5\dfrac{5}{7}$

It would take $5\dfrac{5}{7}$ hours for 7 people to clean the stadium.

Practice Exercises

Solve each problem using a proportion.

1. A company is remodeling its offices. Five desks were purchased for a total cost of $850. What would have been the cost if 8 desks had been purchased?

2. Three people can pick 20 quarts of strawberries in 1 hour. About how many quarts of strawberries could 5 people pick in 1 hour?

3. Driving at an average rate of 40 miles per hour, Mitch can get to work in 25 minutes. If he has to be at work one morning in 20 minutes, what should be his average speed?

4. Twenty-five pounds of fertilizer are needed for 1,600 square feet of lawn. About how much fertilizer is needed for 2,500 square feet of lawn?

Solutions to Practice Exercises

1. $\dfrac{5}{8}$ (Desks) $\dfrac{850}{x}$ (Cost)

More desks = more cost. This is a direct proportion problem.

$$\dfrac{5}{8} = \dfrac{850}{x}$$

$$5x = 8 \times 850$$

$$x = \dfrac{8 \times 850}{5} = \dfrac{8 \times \overset{170}{\cancel{850}}}{\underset{1}{\cancel{5}}} = 1{,}360$$

Eight desks would cost $1,360.

2. $\dfrac{3}{5}$ (people) $\dfrac{20}{x}$ (quarts)

More people = more quarts. Another direct proportion.

$$\dfrac{3}{5} = \dfrac{20}{x}$$

$$3x = 100$$

$$x = 33\dfrac{1}{3}$$

Five people could pick about $33\dfrac{1}{3}$ quarts of strawberries in 1 hour.

3. $\dfrac{40}{x}$ (miles per hour) $\dfrac{25}{20}$ (minutes)

Increased speed = decreased time.

This is an indirect proportion. Turn one of the ratios over.

$$\dfrac{40}{x} = \dfrac{20}{25}$$

$$20x = 40 \times 25$$

$$x = \dfrac{40 \times 25}{20} = \dfrac{\overset{2}{\cancel{40}} \times 25}{\underset{1}{\cancel{20}}} = 50$$

Mitch would have to average 50 miles per hour to get to work in 20 minutes.

4. $\dfrac{25}{x}$ (pounds of fertilizer) $\dfrac{1{,}600}{2{,}500}$ (square feet of lawn)

More lawn = more fertilizer. This is a direct proportion.

$$\frac{25}{x} = \frac{1,600}{2,500} = \frac{16}{25} \text{ (Why not reduce the fraction?)}$$

$$16x = 25 \times 25 = 625$$

$$x = \frac{625}{16} = 39\frac{1}{16}$$

Notice the word *about* in the problem. It implies that you should round off. You would need about 39 pounds of fertilizer for 2,500 square feet of lawn.

DECIMALS

Place values for digits in our system of numeration are as follows.

4	2	7	.	2	9	3	5	2	4
HUNDREDS	TENS	UNITS	DECIMAL	TENTHS	HUNDREDTHS	THOUSANDTHS	TENTHOUSANDTHS	HUNDREDTHOUSANDTHS	MILLIONTHS

The proper way to read the number at the top of the table is *four hundred twenty-seven and two hundred ninety-three thousand five hundred twenty-four millionths*. The only place to use the word *and* when reading any number is at the location of the decimal point.

The place values that continue to the left of the table are:

Thousands

Ten-thousands

Hundred-thousands

Millions

Ten-millions

Hundred-millions

The place values that continue to the right of the table are:

Ten-millionths

Hundred-millionths

Billionths

Ten-billionths

Hundred-billionths

After billionths is trillionths, quadrillionths, and so on.

Zeroes to the right of the right-most nonzero digit to the right of the decimal point can always be deleted without changing the value of the number.

34.27096000 = 34.27096

Zeroes beginning a number to the left of the decimal point are also unnecessary.

032.785 = 32.785

If the whole number part of a decimal number is zero, it may be deleted.

0.34 = .34

In printed material, such zeroes are normally included for clarity.

Rounding Off

The words *about* and *approximately* in a word problem indicate that you should be rounding off the answer in some way. There are two different rules for rounding off—one for whole numbers and one for decimal numbers.

Rounding Numbers Off to a Place Value Left of the Decimal Point

To round off a whole number to a specified place value, first identify that position, and examine the next digit to the right. If the digit to the right is five or more, add one to the digit in the desired position and replace all digits to the right with zeroes. If the digit to the right is less than five, replace all digits to the right with zeroes.

For example, round 594,372 to the nearest:

Hundred thousand—600,000

Ten thousand—590,000

Thousand—594,000

Hundred—594,400

Ten—594,370

Million—1,000,000

Ten million—0

Rounding Numbers Off to a Place Value Right of the Decimal Point

To round off a decimal number to a specified place value right of the decimal point, first identify that position, and examine the next digit to its right. If that digit is five or more, add one to the digit in the desired position, and delete all digits to its right. If the digit to the right of the desired position is less than five, delete all digits to the right of that position.

For example, round 5.40959 to the nearest:

Tenth—5.4

Hundredth—5.41

Thousandth—5.410

Ten-thousandths—5.4096

Two decimal places—5.41

Addition and Subtraction of Decimals

Addition and subtraction of decimal numbers is exactly the same as addition and subtraction of whole numbers except that the decimal points must first be aligned.

Subtract 15.4803 − 2.315.

15.4803
2.315
13.1653

Multiplication of Decimal Numbers

It is not necessary to align decimal places to perform multiplication, but the number of decimal places in the product must be equal to the total number of decimal places in the numbers being multiplied. Otherwise, the process is the same as multiplying whole numbers.

Multiply (3.14)(1.6).

3.14	Two decimal places
1.6	One decimal place
1884	
314	
5.024	Three decimal places

Division of Decimal Numbers

We will give the rule for division in the context of doing an example.

Divide 170.52 by 0.4.   Move the decimal point in the divisor enough places to the right to make a whole number.

$$0.4 \overline{)170.52}$$

$$4 \overline{)1705.2}$$ Move the decimal point in the dividend the same number of places to the right as you moved it in the divisor.

$$\overset{426.3}{4 \overline{)1705.2}}$$ Perform the division as a whole number division. Place the decimal point immediately above the decimal point in the dividend.

Practice Exercises

Perform the indicated operations.

1. Round 63.04832 to the nearest:
   - a. hundred
   - b. ten
   - c. one (unit)
   - d. tenth
   - e. hundredth
   - f. thousandth

2. $403.5 + 5.32 + 0.108$

3. $20.3 - 0.93$

4. $2 - 0.0024$

5. $(0.213)(0.14)$

6. $(35)(0.25)$

7. $1,000(2.31)$

8. $17 \div 4$

9. $1.008 \div 4.2$

10. $\dfrac{4.732}{100}$

Solutions to Practice Exercises

1. a. 100   d. 63.0
   b. 60   e. 63.05
   c. 63   f. 63.048

2. 408.928

3. 19.37

4. 1.9976

5. 0.02982

6. 8.75

7. 2,310

8. 4.25

9. 0.24

10. 0.04732

CONVERTING FRACTIONS TO DECIMALS AND VICE VERSA

All fractions can be converted into decimal form by interpreting the fraction as a division of whole numbers. For example, to convert $\frac{1}{4}$ to a decimal, divide 4 into 1.

$$4\overline{)1.00} \quad \substack{.25}$$

This decimal terminates—it stops after two decimal places. Some decimals obtained in this way do not terminate, but if they do not terminate, they will repeat in some fashion. We can show repetition by drawing a bar over the repeating part.

$$\frac{1}{3} = 0.333333\ldots = 0.\overline{3}$$

$$\frac{7}{9} = 0.7777777\ldots = 0.\overline{7}$$

$$\frac{3}{11} = 0.27272727\ldots = 0.\overline{27}$$

$$\frac{511}{999} = 0.511511511\ldots = 0.\overline{511}$$

To convert a terminating decimal to a fraction, the easiest thing to do is to place the digits over the power of ten that contains the same number of zeros. For example, 0.8 is $\frac{8}{10}$, 10 is the power of ten that contains one zero; 0.24 is $\frac{24}{100} = \frac{6}{25}$, 100 is the power of ten that contains two zeros; 0.725 $\frac{725}{1,000} = \frac{29}{40}$, 1,000 is the power of ten that contains three zeros.

Repeating decimals can all be represented as fractions also. For all repeating decimals in which the repeating part consists of one digit, place that digit over 9 and simplify if possible. If the repeating part has two digits, place those digits over 99. If the repeating part has three digits, place those digits over 999, and so on. For example,

$$0.\overline{3} = \frac{3}{9} = \frac{1}{3}$$

$$0.\overline{7} = \frac{7}{9}$$

$$0.\overline{24} = \frac{24}{99} = \frac{8}{33}$$

$$0.\overline{705} = \frac{705}{999} = \frac{235}{33}$$

Practice Exercises

Convert each fraction to a decimal.

1. $\frac{3}{8}$　　　　3. $\frac{2}{3}$

2. $\frac{7}{20}$　　　　4. $\frac{8}{11}$

Convert each decimal to a fraction in simplest form.

5. 0.95　　　　8. $0.\overline{18}$

6. $0.\overline{2}$　　　　9. 2.75

7. 0.045　　　　10. $0.\overline{9}$

Solutions to Practice Exercises

1. 0.375

2. 0.35

3. $0.\overline{6}$

4. $0.\overline{72}$

5. $\frac{95}{100} = \frac{19}{20}$

6. $\frac{2}{9}$

7. $\frac{45}{1,000} = \frac{9}{200}$

8. $\frac{18}{99} = \frac{2}{11}$

9. $2\frac{3}{4}$

10. $\frac{9}{9} = 1$

COMPARING FRACTIONS AND DECIMALS

To determine which of two fractions is larger, rewrite them so that they have a common denominator. The fraction with the larger numerator is the larger fraction. For example, which is larger $\frac{7}{9}$ or $\frac{4}{5}$? Rewrite both fractions with common denominator 45.

$$\frac{7}{9} = \frac{35}{45} \text{ and } \frac{4}{5} = \frac{36}{45}$$

It is clear that $\frac{4}{5}$ is the larger fraction.

To determine which of two decimals is larger, compare position by position from left to right. The first decimal that has a larger digit in a given position is the larger decimal. Which is larger: 0.321584 or 0.32261? 0.32261 has a larger digit in the third decimal position; therefore, it is the larger decimal.

To compare a fraction with a decimal, first convert one to the other form so that you have either two fractions or two decimals. Then, follow the rules above. Which is larger: $\frac{5}{8}$ or 0.64? The decimal form of $\frac{5}{8}$ is 0.625. We see then that 0.64 is the larger number.

Practice Exercises

For each pair of numbers, determine which is larger.

1. $\frac{7}{8}, \frac{8}{9}$

2. $0.2, 0.\overline{2}$

3. $0.7, \frac{8}{11}$

4. $3.14, 3.1416$

Solutions to Practice Exercises

1. Rewrite both fractions with a common denominator 72
   $\frac{7}{8} = \frac{63}{72}$ and $\frac{8}{9} = \frac{64}{72}$. So $\frac{8}{9}$ is larger.
2. $0.\overline{2} = 0.2222\ldots$ is the larger decimal.
3. $\frac{8}{11} = 0.\overline{72}$ is the larger number.
4. 3.1416 is the larger number.

PERCENTS

The word **percent** means hundredths.

$$23\% = \frac{23}{100} = 0.23$$

For some percents it is better to interpret "hundredths" as meaning "divided by 100."

$$83\frac{1}{3}\% = 83\frac{1}{3} \div 100 = \frac{250}{3} \div \frac{100}{1} = \frac{250}{3} \times \frac{1}{100} = \frac{5}{6} = 0.8\overline{3}$$

$$12\frac{1}{2}\% = 12\frac{1}{2} \div 100 = \frac{25}{2} \div \frac{100}{1} = \frac{25}{2} \times \frac{1}{100} = \frac{1}{8} = 0.125$$

KAPLAN

Changing Percents to Decimals and Fractions

- To change simple percents to decimals, move the decimal point two places to the left, and drop the percent sign.
- To change simple percents to fractions, place the percent number over 100, drop the percent sign, and simplify as needed.

When using percents in calculations, you must always change the percent to either a fraction or a decimal first. For some percents, you could reasonably use either the fraction or the decimal form such as 23% (0.23) or $12\frac{1}{2}$% ($\frac{1}{8}$). Those percents whose decimal forms are repeating decimals such as $83\frac{1}{3}$% are best converted to fraction form.

Practice Exercises

Convert each percent to both a fraction and a decimal.

1. 80%

2. 20.4%

3. 7%

4. $87\frac{1}{2}$%

5. $16\frac{2}{3}$%

6. 125%

Solutions to Practice Exercises

1. Fraction: $\frac{80}{100} = \frac{4}{5}$
   Decimal: 0.8

2. Fraction: $\frac{20.4}{100} = \frac{204}{1,000} = \frac{51}{250}$
   Decimal: 0.204

3. Fraction: $\frac{7}{100}$
   Decimal: 0.07

4. Fraction: $87\frac{1}{2} \div 100 = \frac{175}{2} \div \frac{100}{1} = \frac{175}{2} \div \frac{1}{100} = \frac{\overset{7}{\cancel{175}}}{2} \div \frac{1}{\underset{100}{\cancel{4}}} = \frac{7}{8}$
   Decimal: Write $87\frac{1}{2}$ as 87.5%. So the decimal is 0.875.

5. Fraction: $16\frac{2}{3} \div 100 = \frac{50}{3} \div \frac{100}{1} = \frac{50}{3} \times \frac{1}{100} = \frac{\overset{1}{\cancel{50}}}{3} \times \frac{1}{\underset{100}{\cancel{2}}} = \frac{1}{6}$
   Decimal: Divide 6 into 1. The decimal is $0.\overline{16}$.

6. Fraction: $\frac{125}{100} = \frac{5}{4} = 1\frac{1}{4}$
   Decimal: 1.25

Changing Decimals and Fractions to Percents

To change a decimal to a percent, move the decimal point two places to the right and attach a percent sign.

To change a fraction to a percent, there are two reasonable procedures. You could first change the fraction, $\frac{a}{b}$, to a decimal by dividing the denominator into the numerator and following the rule above, or you could set up a proportion like $\frac{a}{b} = \frac{P}{100}$. Solve this proportion for P, and attach a percent sign.

Some examples:

Change 0.35 to a percent.

Move the decimal point 2 places to the right. Attach a percent sign. The answer is 35%.

Change 2.5 to a percent.

You use the same rule, but you must supply a 0. The answer is 250%.

Change 0.027 to a percent.

Two places to the right; attach a percent sign. 2.7%.

Change $\frac{3}{8}$ to a percent.

$\frac{3}{8}$ written as a decimal is 0.375. Move the decimal point two places to the right and attach a percent sign. The answer is 37.5%. This could also be written as $37\frac{1}{2}$%.

Change $\frac{5}{6}$ to a percent.

This time let's set up a proportion.

$\frac{5}{6} = \frac{P}{100}$ Cross multiply.

$6P = 500$ Divide by 6. Carry out to two places. Write the remainders as a fraction.

$P = 83\frac{1}{3}$

The answer is $83\frac{1}{3}$%.

Change $\frac{5}{4}$ as a percent.

Write a proportion. $\frac{5}{4} = \frac{P}{100}$

$4P = 500$

$P = 125$

The answer is 125%.

KAPLAN

Practice Exercises

Write each fraction or decimal as a percent.

1. $\dfrac{1}{20}$ 6. 0.37

2. $\dfrac{4}{5}$ 7. 2.75

3. $\dfrac{5}{16}$ 8. 1

4. $\dfrac{3}{7}$ 9. 0.062

5. $\dfrac{27}{100}$ 10. 0.01

Solutions to Practice Exercises

1. $\dfrac{1}{20}$ written as a decimal is 0.05. The answer is 5%

2. $\dfrac{4}{5} = 0.8$ The answer is 80%.

3. Write a proportion: $\dfrac{5}{16} = \dfrac{P}{100}$

   $16P = 500$

   $P = 31\dfrac{1}{4}$ The answer is $31\dfrac{1}{4}$%.

   The answer could also be written 31.25%.

4. $\dfrac{3}{7} = \dfrac{P}{100}$

   $7P = 300$ Divide by 7. Move two places. Write remainder as a fraction.

   $P = 42\dfrac{6}{7}$

   The answer is $42\dfrac{6}{7}$%. (This could be written $42.\overline{857142}$%. Not very convenient.)

5. $\dfrac{27}{100} = \dfrac{P}{100}$ The answer is obvious, 27%.

6. 37%

7. 275%

8. 100%   You have to attach two zeroes.

9. 6.2%

10. 1%

THE PERCENT PROPORTION

All percent problems can be rephrased to read

A is $P\%$ of B.

This can then be translated into the proportion

$$\frac{A}{B} = \frac{P}{100}.$$

If any two values of A, B, or P are known, then the third value can be found.

Here are some examples.

What number is 25% of 96?

In this question, we are asked to find A, P is 25, and B is 96, so the proportion is

$$\frac{A}{96} = \frac{25}{100} \qquad \text{Cross multiply.}$$

$$100A = 25 \times 96 \qquad \text{Divide by 100.}$$

$$A = \frac{25 \times 96}{100} \quad \frac{\overset{1}{\cancel{25}} \times 96}{\underset{4}{\cancel{100}}} = \frac{96}{4} = 24 \qquad \text{Notice how cancellation can save time.}$$

The answer is 24, so 24 is 25% of 96.

28.8 is 60% of what number?

In this question, A is 28.8, P is 60, and B is unknown. The proportion is

$$\frac{28.8}{B} = \frac{60}{100} \qquad \text{Simplify the fraction on the right side.}$$

$$\frac{28.8}{B} = \frac{3}{5} \qquad \text{Cross multiply.}$$

$$3B = 28.8 \times 5 \qquad \text{Divide by 3.}$$

$$B = \frac{28.8 \times 5}{3} = \frac{\overset{9.6}{\cancel{28.8}} \times 5}{\underset{1}{\cancel{3}}} = 48$$

So 28.8 is 60% of 48.

96 is what percent of 80?

In this question, A is 96, P is unknown, and B is 80. The proportion is

$$\frac{96}{80} = \frac{P}{100}$$

$$80P = 9,600$$

$$P = 120$$

So 96 is 120% of 80.

What is $83\frac{1}{3}\%$ of 60?

A is unknown, P is $83\frac{1}{3}$, and B is 60. When P is a fraction such as this one, it is better to determine its fraction equivalent and replace the entire right side of the percent proportion by that fraction. We determined previously that the fraction equivalent for $83\frac{1}{3}\%$ is $\frac{5}{6}$. So write the proportion

$$\frac{A}{60} = \frac{5}{6}$$

$$6A = 300$$

$$A = 50$$

50 is $83\frac{1}{3}\%$ of 60.

Practice Exercises

Find the missing part, A, P, or B for each of these percent problems.

1. What is 5% of 90?

2. 40 is 80% of what number?

3. What number is 225% of 16?

4. 10 is $12\frac{1}{2}\%$ of what number?

5. 15 is what percent of 90?

6. 4 is $66\frac{2}{3}\%$ of what number?

7. 25 is what percent of 80?

Solutions to Practice Exercises

1. $$\frac{A}{90} = \frac{5}{100}$$

   $$100A = 450$$

   $$A = 4.5$$

2. $$\frac{40}{B} = \frac{80}{100} = \frac{4}{5}$$

   $$4B = 200$$

   $$B = 50$$

3. $$\frac{A}{16} = \frac{225}{100} = \frac{9}{4}$$

   $$4A = 144$$

   $$A = 36$$

4. $\dfrac{10}{B} = \dfrac{1}{8}$ The fraction equivalent of $12\dfrac{1}{2}\%$ is $\dfrac{1}{8}$.

$B = 80$

5. $\dfrac{15}{90} = \dfrac{P}{100}$

$90P = 1,500$

$P = 16\dfrac{2}{3}$ 15 is $16\dfrac{2}{3}\%$ of 90.

6. $\dfrac{4}{B} = \dfrac{2}{3}$ The fraction equivalent of $66\dfrac{2}{3}\%$ is $\dfrac{2}{3}$.

$2B = 12$

$B = 6$

7. $\dfrac{25}{80} = \dfrac{P}{100}$

$80P = 2,500$

$P = 31\dfrac{1}{4}$ 25 is $31\dfrac{1}{4}\%$ of 80.

APPLICATIONS OF THE PERCENT PROPORTION

The usefulness of the percent proportion depends on your ability to restate the problem in the form A is P% of B. In this part of the chapter, you will practice interpreting percent problems in the correct way so that you can solve them. We do not pretend that this is the only way to do percent problems. If you are confident in your ability to solve these problems, feel free to use your method. If you have any doubts, you should practice our method so that you have a place to begin. Much time is wasted in searching for a place to begin solving a word problem.

Examples

1. On a test of 50 questions, Joni got 42 correct. What percent of the questions did she get correct? What percent did she get incorrect?

We can restate this problem as follows:

42 is what percent of 50?

Then the proportion is

$\dfrac{42}{50} = \dfrac{P}{100}$

$50P = 4,200$

$P = 84$

Joni got 84% of the questions correct. It is not necessary to solve another percent problem to answer the second question. All that is needed is to subtract 84% from 100%. She got 16% of the questions incorrect.

2. In your chemistry class you need 720 mL of an acid solution. If 5% of the solution is to be pure acid, how many milliliters of the solution is acid?

We can restate this problem as follows:

The number of milliliters of acid is 5% of 720

The proportion is

$$\frac{A}{720} = \frac{5}{100}$$

$$100A = 3,600$$

$$A = 36$$

There are 36 mL of pure acid in the solution.

3. Brian's salary increased from $7,200 to $7,560. What was his percent increase in salary?

Brian's salary increased $360, so the restatement of the problem is:

360 is what percent of 7,200?

So the proportion is:

$$\frac{360}{7,200} = \frac{P}{100}$$

The left side of this proportion reduces.

$$\frac{1}{20} = \frac{P}{100}$$

$$20P = 100$$

$$P = 5$$

Brian got a 5% increase in salary.

You might have done this problem by restating the problem:

7,560 is what percent of 7,200?

The answer to this question is 105%, so you would have to subtract 100% in order to get the same answer.

4. At $3\frac{1}{2}$ months of age, Lucy weighed 13 pounds. This represented a 60% increase over her weight at one month. What was her weight at one month?

Because 13 pounds represents her weight at one month plus a 60% increase of her weight at one month, we could say:

13 is 160% of her weight at one month.

We could write this proportion:

$$\frac{13}{B} = \frac{160}{100} = \frac{8}{5}$$

$$8B = 65$$

$$B = \frac{65}{8} = 8\frac{1}{8}$$

Lucy's weight at one month was $8\frac{1}{8}$ pounds.

Practice Exercises

1. Robert went on a diet with the intention of losing 15% of his weight. When he reached his goal he weighed 187 pounds. What did he weigh when he started his diet?

2. Jill took a test with 60 questions on it. She got 80% of the questions correct. How many questions did she get wrong?

3. A jeweler discounts a ring 20%. After a week, he discounts the ring another 10%. If the original price of the ring is $256, what is the selling price?

4. A $1,250 investment grew to $1,325 in one year. What is the percent increase for this investment?

Solutions to Practice Exercises

1. If Robert lost 15% of his weight, then he weighs 85% (= 100% - 15%) of his original weight. So *187 is 85% of his original weight.*

$$\frac{187}{B} = \frac{85}{100}$$

$$85B = 18,700$$

$$B = 220$$

Robert weighed 220 pounds when he started his diet.

2. If Jill got 80% correct, then she got 20% wrong. So *the number wrong is 20% of 60.*

$$\frac{A}{60} = \frac{20}{100} = \frac{1}{5}$$

$$5A = 60$$

$$A = 12$$

Jill got 12 questions wrong.

3. If the ring had sold with the first discount, the customer would have paid 80% of the original price. So *the selling price would have been 80% of $256.*

$$\frac{A_1}{256} = \frac{80}{100} = \frac{4}{5}$$

$$5A_1 = 1,024$$

$$A_1 = 204.80$$

So with the first discount, the ring would have sold for $204.80.

Now with the second discount of 10%, the customer will pay 90% of the previous sale price. *The sale price is 90% of 204.80.*

$$\frac{A_2}{204.80} = \frac{90}{100} = \frac{9}{10}$$

$$10A_2 = 1,843.20$$

$$A_2 = 184.32$$

The final selling price is $184.32

4. The actual increase is $75. So *75 is what percent of 1,250*?

$$\frac{75}{1,250} = \frac{P}{100}$$

$$1250P = 7500$$

$$P = 6$$

The investment increased 6%.

Chapter Nine: **Measurement, Geometry, and Statistics**

BASIC MEASUREMENT FACTS

There are some basic measurements that you'll be expected to know on the CBEST. Note that the equals sign (=) is used here to indicate the same measurement, not equal numbers.

Length:

1 foot = 12 inches

1 yard = 3 feet = 36 inches

1 mile = 5,280 feet

Capacity:

1 cup = 8 fluid ounces

1 pint = 2 cups = 16 fluid ounces

1 quart = 2 pints

1 gallon = 4 quarts

Weight:

1 pound = 16 ounces

1 ton = 2,000 pounds

Time:

1 minute = 60 seconds

1 hour = 60 minutes

1 day = 24 hours

1 week = 7 days

1 year = 365 days (a leap year is 366 days)

1 decade = 10 years

1 century = 100 years

UNIT FRACTIONS AND CONVERSIONS

A *unit fraction* is a fraction representing the number 1. Each item above can be expressed as two different unit fractions. For example, 1 foot = 12 inches can be expressed as:

$$\frac{1 \text{ foot}}{12 \text{ inches}} \text{ or } \frac{12 \text{ inches}}{1 \text{ foot}}$$

Similarly, 1 gallon = 4 quarts can be expressed as:

$$\frac{1 \text{ gallon}}{4 \text{ quarts}} \text{ or } \frac{4 \text{ quarts}}{1 \text{ gallon}}$$

These unit fractions are useful in converting one unit of measurement to another.

Let's change 32 quarts to gallons. First, choose the unit fraction that has gallons on top and quarts on bottom. Then, multiply it by the original measurement that is also written as a fraction. Next, cancel the units as if they were factors in the numerators and denominators of the fractions, and perform the operations with the numbers as indicated.

$$\frac{32 \text{ quarts}}{1} \times \frac{1 \text{ gallon}}{4 \text{ quarts}}$$

Canceling the word quarts as if it were a number, you are left with dividing 4 into 32. So 32 quarts equals 8 gallons.

Let's look at another example. Convert $\frac{1}{2}$ mile to yards. Here, we'll use two unit fractions.

$$\frac{1}{2} \frac{\text{mile}}{1} \times \frac{5{,}280 \text{ feet}}{1 \text{ mile}} \times \frac{1 \text{ yard}}{3 \text{ feet}}$$

The first unit fraction gets rid of the unit *mile*, and the second gets rid of *feet* and introduces the *yard* unit that is desired. Now we see that you need to divide 2 and 3 into 5,280, one at a time.

$$\frac{1}{2} \text{ mile} = \frac{1}{2} \times \frac{5{,}280}{1} \frac{1 \text{ yard}}{3} = \frac{1}{\cancel{2}} \times \frac{\overset{2{,}640}{\cancel{5{,}280}}}{1} \times \frac{1 \text{ yard}}{3} \frac{\overset{880}{\cancel{2{,}640}}}{1} \times \frac{1 \text{ yard}}{\cancel{3}} = 880 \text{ yards}$$

Practice Exercises

1. Convert 4 yards to feet.

2. Convert 156 inches to feet.

3. Convert 56 pints to gallons.

4. Convert $2\frac{1}{2}$ pounds to ounces.

5. Convert 3,000 seconds to hours.

Solutions to Practice Exercises

1. $\dfrac{4 \text{ yards}}{1} \times \dfrac{3 \text{ feet}}{1 \text{ yard}} = \dfrac{4}{1} \times \dfrac{3 \text{ feet}}{1} = 12 \text{ feet}$

2. $\dfrac{156 \text{ inches}}{1} \times \dfrac{1 \text{ foot}}{12 \text{ inches}} \times \dfrac{156}{1} \times \dfrac{1 \text{ foot}}{12} = 13 \text{ feet}$

3. Use two unit fractions for this one.

   $\dfrac{56 \text{ pints}}{1} \times \dfrac{1 \text{ quart}}{2 \text{ pints}} \times \dfrac{1 \text{ gallon}}{4 \text{ quarts}} = 7 \text{ gallons}$

4. $2\frac{1}{2} \text{ pounds} = \dfrac{5}{2} \dfrac{\text{pounds}}{1} \times \dfrac{16 \text{ ounces}}{1 \text{ pound}} = \dfrac{5}{2} \times \dfrac{16 \text{ ounces}}{1} = \dfrac{5}{\frac{1}{\cancel{2}}} \dfrac{\overset{8}{\cancel{16}} \text{ ounces}}{1} = 40 \text{ ounces}$

5. $\dfrac{3{,}000 \text{ seconds}}{1} \times \dfrac{1 \text{ minute}}{60 \text{ seconds}} \times \dfrac{1 \text{ hour}}{60 \text{ minutes}} = \dfrac{3{,}000}{1} \times \dfrac{1}{60} \times \dfrac{1 \text{ hour}}{60} =$

   $\dfrac{\overset{50}{\cancel{3000}}}{1} \times \dfrac{1}{\frac{1}{\cancel{60}}} \times \dfrac{1 \text{ hour}}{60} = \dfrac{50}{1} \times \dfrac{1 \text{ hour}}{\cancel{60}} = \dfrac{5}{6} \text{ hour}$

PERIMETERS AND AREAS

A **polygon** is a plane geometric figure with three or more sides. If the sides are all the same length and the angles all have the same measure, the polygon is called *regular*. A regular four-sided polygon is a square.

The **perimeter** of a polygon is the sum of the lengths of the sides. You can calculate the perimeter of any polygon by adding the lengths of the sides, although squares and rectangles have special rules: Because a square has four sides all the same length, just multiply the length of one side by four. The formula for the perimeter of a square is $p = 4s$. As for a rectangle, its side lengths are equal in pairs, so that formula is $p = 2l + 2w$.

The **area** of a polygon is the measure of its surface. For a square, the formula would be $a = s^2$ (multiply the length of a side by itself). So if the sides of a square are 3 inches, then its area is 9 square inches. Saying that the area is 9 square inches means that 9 smaller squares—each 1 inch on each side—would fit inside the original square. For a rectangle, finding the area requires multiplying the length times the width: $a = lw$.

In order to to apply the perimeter or area formula to a rectangle, the lengths of the sides must be in the same unit of measure. It would not make sense to multiply 9 *inches* by 2 *feet*. Although you could convert inches to feet or feet to inches to find the area, you are better off glancing at the answer choices on a CBEST question to guide you about which conversion to use. In either case, 9 inches $= \frac{3}{4}$ feet, so the area is $\frac{3}{4}$ feet x 2 feet $= \frac{3}{2}$ square feet $= 1\frac{1}{2}$ square feet, or 2 feet $=$ 24 inches.

So the area is also 9 inches x 24 inches $=$ 216 square inches.

Both answers are correct.

Many other regions can be subdivided into squares or rectangles to find the area. The area of this region is the sum of the areas of the rectangle and the square.

To find the area of a triangle, use the following formular: $A = \frac{1}{2}bh$.

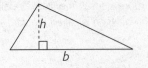

In this triangle, h is the height or altitude to the base b.

Practice Exercises

For questions 1–5, for each value of s for the square or w and l for the rectangle, determine both the perimeter and the area of the polygon.

1. $s = 7$ inches

2. $w = 3$ feet and $l = 5$ feet

3. $s = 1.4$ feet

4. $w = 6$ inches and $l = 4$ feet

5. $s = 2$ feet 3 inches

6. A triangle has one side of 8 inches, and the altitude to that side is 5 inches. Determine the area of the triangle.

Solutions to Practice Exercises

1. Perimeter: 4(7 inches) = 28 inches
   Area: $(7 \text{ inches})^2$ = 49 square inches

2. Perimeter: 2(3 feet) + 2(5 feet) = 6 feet + 10 feet = 16 feet
   Area: (3 feet)(5 feet) = 15 square feet

3. Perimeter: 4(1.4 feet) = 5.6 feet
   Area: $(1.4 \text{ feet})^2$ = 1.96 square feet

4. Perimeter: In feet: $\left(6 \text{ inches} = \frac{1}{2} \text{ feet}\right) 2\left(\frac{1}{2} \text{ ft}\right) + 2(4 \text{ ft}) = 1 \text{ ft} + 8 \text{ ft} = 9 \text{ ft}$

   In inches: (4 ft = 48 in)2(6 in) + 2(48 in) = 12 in + 96 in = 108 in

   Area: In feet: $\left(\frac{1}{2} \text{ ft}\right)(4 \text{ ft}) = 2$ square feet

   In inches: (6 in)(48 in) = 288 square inches

5.   Perimeter: In feet: $4\left(2\frac{1}{4}\ \text{ft}\right) = 4\left(\frac{9}{4}\ \text{ft}\right) = 9\ \text{ft}$

   In inches: $4(27\ \text{in}) = 108\ \text{in}$

   Area: In feet: $\left(2\frac{1}{4}\ \text{ft}\right)^2 = \left(\frac{9}{4}\ \text{ft}\right)^2 = \frac{81}{16}\ \text{sq. ft} = 5\frac{1}{16}\ \text{sq. ft}$

   In inches: $(27\ \text{in})^2 = 729\ \text{sq. in}$

6.   The area is $\frac{1}{2}(8)(5) = 20\ \text{sq. in}$

CIRCLES

A **diameter** is a line segment that passes through the center of a circle and has its endpoints on the circle. A **radius** is a segment that has one endpoint at the center of a circle and the other endpoint on the circle. The length of a radius of a circle is half of the length of a diameter: $r = \frac{1}{2}d$.

The **circumference** of a circle is the length of the arc of the circle. Its length is pi (π) times the length of the diameter or two times π times the length of the radius of the circle: $c = \pi d = 2\pi r$. (π is a number for which there are three commonly used approximations: $\pi \approx 3.14$, or $\pi \approx 3.1416$, or $\pi \approx \frac{22}{7}$.)

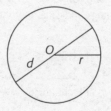

The **area** of a circle is π times the square of the length of the radius: $A = \pi r^2$.

Practice Exercises

For questions 1–4, determine the circumference and area of a circle with the given radius or diameter. Use 3.14 as the approximation of π. Round decimal answers to the nearest hundredth.

1.   Radius 10 inches.

2.   Radius 4.1 feet.

3.   Diameter 6 inches.

4.   Diameter 10 miles.

5.   Determine the radius of a circle if its circumference is 25.12 inches.

Solutions to Practice Exercises

1. Circumference: 2(3.14)(10 inches) = 62.8 inches

   Area: (3.14)(10 inches)^2 = 3.14(100 square inches) = 314 square inches

2. Circumference: 2(3.14)(4.1 feet) = 25.748 feet ≈ 25.75 feet

   Area: (3.14)(4.1 feet)^2 = 3.14(16.81 square feet) = 52.7834 sq. ft ≈ 52.78 sq. ft

3. If the diameter is 6 inches, then the radius is 3 inches.

   Circumference: 2(3.14)(3 inches) = 18.84 inches

   Area: (3.14)(3 inches)^2 = 3.14(9 sq. in) = 28.26 sq. in

4. If the diameter is 10 miles, then the radius is 5 miles.

   Circumference: 2(3.14)(5 miles) = 31.4 miles

   Area: (3.14)(5 miles)^2 = 3.14(25 square miles) = 78.5 square miles

5. The circumference is found by multiplying the radius by 2π, so divide the circumference by 2π. The radius is 25.12 inches ÷ (2 × 3.14) = 25.12 inches ÷ 6.28 = 4 inches.

ANGLE MEASUREMENT

The most common unit of angle measurement is the **degree**. There are 360 degrees in one revolution. So an angle that is one-fourth of a revolution—a right angle—measures 90 degrees (90°). The little box inside the corner of the angle indicates that the angle measures 90°.

Right angle

Angles that measure less than 90° are called **acute**. Angles that measure more than 90° but less than 180° are **obtuse**, and angles that measure 180° exactly are **straight angles**.

Acute angle   Obtuse angle   Straight angle

Two angles whose sum is 90° are **complementary**. If their sum is 180°, they are **supplementary**.

Complementary angle

Supplementary angle

PARALLEL LINES

If two parallel lines are intersected by a third line, called a transversal, there are several angle relationships formed.

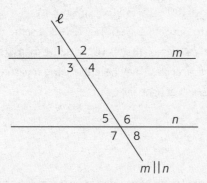

∠1 and ∠4 are **vertical** angles. (Equal measure.)

∠1 and ∠5 are **corresponding** angles. (Equal measure.)

∠4 and ∠5 are **alternate interior** angles. (Equal measure.)

∠1 and ∠8 are **alternate exterior** angles. (Equal measure.)

∠3 and ∠5 are **interior angles on the same side of the transversal**. These angles are supplementary.

∠2 and ∠8 are **exterior angles on the same side of the transversal**. These angles are supplementary.

Also, if any of these angle relationships can be shown to be true, then the lines are parallel.

Practice Exercises

If ∠2 measures 25°, determine the measure of the following angles.

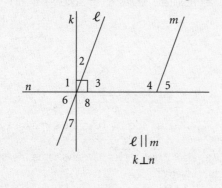

1. ∠1

2. ∠3

3. ∠4

4. ∠5

5. ∠6

6. ∠7

7. ∠8

Solutions to Practice Exercises

1. 90°: Perpendicular lines intersect at right angles.

2. 65°: Angles 2 and 3 are complementary, so subtract 90 − 25 = 65.

3. 115°: Angles 3 and 4 are interior angles on the same side of the transversal. These angles are supplementary, so subtract 180 − 65 = 115.

4. 65°: Angles 3 and 5 are corresponding angles. They have the same measure.

5. 65°: Angles 3 and 6 are vertical angles. They have the same measure.

6. 25°: Angles 2 and 7 are vertical angles. They have the same measure.

7. 90°: Perpendicular lines intersect at right angles.

TRIANGLES

A triangle can be categorized by the length of its sides or by the measurement of its angles. If no two sides are the same length, the triangle is said to be **scalene**. If at least two sides are the same length, it is **isosceles**, and if all three sides are the same, the triangle is **equilateral**.

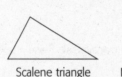

Scalene triangle   Isosceles triangle   Equilateral triangle

The sum of the three angles of every triangle is 180°. If all three angles of a triangle are acute, the triangle is said to be acute. If one angle is 90°, it is a right triangle. If one angle is more than 90°, it is obtuse. If all three angles of a triangle have the same measure, the triangle is **equiangular**. All equiangular triangles are also equilateral.

If an isosceles triangle has exactly two sides of the same length, then the angles opposite those sides also have the same measure. (Base angles of an isosceles triangle are equal in measure.)

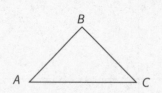

If $AB = BC$, then ∠A and ∠C have the same measure.

This rule works in the other way also: If two angles have the same measure, then the sides opposite those angles are equal in length.

At this point, it is easy to see that all three of the angles of an equilateral triangle are 60°. By dividing any polygon into triangles, the sum of its angles can be determined. Draw as many diagonals as possible from one vertex to form a triangle.

This pentagon can be divided into three triangles, so the sum of all five angles is $3(180°) = 540°$.

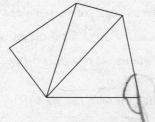

complementary

If one side of a triangle is extended at a vertex, an **exterior angle** is formed. The exterior angle is supplementary to the interior angle at that vertex. Its measure also equals the sum of the other two angles of the triangle.

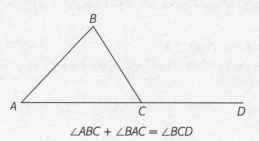

$$\angle ABC + \angle BAC = \angle BCD$$

If one exterior angle is formed at every vertex of a polygon, their sum is always 360°.

Pythagorean Theorem

The two sides of a right triangle that form the right angle are called the *legs,* and the side opposite the right angle is the *hypotenuse*. If the lengths of the legs of a right triangle are a and b, and the hypotenuse is c, then $a^2 + b^2 = c^2$. The Pythagorean theorem is also useful for showing that a triangle is a right triangle. If the lengths of the sides satisfy the equation $a^2 + b^2 = c^2$, then you have a right triangle. So a triangle with sides 3, 4, and 5 inches is a right triangle because $3^2 + 4^2 = 9 + 16 = 25 = 5^2$.

For another application of the Pythagorean theorem, suppose a man drove 5 miles north, and then turned and drove 12 miles east. How far is he from his starting point?

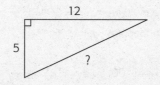

Let the unknown distance be c. Then:

$5^2 + 12^2 = c^2$

$25 + 144 = c^2$

$169 = c^2$

Then take the square root of 169. The man is 13 miles from his starting point.

Practice Exercises

1. What is the sum of the interior angles of a seven-sided polygon, a heptagon?

2. In $\triangle ABC$, if $AB = BC$ and $m\angle B = 30°$, what is the measure of $\angle A$?

3. What is the length of the hypotenuse of a right triangle if the legs are 6 inches and 8 inches?

4. What is the length of the unknown leg of a right triangle if the other leg is 24 feet and the hypotenuse is 26 feet?

5. The sides of triangle are 4, 5, and 6 inches. Determine whether or not this is a right triangle.

6. What is the measure of one exterior angle of a regular pentagon?

Solutions to Practice Exercises

1. 900°: Five triangles are formed by drawing as many diagonals as possible from one vertex. So the sum of the angles is 5(180) = 900.

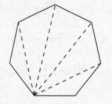

2. 75°: Because the sum of all three angles of a triangle is 180°, the sum of the two base angles is 180 - 30 = 150. Because the base angles have the same measure, they must each be half of 150.

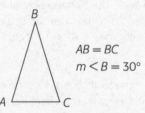

$AB = BC$
$m < B = 30°$

3. 10 inches: Use the Pythagorean theorem: $c^2 = 6^2 + 8^2 = 36 + 64 = 100$. So $c = 10$.

4. 10 feet: Use the Pythagorean theorem:

    $a^2 + 24^2 = 26^2$

    $a^2 = 26^2 - 24^2 = 676 - 576 = 100$. So $a = 10$.

5. No, this is not a right triangle. Do these lengths satisfy the Pythagorean theorem?

    $4^2 + 5^2 = 6^2$

    $16 + 25 = 36$

    $41 \neq 36$

6. 72°: A pentagon can be divided into three triangles by drawing diagonals from one vertex, so the sum of the angles is $3(180) = 540$ degrees. Because the angles of a regular pentagon are all the same, one of the interior angles is $\frac{1}{5}(540) = 108$ degrees. The exterior angle is the supplement of the interior angle, and its measure is $180 - 108 = 72$ degrees. It is also true that the sum of the exterior angles, taking one at each vertex, is 360°. This answer could have been found more easily by just dividing 360 by 5.

LINES, SEGMENTS, AND ANGLES IN CIRCLES

There are 360 degrees of arc in every circle. A **central angle** is an angle that has its vertex at the center of a circle. The degree measure of a central angle equals the degree measure in its intercepted arc.

An angle that has its vertex on the circle is an **inscribed angle**. The measure of an inscribed angle is half of the measure of the intercepted arc. Because of this rule, an angle inscribed in a semicircle is a right angle.

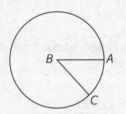 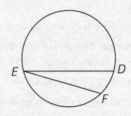

$$m\angle ABC = m(arc\ AC) \qquad m\angle DEF = \frac{1}{2}\ m(arc\ DF)$$

Practice Exercises

Find the following:

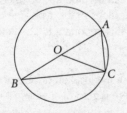

O is the center
$m(\text{arc }AC) = 50°$

1. $m(\text{arc }BC)$ 4. $m\angle OCB$

2. $m\angle AOC$ 5. $m\angle ACB$

3. $m\angle ABC$

Solutions to Practice Exercises

1. 130°: $\overline{AB}$ is a diameter because it passes through the center of the circle. A diameter separates the arc of the circle into two arcs of equal measure, each 180°. The sum of the measures of arcs AC and BC is 180°. So $m(arc\ BC) = 180° - 50° = 130°$.

2. 50°: A central angle has the same measure as its intercepted arc.

3. 25°: The measure of an inscribed angle is half the measure of its intercepted arc.

4. 25°: $\triangle OBC$ is isosceles because all radii of a circle have the same length. So $m\angle OBC = m\angle OCB$. Base angles of an isosceles triangle have the same measure.

5. 90°: An angle inscribed in a semicircle is a right angle.

STATISTICS

Levels of Data

One of the purposes of statistics is to try to make sense out of a collection of data. Any set of data is the result of performing some statistical experiment. Consider a survey that includes the following questions:

1. What is the high school from which you graduated?

2. What is your opinion of the quality of instruction at your high school: Excellent, Above Average, Average, Below Average, or Poor?

3. What was your year of graduation?

4. What was the number of classmates in your graduating class?

The data obtained in question 1 are the *collection* of names of high schools of the people who took the survey. This type of data is **nominal** data—just the name of something. Many times nominal data is tabulated, counted, and reported with the count for each item of data. These numbers are not the data; the data are the names.

In question 2, the data obtained are **ordinal** data—data that can be ordered—but it is not numeric. Sometimes numbers are assigned to the responses to questions of this type. The mere presence of numbers doesn't mean that it is then numeric data. It is important to keep the original question in mind when determining the type of data.

In question 3, **interval** data is obtained. It is numeric data, but the location of zero on the scale of the data is an arbitrary choice. It does not indicate that there is zero of anything. It is just a starting point for measuring years.

It makes sense to subtract interval data—one person graduates five years later than another, for instance—but addition and multiplication make no sense. You could average data, but you could not divide one item of data by another.

In question 4, the number of classmates is an example of **ratio** data, numeric data that has a meaningful zero. If one had given zero as a response to this question, it would mean that he had no classmates. All of the mathematical operations could conceivably be performed. Ratio data are considered to be the highest level of statistical data.

Averages

The purpose of an average is to give some idea of the middle of a body of data. An average is a measure of central tendency. In statistics, there are three types of averages. The most common one is the **mean**, the number obtained by adding all the items in a numerical data set and dividing by the number of items. Take this small data set: 3, 6, 8, 1, 3. The mean is $\frac{3 + 6 + 8 + 1 + 3}{5} = \frac{21}{5} = 4.2$. There is no mean for nominal or ordinal data.

The second type of average is the **median**, the middle number in a data set that is ranked from smallest to largest. If the data set given above were ranked, we would see that the middle number is 3. The median is 3: 1, 3, 3, 6, 8.

Finding the median can always be done as long as there is an odd number of items of data. With 55 items, you would first set them in order from smallest to largest, and then count to the 28th item. ($28 = \frac{55 + 1}{2}$) The item of data that sits in the 28th position is the median. Note that the median is *not* 28.

If there is an even number of items of data, there is no middle number. In this case, add the two numbers in the middle and divide by 2.

Suppose there had been one additional item of data in the data set given above: 1, 3, 3, 6, 8, 12. The two middle numbers are 3 and 6, so the median is $\frac{3 + 6}{2} = \frac{9}{2} = 4.5$. If the data set had 98 items of data, first rank the data from smallest to largest. The positions of the two middle numbers are 49 and 50, so add these numbers and divide by 2.

The quotient is the position of the first of the two numbers in the middle; take that number and the next one, add, and then divide by 2. The result is the median.

The third, and most frequently occurring type of average, is **mode**. Of the three types of averages, this is the only one that can be used for all levels of data. Going back to the original set of data above (1, 3, 3, 6, 8), the number 3 occurs twice, and no other number occurs that many times, so 3 is the mode. If no item of data occurs more frequently than any other, there is no mode.

Practice Exercises

A polling group conducted a survey that included the following questions.

I. What is your political affiliation?

II. What temperature do you consider to be ideal for comfort?

III. What is your opinion of the governor's performance? (0–5, from disapprove strongly through approve wholeheartedly)

IV. How many cars do you own?

Determine the level of data obtained in each question in this survey.

1. Question I

2. Question II

3. Question III

4. Question IV

5. Determine the mean, median, and mode of the following data: 4, 1, 5, 2, 5, 7, 2, 1

6. Determine the mean median, and mode of the following data: 3, 3, 3, 3, 3, 3, 3, 3, 3

Solutions to Practice Exercises

1. Names of political parties are nominal data.

2. Temperature—regardless of thermometer scale used—is interval data. The temperature identified as zero is completely arbitrary: It doesn't indicate that there is no temperature; it's just a place to begin. It would make sense to subtract temperatures—65°F is 5 degrees cooler than 70°—but addition makes no sense. Averages (means) make sense, but not multiplication.

3. This is ordinal data. Though there are numbers assigned to the responses, it is not numeric data. The numbers are completely arbitrary—they could just as well have been 1–10 or 0–100.

4. The number of cars is ratio data. The number zero is certainly meaningful, and all other mathematical operations can be performed on the data.

5. First rank the data: 1, 1, 2, 2, 4, 5, 5, 7

   Mean: Add the numbers together and divide by the number of items. You should get 27 for your total, and then 27 divided by 8 items is 3.375.

   Median: Divide 8 by 2. The fourth number is the first of the two in the middle. The fourth number in the ranked data is 2; the next number is 4. Add and divide by 2:
   $$\frac{2+4}{2} = \frac{6}{2} = 3.$$

   Mode: There is no mode because no one number occurs more frequently than any other.

6. All three averages are the same: 3.

Weighted Averages

Sometimes scores are to be weighted in some way to determine the mean. The **weighted average** is calculated by multiplying the scores by the corresponding weights, adding the results, and dividing by the total weight. Take a teacher's scheme for determining class grades. The syllabus for the class states the following breakdown for determining a grade:

Quiz 1   5% of the grade

Quiz 2   10% of the grade

Midterm   25% of the grade

Quiz 3   10% of the grade

Final exam   50% of the grade

Suppose one student had the following scores:

Quiz 1   73

Quiz 2   89

Midterm   84

Quiz 3   95

Final exam   88

Not including the final exam, her scores would be:

$$\frac{0.05(73) + 0.10(89) + 0.25(84) + 0.10(95)}{0.05 + 0.10 + 0.25 + 0.10} = \frac{43.05}{0.50} = 86.1$$

Including the final exam, her scores would be:

$$\frac{0.05(73) + 0.10(89) + 0.25(84) + 0.10(95) + 0.50(88)}{0.05 + 0.10 + 0.25 + 0.10 + 0.50} = \frac{87.05}{1.00} = 87.05$$

Practice Exercises

1. Using the grade point average (GPA) assignment of 4 points for an A, 3 points for a B, 2 for a C, 1 for a D, and 0 for an F, determine the GPA—rounded to the nearest hundredth—of a student whose grade report for a semester is:

   Intermediate Algebra (5 units)   A

   Psychology (3 units)   B

   Phys. Ed. (2 units)   C

   History (3 units)   B

2. If Phys. Ed. is not counted, determine the GPA, rounded to the nearest hundredth, of the student above.

Solutions to Practice Exercises

1. The GPA is $\dfrac{5(4) + 3(3) + 2(2) + 3(3)}{5 + 3 + 2 + 3} = \dfrac{20 + 9 + 4 + 9}{13} = \dfrac{42}{13} = 3.23$

2. The GPA not counting Phys. Ed. is $\dfrac{5(4) + 3(3) + 3(3)}{5 + 3 + 3} = \dfrac{38}{11} = 3.45$

MEASURES OF RELATIVE STANDING

Most schools report the results of standardized tests in **percentiles** or **stanines**. That way, one person's score can be compared with the scores of the others who took the test. If you have a percentile rank of 62, then your score is better than 62 percent of the students who took the test.

Logically, then, the 50th percentile is the median—it separates the scores into equal halves. Half the scores are higher; half are lower. We could also say that 20 percent of the scores fall between those with percentile ranks of 60 and 80, for example.

Stanines are used almost exclusively in education. Stanines are nine intervals constructed in such a way that the first and ninth stanines contain 4% of the scores each; the first contains the lowest 4%, and the ninth contains the highest 4%. The middle stanine—the fifth—contains the middle 20% of the scores. The middle three stanines—the fourth, fifth, and sixth—are usually considered to be average.

Practice Exercises

Following are the scores of 20 students on a statistics test: 48, 50, 53, 57, 63, 65, 68, 69, 70, 72, 75, 76, 78, 80, 83, 85, 88, 90, 91, 94.

1. Determine the median.

2. Determine the 10th percentile.

3. Determine the 60th percentile.

4. Determine the first and ninth stanines.

5. Determine the fifth stanine.

Solutions to Practice Exercises

1. Add the 10th and 11th numbers and divide by 2. $\frac{72 + 75}{2} = \frac{147}{2} = 73.5$

2. The 10th percentile is the number such that 10% of the data is less than that value. Ten percent of 20 numbers is two numbers. There are two numbers less than 53 in the ranked data.

3. Sixty percent of 20 numbers is 12. Count the first 12 numbers: 76 is the 12th number. So 78 is the 60th percentile.

4. The first and ninth stanines contain 4% of the data each. Four percent of 20 is 0.8, which can be rounded to one. The first stanine contains the number 48, and the ninth stanine contains the number 94.

5. The fifth stanine contains 20% of the middle data. Twenty percent of 20 numbers is 4—we want the middle 4 numbers. They are the 9th, 10th, 11th, and 12th numbers: 70, 72, 75, and 76.

PROBABILITY

The **probability** of an event happening is a number between 0 and 1, inclusively, that represents the likelihood of the event occurring. Events are less likely to occur if their probability is close to 0 and are more likely to occur if their probability is close to 1. Events that are as likely to happen as not have a probability of $\frac{1}{2}$.

The list of all possible outcomes in a statistical experiment is the **sample space**. An **event** is any subset of the sample space. If the sample space has n outcomes in it, and the event A has f outcomes, then the probability of event A occurring is $P(A) = \frac{f}{n}$.

For example, the sample space for the experiment of flipping two fair coins and noting heads (H) or tails (T) is:

HH

HT

TH

TT

Let an event be the outcomes identified by the phrase *same on both coins*. The outcomes HH and TT are the only ones that have the same on both coins. So the probability of flipping two coins and getting the same result for both coins is $P(\text{same on both coins}) = \frac{2}{4} = \frac{1}{2}$. Let another event be identified by *at least one head*. The outcomes in this event are HH, HT, and TH. So the probability of obtaining at least one head is $P(\text{at least one head}) = \frac{3}{4}$.

The sample space for the experiment of drawing one card from a well-shuffled standard deck of cards is the list of all 52 cards. Be careful not to confuse the sample space with the number of outcomes in the sample space. The sample space is the *list* of all possible outcomes. The event of picking a heart contains 13 items from the sample space, so the probability of drawing one card from a standard deck and getting a heart is $P(\text{heart}) = \frac{13}{52} = \frac{1}{4}$.

The probability of drawing one card from a standard deck and getting an ace is $P(\text{ace}) = \frac{4}{52} = \frac{1}{13}$. There are four aces in a deck.

The probability of drawing one card from a standard deck and getting a red card is $P(\text{red}) = \frac{26}{52} = \frac{1}{2}$. There are 26 red cards in the deck.

The probability of drawing one card from a standard deck and getting a face card or an ace is $P(\text{face card or ace}) = \frac{12+4}{52} = \frac{16}{52} = \frac{4}{13}$. There are 12 face cards and 4 aces in the deck.

The probability of drawing one card from a standard deck and getting a face card or a club is

$P(face\ card\ or\ club) = \dfrac{12 + 13 - 3}{52} = \dfrac{22}{52} = \dfrac{11}{26}$. There are 12 face cards and 13 clubs, but three of these cards are counted twice—the three club face cards. So that every card is counted only once, three must be subtracted from the total to get the correct number in the event.

A survey was conducted in a city to determine the annual income of 100 individuals. The results are summarized for publication in the following table.

Annual Incomes	Number of people (frequency)
Less than $15,000	5
$15,000 – 19,999	18
$20,000 – 24,999	25
$25,000 – 29,999	31
$30,000 – 34,999	12
$35,000 or more	9

If one person who participated in this survey is chosen at random, the probability that his income is between $20,000 and $24,999 is $P(between\ \$20,000\ and\ \$24,999) = \dfrac{25}{100} = \dfrac{1}{4}$. There were 25 people whose income fell into this range.

If one person who participated in this survey is chosen at random, the probability that his income is $30,000 or more is $P(\$30,000\ or\ more) = \dfrac{12 + 9}{100} = \dfrac{21}{100}$.

If one person who participated in this survey is chosen at random, the probability that his income is exactly $27,512.65 cannot be determined from the information in the table, but it's very likely to be zero. Most probably no one from the original group of 100 people had exactly that income.

Practice Exercises

A single die is rolled once. The die has six sides with 1, 2, 3, 4, 5, and 6 spots. Determine the following probabilities:

1. *P(5)*

2. *P(even number)*

3. *P(prime number)*

4. *P(number greater than 2)*

   One card is drawn from a well-shuffled standard deck of cards. Determine the following probabilities:

5. *P(club)*

6. *P(king)*

7. *P(king of clubs)*

8. *P(king or club)*

9. Determine the sample space for the experiment of flipping three fair coins.

10. Using the sample space from question 9, determine *P(exactly two heads)*

Solutions to Practice Exercises

1. $P(5) = \frac{1}{6}$

2. $P(\textit{even number}) = \frac{3}{6} = \frac{1}{2}$. The event *even* has 3 outcomes: 2, 4, and 6.

3. $P(\textit{prime number}) = \frac{3}{6} = \frac{1}{2}$. The event *prime* has 3 outcomes: 2, 3, and 5.

4. $P(\textit{number greater than 2}) = \frac{4}{6} = \frac{2}{3}$. The event *greater than 2* has 4 outcomes: 3, 4, 5, and 6.

5. $P(\textit{club}) = \frac{13}{52} = \frac{1}{4}$. The event *club* has 13 outcomes.

6. $P(\textit{king}) = \frac{4}{52} = \frac{1}{13}$. The event *king* has 4 outcomes.

7. There is only one king of clubs. $P\,(\textit{king of clubs}) = \frac{1}{52}$

8. $P(\textit{king or club}) = \frac{4 + 13 - 1}{52} = \frac{16}{52} = \frac{4}{13}$. There are four kings, 13 clubs, but the king of clubs is counted twice.

9.
HHH	HHT
HTH	HTT
THH	THT
TTH	TTT

10. $P(\textit{exactly two heads}) = \frac{3}{8}$. The event *exactly two heads* contains the outcomes HTH, THH, and HHT.

Chapter Ten: **Algebra and Graphic Relations**

THREE MEANINGS OF THE − SIGN

In the English language there are many examples of different meanings for the same or similar-sounding words. Consider the words *there, their,* and *they're.* In the same way, the symbol − has the same problem in algebra; it has different meanings depending on where its location is in an expression.

Meaning 1. If the symbol appears to the left of a number, it is properly read *negative*. So −7 is *negative seven*. And $-\frac{4}{5}$ is *negative four-fifths*.

Meaning 2. If the symbol appears between two numbers, it is a subtraction sign. So 9 − 5 is *nine minus five*.

Meaning 3. If the symbol appears any other place, it is properly read *opposite*. The opposite of any number is that number located the same distance from zero on the opposite side of zero on the number line. To the left of any variable: $-x$ is the *opposite of x*. To the left of parentheses, $-(x + 5)$ is the *opposite of x + 5*. To the left of another operation, -2^2 is the *opposite of 2^2*.

ABSOLUTE VALUE

The absolute value of a number is its distance from zero on the number line. Distance is never negative, so the absolute value of a number is always zero or a positive number. The symbol for absolute value is two vertical lines surrounding a number: $|-5| = 5$ or $|-3| = 3$.

SIGNED NUMBERS

Addition of Signed Numbers

Rule 1: To add two numbers with the same sign, add their absolute values, and attach the common sign to the answer.

$+5 + (+7) = +12$ Add 5 and 7. The common sign is +.

If a number is positive, its sign is optional. If a number is negative, its sign is never optional.

$-4 + (-3) = -7$ Add 3 and 4. The common sign is –.

$-8 + (-3) = -11$ Add 8 and 3. The common sign is –.

Rule 2: To add two numbers with different signs, subtract their absolute values, and attach the sign of the number with the larger absolute value to the answer.

$5 + (-8) = -3$ Subtract 5 from 8. –8 has the larger absolute value, so attach the – sign to the answer.

$-6 + 9 = 3$ Subtract 6 from 9. 9 has the larger absolute value, so the answer is positive.

Subtraction of Signed Numbers

To subtract two signed numbers, change the sign of the number *after* the subtraction sign to its opposite, and change the sign of the operation to addition. Follow Rules 1 and 2 for addition above.

$$a - b = a + (-b)$$

In other words, *a* minus *b* equals *a* plus the opposite of *b*. The expression $(-b)$ is not *negative b* here. It is merely the *opposite* of the number that follows the subtraction sign.

$9 - 3 = 9 + (-3) = 6$ Change the operation to addition. Change the sign of the number following the subtraction sign. Then add.

$6 - (-4) = 6 + 4 = 10$ Always change two things: the operation to addition and the sign of the number after the subtraction sign to its opposite.

$-7 - 3 = -7 + (-3) = -10$

$-4 - (-9) = -4 + 9 = 5$

Practice Exercises

Perform the indicated operations.

1. $-[-(-7)]$

2. $-7 + (-3)$

3. $-7 - 6$

4. $-12 - (-4)$

5. $-1.2 - 3.5$

6. $\dfrac{-2}{3} + \dfrac{3}{4}$

Solutions to Practice Exercises

1. $-[-(-7)] = -[7] = -7$ Work from the inside out.

2. $-7 + (-3) = -10$

3. $-7 - 6 = -7 + (-6) = -13$

4. $-12 - (-4) = -12 + 4 = -8$ Add absolute values. Attach the common sign

5. $-1.2 - 3.5 = -1.2 + (-3.5) = -4.7$

6. $\dfrac{-2}{3} + \dfrac{3}{4} = \dfrac{-8}{12} + \dfrac{9}{12} = \dfrac{1}{12}$

Multiplication of Signed Numbers

To multiply two signed numbers, multiply their absolute values, and attach a sign to the answer according the following rules.

Rule 1: If the two numbers have the same sign, the answer is positive.

Rule 2: If the two numbers have opposite signs, the answer is negative.

$(-5)(6) = -30$ Rule 2

$(-8)(-5) = 40$ Rule 1

Division of Signed Numbers

To divide two signed numbers, divide their absolute values, and attach a sign as determined by the same rules given above for multiplication.

$-20 \div (-10) = 2$ Rule 1

$\dfrac{-28}{4} = -7$ Rule 2

EXPONENTS

For whole numbers n:

$a^n = a \cdot a \cdot a \cdot \cdots \cdot a$ n factors of a

The number a is called the base, and the small raised number n is called the exponent. Expressions of this type are read *a to the nth power*. So 7^4 is read *7 to the fourth power*. When the exponent is 2, we commonly say *squared*. So 5^2 is read *five squared*. When the exponent is 3, we say *cubed*.

There are two special cases of this rule. If $n = 1$, there is no actual multiplication, but $a^1 = a$. For values where $a \neq 0$, if $n = 0$, then $a^0 = 1$.

$3^2 = 3 \times 3 = 9$

$5^4 = 5 \times 5 \times 5 \times 5 = 625$

$(-2)^2 = (-2)(-2) = 4$

$$(-2)^3 = (-2)(-2)(-2) = 4(-2) = -8 \qquad \text{Multiply two at a time}$$
$$-2^2 = -(2 \times 2) = -(4) = -4 \qquad \text{Opposite of } 2^2$$

SQUARE ROOT

a is a square root of b if and only if $a^2 = b$. With this definition, there are two square roots of 25; it is true that both 5^2 and $(-5)^2$ equal 25. So both 5 and −5 are square roots of 25. Similarly, there are two square roots of every positive number. Because any number squared becomes either positive or zero, there are no square roots of negative numbers.

The ***radical sign*** symbol $\sqrt{}$ is used in the operation square root. The number underneath the bar of the radical sign is called the radicand. Keep in mind that when this symbol is used, the answer indicates the positive square root (or zero) only, never the negative value.

$$\sqrt{25} = 5$$
$$\sqrt{0} = 0$$
$\sqrt{-9}$ does not exist.   Negative numbers do not have square roots.
$-\sqrt{49} = -(7) = -7$ Opposite of the square root of 49

Practice Exercises

Perform the indicated operations.

1. $-8(-3)$

2. $\dfrac{-42}{-7}$

3. $\dfrac{32}{-8}$

4. 5^3

5. $(-3)^4$

6. 7^0

7. $\sqrt{64}$

Solutions to Practice Exercises

1. $-8(-3) = 24$

2. $\dfrac{-42}{-7} = 6$

3. $\dfrac{32}{-8} = -4$

4. $5^3 = 5 \times 5 \times 5 = 125$

5. $(-3)^4 = (-3)\,(-3)\,(-3)\,(-3) = 9(-3)\,(-3) = -27(-3) = 81$

6. $7^0 = 1$ Any number except 0^0 equals 1

7. $\sqrt{64} = 8$

ORDER OF OPERATIONS

Expressions that include several operations require that the operations be done in a certain order. Use the following process:

1. Do all operations inside grouping symbols first. That means anything inside parentheses, brackets, braces, or grouped as a unit, as in $\dfrac{3+9}{4+8}$ or $\sqrt{16+9}$.

2. Do all roots and exponents in order from left to right.

3. Do multiplications and divisions from left to right. This doesn't mean *do all multiplications and then all divisions*. It means do the operations one-by-one as they appear from left to right.

4. Do additions and subtractions in order from left to right.

Examples:

- $12 + 2 \times 4 = 12 + 8 = 20$ Multiplication before addition

- $3 \times 5^2 = 3 \times 25 = 75$ Exponents before multiplication

- $5 - 14 \div 2 \times 3 + 8$
  $= 5 - 7 \times 3 + 8$
  $= 5 - 21 + 8$
  $= 5 + (-21) + 8$
  $= -16 + 8 = -8$

- $2\{4 - 3[5 - (3 - 6)]\}$
  $= 2\{4 - 3[5 - (3 + (-6))]\}$ Innermost grouping symbols first
  $= 2\{4 - 3[5 - (-3)]\}$
  $= 2\{4 - 3[5 + 3]\}$
  $= 2\{4 - 3[8]\}$
  $= 2\{4 - 24\}$
  $= 2\{4 + (-24)\}$
  $= 2\{-20\} = -40$

Practice Exercises

Perform the indicated operations.

1. $5 + 2(3 - 5)$

2. $-4 - 2\{3 - [4 - 2(1 - 3)]\}$

3. $-3^2 + (-2)^2 \times 5$

Solutions to Practice Exercises

1. $5 + 2(3 - 5) = 5 + 2(3 + (-5)) = 5 + 2(-2) = 5 - 4 = 1$

2. $-4 - 2\{3 - [4 - 2(1 - 3)]\}$

    $= -4 - 2\{3 - [4 - 2(1 + (-3))]\}$

    $= -4 - 2\{3 - [4 - 2(-2)]\}$

    $= -4 - 2\{3 - [4 - (-4)]\}$

    $= -4 - 2\{3 - [4 + 4]\}$

    $= -4 - 2\{3 - 8\}$

    $= -4 - 2\{3 + (-8)\}$

    $= -4 - 2\{-5\}$

    $= -4 - (-10)$

    $= -4 + 10 = 6$

3. $-3^2 + (-2)^2 \times 5 = -9 + 4 \times 5 = -9 + 20 = 11$

SIMPLIFYING RADICALS

If a radicand has a square factor other than 1, it can be simplified. The rule that allows this simplification is as follows.

The Rule: As long as none of the radicands are negative, radicands can be multiplied. In other words, $\sqrt{xy} = \sqrt{x} \times \sqrt{y}$.

$$\sqrt{12} = \sqrt{4 \times 3} = \sqrt{4} \times \sqrt{3} = 2\sqrt{3}$$
$$\sqrt{72} = \sqrt{36 \times 2} = \sqrt{36} \times \sqrt{2} = 6\sqrt{2} \qquad \text{Always use the largest square factor}$$

Practice Exercises

Simplify.

1. $\sqrt{500}$

2. $\sqrt{320}$

3. $3\sqrt{75}$

4. $\frac{2}{3}\sqrt{24}$

Solutions to Practice Exercises

1. $\sqrt{500} = \sqrt{100 \times 5} = \sqrt{100} \times \sqrt{5} = 10\sqrt{5}$

2. $\sqrt{320} = \sqrt{64 \times 5} = \sqrt{64} \times \sqrt{5} = 8\sqrt{5}$

3. $3\sqrt{75} = 3\sqrt{25 \times 3} = 3\sqrt{25} \times \sqrt{3} = 3 \times 5\sqrt{3} = 15\sqrt{3}$

4. $\frac{2}{3}\sqrt{24} = \frac{2}{3}\sqrt{4 \times 6} = \frac{2}{3}\sqrt{4} \times \sqrt{6} = \frac{2}{3} \times 2\sqrt{6} = \frac{4}{3}\sqrt{6}$

Simplification

To *simplify* in math means to eliminate parentheses by using the distributive property and then to combine similar terms. So $a(b + c) = ab + ac$.

Examples:

- $3(2x + 5) = 6x + 15$
- $-4(3x - 6) = -12x + 24$
- $2(x - 3) + 5(x + 2) = 2x - 6 + 5x + 10 = 7x + 4$
- $4(x - 2) - (2x + 5) = 4x - 8 - 2x - 5 = 2x - 13$

SOLVING EQUATIONS

There are two rules used to solve equations.

Rule 1: You may add or subtract any number from both sides of an equation.

Rule 2: You may multiply or divide both sides of an equation by any number except zero.

Applying either rule will result in a new equation that will have the same solution as the original equation. The goal is to produce an equation of the type $x = a$ from which it is obvious that the solution set is {a}.

Example 1: $2x + 1 = 5$ Subtract 1 from both sides.

  $2x = 4$ Divide both sides by 2.

  $x = 2$

Example 2: $2(x + 3) - 9 = 7$ Simplify both sides separately.

  $2x + 6 - 9 = 7$

  $2x - 3 = 7$ Add 3 to both sides.

  $2x = 10$ Divide both sides by 2.

  $x = 5$

Example 3: $\dfrac{x + 1}{2} + \dfrac{x + 2}{3} = \dfrac{7}{6}$ Multiply both sides by 6.

  $6\left(\dfrac{x + 1}{2} + \dfrac{x + 2}{3}\right) = 6\left(\dfrac{7}{6}\right)$

  $3(x + 1) + 2(x + 2) = 7$ Simplify the left side.

  $3x + 3 + 2x + 4 = 7$

  $5x + 7 = 7$ Subtract 7 from both sides.

  $5x = 0$ Divide both sides by 5.

  $x = 0$

Practice Exercises

Solve each equation.

1. $4x - 3 = 13$

2. $7 - (2x + 1) = 5 + 3(x - 4)$

3. $2 + x = 3 - 2[1 - 2(x + 1)]$

4. $\dfrac{x}{5} - \dfrac{x}{4} = \dfrac{-1}{2}$

Solutions to Practice Exercises

1. $4x - 3 = 13$ Add 3

   $4x = 16$ Divide by 4

   $x = 4$

2. $7 - (2x + 1) = 5 + 3(x - 4)$ Simplify both sides

   $7 - 2x - 1 = 5 + 3x - 12$

   $6 - 2x = 3x - 7$ Add $2x$ to both sides

   $6 = 5x - 7$ Add 7 to both sides

   $13 = 5x$ Divide both sides by 5

   $\dfrac{13}{5} = x$

3. $2 + x = 3 - 2[1 - 2(x + 1)]$ Simplify the right side. Inner parentheses first

   $2 + x = 3 - 2[1 - 2x - 2]$

   $2 + x = 3 - 2 + 4x + 4$

   $2 + x = 5 + 4x$ Subtract x from both sides

   $2 = 5 + 3x$ Subtract 5 from both sides

   $-3 = 3x$ Divide by 3

   $-1 = x$

4. $\dfrac{x}{5} - \dfrac{x}{4} = \dfrac{-1}{2}$ Multiply both sides by 20

   $20\left(\dfrac{x}{5} - \dfrac{x}{4}\right) = 20\left(\dfrac{-1}{2}\right)$

   $4x - 5x = -10$

   $-x = -10$ Divide both sides by -1.

   $x = 10$

POLYNOMIALS

Addition and subtraction of polynomials is easy. It is merely combining similar terms.

$$(3x^2 + 4x - 7) - (5x^2 - 3x - 9)$$
$$= 3x^2 + 4x - 7 - 5x^2 + 3x + 9$$
$$= -2x^2 + 7x + 2$$

Multiplication of binomials is an extension of the distributive property commonly known as the FOIL method. FOIL means:

F: Multiply the <u>f</u>irst terms of the binomials.

O: Multiply the <u>o</u>uter terms.

I: Multiply the <u>i</u>nner terms.

L: Multiply the <u>l</u>ast terms.

$$(x + 3)(x + 5) = x^2 + 5x + 3x + 15 = x^2 + 8x + 15$$
$$(x - 4)(2x + 3) = 2x^2 + 3x - 8x - 12 = 2x^2 - 5x - 12$$
$$(3x - 5)(2x - 7) = 6x^2 - 21x - 10x + 35 = 6x^2 - 31x + 35$$
$$(4x + 5)(4x - 5) = 16x^2 - 20x + 20x - 25 = 16x^2 - 25$$

Practice Exercises

Simplify.

1. Subtract $(x^2 - 3x + 2)$ from $(4x^2 - 5x - 4)$.

2. $(x - 5)(x - 6)$

3. $(x + 6)(x - 1)$

4. $(2x - 5)(3x + 1)$

5. $(2x - 7)(2x + 7)$

Solutions to Practice Exercises

1. $(4x^2 - 5x - 4) - (x^2 - 3x + 2) = 4x^2 - 5x - 4 - x^2 + 3x - 2 = 3x^2 - 2x - 6$

2. $(x - 5)(x - 6) = x^2 - 6x - 5x + 30 = x^2 - 11x + 30$

3. $(x + 6)(x - 1) = x^2 - x + 6x - 6 = x^2 + 5x - 6$

4. $(2x - 5)(3x + 1) = 6x^2 + 2x - 15x - 5 = 6x^2 - 13x - 5$

5. $(2x - 7)(2x + 7) = 4x^2 - 49$

KAPLAN

FACTORING

Factoring is the process of changing a polynomial into the product of other polynomials. Following are some methods of factoring polynomials.

Greatest Common Factor

If all the terms of a polynomial contain a common factor, use the distributive property to remove the greatest common factor.

$$3x - 12 = 3(x - 4)$$
$$15x^3 - 20x^2 = 5x^2(3x - 4)$$
$$24a^4b - 30a^3b^2 + 12a^2b^3 = 6a^2b(4a^2 - 5ab + 2b^2)$$

Difference of Squares

A polynomial of the type $A^2 - B^2$, that is, two terms both of which are squares with a subtraction sign between them, is called a *difference of squares*. Polynomials of this type can be factored according to the following pattern:

$$A^2 - B^2 = (A - B)(A + B)$$
$$x^2 - 25 = (x - 5)(x + 5)$$
$$4x^2 - 49 = (2x - 7)(2x + 7)$$
$$25x^2 - 100 = 25(x^2 - 4) = 25(x - 2)(x + 2) \qquad \text{Do the greatest common factor first}$$
$$x^4 - 81 = (x^2 - 9)(x^2 + 9) = (x - 3)(x + 3)(x^2 + 9)$$
$$36x^2 + 25 \qquad \text{This polynomial is not factorable}$$

Factoring Polynomials of the Type $x^2 + bx + c$

The coefficient of the first term in this type of polynomial is always 1. To do this type of factoring, look for factors of the last term whose sum or difference (depending on the sign of the third term) is equal to the coefficient of the middle term. These numbers are the second terms of the two binomial factors.

Example 1: $\quad x^2 - 8x = 15 \qquad$ Factors of 15 whose *sum* is 8: 3 and 5
$\qquad\qquad\quad = (x - 3)(x - 5)$

Example 2: $\quad x^2 - 3x - 40 \qquad$ Factors of 40 whose *difference* is 3: 5 and 8
$\qquad\qquad\quad = (x + 5)(x - 8) \qquad$ The larger number gets the sign of the middle term.

Example 3: $\quad 3x^2 - 3x - 18 \qquad$ Do the greatest common factor first
$\qquad\qquad\quad = 3(x^2 - x - 6) \qquad$ Factors of 6 whose *difference* is 1: 2 and 3
$\qquad\qquad\quad = 3(x + 2)(x - 3)$

Factoring Polynomials of the Type $ax^2 + bx + c$

The coefficient of the first term of this type of polynomial is a number other than 0 or 1. $a \neq 0$ or 1. First multiply the first and last coefficients, ac. Look for factors of that number whose sum or difference, depending on the sign of the last term, equals the coefficient of the middle term. Then rewrite the middle term using those numbers, group, and factor.

Example 1: $2x^2 + 5x - 12$ Multiply 2 times 12. Factors of 24 whose difference is 5: 3 and 8. Rewrite the middle term using 3 and 8

$= 2x^2 - 3x + 8x - 12$ Group the first two and the last two terms

$= (2x^2 - 3x) + (8x - 12)$ Find common factors in each group

$= x(2x - 3) + 4(2x - 3)$ Now $(2x - 3)$ is a common factor

$= (2x - 3) + (x + 4)$

Example 2: $8x^2 + 2x - 3$ 8 times 3 = 24. Look for factors of 24 whose difference is 2: 4 and 6. Rewrite the middle term using these numbers.

$= 8x^2 - 4x + 6x - 3$ Group and factor

$= 4x(2x - 1) + 3(2x - 1)$ Now $(2x - 1)$ is a common factor

$= (2x - 1)(4x + 3)$

Example 3: $6x^2 + 19x + 10$ 6 times 10 = 60. Factors of 60 whose sum is 19: 4 and 15. Rewrite middle term.

$= 6x^2 + 4x + 15x + 10$ Group and factor

$= 2x(3x + 2) + 5(3x + 2)$ Now $(3x + 2)$ is a common factor

$= (3x + 2)(2x + 5)$

Practice Exercises

Factor completely.

1. $4x^2 - 20x$

2. $3x^2 - 27$

3. $a^2 - 3a - 10$

4. $x^2 - 14x + 49$

5. $2x^2 + 13x + 18$

Solutions to Practice Exercises

1. $4x^2 - 20x = 4x(x - 5)$ Greatest common factor

2. $3x^2 - 27 = 3(x^2 - 9)$ Greatest common factor
    $= 3(x - 3)(x + 3)$ Difference of squares

3. $a^2 - 3a - 10 = (a - 5)(a + 2)$ Factors of 10 whose difference is 3: 2 and 5

4. $x^2 - 14x + 49 = (x - 7)(x - 7) = (x - 7)^2$ Factors of 49 whose sum is 14: 7 and 7
    (Perfect square trinomial)

5. $2x^2 + 13x + 18$ Multiply 2 times 18. Factors of 36 whose sum is 13

    $= 2x^2 + 4x + 9x + 18$ Group and factor
    $= 2x(x + 2) + 9(x + 2)$ Now $(x + 2)$ is a common factor

GRAPHING

The common method of graphing is called the *rectangular coordinate system*. It consists of two number lines at right angles to each other. The horizontal line is the *x*-axis, and the vertical line is the *y*-axis. These two lines separate the plane into four quadrants numbered I, II, III, and IV, beginning with the upper right quadrant and numbered counterclockwise.

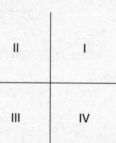

The points on the graphs in the rectangular coordinate system are identified with ordered pairs of real numbers. An ordered pair consists of two real numbers separated by a comma, set within parenthesis: (x, y). The first number is the *x*-axis measure, and the second number is the *y*-axis measure.

The source of the ordered pairs is usually an equation with two variables such as $2x + 5y = 9$. The ordered pair $(2,1)$ satisfies the equation in the sense that if 2 is substituted for *x* and 1 is substituted for *y*, the equation becomes true:

$$2(2) + 5(1) = 4 + 5 = 9$$

Other ordered pairs can be found by choosing some number (any number) for *x* (or *y*) and solving for the other variable. Let's pick $x = 7$.

$2(7) + 5y = 9$

$14 + 5y = 9$ Subtract 14 from both sides

$5y = -5$ Divide both sides by 5

$y = -1$ $(7,-1)$ satisfies the equation

Now pick $x = -1$.

$$2(-1) + 5y = 9$$
$$-2 + 5y = 9 \qquad \text{Add 2 to both sides}$$
$$5y = 11 \qquad \text{Divide both sides by 5}$$
$$y = \frac{11}{5} \qquad \left(-1, \frac{11}{5}\right) \text{ satisfies the equation}$$

If the ordered pairs are located on a rectangular coordinate system, they fall on a line. By drawing the line through the points, you have a picture of all the ordered pairs that satisfy the equation. More complicated equations give graphs other than lines. No matter what the graph, it is a picture of all ordered pairs that satisfy the equation. The CBEST may ask you to find certain ordered pairs or to judge whether an ordered pair satisfies an equation.

Practice Exercises

1. Is $(2,-3)$ a solution of $3x - 2y = 0$?

2. In the equation $y = 4x - 3$, find y if $x = -1$.

Use the equation $x - 3y = 5$ to complete the following ordered pairs:

3. $(5, \ )$

4. $(8, \ )$

5. $(-3, \ )$

Solutions to Practice Exercises

1. $3x - 2y = 0$ Substitute
   $3(2) - 2(-3) = 6 - (-6) = 6 + 6 = 12 \neq 0$ No, $(2,-3)$ is not a solution.

2. $y = 4x - 3$ Substitute
   $y = 4(-1) - 3 = -4 - 3 = -7$ If $x = -1$, then $y = -7$

3. $x - 3y = 5$
   $5 - 3y = 5$ Subtract 5 from both sides
   $-3y = 0$ Divide both sides by -3
   $y = 0$ The ordered pair is $(5,0)$

4. $x - 3y = 5$
   $8 - 3y = 5$ Subtract 8 from both sides
   $-3y = -3$ Divide both sides by -3
   $y = 1$ The ordered pair is $(8,1)$

5. $x - 3y = 5$
   $-3 - 3y = 5$ Add 3 to both sides
   $-3y = 8$ Divide both sides by -3
   $y = \frac{-8}{3}$ The ordered pair is $\left(-3, \frac{-8}{3}\right)$

KAPLAN

APPLICATIONS OF GRAPHING

Graphs can represent changes between two related quantities. Suppose Steve leaves for work, 20 miles away, starting out very fast and gradually slows down, the graph might look like the one below. The horizontal axis represents time and the vertical axis represents distance from Steve's home.

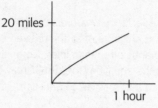

Consider another situation: a short airplane trip on which a constant speed is maintained, but the pilot had to circle the airport a few times before landing. That graph might look like this:

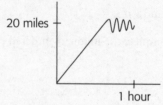

Practice Exercises

Draw a graph for each of the following trips.

1. Corey drove quickly to a park 20 miles away for a picnic. The trip took 30 minutes. The picnic lasted two hours, and the return trip from the park was much slower than the trip to the park. Corey arrived home 5 hours after he left home.

2. Joel left work to drive the 20 miles home. He drove 10 minutes slowly through the city, stopping at one stoplight for 5 minutes. He then got on the freeway and drove quickly to his exit in 30 minutes. He drove slowly for 5 minutes, stopped at another stoplight for 5 minutes, and then drove home in another 5 minutes.

Solutions to Practice Exercises

1.

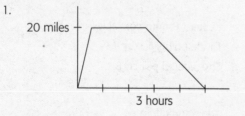

2.

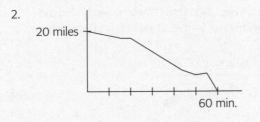

WORD PROBLEMS

Almost all of the questions on the CBEST are presented as word problems. Perhaps the most important thing to remember when solving a word problem is to read the question carefully. Underline or circle important words. (You are allowed to write in the test booklet on the CBEST.)

Most word problems will fit into one of several categories. Some problems are purely arithmetic in nature. Key phrases may be:

How many more…?	Subtract
What is the area…?	Multiply
How many of _____ are in…?	Divide

Some problems describe quantities that vary in relation to each other. These can be solved by using a proportion. Proportions and their solutions are reviewed earlier in this book.

Time and distance of a traveling object

Juice and number of people drinking the juice

Length between points on a map and distance on the ground

Yes, other problems are algebraic in nature, meaning that you'll need to set up and solve an equation. The general plan of attack should be:

1. Read the problem, usually more than once. Circle and underline important words. Draw diagrams as needed.

2. Choose a variable to represent the quantity being sought. Choose a variable that will be easy to remember, such as t for time or B for Bill's age. Represent all other numbers described in the problem in terms of the same variable.

3. Write an equation. This is the difficult step. The equation is a direct interpretation of the words of the problem, but sometimes a well-known formula—such as that for perimeter or area—will apply. In addition, there are schemes for solving mixture, distance–rate–time, and age problems.

4. Solve the equation.

5. Answer the question.

Example 1: The length of a rectangle is 5 feet less than three times the width. Find the length and the width if the perimeter is 54 feet. Draw a diagram, and label it appropriately.

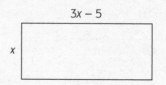

The formula for the perimeter of a rectangle is: $p = 2w + 2l$.
So,

$54 = 2x + 2(3x - 5)$ Simplify the right side

$54 = 2x + 6x - 10$

$54 = 8x - 10$ Add 10 to both sides

$64 = 8x$ Divide both sides by 8

$8 = x$

The width of the rectangle is 8 feet and the length is $3(8) - 5 = 24 - 5 = 19$ feet.

Example 2: The area of a triangle is 60 square inches. The base of the triangle is 10 inches, and the angle opposite the base is 27°. Find the length of the altitude to the base.

The measure of the angle is unnecessary information here, perhaps included to trick you. Draw a diagram and label it.

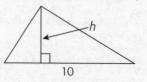

The formula for the area of a triangle is: $a = \frac{1}{2}bh$.
So,

$60 = \frac{1}{2}(10)h$ Simplify the right side

$60 = 5h$ Divide both sides by 5

$12 = h$

The altitude is 12 inches.

Example 3: Carol has $800 to invest. She invests part of the money in an account at 4% and the remainder in another account at 6% simple interest. If her total interest for one year is $38, how much did she invest at each rate?

Let the amount of money invested at 4% be x. Since the sum of the two investments is $800, the amount of money invested at 6% is $800 - x$. The formula for simple interest is: $i = prt$, where p represents the principal— the amount of money invested; r represents the rate of interest always expressed as a percent; and t represents time measured in years.

Since there are two different interest-bearing accounts here, we have to calculate each account separately.

$x(0.04)(1) = 0.04x$	Interest on the 4% account
$(800 - x)(0.06)(1) = 0.06(800 - x)$	Interest on the 6% account

Since the total interest is $38, the equation for this problem is:

$0.04x + 0.06(800 - x) = 38$	Multiply both sides by 100
$4x + 6(800 - x) = 3,800$	Simplify the left side
$4x + 4800 - 6x = 3,800$	
$-2x + 4800 = 3,800$	Subtract 4,800 from both sides
$-2x = -1,000$	Divide both sides by -2
$x = 500$	

Carol invested $500 at 4% and $800 - 500 = $300 at 6%.

Practice Exercises

1. Larry wants to build a rectangular garden such that the length is two feet more than three times the width. He also wants to separate the garden into two regions by building another fence parallel to the width as in the diagram. Find the width and length of the garden if it takes 94 feet of fencing to build it.

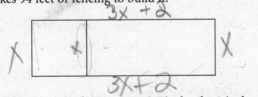

2. The base of a closed rectangular box measures 5 inches by 8 inches. What should the height of the box be if the total outside surface area is 158 square inches?

3. A certain amount of money is invested at 3% simple interest, and $100 more than twice that amount is invested at 5%. If the total interest in one year is $44, how much is invested at each rate?

4. How much distilled water must be mixed with 5 quarts of a 4% acid solution to make a 3% solution?

Solutions to Practice Exercises

1. Using the diagram, label each of the three parallel fences x. Then the two longer sides become $3x + 2$.

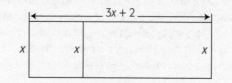

So,

$3x + 2(3x + 2) = 94$	Simplify the left side
$3x + 6x + 4 = 94$	
$9x + 4 = 94$	Subtract 4 from both sides
$9x = 90$	Divide both sides by 9
$x = 10$	

The garden is 10 feet by $3(10) + 2 = 32$ feet.

2. A rectangular box has three pairs of identical sides. The top and bottom are two rectangles with area $5 \times 8 = 40$ square inches each. The front face and the back are rectangles with area $5x$ each. The left and right sides are rectangles with area $8x$ each.

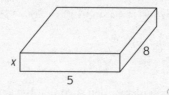

So,

$2(40) + 2(5x) + 2(8x) = 158$	Simplify the left side
$80 + 10x + 16x = 158$	
$80 + 26x = 158$	Subtract 80 from both sides
$26x = 78$	Divide both sides by 26
$x = 3$	

The height of the box is 3 inches.

3. Let the amount of money invested at 3% be x. Then the amount invested at 5% is $2x + 100$.

So,

$0.03x + 0.05(2x + 100) = 44$ Multiply both sides by 100.

$3x + 5(2x + 100) = 4,400$ Simplify the left side

$3x + 10x + 500 = 4,400$

$13x + 500 = 4,400$ Subtract 500 from both sides

$13x = 3,900$ Divide both sides by 13

$x = 300$

$300 is invested at 3%, and $(2(300) + 100) = \$700$ is invested at 5%.

4. Fill in the diagram. Notice that distilled water has no acid in it—0%. So,

$$\boxed{5} \ + \ \boxed{x} \ = \ \boxed{5 + x}$$
$$4\% \qquad\qquad 0\% \qquad\qquad 3\%$$

$0.04(5) + 0 = 0.03(5 + x)$ Multiply both sides by 100

$4(5) = 3(5 + x)$ Simplify both sides

$20 = 15 + 3x$ Subtract 15 from both sides

$5 = 3x$ Divide both sides by 3

$\dfrac{5}{3} = 1\dfrac{2}{3} = x$

You need to add $1\dfrac{2}{3}$ quarts of distilled water.

| SECTION FOUR |

Writing

Chapter Eleven: **Writing Section Overview**

The writing test is designed to measure your thinking skills, how well you can organize ideas, and how well you use American English. These are skills every teacher needs to organize and present information and model the correct use of language for students.

FORMAT

The writing section of the CBEST is made up of two essay questions that you can answer based on your own personal experience or your opinion. In other words, you do not need to know any specific information to answer the questions in this section of the test. The essay questions usually require one descriptive/narrative and one analytical/expository essay.

You will have four hours to answer all of the questions on the CBEST. There is no specific time limit for any one section. If you wish to repeat a section on a later test, you can do so. In that case, you could have four hours to do the writing section. However, if you are taking the CBEST for the first time, save an hour to do the writing section. Dividing the hour into 30-minute segments is probably the best strategy, but you will want to allocate time within that 30 minutes for organizing your ideas, writing the response, and proofreading your essay.

The essay readers will score your essays on your ability to do the following:

- respond to the specific question or topic assigned
- develop and organize ideas using various types of supporting details (specific examples or facts)
- demonstrate an awareness of the intended audience
- use language well, including correct paragraphing and mechanics

SCORING

Each essay will be scored on a scale of 1 to 4, with 4 being best. A score of 3 is a marginal pass, 2 a marginal fail, and one is a definite fail. Because each essay is scored twice, combinations of scores can range from 4 to 16.

The graders will be looking for certain attributes in your essay:
- Does it answer the questions?
- Is it well organized?
- Does it develop the ideas within?
- Is it generally grammatically correct?
- Does it use language well?
- Is it legible?

Taking Charge of the Essay Questions

Let's look at those attributes again. How can you manage them?

Does your essay answer the question?

Read the topic carefully, two or three times. Are you sure you understand what is being asked? It may help you to circle or underline key words. You may want to rephrase the question to help you gain clarity about what is being asked. Remember, you can write in the test booklet.

Is your essay well organized?

To help you to organize your thoughts, take time for prewriting in the space provided in the exam booklet. Prewriting can mean clustering, brainstorming, outlining, or all three, but while you want to get your creative juices flowing, you need to limit yourself to about 5 minutes of prewriting before you begin the actual essay.

Does it develop the ideas you present?

Be sure you have 2 or 3 examples to support each idea. Your examples may include facts that you happen to remember, observations based on experiences you have had, descriptions, or other details. The prewriting you have done should provide you with those examples.

Is it generally grammatically correct?

Check your essay for errors after you have finished. While you are writing, don't slow down to check for or correct errors. Keep your ideas flowing. You can take the last 5 minutes of the half-hour to go over your essay and make minor corrections, inserting commas or periods as needed and correcting spelling.

Does it use language well?

This element is something you can practice far ahead of the exam by doing lots of writing and by fine-tuning your use of language so that when you take the exam, a graceful use of language is natural for you.

Language usage can be classified as **formal** (for college papers and for business letters to people whom you don't know), **informal** (for personal essays, popular magazine articles, and letters to friends), and **nonstandard** (slang or jargon). The essay question that asks you to analyze or argue a point should be written using more formal language than you would use in the personal essay.

Is it legible?

You cannot expect to get credit for something no one can read. Practice penmanship in advance if you need to. Don't write too large or too small. Use appropriate margins (no more than 1 inch on each side) and write on every line. Just as you would dress well for a job interview, present your writing at its best.

Before you begin writing, check to see how much space is provided in the exam booklet for you to write your essay in. Then you can judge how to develop your essay. Some writers tend to write too much. Others don't write enough. Be sure your essay will be complete within the available space.

Now that you have read about the format of the Writing section and how your essays will be scored, let's move on to how you will go about writing your essay on test day. The next chapter provides you with proven strategies to help you manage your time and skills effectively.

Chapter Twelve: **Writing Section Strategies**

USEFUL STRATEGIES FOR APPROACHING THE WRITING TEST

Outline Your Ideas, and Stick to Them

When you have a good outline, your paper will practically write itself. Assume the test maker's mindset, i.e., write in an objective tone unless the question you are responding to specifically asks for a personal response.

Manage Your Time

Practicing in advance under simulated test conditions, including using a timer, will help to ease your anxiety during the test, and you will perform better.

Preparing for the Essay

Producing a good short essay on demand is a skill that you can develop and improve with practice.

A good essay will have several characteristics: a good thesis statement, good organization, correct mechanics, and readable style. It should also reflect clear thinking and logical development. In this section, we will discuss all of these characteristics and give you a few tips to help your writing improve beyond these basics.

Begin With a Strong Thesis Statement

The thesis statement will answer the question or address the topic assigned. It should be short and simple. Brevity and simplicity reflect a clear and focused mind and will help you develop your essay in a straightforward manner. The more clarity you bring to your essay, the easier it will be for the reader to understand it. Remember, you are trying to communicate as effectively and efficiently as possible.

A good thesis statement, besides being simple and brief, will be limited to one main idea. It should also grab the interest of the reader. Don't be boring. Create a statement that will catch the reader's attention.

Good organization results from an essay that has unity, which can be achieved by beginning with a good thesis statement that expresses your main idea. Beginning that way will automatically help you know what to include and what to leave out. If you only include ideas relevant to your thesis statement, you will have taken a big step toward your goal of writing a good essay.

A Well-Organized Essay is Coherent

To achieve coherence, always be sure you finish one idea before you introduce another one. Don't confuse the reader. The orderly progression of ideas in your essay helps the reader stay focused, and you will want to do everything you can to help the reader understand your message. In addition to a logical, orderly presentation of ideas, you can insert helpful words or phrases to serve as guideposts to changes in ideas. Examples are:

Additionally,	By contrast,
In addition to	Second,
On the other hand,	Third,

Good organization will also put your ideas in their proper place in the essay. The most important supporting detail should come at the end of the essay and the next most important at the beginning. Ideas of lesser importance can be placed in between. Furthermore, important ideas should be given more space than ideas of lesser importance because you will want to develop them more fully.

Elaborating on the most important ideas will help you develop an effective response to the question. Use examples, explanations, description, and definition to clarify your ideas.

Be Stylistically Interesting

Developing a readable style seems to come easily to people who have read a lot, especially to people who have read a lot of good writing. Of course, you should read as much good writing as you can. You can work on your own style by making it sound as natural as possible. Do you speak easily and well? Let your writing sound like you. It will have your own personal style imprinted on it.

Another style enhancer is to strive for brevity. Practice expressing your thoughts succinctly, avoiding choppy sentences, and use simple words whenever you can. Many writers believe using long words will make them sound intelligent, but the goal of your essay should be to communicate effectively, not to use a lot of long words.

Using a variety of sentence structures and well-chosen, colorful words will encourage your reader to stay with you throughout the essay. Who can put down writing that is lively and interesting? This kind of writing will hold the reader's attention throughout.

To achieve sentence variety, use a combination of simple and compound and complex sentences.

Simple sentences generally follow a pattern of subject > verb > object.

Example

My dog chased the mailman.

$$\underbrace{\text{My dog}}_{\text{Subject}}\ \underbrace{\text{chased}}_{\text{Verb}}\ \underbrace{\text{the mailman.}}_{\text{Object}}$$

Compound sentences join two independent clauses (complete ideas) together using commas and conjunctions or semicolons and conjunctions. Look at the following example.

My dog chased the mailman, and she caught him.

The comma and the "and" join the two ideas.

Here are some ways to join two independent clauses and form compound sentences:

My dog chased the mailman, *and* she caught him.

My dog chased the mailman, *but* she didn't catch him.

You could come with us, *or* you could stay home.

Other coordinating conjunctions are: *nor*, *for*, *so*, *yet*.

Another way to join two independent clauses and form compound sentences is with semi-colons. The correct and effective use of semicolons will give your writing a sophisticated quality.

My dog chased the mailman; however, she failed to anticipate his surprising response.

However is called a conjunctive adverb. Other conjunctive adverbs that can be used with semi-colons are *therefore* and *moreover*. When you form compound sentences by using semicolons, be sure the ideas are closely related.

Two independent clauses whose ideas are merely related within the scope of the paragraph should stand alone with a period at the end of one and a capital at the beginning of the next.

Try punctuating these independent clauses according to the ideas they express. Check your answers on the next page.

Dad loved to watch football. He never missed a game.

Dad loved to watch football. He loved to watch basketball even more.

Dad loved to watch football. He often had to work when games were broadcast.

Dad loved to watch football. He kept up with all the players.

Coordinating conjunctions (*and*, *but*, *or*, *nor*, *for*, *so*, and *yet*) have another use in good writing. They show the equality of two or more ideas. They can be especially helpful in creating parallel structures.

Parallelism

Parallelism is a technique that elevates the level of your writing. It helps to achieve brevity and grace in style, but most important, it helps to order ideas logically, and therefore, it assists the reader in understanding what you have to say.

Parallel ideas should be expressed in parallel form. Balance single words with single words, phrases with phrases, and clauses with clauses.

Examples

Singing, dancing, and acting are all important skills for a performer to master.

Children at play, flowers in bloom, voices in song all bring joy to the heart.

He walked quickly, turned suddenly, and mysteriously, disappeared.

Subordination and Complex Sentences

In sentences that express two or more unequal ideas, place the main ideas in independent clauses and less important ideas in subordinate clauses or phrases.

Subordinate clauses cannot stand alone and usually begin with an introductory word. You decide which idea is the most important, and structure your sentence accordingly.

Common introductory words to subordinate ideas in clauses are:

after	Because	Since	unless
although	Before	That	until
as	If	Though	when
where	Whether	Which	while
who	Whom	Whose	

Finally, mechanics (spelling, punctuation, and syntax) give legitimacy to your efforts. It's difficult for a reader to respect a writer's thinking if the paper is filled with grammatical errors.

Dad loved to watch football, and he kept up with all the players.

Dad loved to watch football; however, he often had to work when games were broadcast.

Dad loved to watch football, but he loved to watch basketball even more.

Dad loved to watch football; he never missed a game.

Answers

KAPLAN'S FIVE-STEP METHOD FOR WRITING ESSAYS

Kaplan's Five-Step Method for Writing Essays will help to give you the confidence you need to keep your cool in the test room. Read through them carefully, and follow the steps closely. Having a plan puts you ahead of the game and the test!

Step 1. Prewriting

Step 2. Outlining

Step 3. Drafting

Step 4. Revising

Step 5. Proofreading

Step 1. Prewriting

Planning your response or prewriting involves 3 steps:

1. Identifying important information in the question

2. Brainstorming your ideas

3. Thinking through your response

You will want to take about 5 minutes to organize your ideas before you begin writing. This is an important part of the writing process. It gives your mind a chance to do the creative work needed to write effectively.

Identify the Topic

Read the prompt. Then identify the general topic you are asked to discuss. Are specific tasks set forth in the question? If so, let that guide your thinking as you brainstorm.

Brainstorming Your Ideas

Once you have a clear idea of the question, ideas will start popping into your head. Start writing them down! There is more than one way to generate ideas for a timed essay: Listing, clustering, and free-writing are effective. As you practice the essay assignments provided here, try each of those methods more than once to see which is most congenial to you. The purpose is to get down on paper all of the ideas you can that may be applicable to your topic. You are looking for the essence of the ideas.

Think Through Your Response

Once you get the ideas down on paper, take some time to think through your possible response. Assume the test maker's mindset. The readers of your answer will want to see an essay that includes the characteristics mentioned earlier in this section:

- A strong thesis statement
- Good organization
- An interesting style

KAPLAN

Try the following types of brainstorming:

Clustering

Write down your topic in the center of the prewriting area (under the question in the test booklet). Then draw a circle around that topic:

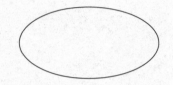

Take the next one or two minutes to jot down all of the ideas that pop into your head related to the topic. Then connect them to the topic:

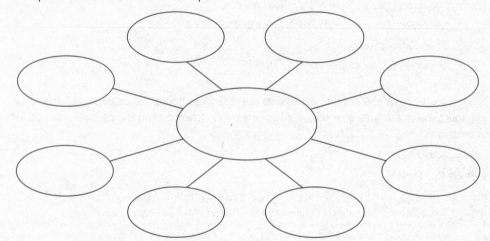

You can practice with the following topics:

1. Identify and discuss a book you have read that significantly influenced your life. Tell how it influenced your life.

2. Compare and/or contrast two international views of the United States. Explain how each may have arisen.

3. Argue the position that participation in sports can help a person to develop important skills for future success.

When you have finished, analyze what you have put down. Cross out all the ideas that don't fit with the others, and then number the remaining ones in an order that will give you an organized essay. You may want to list them quickly in order off to the side just to have an easy reference as you write.

Next, spend 2 to 3 minutes outlining to help organize your ideas. At the end of 5 minutes, you should be ready to begin your essay. Don't take too much time. Your goal is to write a well-organized essay, not a masterpiece.

Free Writing

If you feel stuck, or clustering isn't working for you, use free writing as a way to get the writing process going. You can write almost anything, even that you don't like the assigned topic, but getting your pencil to the paper will help you get started. Then you can quickly move to clustering or outlining. Remember to do this in the space provided for prewriting.

A freewriting sample might look like this:

> I can't think of a thing to say. Nothing important has ever happened to me. I've had an ordinary life. What can I possibly write? My jobs have been boring and my life has been ok, except maybe for the summer my little cousin came to visit, 'cuz that's when I first realized I liked little children and it was after that I thought of being a teacher...

Step 2. Outlining

Outlining is good way to organize your thoughts, and for some people, it is the best way. The better organized your outline is, the easier it will be to write your essay. Read through the ideas you have generated, and determine which you will use in your essay and where each one will go.

An informal outline is perfect for an informal essay. Get at least three main points down on paper. If you have more, select the three that go together best, and jot down some subpoints under each. The subpoints can be examples or descriptive elements. Remember, you should have at least two subpoints beneath each main point.

Your outline may look somewhat like this one:

My First Boss

I. Taught me a lot about the value of work

   A. He worked hard around his house, kept plants trimmed, house painted

   B. Seemed to enjoy having everything look good

   C. Seemed to enjoy working

II. Appreciated my helping him

   A. Always gave me jobs I could do easily

      1. Picking up papers or trash or leaves when I was 10

      2. Walking his big German Shepherd when I was 12

      3. Painting when I was 15

   B. Paid and thanked me immediately after I had finished my work.

III. I learned at a young age that I could earn money for things I wanted to buy by working

   A. Soon, I asked him if he had work he needed help with

   B. I began to look around for things that needed to be done at his house

Step 3. Drafting

The Opening Paragraph

One very important factor in writing a good essay is a strong opening paragraph. A good first paragraph will not only catch the reader's attention, but it will also tell the reader what to expect in the essay.

Details and specific examples will enrich your writing by clarifying your meaning and communicating your ideas effectively.

Plan to write several paragraphs. They can be of varying length, but most should be at least three sentences long. Many short paragraphs can make your essay appear thin, choppy, or lacking in development, but an infrequent short paragraph can be used for emphasis or impact.

Just as you should vary your paragraphs, your sentences should be varied in pattern. Short, punchy sentences can be forceful, but an essay that is filled with short, declarative sentences will be boring. Varying the length and structure of your sentences will keep your reader interested.

Compare the following two paragraphs:

> One of my neighbors taught me the value of hard work. He worked very hard when he was home. He mowed his lawn every week. He trimmed the hedge once a month. He painted his window sills. He always did a lot of work. He worked all weekend.

The repetitive structure is boring and too general. The same sentence pattern is used throughout.

> I learned the value of hard work at an early age. One of my neighbors, a judge, spent his weekends working around his house. He mowed the lawn, trimmed hedges, planted flowers, and seemed to enjoy doing it. Every Saturday and Sunday I could see him in his yard, happily making things look better. If he wasn't gardening, he was painting. I often talked to him as he was going about his tasks, and soon I was helping him and getting paid for it.

Better. It has sentence variety and details.

The Body

Stick to your outline, writing one paragraph at a time, fully developing the idea in each paragraph. Paragraphs can be any length, but they must have no more than one topic within each.

Conclusion

The conclusion to your essay should bring your ideas to completion so that the reader is not left hanging in mid-air. Use it to finish your essay neatly, wrap up your ideas, add information that is relevant, or carry your reader's thoughts toward the future. Be careful, however, to not introduce an entirely new idea. The reader will be puzzled and disappointed if the conclusion suggests something entirely new.

Step 4. Revising

Your draft should include all of your ideas from the outline, but you may need to fine-tune it. As you revise, you can check to see whether you have developed every idea as fully as you wish. Revising the essay involves:

1. Checking the structure—are all ideas included?
   Is your response clear, complete, and logical?
2. Checking the content—did you respond to the question?
   Does all of the information relate to the topic?

Step 5. Proofreading

As you write, keep an eye on the clock now and then so that you have time at the end of the test period to proofread. This is the stage where you polish your essay. When you are finished, look for errors in **spelling, punctuation, usage,** and **grammar**. Did you leave out a word or a letter?

Spelling—Watch out for commonly misused homonyms such as *there, their,* and *they're* and other easily confused spellings such as *ei* and *ie*. The rule generally is *i* before *e* except after *c*.

Punctuation—Be sure your sentences end with a period or question mark. Other end punctuation should be used only rarely. Commas and semicolons should be used appropriately (simple guidelines are included in this text).

Usage—Do subjects and verbs agree? Are nouns and pronouns interchanged correctly?

Grammar—Does every sentence express a complete thought?

Correct your essay neatly by carefully erasing the error or by lining it out and writing in the correction. Ask yourself if your writing is legible; can it be read easily?

WHAT WILL THE EVALUATOR LOOK FOR?

The essay evaluators who read your essay will look for the following key points:

- details, facts, examples, and logical reasons that support the thesis
- paragraphs that display unity leading to a logical conclusion
- sentences that are varied in structure, use lively verbs, adjectives, and adverbs, and hold the reader's interest
- few grammatical, mechanical, or spelling errors

Your writing will display your level of thinking. Poor grammar or mechanics impedes understanding and makes it difficult to tell whether or not you are a clear and logical thinker.

HOW CAN YOU BE IN TOP FORM?

At the beginning of this book we talked about test takers who view tests as a challenge and rise to the occasion with a determination to *beat the test*. You can do that with the writing section as well, even though memorization is generally not a skill that will help you in the writing section of the CBEST.

What will help is being in a mental state of heightened alertness—being on your toes, so to speak.

To prepare: PRACTICE, PRACTICE, PRACTICE.

If you have a month to prepare, set aside half an hour three to four days a week in a quiet place (no television, radio, children, or barking dogs) with a timer. In that half hour, write an essay. By the time you have written six essays you will be ready to spend an hour writing. In that hour, write two essays. You will want to practice the two-essay hour every other day for at least two weeks before the test.

Practice getting started through clustering, freewriting, or outlining, remembering to allow about 5 minutes to organize your ideas.

Then write your essay. Stop after 25 minutes to reread and edit your essay. Check for left out words, misspellings, incorrect punctuation, and awkward or unclear sentences. Make neat and careful corrections.

Put your essay away until the next day. Then, take your essay out, reread it, and analyze it according to the following checklist:

- Does it have a simple, clear thesis statement limited to one main idea?
- Are all the ideas related to the main idea?
- Is the most important point near the end of the essay, and is it fully developed?
- Is the second most important point at the beginning of the essay?
- Are the ideas as fully developed as possible using details, facts, and examples.
- Are sentences varied in structure, and do they use well-chosen, colorful, and lively words?
- Are the paragraphs unified and coherent?

Next, mark up your essay with comments on your strengths and your weaknesses as a writer. If you have a friend, teacher, or mentor you can call on to read and evaluate your practice essay, do so. Sometimes another reader will spot weaknesses you miss. Remember, you want to do your best, so make use of all the resources you have.

You may be surprised at how your writing improves as you regularly do self-evaluations of your practice essays using the above specific guidelines.

In addition to the practice essays, write as often as you can to friends or in a journal, or take a writing course if it's convenient. Your hand and arm muscles will become accustomed to writing for an hour at a time, and your mind will get used to forming and expressing ideas in an organized and logical way.

An Example of a Poor Essay

repetitive sentence structure

coherence (unrelated idea)

another unrelated idea

spelling

awkward sentence structure

run-on sentence, comma fault

run-on sentence

reference unclear

comma fault

syntax

One teacher had the most influence on my life. I had her in high school for social studies. She wasn't pretty, but she was really smart and knew a lot. She was also full of energy and seemed to like to sit on the desk and talk to us person to person. I don't think she had any children but I know she had a husband. I actually don't remember which class I had her for maybe American Government, but I know I liked to go there. It was her personality I guess.

Isn't it funny that someone can have an influence on you and you don't even remember the class?

There were several teachers I liked, but she was my favorite. I remember she would correct my spelling whenever I made a misteak and over and over if I made the mistake again.

I hope I'll be patient like her to help students who keep making mistakes.

Comments on the Essay

This essay vaguely describes a person, but does not tell anything about how the teacher influenced the writer's life. It lacks focus, and the writer seems to have an unclear memory. The essay does not address the question. In fact, it is boring. The thesis statement does not grab the reader's attention. The language is not lively. The paragraphs are too short, and the conclusion is very weak.

You can do much better than that. Use the following pages to begin practicing your essay writing skills.

TWO TYPES OF ESSAYS ON THE CBEST

The CBEST writing questions are usually of two types. The first is a personal essay in which you use description and narration (telling a story) about some important experience or aspect of your life. This is an informal essay that allows you to be informal in style. Use first person ("I") in this form of essay, but avoid slang or informal language.

To be effective:

1. Set a context.
   Describe a place and time in which the event occurred.

2. Use chronological order.
   Start at the beginning, and end at the end.

3. If you are describing a place or person, use a lot of detail, and present it in an order that is simple to understand and will be easy for the reader to picture.

The second type is an expository essay focused on explaining or analyzing a situation or an issue. The style of this type of essay can also be informal, but you must not use first person ("I") in writing it. Because its purpose is to inform, explain, or analyze, it should be impersonal. It is too easy to slip into opinion-giving if you use first person constructions.

A general guideline for good writing here is to use active voice as much as possible. It is more emphatic than passive voice and, therefore, sounds more authoritative.

> **Active voice:** The subject is the doer of the action.
>
> Michael Crichton wrote one of his books in six days.

> **Passive voice:** The subject receives the action of the verb.
>
> The book was written (by Michael Crichton) in six days.

Use of the passive voice omits the actor or doer and so is often vague or confusing.

Remember, clear, effective communication is your goal.

WRITING PRACTICE WITH SAMPLE ESSAYS

Topic 1

There have been many articles and some books written that suggest that children who watch too much television do not perform well in school. One author has even questioned the value of "Sesame Street." Explain whether you agree or disagree with this criticism, using your own observations and experience in your answer.

_____

_____

_____

_____

_____

_____

_____

_____

_____

Use this checklist to evaluate your essay:

- Does it have a simple, clear thesis statement limited to one main idea?
- Are all the ideas related to the main idea?
- Is the most important point near the end of the essay, and is it fully developed?
- Is the second most important point at the beginning of the essay?
- Are the ideas as fully developed as possible using details, facts, and examples?
- Are sentences varied in structure, and do they use well-chosen, colorful, and lively words?
- Are the paragraphs unified and coherent?

List the strengths of your essay and areas for improvement:

Strengths   **Areas for Improvement**

_____   _____

_____   _____

_____   _____

_____   _____

_____   _____

_____   _____

_____   _____

Sample Essay

Certainly there is persuasive data to support the claim that children who watch too much television do not do well in school. Certain questions should be asked, however, before launching into a discussion of this subject:

1. How much is too much?
2. What types of shows do children watch who underperform?
3. Who watches *with* them?
4. Do they discuss the ideas presented and the language used in the program?

Elementary school teachers noticed years ago that children began to be able to spell "headache" correctly on spelling tests. That change was clearly the result of the children's seeing advertisements for headache medications on television.

However, the main criticism today is that television programs offer little more than "sound bites" and do not foster long attention spans or the ability to think about complex ideas. Years ago, when children read long English and American novels that used complex sentences, descriptive vocabulary, and presented sophisticated ideas, children developed the ability to sustain attention and understand complex and sophisticated ideas.

My children, who both earned college degrees, watched a lot of television as they were growing up, but they were also read to and encouraged to read. Helping them find books they enjoyed was a challenge. They had very different tastes in reading as in everything else. Other factors also probably helped them. They played sports and musical instruments, traveled, visited museums, and generally had lives that helped them engage with the world.

Based on that experience, one might think that I would disagree with the statement. However, that is not the case. Not all parents are interested in helping their children develop their minds, nor are they skilled in doing so.

There are many factors that contribute to a child's success in school: poverty or wealth, values within the family, parents' self involvement or other involvement, parents' level of education, a child's intelligence, and more. If the necessary structures are not in place, excessive television watching can, in fact, have a deleterious effect on a child's ability to learn. Children who are watching television are not reading, discussing, or thinking during that time, nor are they interacting with friends or mastering skills they will need as adults.

If one believes time is precious, then time well spent has value. It is better to say that excessive television watching is the result of poor parenting and that parents need to be trained in good parenting skills in order help give their children a good start in life.

Commentary

The writer begins with a simple thesis statement, but using the word "certainly" as an introductory word suggests that there will be disagreement somewhere along the line.

The writer employs the technique of asking several questions to help order ideas to be brought forth in the body of the essay. For the most part, the language is formal. The personal example responds to a specific aspect of the question. Questions 3 through 7 are all met. The conclusion brings the essay full circle with a restatement of the topic in a form the writer can accept. This is a generally well written essay that shows clear thinking and skill in development and use of language.

Topic 2

Describe and explain the factors that have influenced your choice of career.

_____

_____

_____

_____

_____

_____

_____

_____

_____

_____

_____

_____

_____

_____

_____

_____

_____

_____

_____

_____

_____

_____

_____

_____

_____

_____

_____

_____

_____

_____

_____

Use this checklist to evaluate your essay:

- Does it have a simple, clear thesis statement limited to one main idea?
- Are all the ideas related to the main idea?
- Is the most important point near the end of the essay, and is it fully developed?
- Is the second most important point at the beginning of the essay?
- Are the ideas as fully developed as possible using details, facts, and examples?
- Are sentences varied in structure, and do they use well-chosen, colorful, and lively words?
- Are the paragraphs unified and coherent?

List the strengths of your essay and areas for improvement:

Strengths	Areas for Improvement
_____	_____
_____	_____
_____	_____
_____	_____
_____	_____
_____	_____
_____	_____

Sample Essay

I decided to become a teacher through no fault of my own. I had always known that I did not want to become a nurse or work with animals. I had thought originally that I might want to be a lawyer, but law school was not what I expected, and I realized I liked the school schedule even if I did not like the subject matter. School is out all summer and over Christmas, leaving a lot of time to do interesting things. I had always wanted to travel. Not only that, but the teachers I had had who were the most interesting traveled every summer. I wanted to be an interesting person and have an interesting life so summers off sounded very good.

When I was in college, I had worked at a junior high teaching reading to students who had difficulty in school. I discovered that I liked them; they were amusing. I realized that I got a lot of satisfaction from interacting with them and seeing them make progress academically. In other words, I took pleasure in someone else's learning. Eventually, I found I enjoyed experimenting with creative ways to help students learn; the preparation process for teaching had become fun as well.

Furthermore, teaching is a field that allows women equality of pay with men, unlike some other professions.

When you add all of these factors together, it's easy to see why I chose to be a teacher. However, I claim the decision was made through no fault of my own because I didn't decide specifically. Rather, over several years life experiences took me in that direction, as I tried on several hats: saleswoman, personnel clerk, law student and teaching aide.

Commentary

This essay is much shorter than the other and could be faulted on brevity. The personal voice is appropriate, as is the informal language. The writer catches the reader's attention with an unexpected statement at the start, but then brings the reader full circle to the conclusion, drawing the ideas together to explain the thesis statement. The paragraphs are well developed, but the punctuation is faulty and could have been improved with more careful proofreading.

Topic 3

Polonius' advice to his son in Hamlet has become famous. He says,

"This above all: to thine own self be true,

And it must follow as the night the day,

Thou canst not then be false to any man."

Explain whether or not you agree with this advice. Support your position as effectively as you can.

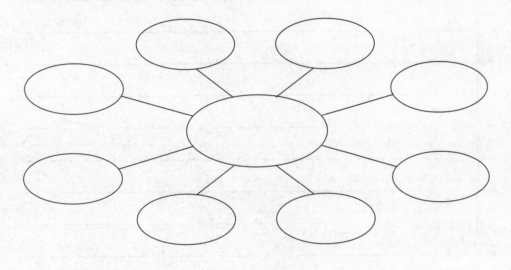

_____

_____

_____

_____

_____

_____

_____

_____

_____

_____

Use this checklist to evaluate your essay:

- Does it have a simple, clear thesis statement limited to one main idea?
- Are all the ideas related to the main idea?
- Is the most important point near the end of the essay, and is it fully developed?
- Is the second most important point at the beginning of the essay?
- Are the ideas as fully developed as possible using details, facts, and examples?
- Are the sentences varied in structure, and do they use well-chosen, colorful, and lively words?
- Are the paragraphs unified and coherent?

List the strengths of your essay and areas for improvement:

Strengths   **Areas for Improvement**

_____   _____

_____   _____

_____   _____

_____   _____

_____   _____

_____   _____

_____   _____

Sample Essay

"This above all: to thine own self be true,

And it must follow as the night the day,

Thou canst not be false to any man."

In theory I agree with this famous statement. If you can be true to yourself, you may offend others by brutal honesty, but you won't be called a liar.

Lying has become pervasive in our culture. It is so pervasive, in fact, that there have even been books written about it. From advertising's misleading statements to people's cheating on their income taxes, almost no one tells the truth. Many people lie to themselves as well, because they can't face who they really are. If they were honest with themselves all their deeds would haunt them. So, Polonius had it right.

What do you do about the person who lies so convincingly that he believes his own lies? He eventually doesn't realize he is lying. That person is really troubling, but is he troubled? Probably not, but good lying doesn't go completely unnoticed. Eventually it's recognized. As P.T. Barnum said, "You can fool all of the people some of the time and some of the people all of the time, but you can't fool all of the people all of the time."

The unconscious but practiced liar will eventually be seen for what he is. As a result, he will lose the respect of friends and acquaintances.

Polonius' advice is valuable for someone who wants peace of mind and a guilt-free life. Being true to yourself, your own values, makes your everyday life stress free. You will not be a "yes man." You can go to sleep at night with a clear conscience.

Commentary

Beginning your essay with a quote from the prompt lets the reader know you are focused on the topic. Referring to Polonius throughout the paper tells the reader you are still focused on the topic.

Bringing in the quote from P.T. Barnum is a good technique, because it is a generally recognized quote within the culture.

The weakest part of this essay is the conclusion. It needs a more powerful conclusion, something with more punch.

Topic 4

Many people recognize a talent within themselves that they value. Discuss one of your talents and explain what that talent has made possible for you and why you value it.

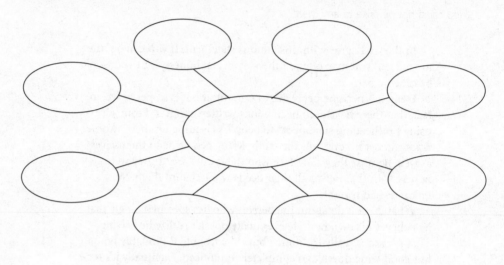

_____

_____

_____

_____

_____

_____

_____

_____

_____

_____

_____

Use this checklist to evaluate your essay:

- Does it have a simple, clear thesis statement limited to one main idea?
- Are all the ideas related to the main idea?
- Is the most important point near the end of the essay, and is it fully developed?
- Is the second most important point at the beginning of the essay?
- Are the ideas as fully developed as possible using details, facts, and examples?
- Are sentences varied in structure, and do they use well-chosen, colorful, and lively words?
- Are the paragraphs unified and coherent?

List the strengths of your essay and areas for improvement:

Strengths   **Areas for Improvement**

_____   _____

_____   _____

_____   _____

_____   _____

_____   _____

_____   _____

_____   _____

Sample Essay

I have always loved music. For years I studied the violin, playing in orchestras in junior high and in high school and in my city's youth symphony. Did I have a talent for music? Perhaps. However, I never thought I was very good, and so eventually I gave up the violin. There was to be no music career for me.

I never gave up my love of music, however. Knowing how difficult it is to play an instrument has made me appreciate the talent and self-discipline of concert artists, and I did develop a refined ear for a good performance which helps me appreciate every good performance even more than I otherwise would have.

For years I have collected records and then CDs that have given me many hours of pleasure. I will never pass up the opportunity to attend a concert, and I enjoy every minute of it.

That "perhaps" talent has made my life rich and enjoyable, partly because I studied an instrument and partly because people value things they have invested time in.

I am very thankful that I love music so much. Often, on hearing a well played piece, a great feeling of joy and pleasure surges up through my chest. It's an irreplaceable feeling and rewarding enough to keep me coming back for more.

Commentary

It takes a couple of sentences to get to the main idea of this essay. The conclusion is strong because it expresses an emotional experience in the physical body. Using words like "surges" is good because it gives the sentence vitality.

The choice of topic in answer to the question may be a little off beat, but if you can develop your ideas well, an unexpected response to a question will be O.K.

Try the next two topics on your own, doing your own evaluation.

FURTHER WRITING PRACTICE

Now, tackle the following topics. Do your own analysis of your writing using the guidelines provided.

Topic 1

Identify a contemporary social problem that you believe needs to be solved in order for young people to have successful lives. Make your answer as complete as you can.

_____

_____

_____

_____

_____

_____

_____

_____

_____

Use this checklist to evaluate your essay:

- Does it have a simple, clear thesis statement limited to one main idea?
- Are all the ideas related to the main idea?
- Is the most important point near the end of the essay, and is it fully developed?
- Is the second most important point at the beginning of the essay?
- Are the ideas as fully developed as possible using details, facts, and examples?
- Are sentences varied in structure, and do they use well-chosen, colorful, and lively words?
- Are the paragraphs unified and coherent?

List the strengths of your essay and areas for improvement:

Strengths   **Areas for Improvement**

_____   _____

_____   _____

_____   _____

_____   _____

_____   _____

_____   _____

_____   _____

Topic 2

Describe a person (relative, friend, or celebrity) who you admired when you were young and who influenced you positively. Describe that person's influence on you in great detail.

_____

_____

_____

_____

_____

_____

_____

_____

_____

_____

_____

_____

_____

_____

_____

_____

_____

_____

_____

_____

_____

_____

_____

_____

_____

_____

_____

_____

_____

_____

_____

_____

KAPLAN

Use this checklist to evaluate your essay:

- Does it have a simple, clear thesis statement limited to one main idea?
- Are all the ideas related to the main idea?
- Is the most important point near the end of the essay, and is it fully developed?
- Is the second most important point at the beginning of the essay?
- Are the ideas as fully developed as possible using details, facts, and examples?
- Are sentences varied in structure, and do they use well-chosen, colorful, and lively words?
- Are the paragraphs unified and coherent?

List the strengths of your essay and areas for improvement:

Strengths   **Areas for Improvement**

_____   _____

_____   _____

_____   _____

_____   _____

_____   _____

_____   _____

_____   _____

Practice Tests

Practice Test One Answer Sheet

Remove (or photocopy) the answer sheet and use it to complete the practice test.
See the answer key following the test when finished.

READING SECTION

1. Ⓐ Ⓑ Ⓒ Ⓓ Ⓔ	14. Ⓐ Ⓑ Ⓒ Ⓓ Ⓔ	27. Ⓐ Ⓑ Ⓒ Ⓓ Ⓔ	40. Ⓐ Ⓑ Ⓒ Ⓓ Ⓔ			
2. Ⓐ Ⓑ Ⓒ Ⓓ Ⓔ	15. Ⓐ Ⓑ Ⓒ Ⓓ Ⓔ	28. Ⓐ Ⓑ Ⓒ Ⓓ Ⓔ	41. Ⓐ Ⓑ Ⓒ Ⓓ Ⓔ			
3. Ⓐ Ⓑ Ⓒ Ⓓ Ⓔ	16. Ⓐ Ⓑ Ⓒ Ⓓ Ⓔ	29. Ⓐ Ⓑ Ⓒ Ⓓ Ⓔ	42. Ⓐ Ⓑ Ⓒ Ⓓ Ⓔ			
4. Ⓐ Ⓑ Ⓒ Ⓓ Ⓔ	17. Ⓐ Ⓑ Ⓒ Ⓓ Ⓔ	30. Ⓐ Ⓑ Ⓒ Ⓓ Ⓔ	43. Ⓐ Ⓑ Ⓒ Ⓓ Ⓔ			# right in Reading Section
5. Ⓐ Ⓑ Ⓒ Ⓓ Ⓔ	18. Ⓐ Ⓑ Ⓒ Ⓓ Ⓔ	31. Ⓐ Ⓑ Ⓒ Ⓓ Ⓔ	44. Ⓐ Ⓑ Ⓒ Ⓓ Ⓔ			
6. Ⓐ Ⓑ Ⓒ Ⓓ Ⓔ	19. Ⓐ Ⓑ Ⓒ Ⓓ Ⓔ	32. Ⓐ Ⓑ Ⓒ Ⓓ Ⓔ	45. Ⓐ Ⓑ Ⓒ Ⓓ Ⓔ			
7. Ⓐ Ⓑ Ⓒ Ⓓ Ⓔ	20. Ⓐ Ⓑ Ⓒ Ⓓ Ⓔ	33. Ⓐ Ⓑ Ⓒ Ⓓ Ⓔ	46. Ⓐ Ⓑ Ⓒ Ⓓ Ⓔ			
8. Ⓐ Ⓑ Ⓒ Ⓓ Ⓔ	21. Ⓐ Ⓑ Ⓒ Ⓓ Ⓔ	34. Ⓐ Ⓑ Ⓒ Ⓓ Ⓔ	47. Ⓐ Ⓑ Ⓒ Ⓓ Ⓔ			# wrong in Reading Section
9. Ⓐ Ⓑ Ⓒ Ⓓ Ⓔ	22. Ⓐ Ⓑ Ⓒ Ⓓ Ⓔ	35. Ⓐ Ⓑ Ⓒ Ⓓ Ⓔ	48. Ⓐ Ⓑ Ⓒ Ⓓ Ⓔ			
10. Ⓐ Ⓑ Ⓒ Ⓓ Ⓔ	23. Ⓐ Ⓑ Ⓒ Ⓓ Ⓔ	36. Ⓐ Ⓑ Ⓒ Ⓓ Ⓔ	49. Ⓐ Ⓑ Ⓒ Ⓓ Ⓔ			
11. Ⓐ Ⓑ Ⓒ Ⓓ Ⓔ	24. Ⓐ Ⓑ Ⓒ Ⓓ Ⓔ	37. Ⓐ Ⓑ Ⓒ Ⓓ Ⓔ	50. Ⓐ Ⓑ Ⓒ Ⓓ Ⓔ			
12. Ⓐ Ⓑ Ⓒ Ⓓ Ⓔ	25. Ⓐ Ⓑ Ⓒ Ⓓ Ⓔ	38. Ⓐ Ⓑ Ⓒ Ⓓ Ⓔ				
13. Ⓐ Ⓑ Ⓒ Ⓓ Ⓔ	26. Ⓐ Ⓑ Ⓒ Ⓓ Ⓔ	39. Ⓐ Ⓑ Ⓒ Ⓓ Ⓔ				

MATH SECTION

1. Ⓐ Ⓑ Ⓒ Ⓓ Ⓔ	14. Ⓐ Ⓑ Ⓒ Ⓓ Ⓔ	27. Ⓐ Ⓑ Ⓒ Ⓓ Ⓔ	40. Ⓐ Ⓑ Ⓒ Ⓓ Ⓔ			
2. Ⓐ Ⓑ Ⓒ Ⓓ Ⓔ	15. Ⓐ Ⓑ Ⓒ Ⓓ Ⓔ	28. Ⓐ Ⓑ Ⓒ Ⓓ Ⓔ	41. Ⓐ Ⓑ Ⓒ Ⓓ Ⓔ			
3. Ⓐ Ⓑ Ⓒ Ⓓ Ⓔ	16. Ⓐ Ⓑ Ⓒ Ⓓ Ⓔ	29. Ⓐ Ⓑ Ⓒ Ⓓ Ⓔ	42. Ⓐ Ⓑ Ⓒ Ⓓ Ⓔ			
4. Ⓐ Ⓑ Ⓒ Ⓓ Ⓔ	17. Ⓐ Ⓑ Ⓒ Ⓓ Ⓔ	30. Ⓐ Ⓑ Ⓒ Ⓓ Ⓔ	43. Ⓐ Ⓑ Ⓒ Ⓓ Ⓔ			# right in Math Section
5. Ⓐ Ⓑ Ⓒ Ⓓ Ⓔ	18. Ⓐ Ⓑ Ⓒ Ⓓ Ⓔ	31. Ⓐ Ⓑ Ⓒ Ⓓ Ⓔ	44. Ⓐ Ⓑ Ⓒ Ⓓ Ⓔ			
6. Ⓐ Ⓑ Ⓒ Ⓓ Ⓔ	19. Ⓐ Ⓑ Ⓒ Ⓓ Ⓔ	32. Ⓐ Ⓑ Ⓒ Ⓓ Ⓔ	45. Ⓐ Ⓑ Ⓒ Ⓓ Ⓔ			
7. Ⓐ Ⓑ Ⓒ Ⓓ Ⓔ	20. Ⓐ Ⓑ Ⓒ Ⓓ Ⓔ	33. Ⓐ Ⓑ Ⓒ Ⓓ Ⓔ	46. Ⓐ Ⓑ Ⓒ Ⓓ Ⓔ			
8. Ⓐ Ⓑ Ⓒ Ⓓ Ⓔ	21. Ⓐ Ⓑ Ⓒ Ⓓ Ⓔ	34. Ⓐ Ⓑ Ⓒ Ⓓ Ⓔ	47. Ⓐ Ⓑ Ⓒ Ⓓ Ⓔ			# wrong in Math Section
9. Ⓐ Ⓑ Ⓒ Ⓓ Ⓔ	22. Ⓐ Ⓑ Ⓒ Ⓓ Ⓔ	35. Ⓐ Ⓑ Ⓒ Ⓓ Ⓔ	48. Ⓐ Ⓑ Ⓒ Ⓓ Ⓔ			
10. Ⓐ Ⓑ Ⓒ Ⓓ Ⓔ	23. Ⓐ Ⓑ Ⓒ Ⓓ Ⓔ	36. Ⓐ Ⓑ Ⓒ Ⓓ Ⓔ	49. Ⓐ Ⓑ Ⓒ Ⓓ Ⓔ			
11. Ⓐ Ⓑ Ⓒ Ⓓ Ⓔ	24. Ⓐ Ⓑ Ⓒ Ⓓ Ⓔ	37. Ⓐ Ⓑ Ⓒ Ⓓ Ⓔ	50. Ⓐ Ⓑ Ⓒ Ⓓ Ⓔ			
12. Ⓐ Ⓑ Ⓒ Ⓓ Ⓔ	25. Ⓐ Ⓑ Ⓒ Ⓓ Ⓔ	38. Ⓐ Ⓑ Ⓒ Ⓓ Ⓔ				
13. Ⓐ Ⓑ Ⓒ Ⓓ Ⓔ	26. Ⓐ Ⓑ Ⓒ Ⓓ Ⓔ	39. Ⓐ Ⓑ Ⓒ Ⓓ Ⓔ				

WRITING SECTION

Lined pages on which you will write your essays can be found in the writing section.

Practice Test One

Reading Section

50 Questions

Directions: Each statement in this test is followed by questions based on its content. After reading a statement or passage, choose the best answer to each question from among the five choices given. Answer all questions following a statement or passage on the basis of what is *stated* or *implied* in the passage. Be sure to mark all of your answers in the reading section of your answer document.

Note: Some passages contain numbered sentences, blank lines, or underlined words that are to be used for your reference in answering the questions that follow those passages.

Questions 1–3

California's destiny is *inextricably* tied to its economy. In order to live the "California Dream," people have to have access to good jobs that pay well. *Otherwise*, they can't afford a house and garage and the proverbial two cars to go inside the garage. In order to have access to jobs, citizens must be well educated so that they have the skills required by employers to get work. That means the schools and colleges must have the money they need to prepare these future employees, and the money must come from taxes on incomes earned by people working today. There is no way to evade these interconnections and have a viable society.

1. The word *inextricably* means

   (A) tending to spread or affect others

   (B) that it cannot be expressed

   (C) unrelenting

   (D) it cannot be disentangled or untied

   (E) unfortunately

2. The author's logical development

   (A) shows sloppy thinking

   (B) shows the economic connections necessary for a successful society

   (C) focuses too much emphasis on education

   (D) doesn't lead to a conclusion

   (E) should include noneconomic factors

3. The word *otherwise* in the second sentence

   (A) joins equal elements in the sentences

   (B) signals the relationship between two independent clauses

   (C) signals a logical relationship between parts of a sentence

   (D) expresses a relationship between two nouns

   (E) shows a state of being

GO ON TO THE NEXT PAGE

Questions 4–6

People who are observant have different experiences of life than those who aren't. What others say and the way they say it can tell us a lot about their true feelings and attitudes. They can recognize people who are bitter or sarcastic as well as those who are pleasant, hopeful, or happy by the signals they give through body or verbal language. Gestures, tone of voice, and facial expressions reveal much about the inner person, *but* if you are only partly attentive, you will miss some or all of those signals.

People train themselves to be observant by learning to focus and by not letting their minds wander. Being relaxed and fully attentive to the other person is a good place to start. Then watch and listen. You can also use your sense of smell, and if you shake hands, notice how the other person's hand feels. In fact, you can involve all of your senses in being observant.

4. The audience this selection is written for is probably

(A) people training to be spies

(B) elementary school teachers

(C) engineers

(D) athletes

(E) college students in a class on perception

5. The probable purpose of the article from which this selection is taken is to

(A) teach techniques for developing observation skills

(B) encourage the reader to be more observant

(C) make the reader aware of differences in perception

(D) convince the reader that being observant is good

(E) make the reader ask more questions

6. The use of *but* in the first paragraph is to introduce

(A) a conclusion

(B) a contrasting idea

(C) a transition to the next paragraph

(D) the topic sentence

(E) a warning to the reader

Questions 7–9

Glaciers around the planet are disappearing at an increasing rate, and whereas they have waxed and waned over eons, their melting seems to be happening very rapidly today. In the past 15 years the rate of shrinkage has more than doubled. Scientists are alarmed at what this may *portend*.

To offer a comparison, glaciers covered a third of the world's surface at the peak of the Ice Age; now only about 10 percent of the surface is covered in glacial ice.

7. The word *portend* as used here means

(A) full or pores through which liquid may pass

(B) to be an omen or warning of

(C) to signify

(D) having many meanings

(E) to think deeply about

8. The purpose of the first phrase in the second paragraph, *to offer a comparison*, is

(A) introductory

(B) to help the reader understand the sentence

(C) explanatory

(D) transitional

(E) to signal the passage is from a comparison and contrast essay

GO ON TO THE NEXT PAGE

9. The second paragraph is

   (A) primarily factual

   (B) exemplary

   (C) solely factual

   (D) persuasive

   (E) a mix of fact and opinion

Questions 10–12

Once upon a time, toys were designed to appeal to parents and to train children for their future adult lives. Girls were given baby dolls to cuddle, bathe, and dress, and boys were given erector sets or Lincoln Logs so they could learn to build things. _____ _____. One of them was that manufacturers and marketers began to see children as consumers. Toy design changed to appeal not to parents, but instead, to children. Then electronic toys came along, and child's play moved away from activities that could be enjoyed with other children or with adults to games that could be played only by the individual child. In a way, these games were training children, too, but for video arcades, not for adult life.

10. The author probably believes

    (A) the change in toy design was a result of cultural changes

    (B) toys of an earlier era were too gender specific

    (C) newer toys prepare children for adolescence, not adulthood

    (D) toy design brought about cultural change

    (E) newer toys are not as worthwhile as older toys

11. The passage begins with *Once upon a time* because

    (A) it is an introductory clause

    (B) it is an introductory phrase

    (C) it signals that this might be a story

    (D) it is suggestive that the content might relate to children

    (E) it is trying to grab the reader's attention

12. Choose from the following sentences the one that fits best in the blank space.

    (A) Children's books are in a different category.

    (B) It's difficult to determine the cause for the changes in toy sales.

    (C) Not all cultures differentiate among girls and boys.

    (D) Then our culture went through many changes.

    (E) You can count the number of changes our culture went through.

Questions 13–15

Obesity in America is recognized by experts and government leaders alike as a major problem. It is not *insoluble*, but it will require *prodigious* and united educational efforts on the part of health professionals, educators, federal, state, and local governments along with the cooperation of food manufacturers, suppliers, and restauranteurs to educate Americans and to support changes in eating habits. As citizens and taxpayers, we need to champion healthy eating for our own well-being and for the well-being of our society.

13. The author's purpose is probably to

    (A) persuade

    (B) negate current eating habits

    (C) inform

    (D) entertain

    (E) criticize

14. The word *insoluble* as used in this passage means

    (A) able to be dissolved

    (B) not able to be dissolved

    (C) solvable

    (D) unsolvable

    (E) difficult

GO ON TO THE NEXT PAGE

KAPLAN

15. As used in this selection, the word *prodigious* means

    (A) wonderful
    (B) amazing
    (C) enormous
    (D) highly competent
    (E) worthy of high standards

Questions 16–18

I. The Earth	100
A. Physical world	110
B. Time Zones	115
C. North America	118
1. United States	121
a. Northeastern US	122
b. Southeastern US	124
c. North Central US	126
d. South Central US	128

Using this partial index from an atlas, determine where you would find:

16. Massachusetts

    (A) 100–110
    (B) 118–120
    (C) 115–117
    (D) 126–127
    (E) 122–123

17. The imaginary line separating Eastern Standard Time from Central Time

    (A) 100–110
    (B) 118–120
    (C) 115–117
    (D) 126–127
    (E) 122–123

18. Maps of North and South America

    (A) 100–110
    (B) 118–120
    (C) 115–117
    (D) 126–127
    (E) 122–123

Questions 19–21

Our galaxy, home to our solar system, is called the "Milky Way" in the west. The Japanese call it the "Silver River of Heaven." It contains 100 billion suns and many more planets, moons, and asteroids than that. The "Milky Way" moves through space like a wheel and carries our sun a full revolution once in every 230 million years.

19. This selection is probably taken from

    (A) a general science text
    (B) an article in a popular magazine
    (C) a story about space travel
    (D) a multicultural text
    (E) a history text

20. The best word to describe the style of this selection is

    (A) poetic
    (B) metaphysical
    (C) descriptive
    (D) factual
    (E) astronomical

21. The author's intent in this passage is probably

    (A) to present many facts
    (B) to capture the reader's attention
    (C) to attract students to the study of astronomy
    (D) to inform and educate
    (E) to impress the reader with numbers

GO ON TO THE NEXT PAGE

Questions 22–24

Can you judge a book by its cover? There is an *adage*, usually applied to people, that says you can't. If we are only talking about books, however, the cover can tell you a lot. Today, book covers are designed to attract your attention and entice you to buy. Is the book a prizewinner or a finalist for an award? The cover will tell you. Is the author famous? If so, you'll find his or her name in large print on the front cover. Has it been praised by well-known writers or been reviewed by the New York Times? The cover will tell you that, too. These are all clues as to whether a book is good or not.

Now, how does that apply to people? What can you tell about a person by hairstyle, jewelry, clothes, or a facelift? What do those attributes suggest about the person?

22. The author's purpose seems to be

    (A) to agree with the old saying

    (B) to challenge the truth of the old saying

    (C) to suggest the reader rethink the truth of the old saying

    (D) to argue that a person's appearance tells a lot about him

    (E) to suggest readers look for books by famous authors

23. As it is used here, *adage* means

    (A) a reasonable theory

    (B) a truth too hard to be broken

    (C) a long held belief

    (D) an old saying that is popularly accepted as truth

    (E) an advertising slogan

24. Which of the following would be the best title of the work?

    (A) You Can't Judge a Book by Its Cover

    (B) People as Well as Books Can be Revealing

    (C) Adages, Beware!

    (D) An Old Saying Reconsidered

    (E) A Book Cover Can Tell the Reader a Lot

Questions 25–27

Mankind has an unquenchable thirst for health and wealth. That thirst drove the Age of Exploration. Explorers sought the Fountain of Youth and the Seven Cities of Cibola, whose streets were supposedly paved with gold.

In circumnavigating the globe in 1522, the voyagers who sailed with Magellan overturned centuries of disbelief, ignorance, and superstition about the nature of our planet. That voyage began the accumulation of the knowledge we have today about animal species, cultures, weather, medicines, geography, and many other things.

We are in a new Age of Exploration to discover the realms of space. Just as early explorers planted the flags of their countries on new lands they discovered, Neil Armstrong planted the American flag on the moon. Now we are ready to advance further into space. Recently, scientists have begun talking about exploration beyond discovery for health and wealth, for medicines that may only be attainable from extra-planetary sources, and for minerals that may be mined for the benefit of mankind. Who can imagine what products we may develop and how our knowledge may *accrete* in the next 500 years?

25. This passage can be classified as

    (A) an argument

    (B) an introduction

    (C) an exposition

    (D) a comparison and contrast piece

    (E) an explanation

26. The word *accrete* as used here means

    (A) expand exponentially

    (B) to grow by being added to

    (C) accumulate

    (D) advance

    (E) gather

GO ON TO THE NEXT PAGE

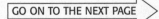

KAPLAN

27. The author's attitude in the selection is

    (A) negative
    (B) factual
    (C) hopeful
    (D) straightforward
    (E) enthusiastic

Questions 28–30

A modification of the traditionally taught science course was to allow students to prepare a presentation using various visual and auditory aids, including PowerPoint, instead of taking a written exam. Another option was for a student to meet with the instructor for discussion instead of taking the usual exam.

Students had to be able to demonstrate their knowledge of course content by explaining a concept map about a preapproved topic and by constructing lesson plans that could be used to teach that topic content in the classroom. Students found that these options gave them an opportunity to search out educational support sources and services and to apply their own creativity in developing a project of practical use to them as teachers.

28. This selection most likely comes from

    (A) a textbook on teaching
    (B) a monograph on preparing science teachers
    (C) an article on visual aids in the classroom
    (D) a science textbook
    (E) an article in a popular magazine

29. The topic relates most closely to

    (A) alternative activities for course content mastery measurement
    (B) special science activities
    (C) student satisfaction with assignments
    (D) alternative test forms
    (E) different kinds of classroom projects

30. Further reading of this article might serve to

    (A) inform future teachers of good science training techniques
    (B) inform teacher trainers of successful practices with trainers
    (C) offer more good suggestions
    (D) help the reader to understand more about science
    (E) encourage students to major in science

Questions 31–33

From the time I was eight years old until I was 12, all the kids in my neighborhood spent every Saturday morning at the movies. We would trudge down the block to the theater, each tightly clutching a quarter in one hand, and watch cartoons, a newsreel, and two westerns. We watched Tom Mix, Gene Autry, Hopalong Cassidy, and Roy Rogers performing good and heroic deeds and riding beautiful horses. At night on the radio, we could listen to The Lone Ranger and his famous farewell, "Hi, ho, Silver." Some of us had subscriptions to comic books about cowboys. I had one to Roy Rogers's comics. He was my favorite.

One of the first full-length books I read was a novel by Zane Grey, "Riders of the Purple Sage."

As I got older, I watched John Wayne movies and westerns on TV such as Death Valley Days, The Rifleman, and Gunsmoke.

Even though I was a girl growing up, the western and its heroes and values formed my view of the world. I believed courage and honesty were important and that there were men who embodied those qualities and could be counted on to step forward to do the right thing to protect society and, especially, the downtrodden.

GO ON TO THE NEXT PAGE

31. The author of this passage uses the following techniques

    (A) analogy and example
    (B) metaphor and simile
    (C) chronological order and analogy
    (D) parallelism and metaphor
    (E) chronological order and parallelism

32. This selection could be classified as

    (A) autobiographical
    (B) persuasive
    (C) descriptive
    (D) analytical
    (E) historical

33. This passage is probably from

    (A) a novel about the American West
    (B) a biography
    (C) an essay on cowboy heroes
    (D) an essay on movies
    (E) an essay on the influence of westerns

Questions 34–36

Native American legends and stories tell us a great deal about each tribe's view of the world and also teach about the proper relationship between man and nature. These were part of what was called "the oral tradition." Many of these stories were only recently written down because most Native Americans had no written language. Their poems, which were used in sacred rituals only known to shamans and told year after year around the campfires to the tribe members, were not only remembered partly by devices such as rhythms and repeated patterns of words, but also by repetition of the stories themselves and the tribal members' understanding of their own culture.

The short days and long nights of the winter months, when hunting was infrequent and fields lay fallow, gave the tribe the opportunity to repeat the old stories—the myths that explained the origin of the world and the source of life—and the opportunity to remind young

and old about the rules for living successfully within the tribal structure.

Dances and songs helped to reinforce understanding and remembering the stories.

Other preliterate cultures around the world functioned in the same way, but the content of the stories and myths differed. Cultural *myths* are interesting to us because of their differences. Those differences help us to understand the structural and perceptual differences among tribes and cultures.

34. As used here, the word *myth* means

    (A) an imaginary, fabricated story about a person
    (B) a traditional story of unknown authorship
    (C) a complex of beliefs
    (D) a story of obscure meaning
    (E) a frequently repeated story

35. This passage is probably

    (A) an introduction to an article on cultural differences
    (B) a summary of an article on cultural differences
    (C) a conclusion of an article on cultural differences
    (D) an introduction to a mythological story
    (E) an excerpt from a book on tribal cultures

GO ON TO THE NEXT PAGE

36. Which of the following best organizes the ideas in the paragraphs?

    (A) I. Characteristics of an "oral tradition"
        II. Differences among "oral traditions"

    (B) I. The purpose of tribal legends and stories
        II. Commonalities and differences of legends around the world and their interest to us

    (C) I. Types of cultural legends
        II. Cultural myths' interest to outsiders

    (D) I. Stories around the campfire were told over and over
        II. Dances and songs helped reinforce learning the legends

    (E) I. How legends were learned and passed down
        II. The importance of dances and songs

Questions 37–39

Use the excerpts below from an index to answer the questions that follow.

	Pages
I. Biographical sketches	35–190
II. Statistics	191–387
III. Hypotheses tests	389–401
IV. Internet projects	401–423
V. Practice exercises	424–457
VI. Standard deviations	452–476

37. Where would you look for data on infant mortality?

    (A) I
    (B) II
    (C) III
    (D) V
    (E) VI

38. Where would you look to gather information on a mathematician?

    (A) I
    (B) II
    (C) III
    (D) V
    (E) VI

39. Where would you find information to help you prepare for a test?

    (A) II
    (B) III
    (C) IV
    (D) V
    (E) VI

Questions 40–42

Sometimes students think they know more than they really seem to know judging by their test scores. This discrepancy can cause enormous frustration to students who believe they have mastered material, but, in fact, haven't. Scientists say that students may recognize some but not all words in a test question and thus believe they know the answer, or they may be able to access partial information in their memory. Furthermore, when questions offer many choices, they are more likely to believe they know the answer than when fewer choices are offered. *In other words*, they may misjudge their level of mastery. The difficulty is that when students believe they know material, they are likely to quit studying rather than trying to "over learn" the material. Guiding students to "over learn" through the use of study guides and by practicing explaining the material to others can be an academic lifesaver for them.

GO ON TO THE NEXT PAGE

40. The author's primary purpose in writing this selection is probably to

    (A) draw students' attention to their learning problems
    (B) assist teachers in instructional effectiveness
    (C) explain why students fail at learning
    (D) ease students' disappointment and frustration
    (E) identify specific learning misjudgments

41. This paragraph could be most improved by adding

    (A) examples from tests to clarify points
    (B) more suggested study activities
    (C) details
    (D) a definition of "overlearning"
    (E) explanations of different kinds of tests

42. The phrase *In other words* is used primarily

    (A) as a transitional phrase
    (B) as an introductory phrase
    (C) as an explanatory phrase
    (D) to provide sentence variety
    (E) to introduce a clarification of previous information

Questions 43–45

The young child entering school for the first time may find the experience disturbing and daunting. A child is faced with having to get along with 20 or sometimes as many as 35 other children. They all have to deal with conflicts, learn to share, participate in competitive activities, face new mental challenges, and do all this while making some friends and being socially accepted by as many children as possible. Young children may enjoy many of the daily activities but still find the school day very stressful and need time in the comfort of home with a parent to gather their personal resources for the next day.

School can be especially difficult for the young child in an environment that includes children who exhibit antisocial behavior, who are verbally aggressive or physically aggressive, and who continue that behavior once it has begun. They may whine frequently, refuse to cooperate, and generally defeat group activities.

43. The author communicates in this passage through

    (A) generalization
    (B) listing characteristics
    (C) definition
    (D) explanations
    (E) assumptions

44. The author's attitude toward young children is best described as

    (A) detached
    (B) informative
    (C) empathetic
    (D) favorable
    (E) sympathetic

45. According to the author, antisocial behavior is

    (A) understandable to other children
    (B) malleable
    (C) frequent
    (D) disturbing to other children
    (E) easily recognizable

GO ON TO THE NEXT PAGE

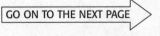

Questions 46–48

Internationally, widespread child labor is a significant problem. One of every four children between the ages of 5 and 14 works, 61% of children who work live in Asia, 32% live in Africa, and 7% live in Latin America. Half of these working children work full time, often in hazardous conditions.

Seventeen percent of the world's children never learn to read, and most of them are girls. They face lives of poverty, hunger, sickness, inadequate housing, poor sanitation, and unemployment.

These conditions challenge the creativity, commitment, and resources of the world. How can these children have better lives? How is education to be provided for them? How can they go to school if they must work? How can their lives be shifted from lives of exploitation to lives of promise and success?

46. The author introduces this passage with

    (A) facts

    (B) statistics

    (C) examples

    (D) details

    (E) a list

47. This selection is probably

    (A) a conclusion to an essay

    (B) an excerpt from a historical document

    (C) a conclusion to a report

    (D) an introduction to an argument

    (E) an introduction to a historical passage

48. One can conclude from the passage that the percentage of children between the ages of 5 and 14 who work is

    (A) 61%

    (B) 7%

    (C) 17%

    (D) 32%

    (E) 25%

Questions 49–50

[1]Advances in scientific knowledge are coming so fast that medicine, technology, and our space program can hardly keep up. [2]New cancer treatments, new knowledge about indicators of heart health, and new methods for dental treatment are being announced seemingly weekly.

Keeping up with all that is new in any field is a challenge. It requires enormous amounts of reading and, often, significant time attending informational meetings and conferences. How does a busy professional manage to stay informed and still work enough to earn a decent living? It is a challenge. Another significant question is, "How is a medical or dental patient to know that the treatment offered by the practitioner is the best available and based on the most recent discoveries?"

The information explosion has improved our lives in many significant ways but may be overwhelming our capacity to absorb and use it.

49. The author's use of sentence two is an example of

    (A) parallelism

    (B) repetition

    (C) exaggeration

    (D) cause and effect

    (E) reasoning

50. The author's main point is

    (A) good professionals will have a hard time earning money

    (B) a well-informed professional may not earn much

    (C) medical patients may not get the best treatment

    (D) the information explosion has presented other problems

    (E) professionals must attend many conferences

GO ON TO THE NEXT PAGE

KAPLAN

Math Section
50 Questions

Directions: Each of the questions in this test is followed by five suggested answers. Select the one that is best in each case. Be sure to mark all of your answers in the Mathematics section of your answer sheet.

1. Which of the following equations gives the relationship shown in the table?

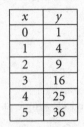

x	y
0	1
1	4
2	9
3	16
4	25
5	36

   (A) $y = x^2$
   (B) $y = x^2 - 1$
   (C) $y = (x + 1)^2$
   (D) $y = 7x + 1$
   (E) $y = x + 3$

2. What is the numerical value of the expression $10 - 12 \div 4 + 3 \times 5$?

   (A) 22
   (B) -8
   (C) $\dfrac{25}{2}$
   (D) 50
   (E) None of these.

3. The Central High School basketball team lost 20% of its games. If the team won 12 games, how many games did they lose?

   (A) 60
   (B) 27
   (C) 15
   (D) 12
   (E) 3

4. This table gives the Fahrenheit temperatures in Chicago at 7:00 A.M. on five days in January.

Mon	Tue	Wed	Thu	Fri
15°	18°	5°	−8°	−3°

   How much colder was it on Friday than it was on Monday?

   (A) 12°
   (B) 18°
   (C) −5°
   (D) −12°
   (E) −45°

5. If a, b, and c are whole numbers that are all divisible by 3, which of the following expressions represent whole numbers that are divisible by 3?

   I. $a + b + c$

   II. $\dfrac{a + b}{c}$

   III. abc

   (A) I only
   (B) II only
   (C) III only
   (D) I and III only
   (E) I, II, and III

6. There are 7 teams in a tournament in which each team plays every other team only once. How many games total will be played in the tournament?

   (A) 7
   (B) 21
   (C) 36
   (D) 42
   (E) 49

GO ON TO THE NEXT PAGE

KAPLAN

7. Which of the following graphs could represent the trip described in the following paragraph? The vertical scales are measured in miles, and the horizontal scales are measured in hours.

   Jon got in his car at home, drove down the street, and stopped at a stoplight. When the light turned green he entered the freeway and continued on his way to work. It took him a total of one hour to make the trip of fifty miles.

   (A)
   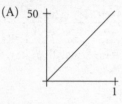

   (B)
   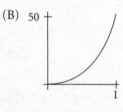

   (C)
   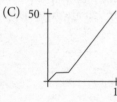

   (D)
   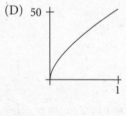

   (E)

8. Which of the following expressions is an interpretation of this sentence?

   Divide a certain number by $\frac{1}{3}$ and then add 1.

   (A) $\dfrac{n+1}{3}$

   (B) $n + \dfrac{1}{\frac{1}{3}}$

   (C) $\dfrac{1}{3}n + 1$

   (D) $\dfrac{n}{\frac{1}{3}} + 1$

   (E) None of these.

9. What is the solution set of the following equation?

   $$3(x + 2) + 5 = 1 - (x + 2)$$

   (A) {–3}

   (B) {–2}

   (C) {–6}

   (D) {0}

   (E) {–5}

10. At DeSoto High School, the number of teachers, t, is seven more than fifteen times the number of administrators, a. Which of the following equations demonstrates this relationship?

    (A) $a = 15t + 7$

    (B) $t = 15a - 7$

    (C) $t + 7 = 15a$

    (D) $t = 15(a + 7)$

    (E) $t = 15a + 7$

11. Twenty seven is 45% of what number?

    (A) 0.1215

    (B) 12.15

    (C) 60

    (D) 121.5

    (E) 600

GO ON TO THE NEXT PAGE

12. If A, B, x, and y are numbers such that $x > y$ and $A \leq B$, then which of the following must be true?

    (A) $x + A = y + B$

    (B) $x + A > y + B$

    (C) $x + B < y + A$

    (D) $x + B > y + A$

    (E) None of these.

13. Which of the following numbers is not equal to the others?

    (A) $\left(\dfrac{1}{2}\right)^2$

    (B) $\dfrac{1}{4}$

    (C) 0.25

    (D) 25%

    (E) $\dfrac{1}{8} \div 2$

14. A board foot is defined to be the volume of wood in a piece that measures 12 inches by 12 inches by 1 inch. What is the number of equivalent board feet in a board that measures 10 feet by 9 inches by 2 inches?

    (A) $7\dfrac{1}{2}$

    (B) 15

    (C) 90

    (D) 180

    (E) 2,160

15. If five workers can clean a stadium after a baseball game in four hours, how long would it take three workers to clean the same stadium?

    (A) $6\dfrac{2}{3}$ hours

    (B) $2\dfrac{2}{5}$ hours

    (C) $3\dfrac{3}{4}$ hours

    (D) 5 hours

    (E) There is not enough information given.

16. Ramona is making curtains that require 2 yards 2 feet of material for each pair. She bought a bolt of material that contains 15 yards. How many complete pairs of curtains can she make from this bolt?

    (A) 7

    (B) 6

    (C) 5

    (D) 4

    (E) 3

17. Christina has taken four tests in her algebra class, and she knows that her average (arithmetic mean) score is 80. She knows that the scores on her first three tests are 92, 80, and 68, but she can't remember the fourth score. What is the score on Christina's fourth algebra test?

    (A) 100

    (B) 95

    (C) 80

    (D) 75

    (E) There is not enough information given.

18. Keith purchases two rolls of ribbon to make awards for a contest. One roll is labeled $5\dfrac{2}{3}$ feet and the other $2\dfrac{3}{4}$ feet. How much more ribbon is on the first roll than on the second?

    (A) 3 feet

    (B) 2 feet 11 inches

    (C) 3 feet 1 inch

    (D) 8 feet 5 inches

    (E) 7 feet 17 inches

GO ON TO THE NEXT PAGE

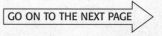

19. When Roland works more than 40 hours in a week, he is paid time-and-a-half for the hours in excess of 40. His normal hourly rate is $12.60 per hour. If he worked 43 hours last week, how much did he earn?

    (A) $504

    (B) $56.70

    (C) $541.80

    (D) $560.70

    (E) $812.70

20. Which of the following numbers is between 0.003 and 0.08?

    (A) 0.0035

    (B) 0.35

    (C) 0.0835

    (D) 0.8

    (E) 0.00035

21. Which of the following expressions is not equivalent to $\frac{xy}{6}$?

    (A) $\frac{1}{6}xy$

    (B) $\frac{x}{2} \times \frac{y}{3}$

    (C) $\frac{1}{2}\left(\frac{xy}{3}\right)$

    (D) $(xy) \div 6$

    (E) $\frac{x}{6} \times \frac{y}{6}$

22. Approximately 3 out of 8 morning glory seeds germinate within 10 days. Out of 500 morning glory seeds, about how many would you expect to germinate within 10 days?

    (A) 60

    (B) 190

    (C) 310

    (D) 440

    (E) 1,330

23. Which of the following expressions represents one of the factors of $3x^2 + x - 4$?

    (A) $x + 1$

    (B) $x - 4$

    (C) $3x - 4$

    (D) $3x + 4$

    (E) $3x + 1$

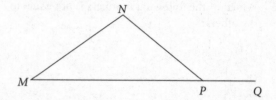

24. In $\triangle MNP$, the measure of $\angle M$ is 32°, and the measure of $\angle N$ is 95°. What is the measure of $\angle NPQ$?

    (A) 63°

    (B) 127°

    (C) 148°

    (D) 85°

    (E) There is not enough information given.

25. The cost per ream of paper is given in the accompanying table.

1 ream	10 reams	30 reams	50 reams	100 or more reams
$5.78	5% disc.	10% disc.	15% disc.	30% disc.

How much did Montague Charter Academy pay for 200 reams of this paper?

    (A) $1,156.00

    (B) $578.00

    (C) $346.80

    (D) $809.20

    (E) $462.40

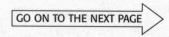

26. An eight-foot vertical post casts a shadow that is 56 inches long. At the same time, a building casts a shadow that is 15 feet 2 inches long. What is the height of the building?

(A) about 106.17 feet

(B) $70\frac{7}{9}$ feet

(C) 26 feet

(D) 2 feet 5 inches

(E) There is not enough information given.

27. Which of the following expressions is equivalent to $\frac{a}{b} - \frac{2}{c}$?

(A) $\frac{a-2}{b-c}$

(B) $\frac{a-2}{bc}$

(C) $a - 2$

(D) $\frac{a}{b} + \frac{c}{2}$

(E) $\frac{ac - 2b}{bc}$

28. It takes Samantha about 35 minutes to translate a page from German to English. Approximately how long would it take her to translate a 15-page essay from German to English?

(A) 8 hours 45 minutes

(B) 7 hours 30 minutes

(C) 17 hours 30 minutes

(D) 2 hours 20 minutes

(E) 10 hours 5 minutes

29. The sum of two numbers is 43. If one of the numbers is x, what expression represents the other number in terms of x?

(A) y

(B) $x - 43$

(C) $x + 43$

(D) $2x - 1$

(E) $43 - x$

30. Which of the following numbers is (are) prime?

  I. 1
  II. 7
  III. 91
  IV. 111

(A) I and II only

(B) II only

(C) I and IV only

(D) II and III only

(E) I, II, and III only

31. The following table gives the results of a certain standardized test for four students.

	Raw score	Percent	Percentile rank
Aaron	75	62.5	71
Anthony	80	66.7	72
Carlynne	90	75	81
Marcus	110	91.7	98

Which of the following statements can you conclude to be true based on this information?

(A) Aaron got 75 percent of the questions correct.

(B) Anthony's raw score of 80 is better than 66.7% of the students who took the test.

(C) Carlynne's percentile rank, 81, means that she got 81% of the questions on the test correct.

(D) Marcus's raw score of 110 is better than 98% of the students who took the test.

(E) None of these statements can be concluded to be true.

GO ON TO THE NEXT PAGE

KAPLAN

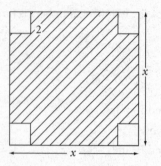

32. A square that is x units on each side has smaller squares 2 units in length cut from each corner, as shown. The area of the shaded center portion can be calculated by subtracting the four corners from the big square.

    $x^2 - 4(2^2)$

    Which of the following expressions represents an alternate approach to find the same area?

    (A) $4(x - 2)^2 + 2(x - 2)$
    (B) $4x - 8$
    (C) $(x - 4)^2 + 4[2(x - 4)]$
    (D) $(x - 4)^2 + 2(x - 2)$
    (E) $(x - 2)^2 + 4[2(x - 2)]$

33. If each side of a rectangle is multiplied by five, the area will be changed in what way?

    (A) The area will be multiplied by five.
    (B) The area will be multiplied by 25.
    (C) The area will be multiplied by 10.
    (D) The area will be multiplied by 100.
    (E) The area will be multiplied by 20.

34. A goat is tied to a stake by means of a rope that is 20 feet long. What is the approximate area of the region that the goat may graze?

    (A) 400π square feet
    (B) 400 square feet
    (C) $(20\pi)^2$ square feet
    (D) 40π square feet
    (E) 62.8 square feet

35. Paul borrowed $500 from his uncle for school supplies. He signed a note to repay the loan in monthly installments of $75. If his uncle does not charge interest on the loan, how much will Paul's final payment be?

    (A) $75
    (B) $200
    (C) $25
    (D) $67
    (E) $50

36. Violent crime statistics for a certain neighborhood are recorded in the table below. What is the approximate annual percent increase for 2003?

Year	Number of Violent crimes
1998	48
1999	40
2000	35
2001	50
2002	55
2003	72

    (A) 31%
    (B) 50%
    (C) 24%
    (D) –17%
    (E) 17%

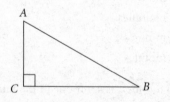

37. In right $\triangle ABC$, $AC = 4$ and $BC = 8$. Express the AB length in simplest radical form.

    (A) $4\sqrt{5}$
    (B) $4\sqrt{3}$
    (C) $2\sqrt{20}$
    (D) $\sqrt{80}$
    (E) $\sqrt{48}$

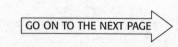
GO ON TO THE NEXT PAGE

38. The Lees want to install a new driveway. They plan to remove the old concrete and excavate an area 15 feet by 30 feet to a depth of 8 inches. What is the volume of excavated material?

    (A) 300 cubic inches

    (B) 518,400 cubic feet

    (C) $11\frac{1}{9}$ cubic yards

    (D) 3,600 cubic inches

    (E) None of these.

39. What is the solution of the equation $0.3x - 2 = 10$?

    (A) {0.04}

    (B) {0.4}

    (C) {4}

    (D) {40}

    (E) {400}

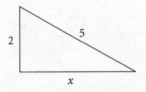

40. What additional information would allow you to determine the length x?

        I. The perimeter of the triangle
        II. The fact that this is a right triangle
        III. $2 \leq x \leq 5$

    (A) I only

    (B) II only

    (C) III only

    (D) I or II

    (E) I, II, or III

41. The relationship between Celsius and Fahrenheit temperatures is given by the formula $C = \frac{5}{9}(F - 32)$. If the Celsius temperature is 30°, what is the corresponding Fahrenheit temperature?

    (A) 30°

    (B) 86°

    (C) 55°

    (D) $1\frac{1}{9}°$

    (E) None of these.

42. Four boxes, each 2 feet 10 inches high, are stacked in a room that has a 12-foot ceiling. How much space remains between the top box and the ceiling?

    (A) 11 feet 4 inches

    (B) 8 feet 40 inches

    (C) 8 inches

    (D) 4 inches

    (E) 6 inches

43. What is the lowest common denominator of the following fractions?

    $\dfrac{2}{3x^2y}$ and $\dfrac{5}{6x^2y^2}$

    (A) 10

    (B) $3x^2y$

    (C) $6x^4y^3$

    (D) $18x^4y^3$

    (E) $6x^2y^2$

44. Mrs. Sanchez gave her class of 30 students a math test. If $\frac{2}{5}$ of her students are male and $\frac{1}{4}$ of the male students received C grades on the test, how many of her male students got a grade of C?

    (A) 2
    (B) 3
    (C) 5
    (D) 10
    (E) 12

45. Which of the following statements is (are) false?

       I. All isosceles triangles are similar.
      II. The three angles of a triangle are supplementary.
     III. All rectangles are quadrilaterals.

    (A) I only
    (B) II only
    (C) III only
    (D) I, II, and III
    (E) I and II only

46. If a negative number is subtracted from a positive number, which of the following will always be the result?

    (A) A number with the same sign as the number with the larger absolute value.
    (B) A number with the same sign as the number with the smaller absolute value.
    (C) Zero.
    (D) A negative number.
    (E) A positive number.

47. If x and y are both positive integers, which of the following is (are) not necessarily (a) positive integer(s)?

       I. $x + y$
      II. $x - y$
     III. x^y
     IV. $\frac{x}{y}$

    (A) II only
    (B) II, III, and IV
    (C) II and IV only
    (D) IV only
    (E) All of these must be positive integers.

48. At Gelson's Market, mangoes are priced at $1.33 each or four for $5.00. How much do you save on each mango by buying four at a time?

    (A) 8 cents
    (B) 32 cents
    (C) $5.32
    (D) $3.67
    (E) None of these.

49. Which of the following equations could be used to solve this word problem?

    The larger of two numbers is three less than five times the smaller number. The sum of four times the smaller number and twice the larger is 36. Find the numbers.

    (A) $2x + 4(5x - 3) = 36$
    (B) $4x + 2(5x + 3) = 36$
    (C) $4x - 3 + 2(5x) = 36$
    (D) $4x + 2(5x - 3) = 36$
    (E) $x + (5x - 3) = 36$

50. Party planners anticipate that three gallons of lemonade will serve 10 kids. How much lemonade should they plan to serve 25 kids?

    (A) $7\frac{1}{2}$ gallons

    (B) $1\frac{1}{5}$ gallons

    (C) 8 gallons

    (D) $2\frac{1}{2}$ gallons

    (E) $83\frac{1}{3}$ gallons

GO ON TO THE NEXT PAGE

KAPLAN

Writing Section

Directions: The Writing section contains two essay topics. Be sure you write about the given topics. Essays on topics of your choosing will not be acceptable. Your written responses must be your work, must be in your own words, and must not be plagiarized from some other work.

The topics are designed to give you an opportunity to demonstrate your skills in writing effectively. Spend some time considering the topics and organizing your ideas before you start. For the essays, be sure to address all parts of the topics, support generalizations with examples, and use multiple paragraphs.

You may use any space provided in the test booklet to write notes or to prepare an outline or rough draft. However, your score will be based solely on the versions written in the space provided in your answer document. Please write as neatly and legibly as possible. To ensure that you have enough space for your essays, do not skip lines, write in large print, or leave large margins.

TOPIC 1

President Lyndon Johnson said in his inaugural speech, "In each generation, with toil and tears, we have had to earn our heritage again." To what extent do you agree or disagree with his remark? Support your opinion with specific examples.

_____

_____

_____

_____

_____

_____

_____

_____

_____

 GO ON TO THE NEXT PAGE

GO ON TO THE NEXT PAGE

TOPIC 2

Some of our most memorable experiences are those that teach us the meaning of courage. Write about one such event in your own life. Identify what you came to believe "courage" means.

GO ON TO THE NEXT PAGE

GO ON TO THE NEXT PAGE

KAPLAN

STOP

Practice Test One: **Answer Key**

READING TEST

1.	D	26.	B
2.	B	27.	C
3.	B	28.	B
4.	E	29.	A
5.	A	30.	B
6.	B	31.	E
7.	B	32.	A
8.	D	33.	E
9.	C	34.	B
10.	C	35.	A
11.	D	36.	B
12.	D	37.	B
13.	A	38.	A
14.	D	39.	D
15.	C	40.	B
16.	E	41.	D
17.	C	42.	E
18.	A	43.	B
19.	B	44.	C
20.	D	45.	D
21.	D	46.	B
22.	C	47.	D
23.	D	48.	E
24.	D	49.	A
25.	C	50.	D

MATH TEST

1.	C	26.	C
2.	A	27.	E
3.	E	28.	A
4.	B	29.	E
5.	D	30.	B
6.	B	31.	D
7.	C	32.	C
8.	D	33.	B
9.	A	34.	A
10.	E	35.	E
11.	C	36.	A
12.	D	37.	A
13.	E	38.	C
14.	B	39.	D
15.	A	40.	D
16.	C	41.	B
17.	C	42.	C
18.	B	43.	E
19.	D	44.	B
20.	A	45.	E
21.	E	46.	E
22.	B	47.	C
23.	D	48.	A
24.	B	49.	D
25.	D	50.	A

WRITING TEST

See Sample Essays on page 246.

KAPLAN

Answers and Explanations

READING SECTION

1. D

Look at the components of the word: The prefix *in* means *not* (*in*capable, *in*competent). The word *extricate* means to be able to free yourself (I couldn't *extricate* myself from the quicksand). *Inextricable* means not able to be extricated. Look at the context. The clue within the sentence is *tied*.

2. B

Choice (A) is simply judgmental, as are choices (C) and (E). Choice (D) is clearly wrong because the conclusion is clearly stated in the last two sentences. By using a process of elimination, we can determine that (B) is the answer.

3. B

Otherwise is not a verb. Therefore, it doesn't show a state of being (E). Nor does it express a relationship between two nouns (D). It introduces a sentence, and therefore cannot signal a logical relationship between parts of a sentence (C). The sentences do not have equal elements to be joined (A). That leaves (B) as the only possible answer. Notice how it is possible to work backwards in answering the question using a process of elimination. There is no rule that says you must proceed in alphabetical order.

4. E

People training to be spies (A) might have much broader training than merely being observant. (B) is not appropriate. *Engineers* (C) might find this information interesting, but not particularly useful in their field. The same is true for *athletes* (D). (E) is the best answer because the article is making the reader aware of using all of the senses and focused attention to be better observers.

5. A

The passage describes techniques for developing observation skills. The other choices do not mention techniques. (C) may look like a good option, but it is too general.

6. B

Since *but* occurs in the middle of a sentence, it cannot be a transition to the next paragraph (C), nor can it introduce the *topic sentence* (D). It is a word that signals a *contrasting idea* (B), not a *conclusion* (A); does it apply to the topic sentence (the first in the paragraph)?

7. B

The word *alarmed* is the clue to this definition, which is *to be an omen or warning of*. The use of the word *may* indicates something happening in the future. (C) might look like an appealing answer, but to signify means *to be a sign of* and is not as specific as (B). (A) is incorrect, as are (D) and (E). Try to fit the choice phrases into the sentence and you discover the sentence does not make sense.

8. D

It is *introductory* (A), but the better answer is (D) because it introduces a second paragraph. It is not *explanatory* (C). It doesn't explain anything, and it is not placed here to enhance understanding (B), although it may help. (E), the final choice, is not appropriate, as the phrase is included for meaning rather than to signal the type of essay the passage is taken from.

9. C

The answer cannot be (A) or (E) because either suggests there is information other than facts that is included in the passage. *Exemplary* (B) means very good but doesn't relate to content as the other choices do. There is nothing *persuasive* (D) about this selection.

10. C

The answer (C) is revealed in the last sentence of the selection. (A) could be true but is not the best answer. Choice (B) is not mentioned. (D) is a poor answer because change comes from changes in the culture. (E) is incorrect because the implication is there but not stated.

11. D

The best choice is (D). By the fifth word it is clear this is not a story (C). It is an introductory phrase (B) but not chosen by the author for a specific grammatical purpose. It is not a clause (A). (E) is incorrect because it is not an attention grabber.

12. D

Read the next sentence. (A) does not make sense in the context, nor does (B). (C) may be true but introduces a new idea, so it is a poor choice. (E) is incorrect because of the second-person usage, which doesn't fit the style of the paragraph.

13. A

(A), to persuade, is the best answer. The phrases it *will require* and *we need to* are clearly intended to move people to action. (B) is incorrect because it is not specific. (C) is incorrect because there are not informative facts. (D) is also incorrect; this is not entertaining. (E) is a poor choice because it does not criticize; rather, it makes suggestions.

14. D

Although the prefix *in* means *not*, just as *un* does, the word *dissolve* is not applicable to this usage, so (A) and (B) are incorrect. (C) is not correct because the prefix is negative. (E), *difficult*, is not an appropriate synonym.

15. C

Use the context of the sentence to determine this answer. Which word, when paired with *efforts*, makes the most sense? (A), *wonderful*, (B) *amazing*, (D) *highly competent*, and (E) *worthy of high standards* do not make sense.

16. E

You need to have an understanding of U.S. geography in order to place this state in the correct geographical area. Choices (A) and (B) are too broad. Choice (C) has to do with time, not location. Choice (D) covers the Midwest, not the Northeastern U.S.

17. C

This is sure to be found in the section on Time Zones, page 115. Choice (A) is too general. Choice (B) is probably an overview of North America unrelated to time. Choices (D) and (E) relate to areas of the U.S., not time.

18. A

To find *both* North and South America, you must find an index item large enough to accommodate it. Choices (B), (D), and (E) are too limited in area. *Time zones* has a limited focus, also. Only (A), the Earth, is a large enough topic to be correct.

19. B

The style is informal, and the content is general but not as specific as it would be in a science text (A). The style is not appropriate to fiction (C). The content does not suggest multiculturalism (D) or history (E).

20. D

Every sentence contains a fact, so the other choices are irrelevant. (A) is incorrect even though some of the language sounds poetic. (B) is incorrect because *metaphysical* refers to a branch of philosophy that tries to explain what reality is. (C) is incorrect because it is not as specific as (D). (E) is incorrect because although the topic relates to astronomy, *astronomical* is not a style.

21. D

(D) is the best answer because of all the information presented. The other answer choices, (A) and (E), are not appropriate purposes. (B) is incorrect because it doesn't capture the reader's attention, and (C) is incorrect because the selection is too brief to attract students to the study of astronomy.

22. C

(C) is best because the author gives many reasons to suggest rethinking the old saying. (A) and (B) are too narrow. (A) is incorrect because the author obviously disagrees. Whereas (B) is possible, it is not as close to the main point as (C). (D) is incorrect because the writer questions appearance but does not argue a position about it. (E) is incorrect because all it says is that famous authors' names are in large print on the cover.

23. D

(D) is the best of the possible choices because it is the most completely defined. (B) and (C) are not the best choices because, while close to the definition, they are still not quite correct. (E) might confuse you because of "ad" appearing in both words, but it is incorrect.

24. D

This choice is the most appropriate to the content, and the reader will have a sense about the content of the article. (A) is incorrect because the writer argues against it. (B) is incorrect. It would be more correct to say *People's Appearance, Like Book Covers, Can Be Revealing*. (C) is a poor choice because the passage does not attach adages. (E) is also poor because the article goes beyond a discussion of book covers.

25. C

(C), an *exposition*, best defines this selection. It attempts to convey information in a clear, straightforward way. The other possible choices do not hit the mark exactly. (A) is incorrect because it is not an argument. (B) is a poor choice because it is impossible to tell if it is an introduction. It does not specifically compare explorations. (E) is incorrect because this is not an explanation.

26. B

(B) is the preferred choice because knowledge will be added to by many scientists in many fields, and the addition will be international. That definitive characteristic is not part of the other possible choices. (A) is incorrect because "exponential" growth is not an accurate definition. (C) and (D) are possible in terms of usage but not specific in terms of definition (E). Replacing *accrete* with *gather* would not make sense.

27. C

(C) is best. The author is not *negative* (A). The presentation could be called *straightforward* (D) or *factual* (B), but they don't address the tone, which is clearly *hopeful* but not *enthusiastic* or gushing (E).

28. B

Because it reports on an experiment in instructional technology, it is more likely to come from this source than any of the others. A textbook on teaching (A) is unlikely to be this specific. The other choices are not specific enough.

29. A

The second paragraph as a whole communicates this. The other choices are not specifically to the point of the question. (B) and (E) are too general. (C) is incorrect because student satisfaction, while important, is not the main point. (D) is incorrect because the article does not discuss forms per se.

30. B

Choice (C) is too general. (D) and (E) are not suggested in the text. (A) has to do with training, not possible testing or measurement methods.

31. E

Chronological order occurs throughout; parallelism is used in the first paragraph. (A) and (C) are incorrect because there is not analogy used herein. (B) and (D) are incorrect because metaphor does not occur in the passage.

32. A

It is written in first person in the style of a personal essay, and, thus, is autobiographical. The other choices cannot be supported by the content of the passage. It is definitely not persuasive, analytical, or historical, and while descriptive, it is more obviously autobiographical.

33. E

Reviewing the full content of the passage brings the reader to an understanding of influence of westerns on contemporary life. As an autobiography, the selection cannot be a novel about the American West (A) or a biography (B). Because it includes more than only cowboy heroes and movies, (C) and (D) are incorrect.

34. B

This is the most specific of the definitions relating to the passage. Choice (A) does not take into account that the person may or may not have existed. Choices (C), (D), and (E) are too general. Myths usually can be interpreted symbolically.

35. A

By the time you have read to the end of the selection you realize this is an article on more than just American Indian myths and stories. It is an *introduction* rather than a *summary* (B) or *conclusion* (C), and it has a broader scope than an individual myth (D). (E) is incorrect because the passage does not describe specific *tribal cultures*.

36. B

(B) is the best answer because it is the most comprehensive and inclusive of the ideas in the passage. (A) is too general, and (C)-II is too general. (D) and (E) are too specific to be useful as organizing topics.

37. B

Select this answer by a process of elimination. Identify which answers are clearly wrong. I (A), V (D), and VI (E) can be eliminated first. Then go back. Probably III (C) and IV (not a choice) don't apply. *Statistics* (B) is the best choice.

38. A

Again, use a process of elimination, but after reading the choices, (A) seems the best. (B), (C), (D), and (E) do not include biography or personal information.

39. D

Hypotheses tests (B) is too specific, and (A), (C), and (E) don't fit. *Practice exercises* are standard test preparation vehicles.

40. B

The last sentence provides the correct answer, directing teachers in effective methods of studying to be better teachers and help students learn. (A) is incorrect as this passage is directed toward teachers, and the other choices don't fit.

41. D

Overlearning in quotation marks may not be fully understood by all readers. (A) is a poor choice because examples from tests would not clarify the writer's main point. (B) and (C) are too general, and (E) is a poor choice because explanations of different kinds of tests would not help.

42. E

It leads to a restatement of previously given information to clarify any possible misunderstanding. It is always used that way. The other choices do not hit the mark. (A) is a poor choice because transitions are usually placed between ideas. *Introductory phrases* (B) are at the beginning of paragraphs; while it does introduce an *explanatory phrase*, it is not explanatory. (D) is poor because sentence variety can be achieved in other ways.

43. B

This is the most specific and therefore the best answer. Choice (A) does not fit at all, since this is not a generalization, nor does (C), (D), or (E) fit. The author does not assume anything, nor does he explain or define.

44. C

This answer requires you to be able to differentiate among dictionary definitions: empathy means the ability to share in another's emotions. Sympathy (E) has to do with understanding another's feelings of hurt. (A) is a poor choice because the attitude of concern is not at all detached. (B) and (D) are incorrect because *informative* is not an attitude, nor is *favorable*.

45. D

This is the most important characteristic in terms of the content of the whole article. (A) is obviously incorrect. (B) and (E) are implied, and (C) is not stated at all.

46. B

Percentages are specifically statistical. The other choices are inappropriate. (A) is a poor choice; it is not as specific as (B). (C) and (D) are also too general. (E) is incorrect because it is not a list.

47. D

The questions stated after the statistics serve to direct the reader toward a proposal or argument to rectify the situation; thus, (A) and (C) (conclusions) are wrong, and (B) and (E) (historical) are also wrong.

48. E

Twenty five percent is *one in every four* found in the second sentence. (A) tells how many Asian children work. (B) tells how many children in Latin America work. (C) tells how many children never learn to read. (D) tells how many working children live in Africa.

49. A

The repetition of syntactic form in the sentence is a characteristic of *parallelism*. Sentence 2 is not repetitive (B), an *exaggeration* (C), or a *cause and effect* (D). (E) is a poor choice because it is too general.

50. D

See the last sentence of the selection. It is more general than the other choices, but better because it is more to the point. (A), (B), (C), and (E) are all mentioned but are not the author's main point.

MATHEMATICS SECTION

1. C

Each y value is the square of one more than the x value. Equation (C), $y = (x + 1)^2$, is the only one that reflects that relationship. (A) Each y-value is not the square of the corresponding x-value. (B) Each y-value is not one more than the square of the corresponding x-value. (D) Only the first and last ordered pairs satisfy this equation. (E) Only (1, 4) satisfies this equation.

2. A

Follow the order of operation rules.

$10 - 12 \div 4 + 3 \times 5$	Multiplication and division in order from right to left
$= 10 - 3 + 15$	Addition and subtraction in order from right to left
$= 7 + 15$	
$= 22$	

Choice (B) indicates that addition was performed before subtraction in violation of the order of operation rules. You would have obtained choice (C) if you performed all operations in order from left to right, also in violation of the order of operation rules. Choice (D) would be obtained if you had assumed, incorrectly, that there were parentheses as in $(10 - 12 \div 4 + 3) \times 5$, or had simply multiplied by 5 as the final step.

3. E

If the team lost 20% of its games, then they won 80% of the games played. So 12 is 80% of the number of games played. Set up a proportion and solve.

$\dfrac{12}{x} = \dfrac{80}{100}$	Cross multiply.
$80x = 1{,}200$	Divide both sides by 80.
$x = 15$	So the team played 15 games, won 12, and lost 3.

Because 20% is equivalent to $\dfrac{1}{5}$, it would be easy to mistakenly multiply 5 times 12 and select (A). Choice (B) is probably just a guess. There were 15 games played in all, so (C) is reasonable in that regard, but that was not the

question. If the team lost 12 games, choice (D), then they won the same number of games that they lost, and they would have lost 50% of their games.

4. B

Find the difference between 15° and −3°. Subtract $15 - (-3) = 15 + 3 = 18$. (A) and (D) "How much colder…" requires subtraction, not addition. (C) The correct operation was not division. (E) The correct operation was not multiplication.

5. D

The sum and product of whole numbers divisible by three are also divisible by three, but, for example, $\dfrac{6 + 9}{3} = \dfrac{15}{3} = 5$, which is not divisible by three. So only I and III represent whole numbers that are divisible by three.

6. B

Let's label the teams a, b, c, d, e, f, and g. The games to be played match teams in this way:

ab bc cd de ef fg

ac bd ce df eg

ad be cf dg

ae bf cg

af bg

ag

Notice that there is no aa, bb, cc, etc.; a team cannot play against itself. And the game identified as ab is the same game as ba. This listing shows all 21 of the games to be played. (A) is just a guess that the number of teams is the number of games to be played. (C) appears to be the square of one less than the number of teams, an incorrect assumption. Choice (D) is the product of the number of teams times one less than the number of teams. Squaring the number of teams, choice (E), also does not give the correct answer.

7. C

Jon drove a short distance to the stoplight to start his trip. When he was stopped at the light his distance did not move—represented by the short horizontal segment. The straight segment (constant speed) represents the freeway trip at a steeper slope (he went faster than on the street). (A) The straight segment indicates that Jon drove at a constant rate for the entire trip. It ignores his stop at the light. (B) This graph indicates that he went very slowly at first and increased speed gradually throughout the trip. (D) This graph shows a very rapid speed at the beginning that gradually decreases over the trip. (E) This graph indicates that Jon started 50 miles from home and returned.

8. D

Only (D) translates as *Divide by $\frac{1}{3}$ and add one.* The expression in (A) translates as *Add one to a certain number, and then divide by 3.* Expression (B) is *Add one to a certain number, and then divide by $\frac{1}{3}$.* Expression (C) is *Multiply a certain number by $\frac{1}{3}$, and then add one.*

9. A

$3(x + 2) + 5 = 1 - (x + 2)$	Use a distributive property.
$3x + 6 + 5 = 1 - x - 2$	Combine similar terms.
$3x + 11 = -x - 1$	Add x to both sides.
$4x + 11 = -1$	Subtract 11 from both sides.
$4x = -12$	Divide both sides by 4.
$x = -3$	

(B) If $x = -2$, the expression in parentheses on both sides of the equation is 0. The result is then that $5 = 1$, which is obviously false. The distributive property was incorrectly applied on the left side of the equation. (C) In the course of solving the equation, you subtracted x from both sides instead of adding. (D) If 0 is substituted into the equation, the result is $11 = -1$, which is obviously false. (E) Substituting -5 results in $-4 = 4$, which is also false.

10. E

Only $t = 15a + 7$ reflects this relationship. (A) This equation represents the inverse relationship: *The number of administrators is seven more than fifteen times the number of teachers.* (B) represents the relationship: *The number of teachers is seven less than fifteen times the number of administrators.* (C) represents the relationship: *Seven more than the number of teachers is fifteen times the number of administrators.* (D) represents the relationship: *The number of teachers is equal to fifteen times the sum of the number of administrators and seven.*

11. C

Set up a proportion and solve.

$\frac{27}{b} = \frac{45}{100}$	Cross multiply.
$45b = 2,700$	Divide both sides by 45.
$b = 60$	

(A) is the result of finding 45% of 27 and then dividing by 100. This is not what is called for in this problem. (B) is 45% of 27. (D) is the result of finding 45% of 27 and then multiplying by 10. (E) is probably the result of dividing wrong.

12. D

Rewrite $A \leq B$ as $B \geq A$. Then add the left and right sides of the two inequalities:

$x > y$

$B \geq A$

$x + B > y + A$

(A) *Equality* cannot be inferred from inequalities. (B) could follow only from $x > y$ and $A > B$. (C) could follow only from $x < y$ and $B \leq A$.

13. E

$\frac{1}{8} \div 2 = \frac{1}{8} \times \frac{1}{2} = \frac{1}{16}$, which is not equal to the others.

(A) $\left(\frac{1}{2}\right)^2 = \frac{1}{4}$

(B) $\frac{1}{4}$

(C) $0.25 = \frac{25}{100} = \frac{1}{4}$

(D) $25\% = \frac{25}{100} = \frac{1}{4}$

14. B

As defined, a board foot is 144 cubic inches. The number of cubic inches in the given board is 120 (10 feet = 120 inches) times 9 times 2. Multiply these numbers, and divide by 144. This operation can more easily be done by leaving the product in factored form and canceling: $\frac{120 \times 9 \times 2}{144}$. (A) The 2-inch thickness of the board was ignored. (C) If the volume of the board were divided by 24 instead of 144, the choice would have been choice (C). (D) If you had divided by 12 instead of 144, the choice would have been (D). (E) is the volume of the board in cubic inches, not the question that was asked.

15. A

This is an indirect proportion problem (also called inverse variation). If, as one variable increases, the other one decreases, then the problem is an indirect proportion. (If both increase, the problem is a direct proportion.) To solve an indirect proportion, establish two ratios, one with workers and the other with hours. Be sure to place corresponding numbers on top and bottom of the ratios. The two ratios for this problem are $\frac{5}{3}$ and $\frac{4}{x}$ in which 5 workers correspond to 4 hours and 3 workers correspond to an unknown number of hours. To establish the correct proportion, turn one of the ratios over.

$\frac{5}{3} = \frac{x}{4}$ Cross multiply.

$3x = 20$ Divide by 3.

$x = 6\frac{2}{3}$

Choice (B) is the result of assuming that this is a direct proportion problem. Choice (C) indicates that the proportion was set up incorrectly, such as $\frac{5}{4} = \frac{x}{3}$. If your choice is (D), you're probably guessing.

16. C

Divide 15 yards by $2\frac{2}{3}$ yards.

$$15 \div 2\frac{2}{3} = \frac{15}{1} \div \frac{8}{3} = \frac{15}{1} \times \frac{3}{8} = \frac{45}{8} = 5\frac{5}{8}$$

So she can make 5 complete pairs of curtains. (A) The 2 feet of material was ignored. (B) In this case, rounding up is not a possibility. A fraction of a pair of curtains is not a pair of curtains. (D) and (E) seem like complete guesses.

17. C

Suppose Christina's unknown score is x. Her mean score is found by adding the four values and dividing by four.

$\frac{92 + 80 + 68 + x}{4} = 80$ Simplify.

$\frac{240 + x}{4} = 80$ Multiply both sides by 4.

$240 + x = 320$ Subtract 240 from both sides.

$x = 80$

(A) If the score on the fourth test were 100, her average would be 85. (B) If the score on the fourth test were 95, her average would be 83.75. (D) If the score on the fourth test were 75, her average would be 78.75.

18. B

Subtract $2\frac{3}{4}$ from $5\frac{2}{3}$.

$5\frac{2}{3} - 2\frac{3}{4}$ Rewrite fractions with a common denominator.

$= 5\frac{8}{12} - 2\frac{9}{12}$ Borrow 1 whole from 5.

$= 4\frac{20}{12} - 2\frac{9}{12}$

$= 2\frac{11}{12}$, which means 2 feet 11 inches.

(A) If the problem had required rounding, this choice would be correct. (C) The subtraction was done incorrectly. (D) is the sum of the mixed numbers; this problem requires subtraction. (E) is the same answer as (D) except it is not in simplest form.

19. D

Roland earns 40($12.60) for the first 40 hours of work and 3(1.5)($12.60) for the next 3 hours.

40(12.60) + 3(1.5)(12.60)

=504 + 56.70 = 560.70

(A) ignores the 3 hours of overtime. (B) is just Roland's overtime pay. (C) ignores the "time and a half" factor for overtime pay. (E) includes the "time and a half" factor for all 43 hours.

20. A

The only one between 0.003 and 0.08 is 0.0035. (B), (C), and (D) .0.35, 0.0835, and 0.8 are all greater than 0.08. (E) 0.00035 is less than 0.003.

21. E

The expression $\frac{x}{6} \times \frac{y}{6}$ equals $\frac{xy}{36}$, which is not equivalent to the others. (A), (B), (C), and (D) are all equivalent to $\frac{xy}{6}$.

22. B

This is a direct proportion problem.

$\frac{3}{8} = \frac{x}{500}$ Cross multiply.

$8x = 1,500$ Divide both sides by 8.

$x = 187.5$ The key word is *about*.

The best approximate answer is 190. (A) If the problem had stated "1 out of 8…" this choice would be correct. (C) If the problem had stated "5 out of 8…" this choice would be correct. (D) If the problem had stated "7 out of 8…" this choice would be correct. (E) You cannot expect more seeds to germinate than the number you begin with.

23. D

Multiply 3 times 4. Factors of 12 whose difference is 1 are 3 and 4. Rewrite the middle term using those numbers. Group and factor.

$3x^2 - 3x + 4x - 4$

$(3x^2 - 3x) + (4x - 4)$

$3x(x - 1) + 4(x - 1) = (3x + 4)(x - 1)$

(A), (B), (C), and (E) are the results of errors in the process above.

24. B

An exterior angle of a triangle is equal to the sum of the two remote interior angles.

$\angle NPQ = \angle M + \angle N = 32 + 95 = 127$

(A) is the *difference* of the given angles. (C) is the supplement of $\angle M$: $180 - 32 = 148$. (D) is the supplement of $\angle N$: $180 - 95 = 85$

25. D

A 30% discount implies that the cost is 70% of the original price. So the total cost should be:

$(200)(\$5.78)(0.7) = \$809.20$

(A) assumes no discount for 200 reams. (B) would be the cost of 100 reams at no discount. (C) is the amount of the discount on 200 reams. (E) is obtained by taking the 30% discount twice.

26. C

This is a direct proportion problem. It is important that you have consistent units in the proportion. Change 15 feet 2 inches to 182 inches.

$\frac{8}{56} = \frac{x}{182}$ Cross multiply.

$56x = 8 \times 182$ Divide by 56.

$x = \frac{8 \times 182}{56} = \frac{\cancel{8} \times 182}{\cancel{56}7} = 26$ feet

(A) would be obtained if the problem were an inverse proportion problem. (B) (182)(56) ÷ 12 ÷ 12 for no logical reason. (D) A doll house, perhaps. A completely unreasonable answer.

27. E

First rewrite each fraction so that they have a common denominator, bc.

$\frac{a}{b} - \frac{2}{c} = \frac{ac}{bc} - \frac{2b}{bc} = \frac{ac - 2b}{bc}$

(A) One does not add fractions by simply adding the numerators and denominators. A common denominator is necessary. (B) is the correct common denominator, but the fractions were not rewritten with the common denominator before subtracting. (C) There is no way to add such fractions and not end up with a fraction in the resulting expression. (D) Just changing subtraction to addition does not perform the operation.

28. A

Multiply 35 times 15 and divide by 60 to change the answer to hours and minutes. $\frac{35 \times 15}{60} = \frac{525}{60} = 8.75$, which means 8 hours and 0.75 of another hour. Multiply $(0.75) \times (60) = 45$ minutes. So the total time is 8 hours 45 minutes. (B) is the result of dividing 15 by 2. (C) is the result of dividing 35 by 2. (D) is the result of dividing 35 by 15. (E) is probably just a guess.

29. E

If you know that $x = 13$, you would subtract $43 - 13$ to find the other number. This is the same operation you would do for any given value of x. So the other number is $43 - x$. (A) The problem specifies "In terms of x..." (B) If $x = 13$, then $x - 43 = 13 - 43 = -30$, not the other number. (C) If $x = 13$, then $x + 43 = 13 + 43 = 56$, not the other number. (D) If $x = 13$, then $2x - 1 = 2(13)$ $26 - 1 = 26 - 1 = 25$, not the other number.

30. B

The only prime number in this list is 7. A prime number must have exactly two factors.

I. The number 1 has only one factor and is neither prime nor composite.

III. Factors of 91 are 1, 7, 13, and 91.

IV. Factors of 111 are 1, 3, 37, and 111.

31. D

Only (D) reflects the correct meaning of percentile. (A) Aaron's raw score is 75; he got 62.5% of the questions correct. (B) Anthony's score is better than 72% of the students who took the test. (C) Carlynne's percentile rank of 81 means that she scored better than 81% of the students who took the test.

32. C

An alternate approach is to find the area of the center square and add the areas of the four rectangles on the sides. The sides of the center square are each $x - 2 - 2 = x - 4$. The sides of each of the rectangles are $x - 4$ and 2. So the total area is $(x - 4)^2 + 4[2(x - 4)]$, which simplifies to $x^2 - 16$. (A) The sides of the center square are $x - 2 - 2 = x - 4$. (B) The expression given in the statement of the problem simplifies to $x^2 - 16$, and the expression $4x - 8$ is not equivalent to that. (D) The expression in this choice simplifies to $x^2 - 6x + 12$, which is not equivalent to $x^2 - 16$. (E) The expression in this choice simplifies to $x^2 + 4x - 12$, which is not equivalent to $x^2 - 16$.

33. B

If the sides of any plane object are each multiplied by c, then the area of the object is multiplied by c^2. So the area of the rectangle will be multiplied by 25. For the choices (A), (C), (D), and (E), consider the rectangle with sides 1 foot by 3 feet. The area of this rectangle is 3 square feet. If the sides are multiplied by 5, the new rectangle is 5 feet by 15 feet. Its area is 75 square feet, which is 25 times the area of the original rectangle.

34. A

The grazing area is the area of a circle with radius 20 feet. Use the formula for the area of a circle.

$A = \pi r^2 = \pi(20)^2 = \pi(400) = 400\pi$

(B) The value of π has been lost in this choice. (C) simplifies to $400\pi^2$. Only the radius should be squared, not the value of π. (D) Twenty squared is 400, not 40. (E) is approximately 20π, not the area.

35. E

Divide 500 by 75. $\frac{500}{75} = 6\frac{2}{3}$. The result of this division means that Paul will make 6 full payments of $75 and one last payment of $\frac{2}{3}$ $75, which is $50. (A) Each full payment is $75, but the last payment is less than a full payment. (B) If Paul still owes $200, he will make two more full payments and then the smaller final payment. (C) The final payment will be $\frac{2}{3}$ of a full payment, not $\frac{1}{3}$. (D) The final payment will be $\frac{2}{3}$ of $75, not $\frac{2}{3}$ of $100.

36. A

The one-year increase in the number of violent crimes for the year 2003 is $72 - 55 = 17$. So the question is, 17 is what percent of 55. Set up a proportion.

$\frac{17}{55} = \frac{x}{100}$

$55x = 1,700$

$x = 30.90$ This can be rounded to about 31%.

(B) is the percent increase from 1998 to 2003. (C) is the result of answering the question: *17 is what percent of 72?* Percent increase problems ask the question: *the difference in values is what percent of the original value?* The original value is 55, not 72. (D) There was an increase, so the answer could not be negative. (E) The difference in the number of violent crimes between 2002 and 2003 is 17; that is not the percent change.

37. A

Use the Pythagorean theorem: In any right triangle with sides a, b, and c (c is the hypotenuse), it is always true that $a^2 + b^2 = c^2$.

$(AB)^2 = 4^2 + 8^2 = 16 + 64 = 80$

So, $\sqrt{AB} = 4^2 + 8^2 = 16 + 64 = 80$

(B) is obtained if the squares had been subtracted instead of added. (C) is not in simplest radical form: $2\sqrt{20} = 2\sqrt{4 \times 5} = 2 \times 2\sqrt{5} = 4\sqrt{5}$. (D) also is not in simplest radical form. (E) is the same choice as (B) except it is not in simplest radical form.

38. C

The volume in cubic feet is the product of length, width, and depth. $(15)(30)\left(\frac{2}{3}\right) = 300$ cubic feet. (Not one of the choices.) There are 27 cubic feet in one cubic yard. To convert cubic feet to cubic yards, divide by 27: $300 \div 27 = 11\frac{1}{9}$ cubic yards. (A) is the number of cubic *feet*, not inches. (B) is the number of cubic *inches*, not feet. (D) To convert cubic feet to cubic inches, you would not multiply by 12.

39. D

$0.3x - 2 = 10$ Multiply both sides by 10.

$3x - 20 = 100$ Add 20 to both sides.

$3x = 120$ Divide both sides by 3.

$x = 40$

(A), (B), (C), and (E) are all different ways of mishandling the decimals in the equation.

40. D

(A), (B), (C), and (E) If you knew the peri... ...ould subtract 7 from the perimeter to find x. If you kn... a right triangle, you could use the Pythagorean theore... find x. Knowing that x is between 2 and 5 is not enough to find x.

41. B

Substitute 30 in place of C in the formula and solve for F.

$30 = \frac{5}{9}(F - 32)$ Multiply both sides by 9.

$270 = 5(F - 32)$ Simplify the right side.

$270 = 5F - 160$ Add 160 to both sides.

$430 = 5F$ Divide both sides by 5.

$86 = F$

(A) The Celsius and Fahrenheit temperatures are not equal at this temperature. (C) appears to be a guess. (D) would be obtained by substituting 30 for the variable F, instead of C, and solving for C.

42. C

Multiply four times the height of a box, and subtract from 12 feet.

12 feet − 4 (2 feet 10 inches) =

12 feet − (8 feet 40 inches) =

12 feet − (11 feet 4 inches) =

(11 feet 12 inches) − (11 feet 4 inches) = 8 inches

(A) and (B) are the heights of the four boxes, not the gap at the top. (D) Perhaps you took the four inches from the 11 feet 4 inches. (E) In the process of subtraction, you must borrow 12 inches not 10.

43. E

The lowest common denominator of fractions is the lowest common multiple of the denominators. To find the lowest common multiple of these denominators, write the prime factorization of each, and use each prime factor the greater number of times it appears in either factorization.

$3x^2y = 3 \times x \times x \times y$

$6x^2y^2 = 2 \times 3 \times x \times x \times y \times y$

So use one factor of 2, one factor of 3, two factors of x:, and two factors of y:

$6x^2y^2$

(A) is the lowest common multiple of the *numerators*. (B) is the greatest common factor of the denominators. (C) is obtained if you used each variable factor the *total* number of times it appears in both denominators. (D) is obtained if you used all factors the total number of times they appear in both denominators.

44. B

In the context of fractions, the word *of* almost always translates as multiplication. You want to find $\frac{1}{4}$ of $\frac{2}{5}$ of Mrs. Sanchez's class.

$\left(\frac{1}{4}\right) \times \left(\frac{2}{5}\right) \times (30) = 3$

(A) If her class had 20 students, 2 of the male students would have received Cs. (C) If her class had 50 students, 5 of the male students would have received Cs.

(D) appears to be a guess. (E) is the result of ignoring the $\frac{1}{4}$. That is $\frac{2}{5} \times 30 = 12$.

45. E

Similar triangles have corresponding sides that are in proportion; they are the same shape but usually a different size. (A), (B), (C), and (D) Here are two isosceles triangles that are not similar. The definition of *supplementary angles* specifically refers to *two* angles. Three angles cannot be supplementary even if their sum is 180°. The statement "All rectangles are quadrilaterals" is true. So the false statements are I and II.

46. E

An example should show the correct answer. 7 − (−9) = 7 + 9 = 16, a positive number. (A) The example above is a counterexample. The number with the larger absolute value is −9, yet the result is not negative. (B) 7 − (−5) = 7 + 5 = 12 is a counterexample for this choice. (C) and (D) Both of the examples above are counterexamples for these choices.

47. C

Suppose $x = 2$ and $y = 4$, then $x − y = 2 − 4 = 2 + (−4)$ $= −2$, which is not a positive integer, and $\frac{x}{y} = \frac{2}{4} = \frac{1}{2}$, which is also not a positive integer. I and III. For all positive integers x and y, both $x + y$ and x^y will be positive integers.

48. A

When you buy four mangoes at a time, you are really paying $5.00 ÷ 4 = $1.25 for each mango. So by buying four at a time, you save $1.33 − $1.25 = $0.08 = 8 cents on each mango. (B) The total saved on all four mangoes is 32 cents. (C) The total cost of four mangoes at the regular price is $3.67. (D) is the result of subtracting $5.00 − 1.33.

49. D

Let x be the smaller number. Then the larger number is $5x - 3$. So the equation would be $4x + 2(5x - 3) = 36$. (A) The 2 and the 4 are interchanged. (B) In this choice, the expression in parentheses is incorrect. It should be $(5x - 3)$. (C) The expressions in the parentheses are both incorrect. (E) The multiples, 2 and 4, are missing completely.

50. A

This is a direct proportion problem. Set up a proportion and solve.

$\dfrac{3}{10} = \dfrac{x}{25}$ Cross multiply.

$10x = 75$ Divide both sides by 10.

$x = 7.5$

(B) and (D) With more kids to serve, you should expect to need more lemonade, not less. (C) There was no hint to round off the answer. (E) is the choice obtained by treating the problem as in inverse proportion.

WRITING SECTION

Topic 1

4 Essay

It's tempting to respond that of course, each generation of Americans earns and defines its own place in our country's history. After all, each generation faces challenges and circumstances that the previous generations could never even have dreamed of. Members of my generation, for example, will need to be computer-proficient in order to hold down virtually any job in the twenty-first century. My parents, on the other hand, still have problems programming their VCR. We all believe we are unique and, consequently, our ways of dealing with adversity must be unique as well.

However, I must respectfully disagree with Mr. Johnson. I believe the founders of our nation are the ones who earned and defined the role Americans play, both domestically and in the global community. It has been up to succeeding generations not to revise this definition, but rather to apply it to the times in which they live.

A defining moment of American history for my generation was the World Trade Center attacks of 2001. None of us will ever forget where we were when we learned of this tragedy, or the way our country came together in its wake. My parents' generation lost its collective innocence with the assassination of President John Fitzgerald Kennedy. My grandmother still remembers exactly where she was when the news of the bombing of Pearl Harbor came over the radio in her family car. Her parents, in turn, raised their children in the shadow of the Great Depression. Each of these events was unique to its time in history, and each required a different response from the American people. But the ability to face each new challenge, determine what needs to be done, and then find the strength and courage to do it is what I believe forms the core of what it means to be an American. Times may change, but not the true American spirit; that merely adapts and moves forward.

There is a reason that our Constitution, a document written more than 200 years ago by men who could never have imagined the world we live in today, remains the blueprint for a viable society. What history requires of us will, of course, change with time. What our country requires of us, however —our best—will not.

Grader's Comments

This essay fully addresses the topic, presents its author's opinion clearly and convincingly, and maintains its focus. It gets off to a strong start by acknowledging that the opposite point of view has some validity, but then, with a clear transition, develops the writer's own, conflicting opinion. Organization is strong and logical. The supporting examples are appropriate, well developed, and presented in a logical sequence.

The writing is good, with variety and some complexity in sentence structure and good word choice. Paragraphs are logically arranged and coherent. There are few distracting errors in spelling or punctuation.

2 Essay

It is important for each generation to both earn and define our sense of heritage and what it means to be an American. Some people believe that your just born here and that makes you an American. But people who were not born here have to work very hard to get citizenship and pass a test that most so-called "Americans" probly couldn't even pass.

It's very different for each generation, what it means to be an American. Some generations have to fight in wars. Some like in the 1900's lived through two world wars. This is harder than a generation that has no wars. They might take there freedom for granted, which you wouldn't do if you had to fight in a war.

Some generations live through a depression and others have economic prosperity. This makes it very different to be an American in these two different generations.

Grader's Comments

This writer has only partially formed a response to the topic and never states a clear position. In fact, it isn't clear even how the writer is interpreting the Johnson quotation. There is some organization, but not enough, and ideas are repeated rather than developed. The supporting examples are all too general, with no specificity or detail offered.

Sentences are often awkward, and there are many careless errors ("your" instead of "you're" in the second line and "probly" instead of "probably" in the last line of the first paragraph, for example).

Topic 2

4 Essay

There are some very courageous people in this world. They are the ones who do things that the rest of us would be afraid to do. I never realized what it meant to be brave until read about the actions of the firefighters on September 11th. After that I formed my own definition of courage: to be without fear.

Firefighters are trained to do things that regular people would be horrified to even think of. When everyone is running away from smoke and flames, firefighters are running right into the heat. They must go through rigorous training, learning to use their ropes and axes, learning what to do when there's not enough air to breathe, and learning to maneuver in dark, tight places. They can be trained to know what to do in a burning building. But there's no training that can teach someone to suppress all their natural instincts to run for safety. That is based on one thing: courage.

I used to take firefighters for granted. Newspaper articles told about them rescuing a family from a third floor bedroom, for example, and I wouldn't really think anything of it. That was just what firefighters were supposed to do.

But when I read accounts of the 9/11 New York attacks, it suddenly struck me how phenomenal it was. When I think back even now, I recall the feeling of that day. Nobody knew what was going on or whether there would be more attacks. Everyone I talked to all across the country was scared. And in the midst of that, firefighters were climbing into their trucks and speeding toward ground zero. They were running from their trucks through ash clouds into the buildings. Instead of just helping people come down the stairs, the firefighters charged up the stairs toward the flames, loaded down with heavy equipment and clothes, hauling themselves up thousands of steps without stopping to wonder what lay ahead—only knowing that, whatever it was, they had to control it.

If these firefighters faced each new challenge with fear, and had to stop to conquer their fear, they would never be able to take quick, decisive, incredible actions like these. Because of the tragedy of September 11th, I have seen that some people truly do have courage, and that courage means to entertain no fear.

Grader's Comments

This author uses a well-developed example to support the stated opinion. Descriptive, active phrases such as "climbing into trucks," "running from smoke and flames," and "hauling themselves up thousands of steps" make the essay both interesting and convincing.

This essay is well planned with an engaging introduction, three tightly structured paragraphs of evidence, and a conclusion that follows from the evidence. The author uses keywords such as "when," "but," "suddenly," and "of course" to link sentences or ideas.

The author wrote and chose words carefully: the spelling, grammar, and diction are consistently correct. However, the writer should be careful of over-using the comma.

1 Essay

What is courage? I have wondered this for myself many times. Does having courage mean you have to climb Mt Everst? Does it mean that you need to go fight in a way? Or can you have corage if you just stay home and lead a kind of quiet life?

I think I'm a pretty brave person. I'm not a race car driver or something like that. But I don't run away from fights. I stick up for what I believe in. When I think I'm right I'm not afraid to tell other people what I feel even if they have the opposite opinion or something. I'm chosing my own course in life not letting other people tell me what to do. I'm going to chose the career I want and not the one my parents want me to. They want me to be an engineer because I like drawing. I don't want to be an engineer. I would consider being an architect but right now I still want to be an artist. I think I'm pretty brave in my own way.

Grader's Comments

This essay suggests that the author didn't read the assignment completely: This essay deals with one part of the assignment, the meaning of courage, but leaves out the crux of the assignment, a specific event that taught this to the writer. That makes this essay off topic. It digresses further toward the end, when the author begins to discuss his/her own personal predicament and fails to bring the discussion back to the general topic.

The vocabulary is easy to understand, but the writing is generally inadequate, and the author adds colloquial words and phrases that slow the reader down without adding meaning, such as: "or something," "in a way," and "kind of." There are a careless errors that may have been corrected with careful proofreading.

Practice Test Two Answer Sheet

Remove (or photocopy) the answer sheet and use it to complete the practice test.
See the answer key following the test when finished.

READING SECTION

1. (A) (B) (C) (D) (E)   14. (A) (B) (C) (D) (E)   27. (A) (B) (C) (D) (E)   40. (A) (B) (C) (D) (E)
2. (A) (B) (C) (D) (E)   15. (A) (B) (C) (D) (E)   28. (A) (B) (C) (D) (E)   41. (A) (B) (C) (D) (E)
3. (A) (B) (C) (D) (E)   16. (A) (B) (C) (D) (E)   29. (A) (B) (C) (D) (E)   42. (A) (B) (C) (D) (E)
4. (A) (B) (C) (D) (E)   17. (A) (B) (C) (D) (E)   30. (A) (B) (C) (D) (E)   43. (A) (B) (C) (D) (E)
5. (A) (B) (C) (D) (E)   18. (A) (B) (C) (D) (E)   31. (A) (B) (C) (D) (E)   44. (A) (B) (C) (D) (E)
6. (A) (B) (C) (D) (E)   19. (A) (B) (C) (D) (E)   32. (A) (B) (C) (D) (E)   45. (A) (B) (C) (D) (E)
7. (A) (B) (C) (D) (E)   20. (A) (B) (C) (D) (E)   33. (A) (B) (C) (D) (E)   46. (A) (B) (C) (D) (E)
8. (A) (B) (C) (D) (E)   21. (A) (B) (C) (D) (E)   34. (A) (B) (C) (D) (E)   47. (A) (B) (C) (D) (E)
9. (A) (B) (C) (D) (E)   22. (A) (B) (C) (D) (E)   35. (A) (B) (C) (D) (E)   48. (A) (B) (C) (D) (E)
10. (A) (B) (C) (D) (E)   23. (A) (B) (C) (D) (E)   36. (A) (B) (C) (D) (E)   49. (A) (B) (C) (D) (E)
11. (A) (B) (C) (D) (E)   24. (A) (B) (C) (D) (E)   37. (A) (B) (C) (D) (E)   50. (A) (B) (C) (D) (E)
12. (A) (B) (C) (D) (E)   25. (A) (B) (C) (D) (E)   38. (A) (B) (C) (D) (E)
13. (A) (B) (C) (D) (E)   26. (A) (B) (C) (D) (E)   39. (A) (B) (C) (D) (E)

right in Reading Section

wrong in Reading Section

MATH SECTION

1. (A) (B) (C) (D) (E)   14. (A) (B) (C) (D) (E)   27. (A) (B) (C) (D) (E)   40. (A) (B) (C) (D) (E)
2. (A) (B) (C) (D) (E)   15. (A) (B) (C) (D) (E)   28. (A) (B) (C) (D) (E)   41. (A) (B) (C) (D) (E)
3. (A) (B) (C) (D) (E)   16. (A) (B) (C) (D) (E)   29. (A) (B) (C) (D) (E)   42. (A) (B) (C) (D) (E)
4. (A) (B) (C) (D) (E)   17. (A) (B) (C) (D) (E)   30. (A) (B) (C) (D) (E)   43. (A) (B) (C) (D) (E)
5. (A) (B) (C) (D) (E)   18. (A) (B) (C) (D) (E)   31. (A) (B) (C) (D) (E)   44. (A) (B) (C) (D) (E)
6. (A) (B) (C) (D) (E)   19. (A) (B) (C) (D) (E)   32. (A) (B) (C) (D) (E)   45. (A) (B) (C) (D) (E)
7. (A) (B) (C) (D) (E)   20. (A) (B) (C) (D) (E)   33. (A) (B) (C) (D) (E)   46. (A) (B) (C) (D) (E)
8. (A) (B) (C) (D) (E)   21. (A) (B) (C) (D) (E)   34. (A) (B) (C) (D) (E)   47. (A) (B) (C) (D) (E)
9. (A) (B) (C) (D) (E)   22. (A) (B) (C) (D) (E)   35. (A) (B) (C) (D) (E)   48. (A) (B) (C) (D) (E)
10. (A) (B) (C) (D) (E)   23. (A) (B) (C) (D) (E)   36. (A) (B) (C) (D) (E)   49. (A) (B) (C) (D) (E)
11. (A) (B) (C) (D) (E)   24. (A) (B) (C) (D) (E)   37. (A) (B) (C) (D) (E)   50. (A) (B) (C) (D) (E)
12. (A) (B) (C) (D) (E)   25. (A) (B) (C) (D) (E)   38. (A) (B) (C) (D) (E)
13. (A) (B) (C) (D) (E)   26. (A) (B) (C) (D) (E)   39. (A) (B) (C) (D) (E)

right in Math Section

wrong in Math Section

WRITING SECTION

Lined pages on which you will write your essays can be found in the writing section.

Practice Test Two

Questions 1–3

Many economists believe that improved education is the best long-term solution to the problem of job losses in America. An alternative solution for the problem of unemployment is to implement trade barriers that might result in retaliation by other countries, thus restricting attempts by American businesses to open plants overseas. Education can provide the skills American workers need to compete with skilled workers in other countries around the world. At present, America has a shortage of highly skilled workers and an abundance of less skilled or unskilled workers. To counter the effects of globalization, equal access to knowledge and information is of *paramount* importance, according to these economists.

1. The author of this selection advocates

   (A) improving access to education in America
   (B) implementing trade barriers
   (C) countering the effects of globalization
   (D) training more highly skilled workers
   (E) creating more jobs for unskilled workers

2. The author's logical development

   (A) shows sloppy thinking
   (B) shows the economic connections necessary for a successful society
   (C) focuses too much emphasis on education
   (D) doesn't lead to a conclusion
   (E) should include noneconomic factors

3. As used here, the word *paramount* means

   (A) being overly suspicious
   (B) ranking higher than any other
   (C) secondary
   (D) outside the range of normal
   (E) double

KAPLAN

Questions 4–6

Exploration of the field of robotics has resulted in an invention called an *exoskeleton* that can be fitted to the lower extremities and, through a system of more than 40 sensors and hydraulic mechanisms, function much like the human nervous system, calculating weight distribution of the wearer and how to distribute it so that the weight of the load being borne is minimized. Users put on a pair of special boots and the attached metal leg braces, a power unit, and a backpack, which weigh approximately a hundred pounds. Carrying a seventy-pound pack on their backs, users feel as if they are carrying only 5 pounds. Inventors claim this device can be useful to soldiers, firemen, and emergency rescue workers.

4. The first sentence is an example of

   (A) a complex sentence

   (B) a compound complex sentence

   (C) a compound sentence

   (D) a periodic sentence

   (E) an extended sentence

5. The term *exoskeleton* as used here means

   (A) going beyond what is right or reasonable

   (B) outside the human body

   (C) an external supporting structure

   (D) to make greater in size or bulk or scope

   (E) to make easy the progress of

6. This selection is most likely an excerpt from

   (A) an article on the science of robotics

   (B) an article on new inventions

   (C) a report on new military equipment

   (D) a science fiction tale

   (E) an engineering text

Questions 7–9

The concept of "emotional intelligence" has entered education and the workplace. Psychologists studying this idea believe it can be more responsible for success in life than mental ability, called the IQ or intelligence quotient. Emotional intelligence has to do with being able to be aware of and managing one's own emotions and being sensitive and responsive to the emotions of others. Some psychologists believe emotional intelligence can be learned by very young children and strengthened throughout their school years so that when they are ready to enter the workforce, they can be more successful than they might have been otherwise. Ideally, parents could begin teaching their children these awareness and perceptual skills from infancy, and then preschools, elementary, and secondary schools would all support the development of these skills.

Of course, parents and probably teachers would need to be taught as well. The effort would be worth it because expansion of this concept holds the possibility of a more harmonious and satisfying culture.

7. Which of the following sentences if inserted into the second paragraph would best fit the author's purpose of intention?

   (A) What parents wouldn't want their children to have the best possible chance of success at school and at work?

   (B) Parent classes would have to be set up at schools, churches, and synagogues.

   (C) As the saying goes, "It's not easy to teach an old dog new tricks."

   (D) Training and practice of these skills would be time consuming.

   (E) Working hard at any skill is important for a successful life.

GO ON TO THE NEXT PAGE

8. The author of this selection seems to believe

    (A) emotional intelligence is more important than other intelligence

    (B) emotional intelligence could change our society for the better

    (C) emotional intelligence is about as valuable as IQ

    (D) emotional intelligence is a new concept in psychology

    (E) it would be difficult to teach children emotional intelligence

9. In this selection the author's tone reflects an attitude toward emotional intelligence that is

    (A) dismissive

    (B) favorable

    (C) neutral

    (D) appreciative

    (E) tolerant

Questions 10–12

Do you get enough sleep? Sleep experts are now claiming that Americans are not only overeaters, but they are also under sleepers. Contrary to previous belief, most people should have eight or more hours of sleep a night, experts claim.

Of course, many people work more than one job, leaving less time for sleep, and students who work and study often get by on fewer hours of sleep than eight. One factor that is just beginning to be looked at is the effect of electric lighting on sleep cycles. The United States has only had widespread electricity for about sixty to seventy years. Before that time, most people went to sleep soon after it got dark and rose with the sun in the morning. Researchers are now examining whether extending "daylight" hours through the use of electricity is affecting Americans' circadian rhythm, causing us to sleep fewer hours every day and thousands of fewer hours over a lifetime.

10. *Circadian rhythm* is a term coined by and used primarily in

    (A) medicine

    (B) psychology

    (C) philosophy

    (D) astronomy

    (E) biology

11. The author of this selection uses which of the following devices to engage the reader's attention?

    (A) choosing an interesting topic

    (B) providing new information

    (C) relying on experts

    (D) asking a direct, personal question

    (E) using complex sentences

12. The reader might infer from this selection that

    (A) electric lights are not good for us

    (B) we all need more sleep

    (C) we have changed our environment without regard to consequences

    (D) Americans are damaging their health by overeating and oversleeping

    (E) Americans are using electricity too much

GO ON TO THE NEXT PAGE

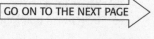

Questions 13–15

Medical research into drugs to treat various ailments often yields lots of "me-too" drugs, medications that mimic the effects of a first successful drug. Similarly, in the fashion industry, many clothing manufacturers create copies or knock-offs of a clever design, which they can sell for less than the original. The movie industry offers other examples of mimicry. Sequels and copycat films always follow films that earn a lot of money. One cannot help but think of the preciousness of human creativity. Imitation is far more often the rule in human endeavor than is inventiveness.

13. The selection exhibits characteristics of which type of essay?

   (A) fictional

   (B) classification

   (C) narrative

   (D) argument

   (E) comparison and contrast

14. As used here, the word "preciousness" is synonymous with

   (A) expensiveness

   (B) precociousness

   (C) special

   (D) rarity

   (E) inventiveness

15. Which of the following sentences offers the best conclusion to the passage?

   (A) Other examples of mimicry can surely be found in other fields.

   (B) True genius, the ability to bring something entirely new to a field, is rare.

   (C) The monetary savings in copying successful products or formats is of greater value than originality.

   (D) You would be in great demand if you had the ability to create a new and successful product.

   (E) There aren't many Einsteins or Newtons to help move mankind forward.

Questions 16–18

Book publishing and reviewing has taken a sharp turn with the advent of the Internet. Readers can review books on various Internet sites and influence sales as much as professional reviewers or critics can. As a result, book sales can increase or decrease sharply based on opinions of everyday readers. Reviews can help publishers find good self-published books that they may have overlooked; on the other hand, writers can see their efforts go for naught as bad reviews cause book sales to *plummet*. Sometimes, the bad reviews are the result of a flame campaign to "get" a writer; sometimes, positive reviews are the result of an author's friends' efforts to help a book's sales. These reader reviews are not as dependable as reviews by independent reviewers. Readers beware! The review you find online may not be very reliable. In the past, readers could count on the quality of a review by a known reviewer and buy a book confident of its quality. Now, anything goes.

16. The writer of the passage seems to be warning readers about online book reviews. The sentence or phrase conveying the warning is

   (A) "… a flame campaign to 'get' a writer"

   (B) "Readers, beware!"

   (C) "Now, anything goes."

   (D) "They are not as dependable as …"

   (E) "… bad reviews cause book sales to plummet"

17. As used in this passage, the word *plummet* means

   (A) to weight heavily

   (B) a token of worth or achievement

   (C) a small plume or tuft

   (D) to plunge

   (E) to float like a feather

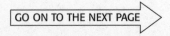
GO ON TO THE NEXT PAGE

18. A phrase that could replace "go for naught" would be

    (A) turn out to be worthless

    (B) turn out to be improper

    (C) cause them to be nauseous

    (D) turn out to leave them at sea

    (E) cause them to want to abandon ship

Questions 19–21

The discovery of water once having been on Mars has reignited intense interest in the red planet once thought to be the home of little green men. Scientists have posited for some time that there are not little green men, but nevertheless, they have looked for some evidence of life forms. The evidence of water is a hopeful sign. While scientists describe the planetary surface they are exploring as *desiccated*, they are looking for striations on rocks that exhibit festooning, tiny curves shaped like smiles on a happy face, and cross bedding, the creation of layers of sedimentary rock at divergent angels. Those telltale signs are from water that has been above ground and that moved slowly over the surface. Scientists have compared the area they are studying to some areas on earth, such as Death Valley in California.

Such interesting data has caused excitement in more than just the scientific community and will probably elicit support from the nation, even the world community, to support further space exploration.

19. This passage could be classified as

    (A) persuasive

    (B) descriptive

    (C) informative

    (D) argumentative

    (E) expository

20. The author of this passage assists the reader in understanding through the use of

    (A) description

    (B) definition

    (C) example

    (D) facts

    (E) new words

21. The word *desiccated* as used in this selection means

    (A) sandy

    (B) gravelly and rocky

    (C) slightly damp

    (D) completely dry

    (E) dry on the surface, but damp below

GO ON TO THE NEXT PAGE

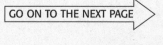

Questions 22–25

Providing a safe care for teenaged drivers doesn't enter the mind of many parents buying their children a first car. Eighteen percent of 16- to 19-year olds own new cars, and 75% own used cars. For many teenagers a car is a status symbol. Instead of looking at factors such as gas mileage, crash test ratings, or whether their teenager has adequate driver training, parents try to find a model that is the most satisfying to their teenager, usually something flashy or fast. Getting a first car is such a significant rite of passage that practical considerations are often thrown to the winds. The fact is that car crashes are the leading cause of death among young people.

Parents would be wise to study their teenager's driving competence and the safety statistics on various models of cars before buying. Certainly they should not give in to their teenager's pleading if the result would be buying an unsafe car.

22. This selection is best described as

   (A) an argument for better driver training methods

   (B) an argument for careful selection of a safe car for teenaged drivers

   (C) an argument for resisting a teenager's pleading for a certain car

   (D) a description of factors involved in selecting a car for a teenager

   (E) an argument for studying accident statistics

23. The phrase "thrown to the winds" in this selection probably means

   (A) tossed like a coin in the air to make a decision

   (B) tossed about like a boat on a stormy sea

   (C) forgotten about

   (D) displeased by other factors

   (E) easily swayed

24. This passage would be improved by

   (A) inclusion of specific safety statistics

   (B) a personal example or story

   (C) a reference to a website

   (D) including names of specific automobile models

   (E) automobile accident data

Questions 25–27

The use of language can be misleading if the speaker and the listener or the writer and the reader do not first agree on a common definition of important words. For example, the word "clean" would seem to be easily understood by everyone. It means not dirty, washed, or sanitized. However, when used regarding pollution by the Environmental Protection Agency in determining which contaminated sites should remain on the superfund list still needing clean up, the meaning becomes vague and unclear to the average person.

Many citizens thought environmental clean up meant removing or sterilizing contaminated soil. In fact, sometimes moving the soil or the damaged waste storage drums was more dangerous than leaving them in place. In those cases, putting a heavy layer of clay over the site was the chosen solution, so that the area remained contaminated, but was to some degree sealed over. Sometimes drains were installed to capture contaminated water before it could percolate down to the water table. These were protective and preventative measures, but did they leave the site *clean*? No.

This is only one example of misunderstanding and misplaced expectations that result from an unclear definition of an important word.

25. Identify which of the following phrases would best introduce the next paragraph in this article.

   (A) Furthermore, another example is …

   (B) On the other hand, people …

   (C) In conclusion, writers and speakers should …

   (D) Following accepted practice, the …

   (E) Another, more serious, example is …

GO ON TO THE NEXT PAGE ⟶

KAPLAN

26. This passage is probably taken from

    (A) an article on environmental solutions

    (B) a handbook for writers

    (C) an article on environmental problems

    (D) an article on clear communication

    (E) a review of environmental policy

27. The writer of this selection seems to be

    (A) arguing for clear communication

    (B) arguing for better government clean up of contaminated sites

    (C) pointing out differences of understanding of words

    (D) describing government obfuscation

    (E) wanting people to agree on definitions

Questions 28–30

Certain cultures place a high value on punctuality. In Japan, Canada, and Scandinavian countries, clocks are always accurate, meetings start on time, and business is done efficiently. In fact, children are trained to be on time from the time they begin school. Interestingly, cultures that value punctuality and live by the clock are more successful economically than cultures that don't. Some countries in South America, the Middle East, and parts of Asia do not value time as highly as others do. People walk more slowly, are routinely late for appointments, and are less economically productive than their more industrialized counterparts. There are many reasons that a culture values tardiness more than timeliness, but the effect on their economy is the same, regardless of the reason.

Estimates are that the habit of tardiness costs Ecuador 10% of its gross national product each year. In recognition of the effect of a lackadaisical attitude toward punctuality, that nation has implemented a national program to be on time. Ecuadorians synchronized their clocks and watches as a first step. Every citizen understands that habitually being on time will produce a stronger economy, and that will mean more money in everyone's pocket. Although the consequence is clear, what is less clear is whether a culture can make such a big shift in behavior over a short period of time.

It may actually be easier now than it was at the start of the Industrial Revolution when people in England had to learn to come to work on the right day as well as at the right time. Before then, the time concept of most people was centered around the seasons and calendar months.

28. Which of the following best organizes the ideas in each paragraph?

    (A) I. Efficiency equals productivity.
        II. A country can lose 10% of its GNP because of tardiness.

    (B) I. Building a strong economy requires timeliness.
        II. It may be easier to teach punctuality now than it once was.

    (C) I. Attitudes toward punctuality determine a country's economic success.
        II. Ecuador is engaged in a major effort to become punctual.

    (D) I. Many counties value tardiness over timeliness.
        II. In Ecuador, people are aware that they are losing money.

    (E) I. Some countries have no concern about punctuality.
        II. Once upon a time, even people in England didn't pay attention to time.

29. The author of this passage seems to

    (A) favor punctuality

    (B) favor a relaxed attitude about time

    (C) have no opinion about punctuality

    (D) think it may be easier now to become punctual than it was 100 years ago

    (E) think certain countries are naturally more punctual

GO ON TO THE NEXT PAGE

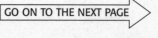

30. One may infer from this selection that

    (A) economic success depends to a great extent on punctuality
    (B) some cultures are basically lazy
    (C) punctuality doesn't make a lot of difference
    (D) to keep a job one must be on time
    (E) countries in the northern hemisphere are more punctual than other countries

Questions 31–33

Although he wanted to be more than a folk singer, he didn't believe at first that he had the life experience or the vocabulary to be a songwriter of any worth, and more than anything, he wanted his work and his name to endure.

Early influences on his performing and his writing were not only the songs of Leadbelly, Elvis Presley, and Woody Guthrie, but also the poetry of Edgar Allen Poe, Lord Byron, John Keats, and John Donne. The work of those poets helped him hone his language. Even the 15th century French poet, Francois Villon, influenced his writing. Imagine a 15th century French poet influencing an American songwriter 500 years later.

31. This selection is most likely taken from

    (A) a music appreciation textbook
    (B) an encyclopedia
    (C) a biographical article in a magazine
    (D) a novel
    (E) an autobiography

32. The style of this selection is

    (A) formal
    (B) informal
    (C) popular
    (D) pedantic
    (E) confessional

33. The author's personal voice is most apparent

    (A) at the end of the first paragraph
    (B) at the end of the second paragraph
    (C) at the beginning of the second paragraph
    (D) throughout the selection
    (E) not at all

Questions 34–36

A recent national survey of middle school, high school, and college teachers revealed interesting but unexpected information. All of those surveyed agreed that English competence is absolutely necessary for students' achievement in college. The surprise came in the differences in teachers' rankings of particular skill importance. College instructors ranked grammar and usage as most important, whereas middle and high school teachers ranked grammar and usage as least important. All agreed that achieving correct sentence structure was the second most important skill. High school teachers ranked writing strategies as most important, whereas college teachers placed that in the position of third importance.

Does this mean that high school students will enter college less well prepared than they should be? Sadly, yes. Teachers tend to teach what they think is important; the study revealed that 30% of high school teachers did not teach grammar and usage at all. It may be postulated that more than 30% of teachers taught very little grammar. It is likely that these nonteaching teachers do not feel comfortable teaching grammar and usage because they don't understand it well themselves. Or they may feel that correcting students' grammar errors and giving individual help is too time consuming. Whatever the reason, students' needs are not being served.

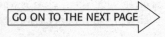
GO ON TO THE NEXT PAGE

34. The author's statements suggest that he assumes

    (A) high school teachers are lazy

    (B) high school teachers don't understand grammar and usage

    (C) some high school teachers don't have time to grade lots of papers

    (D) high school teachers should take grammar courses

    (E) some high school teachers don't feel comfortable teaching grammar and usage

35. The data presented in the passage indicates that

    (A) teachers agree that English proficiency is weak among students

    (B) college teachers don't think grammar is important

    (C) high school teachers disagree with college teachers about the importance of sentence structure

    (D) 30% of high school teachers teach grammar

    (E) all teachers agree that college students must be competent in order to succeed in college

36. A reader of this passage might infer that

    (A) most high school graduates have learned enough grammar

    (B) more teaching of grammar in high school is needed

    (C) college teachers can teach what students don't know

    (D) high school and college teachers need to come to an agreement about the importance of grammar instruction

    (E) the author is only presenting information and not implying anything

Questions 37–39

Can teachers help students learn to think "outside the box?" If they could, human progress in science, politics, relationships, and, in fact, progress in any field would explode. In science, for example, asking unusual or probing questions often leads to new discoveries that improve medical treatment or to new devices that make manufacturing production more efficient.

Medical researchers might ask questions like, "How can drugs we already use be applied in different dosages to a myriad of medical conditions?" Questions *of that ilk* have led to tests of what was originally an antiseizure drug for use as a weight loss drug. Weight loss was an undesirable side effect of the antiseizure drug but might be a desirable characteristic for someone who is obese.

Another different kind of question that stimulated new discoveries was, "Could drugs be added to surgically implanted devices to enhance their performance or longevity, and thus, their effectiveness?" The answer was yes. The question led to further questions about how that answer may be applied.

Teachers need to be alert to students' questions that are unusual or are not easily answered. Rather than saying "no" or stifling the questioner, a good teacher will encourage exploration of ideas and the continual asking of questions as one idea leads to another.

37. This selection is probably taken from

    (A) an article or book chapter on developing creative thinking

    (B) an article about science research

    (C) an article exploring expansion of human progress

    (D) an article about medical science

    (E) an article on how to be a better teacher

GO ON TO THE NEXT PAGE

38. The phrase *of that ilk* means

    (A) of an unusual nature

    (B) being scientific

    (C) in the medical field

    (D) of the same sort or class

    (E) of similar appearance

39. Which of the following sentences inserted in the first paragraph would best fit the author's intention?

    (A) Teachers could try to train students to think creatively.

    (B) Frustrating as students can be, teachers should make every effort to stimulate thinking.

    (C) Routine memorization of information leads in the wrong direction.

    (D) You could become successful by asking the right questions.

    (E) Some thinkers seem to have a gift for creative thinking.

Questions 40–42

December is summer in Antarctica, but that doesn't mean there are meadows of grass and fields of flowers. In fact, ice can be a formidable barrier to exploration if it moves and makes an ocean route impossible to traverse. Recently, a band of fossil explorers on their way to excavate and retrieve a rare dinosaur skeleton found their way blocked by ice and were forced to explore another, more accessible area instead. Imagine their surprise when they found jaw and feet fragments from a meat-eating dinosaur. Why surprise? Scientists have only found a few dinosaurs in that area and never a meat eater as old as this one.

The new find was a marine mammal of some 70 million or more years ago. Perhaps it could be called a prehistoric sea monster.

The *intrepid* explorers had to travel 10 miles a day from their camp to the excavation site. Their effort and persistence paid off, however, as they brought back a significant find.

40. The phrase, "meadows of grass and fields of flowers" is an example of

    (A) descriptive detail

    (B) parallel structure

    (C) naturalism

    (D) coordinating structure

    (E) creative phrasing

41. *Intrepid* as used in this selection means

    (A) fearless, dauntless

    (B) trapped, blocked

    (C) frustrated

    (D) fossil, dinosaur

    (E) energetic, healthy

42. What was most significant about the find described in the selection?

    (A) it was unexpected

    (B) it was an ocean mammal

    (C) it was a surprise

    (D) it was a meat-eating dinosaur

    (E) it was older than other dinosaurs

GO ON TO THE NEXT PAGE

KAPLAN

Questions 43–45

Among the planets in the solar system, earth is unique. It is solid and also active. The surface constantly changes through volcanic and tectonic actions, not to mention the more subtle change caused by storms, wind, and water erosion. Gross geologic charges gradually fold surface material beneath the earth's crust, and thus, our understanding of the earth's history is very limited. Rock and fossil records are unavailable, having been buried over millennia, and we have only been able to send any kind of exploratory device down seven and one-half miles. The center of earth is 4,000 miles below the surface.

Scientists are trying to deal with this lack of information by attempting to create an organism that might have existed even earlier than DNA. Even at that, we are only "scratching the surface" of the knowledge we could have if we could only find a way to *glean* it.

43. Which of the following sentences, inserted at the end of the first paragraph, would best fit the author's intention?

(A) The bulk of the earth's geologic and biological history is unavailable with the techniques we now have.

(B) That means over 90% of the earth's records are unavailable to us.

(C) Therefore, retrieving the oldest information is not only very difficult, it is impossible.

(D) If scientists can develop an early organism, they may be on to the way to creating life.

(E) Finding answers is the purpose of scientific research.

44. The word *glean* as used in this passage means

(A) a flash or beam of light

(B) a brief or slight manifestation or appearance

(C) to gather what is left by reapers

(D) to gather, learn, or find out

(E) to move slowly or cautiously along

45. According to the selection, earth is unique in the solar system because

(A) it is both solid and active

(B) the surface changes through volcanic action

(C) wind and water erosion from its surface

(D) we are able to only "scratch" the surface

(E) surface material is folded beneath the earth's crust

Questions 46–47

"Good night, sleep tight, don't let the bedbugs bite" or "You're snug as a bug in a rug". These are sayings most American children have heard as they were tucked into bed each night. For us as little children, bedbugs were part of our fantasy life. We had never seen them as real characters in fairy tales. They seemed to be from another, older culture when people weren't as clean as they are now.

But bedbugs are not gone. They emerge at night from the walls of houses or old furniture or bedding to bite us and suck our blood. You may never see a bedbug, but you can tell if there might have been one in your bed if you find tiny spots of blood when you get up in the morning. People have been warned that they may pick them up in motel rooms or carry them home in their luggage from foreign travels. They do not carry disease but are repugnant to most people. No one likes to think of sleeping with bugs, fleas, or lice.

46. The author implies that

(A) bedbugs are in walls and old furniture

(B) bedbugs are more present than we have believed

(C) bedbugs come home with travelers in their suitcases

(D) no one likes to sleep with bugs or lice

(E) the old sayings about bedbugs were wrong

GO ON TO THE NEXT PAGE

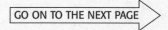

47. The author's purpose seems to be

    (A) to inform the reader
    (B) to disabuse the reader of false beliefs
    (C) to explain that bedbugs are not harmful
    (D) to remind the reader of old sayings
    (E) to frighten the reader

Questions 48–50

Index

Percentage of a class	53
Percentiles	121
Pictogram	73
Pie chart	54
Placebo effect	27
Point estimate	350,354
Poison distribution	153
Poison, Simeon	153,310
Pool	419
Population data	79–81

48. On which page(s) would you look for information on bar graphs and pie charts?

    (A) 350, 354
    (B) 73
    (C) 53
    (D) 121
    (E) 54

49. Where would one look to compare mortality data for two countries?

    (A) 79–81
    (B) 73
    (C) 53
    (D) 121
    (E) 54

50. On which page(s) would you look to find information on a substance having no pharmacological effect?

    (A) 121
    (B) 153
    (C) 79–81
    (D) 73
    (E) 27

GO ON TO THE NEXT PAGE

KAPLAN

Math Section

50 Questions

Directions: Each of the questions in this test is followed by five suggested answers. Select the one that is best in each case. Be sure to mark all of your answers in the Mathematics section of your answer sheet.

1. A caterer estimates that five gallons of potato salad will serve 100 people. If potato salad is prepared only in gallon quantities, how many gallons should be prepared to serve 35 people?

   (A) 7 gallons
   (B) 1.75 gallons
   (C) 1 gallon
   (D) 15 gallons
   (E) 2 gallons

2. Which of the following numbers is (are) prime?

   I. 17
   II. 71
   III. 117

   (A) I only
   (B) II only
   (C) I and II only
   (D) III only
   (E) All three of these numbers are prime.

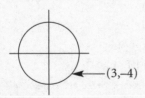

3. The ordered pair $(3, -4)$ represents a point on a circle that has its center at the origin. The point with ordered pair $(0, y)$ is also on the circle. What is a possible value of y?

   (A) 5
   (B) 0
   (C) −1
   (D) 7
   (E) −4

4. One number is one more than twice another number. Five times the smaller number plus three times the larger number is equal to 25. Find the numbers.

   Which of the following equations may be used to solve the problem above?

   (A) $x + (2x + 1) = 25$
   (B) $5x + 3(2x + 1) = 25$
   (C) $3x + 5(2x + 1) = 25$
   (D) $5(x + 1) + 3(2x) = 25$
   (E) $5x + 3(2x - 1) = 25$

5. Perform the indicated operations: $5 - 3(4 + 1) =$

   (A) −4
   (B) 10
   (C) 20
   (D) −10
   (E) None of these.

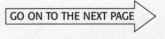

GO ON TO THE NEXT PAGE

KAPLAN

6. Six people were asked, "How many brothers and sisters do you have?"

Barbara	3
Roxanne	1
Denise	3
Scott	2
Laurie	1
Bobby	3

   One person from this group of six is chosen at random. What is the probability that this person had 3 brothers and sisters?

   (A) $\frac{1}{2}$

   (B) $\frac{1}{6}$

   (C) $\frac{1}{3}$

   (D) $\frac{5}{6}$

   (E) 3

7. Tom has been hired to paint a house. He has measured the house and determined that there are approximately 2,600 square feet of siding to be painted with two coats of paint. In order to calculate the number of gallons of paint he will need for the entire job, what additional information must Tom know?

   (A) the approximate amount of time it takes for Tom to apply one gallon of paint

   (B) the amount of time Tom estimates it will take him to complete the job

   (C) the approximate number of square feet one gallon of paint will cover

   (D) the approximate cost of one gallon of paint

   (E) the type of siding, clapboard, or stucco to be painted

8. Which of the following numbers is not between $\frac{3}{8}$ and $\frac{5}{6}$?

   (A) $\frac{1}{2}$

   (B) $\frac{3}{4}$

   (C) $\frac{2}{3}$

   (D) $\frac{1}{3}$

   (E) $\frac{5}{8}$

9. The catch in Placid Lake on a Sunday included 45 trout, 125 bass, and 30 catfish. What percent of the catch was catfish?

   (A) 30%

   (B) 15%

   (C) 60%

   (D) 22.5%

   (E) 24%

10. If x is a whole number and x^2 is odd, which of the following is (are) true?

    I. x is odd.
    II. $x + 2$ is even.
    III. $2x$ is even.

    (A) I only

    (B) II only

    (C) I and II only

    (D) I and III only

    (E) All three of these are true.

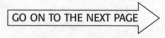
GO ON TO THE NEXT PAGE

KAPLAN

11. When Russell's gas tank showed $\frac{1}{4}$ full, he stopped to fill the tank. If it took 9 gallons to fill the tank, what is the capacity of the tank?

    (A) $6\frac{3}{4}$ gallons

    (B) 12 gallons

    (C) 16 gallons

    (D) 36 gallons

    (E) 27 gallons

12. If x, y, and z are whole numbers that are multiples of 5, which of the following expressions represent whole numbers that are also multiples of 5.

    I. $x + y - z$
    II. $x^2 + y^2 - z^2$
    III. $\frac{xy}{z}$

    (A) I only

    (B) I and II only

    (C) III only

    (D) II and III only

    (E) All three of these.

13. Six people meet at a party. If each person shakes hands with each other person once, how many handshakes will there be?

    (A) 6

    (B) 12

    (C) 15

    (D) 21

    (E) 36

14. Which of the following algebraic expressions is an interpretation of the following phrase?

    One less than two-thirds of a certain number.

    (A) $\frac{2n - 1}{3}$

    (B) $1 - \frac{2}{3}n$

    (C) $\frac{2}{3}n - 1$

    (D) $\frac{1 - 2n}{3}$

    (E) $\frac{2}{3}(n - 1)$

15. Which of the following numbers is not equal to the others?

    (A) 0.2

    (B) $\frac{1}{5}$

    (C) 20%

    (D) $\frac{2}{5} \div 2$

    (E) $2 \div \frac{2}{5}$

16. If $x + y + z = 70$ and $x < 5$, then which of the following must be true?

    (A) $y + z > 65$

    (B) $y + z < 75$

    (C) $y + z > 75$

    (D) $y + z < 65$

    (E) None of these.

GO ON TO THE NEXT PAGE

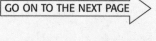

17. Diane bought 8 yards of material. She intends to make blouses from the material that require 1 yard 2 feet for each blouse. How many blouses can she make?

    (A) 3

    (B) 4

    (C) $4\frac{4}{5}$

    (D) 5

    (E) 8

18. The following information is known about five people who took a standardized test.

	Score	Percent	Percentile rank
Tom	45	56	60
Kim	72	90	92
Jim	40	50	56
Brian	63	79	75
Steve	69	86	80

    Which of the following statements is true regarding this information?

    (A) Each of these five people scored above the median.

    (B) Each of these five people scored above the mean.

    (C) No one who took the test got a perfect score.

    (D) Tom scored better than 56 percent of the people who took the test.

    (E) Eighty percent of the people who took the test scored better than Steve.

19. The total cost of lunch is $16.38, including 5% sales tax. How much of the total bill is tax?

    (A) 82 cents

    (B) $15.60

    (C) 78 cents

    (D) $17.20

    (E) $8.19

20. What is the simplified form of $(x + 1)(x - 5)$?

    (A) $x^2 - 5$

    (B) $x^2 + 4x - 5$

    (C) $x^2 + 4x + 5$

    (D) $x^2 + 5$

    (E) $x^2 - 4x - 5$

21. Given a circle with center at O and inscribed $\angle ACB$, if the measure of $\angle AOB$ is 80°, what is the measure of $\angle ACB$?

    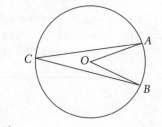

    (A) 80°

    (B) 15°

    (C) 20°

    (D) 40°

    (E) There is not enough information given to determine the measure of $\angle ACB$.

22. When Ray commutes to work at 50 miles per hour, he gets to work in 30 minutes. Bad weather one day forced him to drive at 40 miles per hour. How long should it take him to get to work at this reduced speed?

    (A) 24 minutes

    (B) 35 minutes

    (C) $42\frac{1}{2}$ minutes

    (D) 40 minutes

    (E) $37\frac{1}{2}$ minutes

GO ON TO THE NEXT PAGE

KAPLAN

23. If x represents an odd whole number, what represents the next larger odd whole number?

    (A) $x + 1$

    (B) $x + 3$

    (C) $x + 2$

    (D) $2x + 1$

    (E) $2x - 1$

24. A line passes through the points $A(0, 5)$ and $B(8, 0)$. Find the y-value at the point $C(5, y)$ on the line.

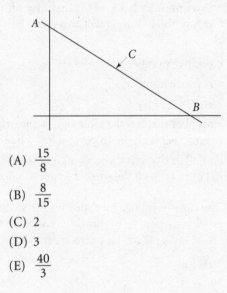

    (A) $\dfrac{15}{8}$

    (B) $\dfrac{8}{15}$

    (C) 2

    (D) 3

    (E) $\dfrac{40}{3}$

25. Which of the following graphs represents the trip described below?

Heather starts slowly on her commute to work 20 miles away. She increases her speed gradually on the freeway. About midway on her commute she has to slow her speed because of an accident. When she passes the accident, she gradually increases her speed until the end of her commute when she gradually slows to a stop at her work. The entire trip took one hour.

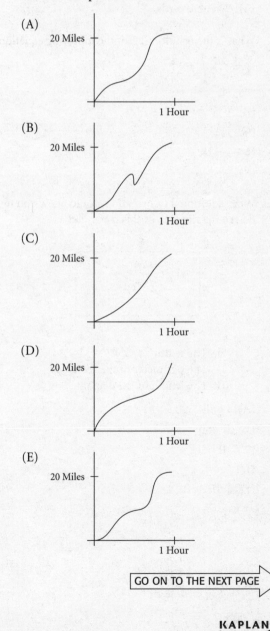

GO ON TO THE NEXT PAGE

KAPLAN

26. The Stewarts are building a circular patio with a diameter of 30 feet. They plan that the concrete slab will be 4 inches thick. If concrete can be ordered as a whole number of cubic yards only, how many cubic yards should they order?

    (A) 8.727 cubic yards

    (B) 9 cubic yards

    (C) 105 cubic yards

    (D) 79 cubic yards

    (E) 27 cubic yards

27. What is the solution set for the following equation?
    $$\frac{x}{3} - \frac{x+1}{2} = \frac{4}{3}$$

    (A) {1}

    (B) {−5}

    (C) {11}

    (D) {−11}

    (E) {−7}

28. What additional information would allow you to determine the area of this rectangle?

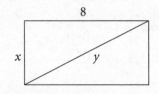

    I. The width
    II. The perimeter of the rectangle
    III. The length of the diagonal

    (A) I only

    (B) II only

    (C) III only

    (D) I or II

    (E) I, II, or III

29. Three-eighth's of Mrs. Weber's class of 40 students is female. Twenty percent of her female students received the grade of A on a recent spelling test. How many of her students were females who got an A on the spelling test?

    (A) 3

    (B) 6

    (C) 8

    (D) 9

    (E) 15

30. If a positive number is added to a negative number, which of the following will always be the result?

    (A) a positive number

    (B) a negative number

    (C) zero

    (D) a number that has the same sign as the original number with the larger absolute value

    (E) a number that has the same sign as the original number with the smaller absolute value

31. *Chili con carne* is on sale for four cans for $6.00. The usual price per can of this chili is $1.69. What is the total saving when four cans are purchased?

    (A) 76 cents

    (B) 19 cents

    (C) $6.76

    (D) $1.50

    (E) None of these.

32. What is the value of $2x^2 - y$ if $x = -3$ and $y = -5$?

    (A) 31

    (B) −31

    (C) 23

    (D) 41

    (E) 53

GO ON TO THE NEXT PAGE

33. On a high school basketball team, the average height of the two guards is 5 feet 9 inches. The average height of the two forwards is 6 feet. The center is 6 feet 4 inches tall. What is the average height of the team?

    (A) $72\frac{1}{3}$ inches

    (B) 6 feet

    (C) 70.5 inches

    (D) 71.6 inches

    (E) 73.2 inches

34. Mary bought the items in this table at the grocery store. If she paid with a twenty dollar bill, how much change did she receive?

2 dozen eggs	$2.75 per dozen
1 gallon milk	$3.80 per gallon
2 boxes cereal	$3.50 per box
4 cans baked beans	89 cents per can

    (A) $19.86

    (B) 14 cents

    (C) $9.06

    (D) $10.94

    (E) None of these.

35. Mike can type five pages in 6 minutes. At this rate, how long will it take him to type 8 pages?

    (A) 3 minutes 45 seconds

    (B) 6 minutes 40 seconds

    (C) 8 minutes 30 seconds

    (D) 10 minutes

    (E) 9 minutes 36 seconds

36. Myrna raised the price of an item in her gift shop 10%. Seeing that it didn't sell at that price, she lowered the price on the item by 10%. How does the final price compare to the initial price?

    (A) The final price is higher than the initial price.

    (B) The final price is lower than the initial price.

    (C) The final price is the same as the original price.

    (D) The comparison of final and initial prices depends on the actual cost of the item.

    (E) There is no way to determine how the final and initial prices compare.

37. How many different amounts of money can be formed by choosing at least one coin from among two pennies, one nickel, and one dime?

    (A) 11

    (B) 8

    (C) 6

    (D) 4

    (E) 3

38. Which of the following sets of three numbers could not be the lengths of the sides of a triangle?

    (A) $\{5, 8, 11\}$

    (B) $\left\{\frac{1}{2}, \frac{2}{3}, \frac{3}{4}\right\}$

    (C) $\sqrt{5}, \sqrt{5}, \sqrt{5}$

    (D) $\{5, 9, 20\}$

    (E) $\{3, 4, 5\}$

GO ON TO THE NEXT PAGE

KAPLAN

39. Prices for regular gasoline during the month of April are given in the accompanying table. What is the approximate weekly percent increase for the fourth week of the month?

Week in April	Price of regular gasoline
1	$2.00
2	$2.10
3	$2.31
4	$2.38

(A) 19%

(B) 7%

(C) 3%

(D) 5%

(E) 38%

40. Which of the following equations can be used to solve the following problem?

At 8:00 A.M. Britney starts out on her bicycle at 15 miles per hour. One-half hour later, Sunny starts out on the same route at 20 miles per hour. At what time will Sunny catch Britney?

(A) $15\left(x - \dfrac{1}{2}\right) = 20x$

(B) $15x = 20\left(x - \dfrac{1}{2}\right)$

(C) $15x + 20\left(x - \dfrac{1}{2}\right) = 8$

(D) $15x = 20(x - 30)$

(E) $15x = 20(x + 30)$

41. The floor of a room that is 10 feet 9 inches wide is to be tiled using square tiles that are 9 by 9 inches. Beginning at the center of the room, 13 tiles are laid out. The same amount is to be trimmed off the tiles that butt up against the wall on both sides of the room. How many inches should be cut off of each of the tiles on the sides of the room?

(A) 3 inches

(B) 6 inches

(C) $4\dfrac{1}{2}$ inches

(D) $7\dfrac{1}{2}$ inches

(E) None of these.

42. What is the simplified form of the following expression?

$(x - 5) + 2[x - 3(x - 1)]$

(A) $-3x - 17$

(B) $-3x - 11$

(C) -6

(D) $-3x + 1$

(E) -2

43. If $a > 0$ and $b < 0$, then which of the following is true?

(A) $ab > 0$

(B) $a + b > 0$

(C) $a - b > 0$

(D) $\dfrac{1}{b} > \dfrac{1}{a}$

(E) $a + b < 0$

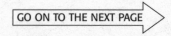
GO ON TO THE NEXT PAGE

KAPLAN

44. An equilateral triangle and a square have the same perimeter. If the area of the square is 36 square inches, what is the length of one side of the triangle?

    (A) 6 inches
    (B) $16\sqrt{3}$ inches
    (C) 18 inches
    (D) 24 inches
    (E) 8 inches

45. What is the number of degrees formed by the hands of a clock at 2:00?

    (A) 60 degrees
    (B) 120 degrees
    (C) 20 degrees
    (D) 30 degrees
    (E) 90 degrees

46. For a craft project, three pieces of rope, each 1 foot 7 inches long, are cut from a spool that had 12 feet to begin with. What length of rope remains on the spool?

    (A) 4 feet 9 inches
    (B) 7 feet 3 inches
    (C) 7 feet 1 inch
    (D) 6 feet 11 inches
    (E) None of these.

47. On January 1, the Henning's fuel tank of 80 gallons was full. During the first week on January, $\frac{2}{5}$ of the fuel was used to heat their house. During the second week, $\frac{1}{3}$ of the remaining fuel was used. How many gallons of fuel remain at the beginning of the third week of January?

    (A) $10\frac{2}{3}$ gallons
    (B) 16 gallons
    (C) 32 gallons
    (D) 48 gallons
    (E) 64 gallons

48. Alex has 15 coins consisting of nickels, dimes, and pennies. He has twice as many pennies as dimes. If the value of his coins is 66 cents, how many dimes does he have?

    (A) 6
    (B) 9
    (C) 1
    (D) 3
    (E) 0

GO ON TO THE NEXT PAGE

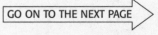

KAPLAN

49. If the diameter of a circle is multiplied by 3, how many times larger will the area of the circle be?

   (A) 9

   (B) 6

   (C) 3

   (D) 27

   (E) 9π

50. A chain that weighs 3 pounds per foot is hanging over the edge of the roof of a building that is 100 feet high. At the end of the chain a bucket is attached that weighs 5 pounds, and the bucket contains water that weighs 62 pounds. If the end of the chain is 70 feet from the ground, what is the total weight that is hanging from the edge of the roof?

   (A) 97 pounds

   (B) 367 pounds

   (C) 277 pounds

   (D) 67 pounds

   (E) 157 pounds

GO ON TO THE NEXT PAGE

Writing Section

Directions: The Writing section contains two essay topics. Be sure you write about the given topics. Essays on topics of your choosing will not be acceptable. Your written responses must be your work, must be in your own words, and must not be plagiarized from some other work.

The topics are designed to give you an opportunity to demonstrate your skills in writing effectively. Spend some time considering the topics and organizing your ideas before you start. For the essays, be sure to address all parts of the topics, support generalizations with examples, and use multiple paragraphs.

You may use any space provided in the test booklet to write notes or to prepare an outline or rough draft. However, your score will be based solely on the versions written in the space provided in your answer document. Please write as neatly and legibly as possible. To ensure that you have enough space for your essays, do not skip lines, write in large print, or leave large margins.

TOPIC 1

According to Katherine Paterson in *The Spying Heart*, "Our fundamental task as human beings is to seek out connections—to exercise our imaginations. It follows, then, that the basic task of education is the care and feeding of the imagination." Do you agree or disagree with this observation, and to what extent? Offer specific examples supporting your opinion.

_____

_____

_____

_____

_____

_____

_____

_____

GO ON TO THE NEXT PAGE

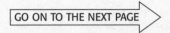

GO ON TO THE NEXT PAGE

KAPLAN

TOPIC 2

Most students had a moment when they first realized for the first time that real education meant more than memorizing facts. Write about a situation that helped you learn this important truth. How has it affected choices you made in life? What other things, besides facts, are important to education?

_____

_____

_____

_____

_____

_____

_____

_____

_____

_____

_____

_____

_____

_____

_____

_____

_____

_____

GO ON TO THE NEXT PAGE ⟩

KAPLAN

STOP

Practice Test Two: **Answer Key**

READING TEST		MATH TEST		WRITING TEST
1. D	26. D	1. E	26. B	See Sample Essays on page 291.
2. B	27. A	2. C	27. D	
3. B	28. C	3. A	28. E	
4. A	29. D	4. B	29. A	
5. C	30. A	5. D	30. D	
6. B	31. A	6. A	31. A	
7. A	32. B	7. C	32. C	
8. B	33. B	8. D	33. D	
9. B	34. E	9. B	34. B	
10. E	35. E	10. D	35. E	
11. D	36. B	11. B	36. B	
12. C	37. E	12. B	37. A	
13. E	38. D	13. C	38. D	
14. D	39. E	14. C	39. C	
15. B	40. B	15. E	40. B	
16. B	41. A	16. A	41. A	
17. D	42. D	17. B	42. D	
18. A	43. B	18. A	43. C	
19. B	44. D	19. C	44. E	
20. B	45. A	20. E	45. A	
21. D	46. B	21. D	46. B	
22. B	47. A	22. E	47. C	
23. C	48. E	23. C	48. D	
24. A	49. A	24. A	49. A	
25. E	50. E	25. E	50. E	

KAPLAN

Answers and Explanations

READING SECTION

1. D

Remember you are looking for the *best* answer. (A) is a possibility, but (D) is best because it is more specific. (B) is obviously wrong; it is called an "alternative solution." (E) is also incorrect, as creating more jobs isn't mentioned.

2. B

The thinking is very clear and logically presented, so (A) is not a possibility. The main point of the passage focuses on education, so (C) is not correct. (D) is not correct because the conclusion is clearly stated in the last sentence. (E) is incorrect since the passage is about education, jobs, and economic and noneconomic factors.

3. B

Look at the structure and meaning of the sentence. *Paramount* (B) is an adjective; (A) is not. (C) is, but the sentence meaning is compromised. (D) and (E) do not fit in terms of meaning in context.

4. A

A *complex sentence* contains a main clause and one subordinate clause. There are no compound sentences in the paragraph, so (B) and (C) are incorrect. A *periodic sentence* (D) saves the main clause until the end of the sentence. An *extended sentence* (E) is not a classification of sentence type.

5. C

(A) is not an appropriate choice because it does not relate to the topic. (B), (D), and (E) might all apply, but (C) is the best answer because it describes the purpose of the exoskeleton. *Exo* means outside.

6. B

The article mentions the field of *robotics* (A), which indicates that the article is from a source outside that field. It is not in the language of *science fiction* (D) nor of *engineering* (E). It will be used by those other than soldiers, so (C) is too narrow a choice.

7. A

(A) is the best answer. (B) an (E), while interesting, do not contribute meaningfully to the passage. Each would need to be more fully developed than one line allows for. (C) is a poor choice because of tone.

8. B

This information is clearly stated in the last sentence of the paragraph. The writer does not actually claim (A), (C), (D) or (E).

9. B

Neither (A), (C), nor (E) is appropriate. Reread the selection carefully. *Appreciative* (D) is possible, but (B) is a better answer.

10. E

Circadian rhythm is used in studying all life forms, so biology is the only appropriate answer. It may be referred to in *medicine* (A), *psychology* (B), or *astronomy* (D) but not in *philosophy* (C).

11. D

Complex sentences (E) do not necessarily hold a reader's attention; neither do the other choices, but asking a direct question at the beginning catches the reader's personal interest.

12. C

This choice is an inference that can be made from reading the whole passage. The other choices are either not implied (A), (D), and (E) or are directly stated (B).

13. E

The writer compares the same phenomenon occurring in several industries. The other choices do not apply. (A) is incorrect because there is no such thing as a fictional essay. (B) is incorrect because information is not being classified as to type. (C) is incorrect because this is not a story (narrative). (D) is incorrect because there is no argument set forth.

14. D

The paragraph says that true creativity or inventiveness is rare. See the last sentence. The other options are not applicable. (A) and (C) are sometimes associated in meaning; (B) is not. It means *a child acting like an adult*. (E) does not make sense.

15. B

(B) is the best choice because it sums up the passage. (A) is not a good choice because it suggests there may be more following it. (C) is a poor choice because it brings in a new idea. (D), using second person, would not fit in with the rest of the passage. (E) is also not a good conclusion because it introduces a new idea.

16. B

Readers, beware! is the only obvious warning. (A), (C), (D), and (E) are phrases, not warnings.

17. D

In context, this is the only choice that fits. Reread the selection carefully. Do not confuse plummet with plume (C) or with (A), which could be associated with *plumb*.

18. A

(A) is the best answer. Naught is a synonym for nothing. Choices (B) and (C) do not make sense in the sentence. (D) and (E) could be misleading because of their association with "nautical."

19. B

The passage primarily describes the surface of Mars. It does not try to persuade (A) and (D). It is *informative* (C), but that is not the best answer. Neither is (E). See the middle of the first paragraph.

20. B

The author defines festooning and cross bedding. He does use examples (C), but that is not the best answer, nor is (A) the best. (E) does not fit because new words are what he is defining.

21. D

The presence of water on Mars is described in the past tense. Present day comparisons are to Death Valley where there is some dampness below the surface. While choices (A), (B), and (D) may appear possible, they are not the best answers, and (C) is obviously wrong.

22. B

The main idea, providing a safe car, is set forth in the first sentence of the first paragraph and in the second paragraph. The other choices are not as complete in scope.

23. C

Read the context. Choices (A), (B), (D), and (E) would not make sense within the sentence. (C) is a less dramatic way to say *thrown to the winds*.

24. A

Good use of statistics will always strengthen an argument. Specific safety statistics on cars would be more useful than general automobile accident data (E) or personal example (B). Choices (C) and (D) would not help clarify or persuade.

25. E

While (A) looks like a possibility, (E) is a better answer in terms of the flow of the argument. (B), (C), and (D) do not follow logically. It's too early for a conclusion.

26. D

The selection talks about the environment, but it is mostly about clear communication. See the beginning and the last sentences. It teaches about writing (B).

27. A

(A) is the best and most straightforward answer. (C) and (E), while close, are not the best. (B) and (D) are not accurate because they are not mentioned.

28. C

(C) is the best answer because it generalizes the points in each paragraph. (A)-I is too general and (A)-II is too specific. The same can be said for (B). (D) and (E) are poor choices because I is vague and II in each case is really a subpoint.

29. D

This answer appears in the second to last sentence of the last paragraph. (A) and (E) are possible answers, but the writer doesn't offer an opinion. So (C), while close, is still not the best.

30. A

This is the most logical inference. The other choices do not necessarily follow from the passage. Laziness (B) is not mentioned. (C) is clearly incorrect from careful reading. (D) is possible but not the best answer. (E) is directly stated.

31. A

While the answer could be (C), (A) is a better choice. The style suggests information given without the usual detail of a magazine biography (C). Neither is the style typical of an *encyclopedia* (B). The other options are not close. (D) is incorrect because it is not in the style of a *novel*. (E) is incorrect because the passage is biographical, not in first person.

32. B

The language used is informal rather than *formal* or *pedantic* (A) and (D). It is biographical, so it cannot be *confessional* (E). *Popular* (C) is not a correct label to apply to style.

33. B

The last sentence in the second paragraph is the author's voice intruding on the informational, impersonal prose (D). (E) is incorrect because there is one personal sentence. Reread the selection carefully.

34. E

This is clearly stated in the second paragraph. (A) and (D) are not stated at all. (B) and (C) are called possibilities, not assumptions.

35. E

See the second sentence of the first paragraph. (A) is not stated. (B) is not stated. (C) is not correct because all teachers agree about sentence structure. (D) is incorrect because 30% did not teach grammar.

36. B

(A) and (C) are discounted in the passage. The passage is not about getting teachers to agree. The author is speculating in the last part of the last paragraph, so (E) is not a viable choice.

37. E

If you read the first and last paragraphs, you will see that the information is set in the context of teaching. (A) is not as good a choice because it is outside the focus of the article. (B) is also not good because the science research is used as an example in the larger context. (C) is a poor choice because it is too broad. (D) is too focused on the details of the article.

38. D

This is not the correct dictionary definition, but it is more to the point in terms of context than (A), (B), (C), or (E).

39. E

(A) is a poor choice because its tone is somewhat passive. (B) is poor because of the word *frustrating*. It introduces a negative tone. (C) is poor because it, like (A) and (B), does not lead the reader logically to the next sentence. (D) is poor because it uses the second person, which is not in line with the rest of the passage.

40. B

Parallel structure is obvious in the repeated grammatical form: a noun followed by a prepositional phrase. (A), while possible, is not accurate. (C) is not correct because naturalism is a type of writing. (D) and (E) are incorrect because they are not accurate labels.

41. A

These explorers did not give up as discussed in the first and third paragraphs. Fearless and dauntless are correct. (B), (C), and (E) are possible in terms of the paragraph content, but not accurate.

42. D

The explorers were surprised (A) and (C), but the most significant fact was that the dinosaur was a meat eater. See the last sentence in paragraph one. (B) and (E) are possible but not the best answers.

43. B

(A) is a fine general statement but does not follow logically from the preceding sentence. (C) is a poor choice because it does sum up the paragraph but does not follow gracefully from the preceding sentence (D) is not acceptable because its topic belongs in the next paragraph. (E) is a true statement but unrelated to the first paragraph.

44. D

Look at the context of the sentence. (A) is incorrect. A flash or beam of light is a gleam. The same could be said for (B), whose definition is glimmer. (C) was the original meaning of *glean*. (E) is plainly incorrect.

45. A

See the second sentence in the first paragraph. (B), (C), (D), and (E) are all possible answers but not complete.

46. B

See the second paragraph. (A), (C), and (D) are directly stated, not implied. (E) is not mentioned.

47. A

There is a lot of information in this passage. The other answer choices, (B), (C), (D), and (E), are not broad enough, although (B) is close. It is best to read the entire passage to grasp the overall meaning.

48. E

Review the chart again. *Bar graphs* are not mentioned in this alphabetical list, but *Pie charts* are. They will be sure to be found on 54. You will need to look at an earlier location in the index to find bar graphs.

49. A

Review the chart again. Mortality (or death rates) will appear under *Population data*.

50. E

Placebo is a term used in pharmacology for an inert substance often used in experiments on the effects of drugs.

MATHEMATICS SECTION

1. E

Set up a proportion:

$\frac{5}{x} = \frac{100}{35}$ Cross multiply.

$100x = 175$ Divide both sides by 100.

$x = 1.75$

Because potato salad is only prepared in gallons, we must round up to 2 gallons. (A) Dividing 35 by 5 is not appropriate in this problem. (B) Because the potato salad is prepared in gallon quantities only, decimal parts of gallons are not possible answers. (C) One gallon of potato salad would serve only $\frac{100}{5} = 20$ people. (D) Setting up an incorrect proportion, $\frac{5}{x} = \frac{35}{100}$, gives this response.

2. C

Both 17 and 71 are prime. (A), (B), (D), and (E). The only factors of 17 are 1 and 17, so 17 is prime. The only factors of 71 are 1 and 71, so 71 is prime. The factors of 117 are 1, 3, 9, 13, 39, and 117; therefore, 117 is not prime.

3. A

The Pythagorean theorem gives the radius of the circle:

$r^2 = 3^2 + 4^2 = 9 + 16 = 25$

$r = 5$

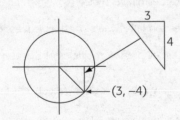

So the y-coordinate of the points where the circle crosses the y-axis is either 5 or –5. (B) The point (0, 0) is the center of the circle, not a point on the circle. (C) is likely the result of merely adding the coordinates of the given point. (D) is probably the sum of the absolute values of the coordinates of the given point. (E) The y-value on the y-axis is not the same as the y-value at the given point that is not on the y-axis.

4. B

The smaller number is x, and the larger number is 2x + 1. The multiples of 5 and 3 are in the right place. (A) This equation ignores the multiples. (C) The multiples are in the wrong place. (D) The quantities in parentheses do not satisfy the relation, *"One number is one more than twice another number."* (E) The quantity in the parentheses is *one less than twice the other number.*

5. D

Follow the order of operation rules. Do the operation inside parentheses first.

$5 - 3(4 + 1)$

$= 5 - 3(5)$ Perform multiplication before subtraction.

$= 5 - 15$ Apply the rule for subtraction.

$= 5 + (-15)$

$= -10$

(A) This choice results from applying the distributive property and getting the sign wrong. (B) If there had been parentheses around 5 – 3, this choice would be correct. (C) would result if the subtraction sign had been changed to an addition sign.

6. A

There are 3 among the 6 people who have 3 brothers and sisters. The probability of randomly choosing a person who has 3 brothers and sisters is $\frac{3}{6} = \frac{1}{2}$. (B) This is the probability of choosing a person with 2 brothers or sisters. (C) is the probability of choosing a person with 1 brother or sister. (D) is the probability of choosing a person with either 1 or 3 brothers and sisters. (E) All probabilities must be numbers between 0 and 1, inclusively.

7. C

The number of gallons of paint can be estimated by dividing the total area in square feet by the number of square feet that one gallon will cover. (A) and (B) Time has nothing to do with amount of paint. (D) Cost of paint does not determine amount of paint. (E) Type of siding, within reason, does not determine amount of paint.

8. D

It is easy to compare fractions if they are all written with a common denominator.

$\frac{3}{8} = \frac{9}{24}$ and $\frac{5}{6} = \frac{20}{24}$

(A) $\frac{1}{2} = \frac{12}{24}$, which is between $\frac{9}{24}$ and $\frac{20}{24}$.

(B) $\frac{3}{4} = \frac{18}{24}$, which is between $\frac{9}{24}$ and $\frac{20}{24}$.

(C) $\frac{2}{3} = \frac{16}{24}$, which is between $\frac{9}{24}$ and $\frac{20}{24}$.

(D) $\frac{1}{3} = \frac{8}{24}$, which is not between $\frac{9}{24}$ and $\frac{20}{24}$.

(E) $\frac{5}{8} = \frac{15}{24}$, which is between $\frac{9}{24}$ and $\frac{20}{24}$.

9. B

The question can be restated, "30 is what percent of 200?" (There was a total of 200 fish caught.) Set up and solve a proportion.

$\frac{30}{200} = \frac{P}{100}$ Cross multiply.

$200P = 3,000$ Divide by 200.

$P = 15$ 30 is 15% percent of 200.

(A) 30 is the number of catfish, not the percent. (C) The percent of catfish is half of the number of catfish, not twice. (D) is the percent of fish that were trout. (E) 30 is 24% of 125, not what the question asks.

10. D

Only I and III are true.

(A), (B), (C), and (E):

    I. If x^2 is odd, then x is odd. (True)

    II. If x is odd then $x + 2$ is also odd. (False)

    III. $2x$ is even for any whole number x. (True)

11. B

Nine gallons represents $\frac{3}{4}$ of the tank. Set up a proportion:

$\frac{3}{4} = \frac{9}{x}$ Cross multiply.

$3x = 36$ Divide both sides by 3.

$x = 12$ The tank holds 12 gallons.

(A) The full tank could certainly not hold less than 9 gallons. (C) appears to be a guess. (D) is the solution to the incorrect proportion $\frac{1}{4} = \frac{9}{x}$. (E) Multiplying 3 times 9 is not the correct operation to solve this problem.

12. B

Let's begin by considering expression I. Since x, y, and z are multiples of 5, $x + y - z$ must be a multiple of 5. Expression I must be part of the correct answer. We can eliminate choices (C) and (D), which do not contain expression I. Let's consider expression II. Since x is a multiple of 5, x^2, which is x times x, is a multiple of 5 times 5, so x^2 is a multiple of 5. Similarly, since y is a multiple of 5, y^2 is a multiple of 5. Thus, x^2, y^2, and z^2 are all multiples of 5. Expression II will be part of the correct answer. We can eliminate choice (C), which does not include expression II. Now lets consider expression III. If x, y, and z are all positive multiples of 5 and xy is less then z, then $\frac{xy}{z}$ will be a positive fraction less than 1, and therefore not a multiple of 5. For example, if $x = 10$, $y = 15$ and $z = 500$, then $\frac{xy}{z} = \frac{(10)(15)}{500} = \frac{150}{500} = \frac{15}{50} = \frac{3}{10}$, which is not a multiple of 5. So expression III will never be part of the correct answer. Choice (B), I and II only, is correct.

13. C

Let the people be identified as *a, b, c, d, e,* and *f,* then the handshakes may be shown as:

ab	bc	cd	de	ef
ac	bd	ce	df	
ad	be	cf		
ae	bf			
af				

There are no handshakes like *aa, bb,* ..., because no one shakes his own hand, and it is not necessary to count *ba, ca,* ..., because they are repetitions of *ab, ac,* ... .(A) No one person shakes 6 hands. (B) A likely guess would be to multiply 6 times 2, but that is not correct. (D) is the choice resulting from counting the pairs *aa, bb,* ..., (E) Another likely incorrect choice is to square 6.

14. C

One less than... means to subtract one, and *of* almost always translates as multiplication in the context of fractions. (A) represents *The quantity one less than twice a certain number divided by 3.* (B) is a misinterpretation of the phrase *One less than...* . (D) represents *The quantity one minus twice a certain number divided by 3.* (E) represents *Two-thirds of the quantity n minus 1.*

15. E

$2 \div \dfrac{2}{5} = \dfrac{2}{1} \times \dfrac{5}{2} = 5$, which is not equal to the others.

(A) $0.2 = \dfrac{2}{10} = \dfrac{1}{5}$

(B) $\dfrac{1}{5}$

(C) $20\% = \dfrac{20}{100} = \dfrac{1}{5}$

(D) $\dfrac{2}{5} \div 2 = \dfrac{2}{5} \times \dfrac{1}{2} = \dfrac{1}{5}$

16. A

$x < 5$ means the same as $5 > x$, so replacing x with 5 in the original equation gives $5 + y + z > x + y + z$. Since $x + y + z = 70$, then $5 + y + z > 70$. By subtracting 5 from each side of this inequality, the result is $y + z > 65$. (B) and (C) You must subtract 5 from both sides of the inequality. (D) The inequality symbol remains the same, $>$.

17. B

One yard 2 feet equals $1\dfrac{2}{3}$ yards. Divide $1\dfrac{2}{3}$ into 8.

$$8 \div 1\dfrac{2}{3} = \dfrac{8}{1} \div \dfrac{5}{3} = \dfrac{8}{1} \times \dfrac{3}{5} = \dfrac{24}{5} = 4\dfrac{4}{5}$$

Because $\dfrac{4}{5}$ of a blouse is not a blouse, discard the fraction part of the mixed number. She can make 4 complete blouses from the material. (A) seems to be a guess. (C) There cannot be a fraction of a blouse. (D) The mixed number cannot be rounded off; just take the whole number part. (E) seems to be a guess.

18. A

The 50th percentile is the median, and each of the five have a percentile rank better than 50. (B) There is no hint about the value of the mean in the table. (C) From the table we have no idea whether or not someone got a perfect score on the test. (D) Tom scored better than 60% of the people who took the test. (E) Steve scored better than 80% of the people who took the test.

19. C

If the sales tax is 5%, then the total bill is 105% of the bill before tax; that is 16.38 is 105% of the cost of dinner. Write a proportion:

$\dfrac{16.38}{x} = \dfrac{105}{100}$ Cross multiply.

$105x = 1,638$ Divide both sides by 105.

$x = 15.60$ Dinner cost $15.60.

Therefore, the amount of tax is $16.38 − 15.60 = $0.78. (A) is 5% of the total bill—not the amount of tax. (B) is the cost of dinner before tax. (D) is the result of applying a second tax to the total bill. (E) If 5% was misinterpreted as 50%, this may be the resulting amount of tax.

20. E

The process to use for this problem is called FOIL.

Multiply the first terms: x^2

Multiply the outer terms: $-5x$

Multiply the inner terms: $+x$

Multiply the last terms: -5

Combine the outer and inner products to simplify to $x^2 - 4x - 5$.
(A) Didn't multiply the outer and inner terms.
(B) Sign error when combining the outer and inner products.
(C) Sign error when multiplying the last terms and when combining the outer and inner products.
(D) Didn't multiply the outer and inner terms and a sign error on the last term.

21. D

The measure of the central angle $\angle AOB$ is equal to the measure of the intercepted arc AB. So the measure of the arc is 80°. The measure of the inscribed angle $\angle ACB$ is half the measure of the intercepted arc. So the measure of $\angle ACB$ is half of 80° or 40°. (A) See the rule above. An inscribed angle is half of its intercepted arc. (B) appears to be a guess. (C) The inscribed angle is half, not one fourth, of the intercepted arc.

22. E

This is an indirect proportion problem, so set up the appropriate proportion:

$\dfrac{50}{40} = \dfrac{x}{30}$ Cross multiply.

$40x = 1,500$ Divide both sides by 40.

$x = 37\dfrac{1}{2}$ He should get to work in $37\dfrac{1}{2}$ minutes.

(A) is the choice that would result by treating the problem as a direct proportion. The time could not be less if the speed is slower. (B), (C), and (D) All of these seem to be guesses.

23. C

The difference between successive odd whole numbers is two. (A) and (B) If an odd number is added to another odd number the result is even, not odd. (D) and (E) Both of these expressions will give an odd number but not necessarily the next consecutive odd number.

24. A

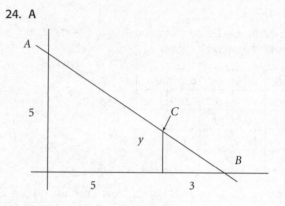

By drawing a vertical segment at point C, similar triangles are formed. Set up a proportion with the corresponding sides of the triangles:

$\dfrac{5}{8} = \dfrac{y}{3}$ Cross multiply.

$8y = 15$ Divide both sides by 8.

$y = \dfrac{15}{8}$

The y-value at the point C is $\dfrac{15}{8}$. (B) The proportion was solved incorrectly. (C) An estimation perhaps by inspecting the diagram. The answer is very close to 2. (D) Three is the base of the smaller triangle, not a y-value. (E) would result by setting up in indirect proportion; this is a direct proportion problem.

25. E

The graph is nearly horizontal at the beginning reflecting *Heather starts slowly*. Then the graph becomes steeper because *she increases her speed gradually*. The graph levels off in the middle because *she has to slow her speed* meaning that her distance from home is not increasing very rapidly during that time. Then the graph becomes steeper as *she gradually increases her speed* until it levels off as *she gradually slows to a stop*. (A) This graph shows that she starts rapidly. (B) The dip in the middle of this graph would indicate that Heather is going back toward her house, whereas she is only slowing her speed on the way to work. (C) This graph does not show the slowing in the middle of the trip. (D) This graph shows a rapid beginning and a rapid ending of the trip.

26. B

The volume of concrete is the area of the patio multiplied by the thickness. Because there are 27 cubic feet in one cubic yard, you have to divide the number of cubic feet by 27 to get the asked for cubic yards.

$$V = (15)^2 \pi \left(\frac{1}{3} \right) = 235.619... \qquad \text{cubic feet}$$

$$V = 235.619... \div 27 = 8.7266... \qquad \text{cubic yards}$$

But because it is delivered in whole number of cubic yards only, round up to 9 cubic yards. (A) The answer must be rounded up. (C) For this choice, the 4 inches was not converted to feet: 4 inches = $\frac{1}{3}$ feet (D) For this choice, you divided by 3 instead of 27. (E) For this choice, you divided by 9 instead of 27.

27. D

First multiply both sides by 6, the lowest common denominator.

$$6 \left(\frac{x}{3} - \frac{x+1}{2} \right) = \left(\frac{4}{3} \right) 6$$

$2x - 3(x + 1) = 8$ Simplify the left side.

$2x - 3x - 3 = 8$

$-x - 3 = 8$ Add 3 to both sides.

$-x = 11$ Divide both sides by -1.

$x = -11$ The solution set is $\{-11\}$.

(A) If the subtraction sign had mistakenly been changed to addition, this would have been the result. (B) If in the application of the distributive property the sign of the 3 was an error, this would have been the choice. (C) $2x - 3x = -x$. (E) The distributive property was misapplied.

28. E

(A), (B), (C), and (D) If x is known, apply the formula for area $A = lw$. If the perimeter is known, you can find x by solving the equation for perimeter $P = 2w + 2l$. Then use the area formula. If the diagonal is known, use the Pythagorean theorem to find x and then use the area formula.

29. A

Twenty percent is equivalent to $\frac{1}{5}$. This problem can be restated, *What is $\frac{1}{5}$ of $\frac{3}{8}$ of 40?* The word *of* typically translates as multiplication in the context of fractions. Therefore, the answer is $\frac{1}{5} \times \frac{3}{8} \times 40 = 3$ females in the class got A's on the test. (B) If the problem had stated, *Forty percent received A's*, this would be correct. (C) is 20% of 40. (D) appears to be a guess. (E) is $\frac{3}{8}$ of 40.

30. D

This is the rule for addition of numbers with different signs. (A) A counterexample: $3 + (-5) = -2$. (B) A counterexample: $5 + (-3) = 2$. (C) Both of the counterexamples above are counterexamples for this also. (E) The counterexample for (A) above works here also.

31. A

Four cans would usually cost $4(\$1.69) = \$6.76$. On sale, they cost $\$6.00$. So the savings is $\$6.76 - 6.00 = \$0.76$. (B) 19 cents is the savings *per can* when bought on sale. (C) is the total cost when 4 cans are purchased when not on sale. (D) $\$1.50$ is the cost per can on sale.

32. C

Substitute the given values and follow the order of operation rules.

$2x^2 - y$

$2(-3)^2 - (-5)$ Evaluate the exponent first.

$= 2(9) - (-5)$ Perform multiplication before subtraction.

$= 18 - (-5)$ Apply the rule of subtraction.

$= 18 + 5$ Add.

$= 23$

(A) indicates that multiplication was done before the exponent, and the subtraction was done incorrectly. (B) Squaring any real number results in a positive answer, even when the multiplication is done before the exponent incorrectly. (D) indicates that multiplication was done before the exponent. (E) The numbers given were substituted for the wrong variables.

33. D

This is a weighted average. The average heights of the guards and forwards must be counted twice.

$$\frac{2(69) + 2(72) + 76}{5} = \frac{358}{5} = 71.6 \text{ inches.}$$

(A) is the result of just averaging the three numbers—not taking into consideration the fact that there are two guards and two forwards. (B) is the answer rounded off to the nearest inch. There was no direction given to round off. (C) is the average of the guards and forwards only. (E) appears to be a guess.

34. B

Extend the table.

2 dozen eggs	$2.75 per dozen	$5.50
1 gallon milk	$3.80 per gallon	$3.80
2 boxes cereal	$3.50 per box	$7.00
4 cans baked beans	89 cents per can	$3.56
		$19.86

Subtract $20.00 − 19.86 = $0.14.

(A) is the total cost of the items—not the question asked. (C) would be the change if only one of each item was purchased. (D) would be the total cost if only one of each item was purchased.

35. E

Set up a direct proportion.

$$\frac{5}{8} = \frac{6}{x} \qquad \text{Cross multiply.}$$

$$5x = 48 \qquad \text{Divide both sides by 5.}$$

$$x = \frac{48}{5} = 9\frac{3}{5} \qquad \frac{3}{5} \text{ of a minute is } \frac{3}{5} \times 60 = 36 \text{ seconds.}$$

Mike can type 8 pages in 9 minutes 36 seconds. (A) is the result of an indirect proportion. (B) is the result of a proportion that means nothing in this problem $\frac{6}{8} = \frac{5}{x}$ (C) and (D) appear to be guesses.

36. B

Use an example. If the item initially cost $100, then a 10% increase would put the new cost at $110. Now, 10% of this new price is $11, so a 10% decrease would put the final price at $99, less than the initial price.

37. A

List all possibilities.

Choosing one coin

1 penny	1 cent
1 nickel	5 cents
1 dime	10 cents

Choosing two coins

2 pennies	2 cents
1 penny and 1 nickel	6 cents
1 penny and 1 dime	11 cents
1 nickel and 1 dime	15 cents

Choosing 3 coins

2 pennies and 1 nickel	7 cents
2 pennies and 1 dime	12 cents
1 penny, 1 nickel, and 1 dime	16 cents

Choosing 4 coins

2 pennies, 1 nickel, and 1 dime	17 cents

There are 11 different amounts of money. (B) is just a miscounting of the different amounts of money. (C) Six is the combination of four things choosing two at a time, but this ignores choosing three and four at a time and the fact that two of the items are identical. (D) There are four coins, but that is not the number of amounts of money. (E) There are three different kinds of coins, but that is not the number of amounts of money.

38. D

For any triangle, the sum of the lengths of any two sides must be greater than the length of the third side. Since $5 + 9 < 20$, these numbers could not be the lengths of the sides of a triangle. (A), (B), (C), and (E) All of these satisfy the rule given above.

39. C

The change in price during the fourth week is 7 cents. The question is: 7 is what percent of 231? Set up a proportion:

$\frac{7}{231} = \frac{P}{100}$ Cross multiply.

$231P = 700$ Divide both sides by 231.

$P\ 3.0303...$ The price increased about 3%.

(A) is the percent increase over the entire month. (B) The increase of 7 cents in price does not mean that the percent increase is 7%. (D) There was a 5% increase during the first week. (E) There was a 38-cent increase over the entire month.

40. B

Create a chart using the formula $d = rt$.

	$d =$	r	t
Britney	$15x$	15	x
Sunny	$20(x - \frac{1}{2})$	20	$x - \frac{1}{2}$

When Sunny catches Britney, they have traveled the same distance. Therefore, the equation is $15x = 20\left(x - \frac{1}{2}\right)$.

(A) It was Sunny who traveled for one-half hour less time, not Britney. (C) Nothing in the problem indicates that the sum of the distances traveled is 8 miles. (D) and (E) Since the units are 15 and 20 miles per *hour,* the units must be consistent. Although one-half hour is equivalent to 30 minutes, you cannot mix units in this way.

41. A

A diagram helps clarify this problem. The difference between the distance between the walls and the length of 13 tiles is 12 inches. Each tile against the wall should be $\frac{1}{2} \times 12 = 6$ inches, so 3 inches should be cut off of the 9-inch squares. (B) Each tile against the wall should be 6 inches. That's not the amount to be cut off. (C) $4\frac{1}{2}$ inches is half a tile—too short to go against the wall. (D) If there had been 14 tiles in the center of the room, this would be correct.

42. D

Use the distributive property to get rid of parentheses and brackets. Get rid of innermost grouping symbols first.

$(x - 5) + 2[x - 3(x - 1)]$
$= x - 5 + 2[x - 3x + 3]$
$= x - 5 + 2x - 6x + 6$ Combine similar terms.
$= -3x + 1$

(A), (B), (C), and (E) All of these are the result of misapplication of the distributive property.

43. C

The rule for subtraction is to add the opposite, so $a - b = a + (-b)$ in which $(-b)$ is a positive number. Therefore, $a - b$ will always result in a positive number: $a - b > 0$. (A) The product of a positive number and a negative number is negative. (B) Here is a counterexample for this choice: If $a = 3$ and $b = -5$, then $a + b = 3 + (-5) = -2$, which is not greater than zero. (D) The reciprocal of a positive number is positive; the reciprocal of a negative number is negative, and a negative number is always less than a positive number. (E) Here is a counterexample for this choice: $a = 5$ and $b = -3$, then $a + b = 5 + (-3) = 2$, which is not less than zero.

44. E

If the square has the area 36 square inches, then the sides of the square are 6 inches, and its perimeter is $6 \times 4 = 24$ inches. The perimeter of the triangle is the same, so one of its sides is $\frac{1}{3} \times 24 = 8$ inches. (A) is one side of the square. (B) is the numerical value of the area of the triangle. (C) is the perimeter of the triangle if its sides were the same as the square. (D) is the perimeter of the square.

45. A

Each hour on the clock represents $\frac{1}{12} \times 360 = 30$ degrees. The angle formed at 2:00 is $2 \times 30 = 60$ degrees. (B) is a guess. (C) If you thought the number of degrees in one revolution is 120 degrees, this would be your choice. (D) is the number of degrees at 1:00. (E) is the number of degrees at 3:00.

46. B

The total length of the three pieces of rope is 3(1 ft 7 in) = 3(19 in) = 57 in = 4 ft 9 in. Subtract: 12 − (4 ft 9 in) = (11 ft 12 in) − (4 ft 9 in) = 7 ft 3 in. (A) is the total length cut from the spool. (C) If you borrowed incorrectly in the subtraction, this would be your answer. Remember 1 foot = 12 inches, not 10. (D) Perhaps just a guess.

47. C

During the first week, the Hennings used $\frac{2}{5} \times 80 = 32$ gallons. Therefore, there were 80 − 32 = 48 gallons left to begin the second week. During the second week, $\frac{1}{3} \times 48$ = 16 gallons were used. To begin the third week, there were 48 − 16 = 32 gallons left. (A) is the result of multiplying the two fractions times 80 gallons, which does not give the correct answer. (B) is the number of gallons used during the second week. (D) is the number of gallons left after the first week. (E) is $\frac{4}{5}$ of 80 gallons.

48. D

Let x be the number of dimes, then the number of pennies is $2x$, and the number of nickels is $15 − 3x$. Therefore, the equation is:

$10x + 1(2x) + 5(15 − 3x) = 66$ Simplify the left side.

$10x + 2x + 75 − 15x = 66$

$−3x + 75 = 66$ Subtract 75 from both sides.

$−3x = −9$ Divide both sides by −3.

$x = 3$ The solution is 3.

Alex has 3 dimes.

(A) There are 6 pennies and 6 nickels but not 6 dimes. (B) There are 9 pennies and dimes together. (C) and (E) These responses appear to be guesses.

49. A

If the diameter is multiplied by 3, so is the radius. The formula for the area of a circle is $A = \pi r^2$. Replace r with $3r$: $A = \pi(3r)^2 = 9\pi r^2$, which is 9 times the original value of A. (B) In the formula above, the radius is squared, not doubled. (C) The radius should be squared. (D) The radius should be squared, not cubed. (E) In this choice, there appears to be some confusion about π.

50. E

There are 30 feet of chain hanging from the roof. Each foot weighs 3 pounds so the chain weighs 90 pounds. The total weight then is 90 + 5 + 62 = 157 pounds. (A) ignores the fact that the chain weighs 3 pounds per foot. (B) is the weight of 100 feet of chain plus the bucket and water. (C) is the weight of 70 feet of chain plus the bucket and water. There is only 30 feet of chain. (D) ignores the chain altogether.

WRITING SECTION

Topic 1

4 Essay

I cannot agree with Katherine Paterson. In the US, all citizens are entitled to a free public education through the end of high school. The decision to continue with higher education in college or beyond is often motivated by a student's desire to learn more about a particular topic. This implies that a student wouldn't be able to learn the same things on her own, without additional classes. The logical explanation for this is that a person's imagination is not enough to provide a sufficient knowledge base, so more "book learning" is required. The value of a "standard" college education is illustrated by examples from medicine and my own family.

Dr. Jonas Salk discovered a vaccine for polio in the middle of the twentieth century, when the disease was epidemic and struck thousands of young people in the US. To achieve this goal, Dr. Salk required extensive years of medical school and research. Without a standard base of medical knowledge, he would not have been able to conduct the experiments he needed to find a successful vaccine. This type of discovery in medicine simply can't be accomplished with imagination alone, because successful medical research requires advanced understanding of anatomy, physiology, chemistry, physics, and biology. Although a doctor may use his imagination to combine chemicals in an innovative way to develop a new treatment, he can't do this if he doesn't already have a foundation of knowledge based on a medical education.

In the same way, a tax specialist can't simply use her creative mind to assist clients. My CPA spent many years studying tax laws and requirements, and she continues to take classes in this field, since federal and state tax laws change often. She can't rely on her imagination to fill out and file tax forms for her clients, because she is legally and ethically obligated to follow the rules. In this case, she needed to have a standard education to learn the basic facts and common knowledge that are relevant to her work as an accountant. Again, if her classes had focused on imagination rather than facts, she would not be able to succeed in her career.

Although some people feel that required classes can be stifling to college students or can discourage them from thinking for themselves, having a standard foundation of knowledge is a necessary part of education for most people. Imagination can help to inspire students as they continue through school, but the primary purpose of education is to teach students what they will need to know to succeed after school.

Grader's Comments

This essay develops the topic consistently and coherently, with a clear introduction, well-developed examples, and a strong conclusion. The author demonstrates that she has understood the prompt by starting off with an interpretation of the issue. She ends the introductory paragraph with a clear transition that informs the reader of the structure and organization of the essay. The author uses transitions throughout the essay, showing that she spent sufficient time planning before starting to write.

The author's writing is strong and clear, and she provides excellent support for her thesis with the diverse examples in the body paragraphs. As suggested by the final sentence of the introductory paragraph, the essay is well organized and follows the author's plan to develop and support her thesis. Finally, the author uses sophisticated language and varied sentence structure to compose this essay and make it interesting to the reader. The lack of grammatical or spelling errors indicates that the author wrote carefully and took time to proofread.

2 Essay

One of the good things about going to college is that you finally get to study more of what you're really interested in instead of just taking the same classes which everyone else takes to graduate from high school. So college classes should encourage students to use their own minds and think more creatively. Encourage imagination not just boring facts or lessons which only ask you to repeat what the textbook says.

Look at Bill Gates. He got a standard education but then used his own ideas and vision to start Microsoft that became a huge success and a standard for computer software. If he had just followed the lessons in his classes and not thought for himself he wouldn't have been able to do what he did with his company.

Bill Gates proves that college should be more supportive of imaginative thinking instead of bland boring repetition. Otherwise everyone is the same and no major advancements or inventions will ever be created. So imagination is a more important part of college education then tradition or common knowledge.

Grader's Comments

This essay begins with a generalization that introduces the author's opinion, showing that the author understood the prompt and providing a thesis statement. However, the next paragraph presents a single example that doesn't provide sufficient support for the thesis. This example needs to be developed further and reinforced with additional details or another example. The author should spend more time planning her essay before writing.

The organization of the essay is satisfactory, with a clear introduction, body paragraph, and conclusion. However, the essay lacks transitions between paragraphs. The language is inconsistent, with some complex sentences interspersed with sentence fragments (second and third sentences of first paragraph, last sentence of third paragraph) and vague phrasing ("…he wouldn't have been able to do what he did…"). Several sentences lack proper punctuation, and the author consistently misuses the pronouns "which" and "that." Another grammatical error appears in the final sentence ("then" instead of "than").

Topic 2

4 Essay

When I began ninth grade, I was terrible at math, but I couldn't understand why. When my math teacher gave the class step-by-step procedures that could solve every possible type of arithmetic problem, I dutifully copied each of the procedures, word-for-word, into my notebook. I memorized every little inch of my notes for the first major test, yet still failed miserably. When the teacher returned my paper, I whined that I hadn't learned anything at all. I had memorized all of the formulas, yet still could not solve the problems. I threw my arms up in defeat.

Fortunately, my teacher was wise enough to recognize that my math education had to go beyond memorization—that a deeper, more complex learning was required. She gave me problem types that I had never seen before: to solve them, I had to be resourceful and use formulas that I had memorized weeks, months, and even years earlier. After I solved the problems, my teacher asked me to develop my own methods for solving this new type of question. For the first time in math class, I did not just parrot another step-by-step process: I had to draw on my past knowledge to create something of my own.

Learning to be resourceful in math quickly led to developing reasoning skills. I began approaching problems like a detective: carefully analyzing each problem, then using logic to determine the most efficient method for solving it. I no longer followed memorized formulas step-by-step, but began to see them simply as helpful tools to be intelligently applied, even outside the classroom. While trying and failing to fix my bicycle one day, I noticed that I was mindlessly following step-by-step instructions. Suddenly, I realized that I could fix my bike just as I solved math problems: by analyzing the problem and then deciding the best way to solve it. Not only did I fix my bike, but I felt I knew for the first time what my math education was all about.

Getting an education does not just involve learning facts and formulas; it involves the acquisition of transferable, less tangible benefits, such as resourcefulness, reasoning ability, and the desire to continue learning. As B.F. Skinner would undoubtedly agree, these benefits are the aspects of education that remain long after memorized facts have been forgotten.

Grader's Comments

This essay clearly and thoroughly addresses the topic. In describing a personal experience with learning math, the author displays a complex, well-developed thought process. The essay is clearly focused and progresses logically from one idea to the next. Support is used appropriately and is relevant to the author's thesis.

This essay was clearly planned and well thought-out before the author began writing. In the first paragraph, the thesis introduces three major components of the author's view of education. In the following paragraphs, the author clearly relates her personal experience to each of these points. The essay concludes neatly by revisiting the original thesis.

Throughout this essay, the author uses a variety of complex sentence structures that contribute to the overall quality of the essay. The essay is free of most errors in spelling, grammar, and usage, and the author demonstrates consistent skill at using vocabulary accurately.

2 Essay

When I began learning how to play the flute in fifth grade, I thought that music education was just memorizing fingerings, key signatures, and the names of symbols. I memorized the names of famous composers from flashcards so that I could pass my multiple-choice tests. I thought that memorizing these things was a waste of time.

My music education really began when I gained the skills that allowed me to progress beyond practicing scales and technical drills. As I practiced a piece, I stopped thinking about fingering and measuring out sincapated rhythms, and instead began to experiment with what the music actually sounded like. I began to understand how rhythms, key changes, and crescendos all worked together to create a particular effect in a piece of music, and how it affected me as I played.

Eventually, I began performing for audiences, and an entirely new chapter of my music education began. As I played, I observed the audience, and tried to understand how different songs and styles of music can evoke different responses. When I began to notice the effects of these details on my audience, I began incorporating more stylistic elements into my pieces. I felt as though I was finally learning why I had been studying music for so many years.

As you can see, my music education had little to do with learning scales and rhythms. True, this foundation was necessary to develop more complex skills, but I believe that my education did not really begin until I learned how to apply the factual knowledge. If I hadn't stopped concentrating on the technical, memorized components of music, I would not have really learned anything about music at all.

Grader's Comments

This essay addresses the topic, but not fully or effectively. The author clearly believes that education means more than acquiring knowledge, and uses an extended, detailed example of his or her own music education to illustrate this point. But the author does not clearly connect this detail to the thesis and never makes clear what other things are important to education.

The essay's overall structure is organized, with an introduction of the author's thesis followed by supporting evidence and an overall conclusion. However, the content of the individual paragraphs focuses on the author's progress in learning music, not on the questions raised in the prompt.

This essay displays well-developed language facility, sentence structure, and use of vocabulary. There are a few minor errors with spelling and parallel structure (in the first sentence), but overall, the writing is satisfactory.

Practice Test Three Answer Sheet

Remove (or photocopy) the answer sheet and use it to complete the practice test.
See the answer key following the test when finished.

READING SECTION

1. Ⓐ Ⓑ Ⓒ Ⓓ Ⓔ	14. Ⓐ Ⓑ Ⓒ Ⓓ Ⓔ	27. Ⓐ Ⓑ Ⓒ Ⓓ Ⓔ	40. Ⓐ Ⓑ Ⓒ Ⓓ Ⓔ
2. Ⓐ Ⓑ Ⓒ Ⓓ Ⓔ	15. Ⓐ Ⓑ Ⓒ Ⓓ Ⓔ	28. Ⓐ Ⓑ Ⓒ Ⓓ Ⓔ	41. Ⓐ Ⓑ Ⓒ Ⓓ Ⓔ
3. Ⓐ Ⓑ Ⓒ Ⓓ Ⓔ	16. Ⓐ Ⓑ Ⓒ Ⓓ Ⓔ	29. Ⓐ Ⓑ Ⓒ Ⓓ Ⓔ	42. Ⓐ Ⓑ Ⓒ Ⓓ Ⓔ
4. Ⓐ Ⓑ Ⓒ Ⓓ Ⓔ	17. Ⓐ Ⓑ Ⓒ Ⓓ Ⓔ	30. Ⓐ Ⓑ Ⓒ Ⓓ Ⓔ	43. Ⓐ Ⓑ Ⓒ Ⓓ Ⓔ
5. Ⓐ Ⓑ Ⓒ Ⓓ Ⓔ	18. Ⓐ Ⓑ Ⓒ Ⓓ Ⓔ	31. Ⓐ Ⓑ Ⓒ Ⓓ Ⓔ	44. Ⓐ Ⓑ Ⓒ Ⓓ Ⓔ
6. Ⓐ Ⓑ Ⓒ Ⓓ Ⓔ	19. Ⓐ Ⓑ Ⓒ Ⓓ Ⓔ	32. Ⓐ Ⓑ Ⓒ Ⓓ Ⓔ	45. Ⓐ Ⓑ Ⓒ Ⓓ Ⓔ
7. Ⓐ Ⓑ Ⓒ Ⓓ Ⓔ	20. Ⓐ Ⓑ Ⓒ Ⓓ Ⓔ	33. Ⓐ Ⓑ Ⓒ Ⓓ Ⓔ	46. Ⓐ Ⓑ Ⓒ Ⓓ Ⓔ
8. Ⓐ Ⓑ Ⓒ Ⓓ Ⓔ	21. Ⓐ Ⓑ Ⓒ Ⓓ Ⓔ	34. Ⓐ Ⓑ Ⓒ Ⓓ Ⓔ	47. Ⓐ Ⓑ Ⓒ Ⓓ Ⓔ
9. Ⓐ Ⓑ Ⓒ Ⓓ Ⓔ	22. Ⓐ Ⓑ Ⓒ Ⓓ Ⓔ	35. Ⓐ Ⓑ Ⓒ Ⓓ Ⓔ	48. Ⓐ Ⓑ Ⓒ Ⓓ Ⓔ
10. Ⓐ Ⓑ Ⓒ Ⓓ Ⓔ	23. Ⓐ Ⓑ Ⓒ Ⓓ Ⓔ	36. Ⓐ Ⓑ Ⓒ Ⓓ Ⓔ	49. Ⓐ Ⓑ Ⓒ Ⓓ Ⓔ
11. Ⓐ Ⓑ Ⓒ Ⓓ Ⓔ	24. Ⓐ Ⓑ Ⓒ Ⓓ Ⓔ	37. Ⓐ Ⓑ Ⓒ Ⓓ Ⓔ	50. Ⓐ Ⓑ Ⓒ Ⓓ Ⓔ
12. Ⓐ Ⓑ Ⓒ Ⓓ Ⓔ	25. Ⓐ Ⓑ Ⓒ Ⓓ Ⓔ	38. Ⓐ Ⓑ Ⓒ Ⓓ Ⓔ	
13. Ⓐ Ⓑ Ⓒ Ⓓ Ⓔ	26. Ⓐ Ⓑ Ⓒ Ⓓ Ⓔ	39. Ⓐ Ⓑ Ⓒ Ⓓ Ⓔ	

☐ # right in Reading Section

☐ # wrong in Reading Section

MATH SECTION

1. Ⓐ Ⓑ Ⓒ Ⓓ Ⓔ	14. Ⓐ Ⓑ Ⓒ Ⓓ Ⓔ	27. Ⓐ Ⓑ Ⓒ Ⓓ Ⓔ	40. Ⓐ Ⓑ Ⓒ Ⓓ Ⓔ
2. Ⓐ Ⓑ Ⓒ Ⓓ Ⓔ	15. Ⓐ Ⓑ Ⓒ Ⓓ Ⓔ	28. Ⓐ Ⓑ Ⓒ Ⓓ Ⓔ	41. Ⓐ Ⓑ Ⓒ Ⓓ Ⓔ
3. Ⓐ Ⓑ Ⓒ Ⓓ Ⓔ	16. Ⓐ Ⓑ Ⓒ Ⓓ Ⓔ	29. Ⓐ Ⓑ Ⓒ Ⓓ Ⓔ	42. Ⓐ Ⓑ Ⓒ Ⓓ Ⓔ
4. Ⓐ Ⓑ Ⓒ Ⓓ Ⓔ	17. Ⓐ Ⓑ Ⓒ Ⓓ Ⓔ	30. Ⓐ Ⓑ Ⓒ Ⓓ Ⓔ	43. Ⓐ Ⓑ Ⓒ Ⓓ Ⓔ
5. Ⓐ Ⓑ Ⓒ Ⓓ Ⓔ	18. Ⓐ Ⓑ Ⓒ Ⓓ Ⓔ	31. Ⓐ Ⓑ Ⓒ Ⓓ Ⓔ	44. Ⓐ Ⓑ Ⓒ Ⓓ Ⓔ
6. Ⓐ Ⓑ Ⓒ Ⓓ Ⓔ	19. Ⓐ Ⓑ Ⓒ Ⓓ Ⓔ	32. Ⓐ Ⓑ Ⓒ Ⓓ Ⓔ	45. Ⓐ Ⓑ Ⓒ Ⓓ Ⓔ
7. Ⓐ Ⓑ Ⓒ Ⓓ Ⓔ	20. Ⓐ Ⓑ Ⓒ Ⓓ Ⓔ	33. Ⓐ Ⓑ Ⓒ Ⓓ Ⓔ	46. Ⓐ Ⓑ Ⓒ Ⓓ Ⓔ
8. Ⓐ Ⓑ Ⓒ Ⓓ Ⓔ	21. Ⓐ Ⓑ Ⓒ Ⓓ Ⓔ	34. Ⓐ Ⓑ Ⓒ Ⓓ Ⓔ	47. Ⓐ Ⓑ Ⓒ Ⓓ Ⓔ
9. Ⓐ Ⓑ Ⓒ Ⓓ Ⓔ	22. Ⓐ Ⓑ Ⓒ Ⓓ Ⓔ	35. Ⓐ Ⓑ Ⓒ Ⓓ Ⓔ	48. Ⓐ Ⓑ Ⓒ Ⓓ Ⓔ
10. Ⓐ Ⓑ Ⓒ Ⓓ Ⓔ	23. Ⓐ Ⓑ Ⓒ Ⓓ Ⓔ	36. Ⓐ Ⓑ Ⓒ Ⓓ Ⓔ	49. Ⓐ Ⓑ Ⓒ Ⓓ Ⓔ
11. Ⓐ Ⓑ Ⓒ Ⓓ Ⓔ	24. Ⓐ Ⓑ Ⓒ Ⓓ Ⓔ	37. Ⓐ Ⓑ Ⓒ Ⓓ Ⓔ	50. Ⓐ Ⓑ Ⓒ Ⓓ Ⓔ
12. Ⓐ Ⓑ Ⓒ Ⓓ Ⓔ	25. Ⓐ Ⓑ Ⓒ Ⓓ Ⓔ	38. Ⓐ Ⓑ Ⓒ Ⓓ Ⓔ	
13. Ⓐ Ⓑ Ⓒ Ⓓ Ⓔ	26. Ⓐ Ⓑ Ⓒ Ⓓ Ⓔ	39. Ⓐ Ⓑ Ⓒ Ⓓ Ⓔ	

☐ # right in Math Section

☐ # wrong in Math Section

WRITING SECTION

Lined pages on which you will write your essays can be found in the writing section.

Practice Test Three

Reading Section

50 Questions

Directions: Each statement in this test is followed by questions based on its content. After reading a statement or passage, choose the answer that best fits each question from among the choices given. Answer all questions on the basis of what is stated or implied in the passage. Be sure to mark all of your answers in the reading section of your answer sheet.

Note: Some passages contain numbered sentences, blank lines, or underlined words that are for your reference in answering the questions that follow those passages.

Questions 1–3

Archeologists can verify what historians and mythologists have written. One famous example is the discovery of the ancient city of Troy. For many years, it was commonly held that the Greek stories and plays about Troy were entirely fanciful. In the 1800s, a retired pharmacist supported an expedition that began to dig in the place where he thought Troy would be, based on the stories. Sure enough, after digging through the remains of the six cities, Trojan artifacts were located.

Recently, archeologists in England found a third-century Roman coin in a *cache* of 5,000 other coins. This coin showed the visage of Domitianus, a little known emperor. His reign was so brief that there isn't much known about him. Only one other coin like this has ever been found, and it was thought to be a hoax. Historians have found only a few vague references to a military officer named Domitianus, who was tried for treason. Whoever he was, his reign was probably so short that only a few coins were minted before it was over. For all the knowledge we have accumulated, it appears there will be many more discoveries to add details to our hoard of information.

1. The main idea expressed in this passage is

   (A) Historians and archeologists arrive at the same conclusions.
   (B) Archeology can contribute to our understanding of history.
   (C) Historians, mythologists, and archeologists must agree to know something is true.
   (D) Archeologists can add information to what we already know.
   (E) Archeology is more important than history or mythology.

2. The author develops the main idea through the use of

   (A) details
   (B) stories
   (C) facts
   (D) historical information
   (E) examples

3. The word *cache* as used in the passage means

    (A) a mark or sign showing something is authentic
    (B) a sign of official approval
    (C) a place in which supplies or stores of food are hidden
    (D) anything stored or hidden in such a place
    (E) a decorative pot or jar

Questions 4–6

Oceanographers know our oceans are in trouble. Many even believe the trouble is worse than they had thought. The U.S. Commission on Ocean Policy, ordered by Congress in 2000, released its 450-page report in 2004. The _____ lists many problems, contaminated seafood, urban runoff of oil, trash and human waste, farm runoff of chemicals that cause growth of algae and suffocate ocean life, and rising sea temperatures that kill coral reefs and enhance the spread of water-born viruses. Those aren't the only problems, however. Commercial fishermen discard up to a quarter of their catch, and yet some fish species have suffered collapse as a result of overfishing. Developers build in ecologically fragile areas and in areas that are vulnerable to severe storms. The report includes 200 recommendations that together may correct this serious situation.

Most of us have not thought about our oceans as more than recreational areas, but we need to see their value and purpose more fully and their problems more fully as well. We must begin to see them as the oceanographer sees them, as having severe problems that have to be addressed in order to save the life within the oceans and our own.

4. This passage is an example of a

    (A) jeremiad
    (B) persuasive essay
    (C) scientific report
    (D) narrative
    (E) review

5. The argument could be made more forceful by including

    (A) statistics on environmental damage
    (B) examples of problems
    (C) testimony by celebrities
    (D) comparison to historical conditions
    (E) use of passive voice

6. Choose the correct word to place in the blank space.

    (A) document
    (B) monograph
    (C) chairman
    (D) study
    (E) report

Questions 7–9

The brain reacts to stress in two different ways. In one reaction, the hypothalamus signals the adrenal glands to release the hormones epinephrine and norepinephrine, which boost the heart rate, breathing, blood pressure, and blood flow to the muscles and brain, providing an extra surge in energy.

In the other reaction, the pituitary gland signals the adrenal glands to release the stress hormone cortisol and other steroids. Both reactions can be helpful to the body, but when they are chronic, their effects can be deadly, contributing to heart attacks, digestive diseases, arthritis, and other autoimmune disorders.

7. What might you infer from the information in this passage?

    (A) the effects of stress can be deadly
    (B) stress reactions can be helpful or harmful
    (C) the effects of chronic stress are harmful
    (D) stress is a fact of life
    (E) people should avoid chronic stress

GO ON TO THE NEXT PAGE ⟶

8. This passage is part of a longer article. The use of words like epinephrine and cortisol suggest that the remainder of the article will be

    (A) very detailed

    (B) only understandable by people with medical training

    (C) more fully explanatory about the physiological effects of stress

    (D) informative about medication

    (E) about the brain

9. An autoimmune disorder results from the production of antibodies that can damage normal components of the body. That would include

    (A) high blood pressure

    (B) arthritis

    (C) fast heartbeat

    (D) ulcers

    (E) headaches

Questions 10–12

Using the table of contents below, find the correct pages to answer the questions that follow:

Table of Contents

10. Where would you look to find an office within a building?

    (A) 12

    (B) 150

    (C) 151

    (D) 152

    (E) 7–11

11. Where would you look to find a specific office?

    (A) 150

    (B) 120–149

    (C) 151

    (D) 152

    (E) 7–11

12. Where would you look first to find the closest place to park to the building you are seeking?

    (A) 150

    (B) 151

    (C) 152

    (D) 153

    (E) 12

GO ON TO THE NEXT PAGE

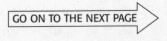

Questions 13–15

A new trend among yuppie parents is immersion method study in a foreign language for their pre- and primary school children. Upwards of 300 language-immersion elementary schools have opened across the country in recent years. Often the students in these schools speak English at home, but write in a second language before they write in English. They study everything in school in their second language: math, science, art, and social studies.

In their early years, these students may not do so well in English language skills, but most recover these skills over time. In fact, by fifth grade they perform as well as or outperform English-only students in vocabulary and grammar.

Some parents would like to be involved in helping their children with homework but don't speak the language, and as a result, some schools are planning to offer beginning language courses to parents so that they can be more involved in their children's school experience.

13. As a result of parents' wanting their children to be bilingual

   (A) parents cannot help children with their homework
   (B) children will be better educated
   (C) parents may end up taking language classes at their children's schools
   (D) the children struggle with two or more languages in school
   (E) parents won't speak English with their children at home

14. The passage seems to imply that

   (A) yuppie parents think being multilingual is a good thing
   (B) more and more children will speak two languages
   (C) yuppie parents want to "keep up with the Joneses"
   (D) preschool is the best time to learn a second language
   (E) yuppie parents are trendy

15. One may deduce from the passage that

   (A) children are at first behind in English
   (B) the immersion method teaches all subjects in a foreign language
   (C) the immersion method is a new method
   (D) the immersion method is a thoroughly tested method
   (E) foreign language instruction is important

Questions 16–18

Building housing for the poor has become an important focus for those who wish to improve our society. Organizations like Habitat for Humanity have begun projects around the world to help provide decent shelter for families that could otherwise not have it.

The Salvation Army has worked in partnership with many groups to provide shelter and job training for the homeless, who would otherwise live hopeless lives on city streets.

Public agencies have begun to build housing for migrant workers who have otherwise had slum-like shelter in many agricultural areas.

All of these efforts have been spearheaded by individuals who care about others and leaving the world a better place. They all share a dream of recognizing human dignity and see housing as an important part of that.

16. One may infer from the passage that an individual with an idea

   (A) can bring about effective change
   (B) can be effective with the support of organizations
   (C) needs to devote their whole life to a dream
   (D) is usually powerless
   (E) may or may not be successful

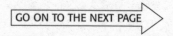

GO ON TO THE NEXT PAGE

17. The argument could be most seriously weakened by

    (A) an opposing argument based on a "pull your-self up by your bootstraps" philosophy

    (B) a listing of costs

    (C) opinions from developers

    (D) evidence that these projects often fail

    (E) bad experience with projects in other countries

18. The author suggests that the individuals who spearheaded these projects think more about

    (A) themselves than others

    (B) the costs of welfare than other things

    (C) the future as opposed to the past

    (D) traditional ideas of government

    (E) recreation than work

Questions 19–21

A recent U.S. government report, *Principal Indications of Student Academic Histories in Postsecondary Education, 1972–2000*, presents data on college student graduation rates that *dispel* some dearly held beliefs and present a fairly positive picture of student persistence.

For years, the public has been told that students cannot get through college in a timely manner. Colleges have made *prodigious* efforts to offer variable scheduling to meet students' needs.

This new report shows that in 1972, 48 percent of students who completed 10 college units earned a bachelor's degree. In 1992, 48.7 percent of an equivalent population earned degrees.

The bad news is that the percentage of men achieving a bachelor's degree declined from 50 to 45.2 percent, but women increased from 45.8 percent in 1972 to 51.8 percent in 1992.

One third of those graduates started at community colleges and transferred to four-year institutions. Surely, the efforts of colleges to schedule classes according to demand has paid off for many students.

19. The conclusion the author draws at the end of paragraph five is

    (A) encouraging

    (B) based on finite data

    (C) too general

    (D) does not follow logically from the prior sentence

    (E) probably valid

20. The word *prodigious* as used in the selection means

    (A) ominous

    (B) abnormal

    (C) extraordinary in size

    (D) inactive

    (E) lavish

21. The word *dispels* as used here means

    (A) to deal out

    (B) to cause to vanish

    (C) to distribute

    (D) to scatter

    (E) to discourage

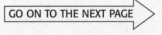

GO ON TO THE NEXT PAGE

KAPLAN)

Questions 22–24

In 1955, students in most secondary schools did not know what honors courses were, and Advanced Placement courses had not been worked out with colleges and universities to give credit. Today, 50% of U.S. teenagers are enrolled in those kinds of courses. Probably these students feel the need to prepare themselves for college and to be as competitive as possible for college admissions.

One can't help but wonder if half of America's students are qualified intellectually for those courses that originally began with 10% or less of a student population.

Most of today's students claim to be self-motivated. Perhaps honors and AP classes should not be limited to only 10% of students—the very high achievers. Perhaps they should be available to all who want to rise to a challenge and study a subject in more depth than they could in the average high school classroom. This is an idea worth considering.

22. The author states that honors and Advanced Placement courses

   (A) have mushroomed over the past 50 years

   (B) enroll too many students

   (C) are probably not challenging

   (D) are too demanding

   (E) will probably be around a long time

23. The author's tone suggests he is

   (A) advocating for honors classes

   (B) open to considering many possible values of honors courses

   (C) opposed to honors courses

   (D) disinterested in honors courses

   (E) differentiating between honors and Advanced Placement courses

24. The author speculates

   (A) very little

   (B) about student motivation

   (C) about data and percentages

   (D) on several issues

   (E) too much

Questions 25–27

Using the Table of Contents below, please locate the information requested.

Contents

GO ON TO THE NEXT PAGE

25. On which page(s) would you look to find plant propagation methods?

    (A) 17 and 23
    (B) 23 and 26
    (C) 26
    (D) 17 and 21
    (E) 15 and 17

26. On what page(s) would one find information on how succulents developed?

    (A) 1 and 17
    (B) 1 and 7
    (C) 33
    (D) 7 and 23
    (E) 15 and 21

27. Where would someone look who wanted to raise succulents and wanted appropriate information?

    (A) 23
    (B) 17
    (C) 18 and 20
    (D) 17–21
    (E) 26

Questions 28–30

   Alexander the Great of Macedonia chose a small fishing village in northern Egypt on the edge of the Mediterranean Sea to be the new capital of his expanding empire. Soon, Alexandria, as it came to be called, was home to a great university whose library contained every known book that had been written. The university was a teaching center that drew scholars from the whole world.

   Euclid wrote the rules of geometry there, and Archimedes invented the spiral-shaped fluid pump that is still used today. Here the diameter of the earth was calculated. This was probably the most significant location in the world at that time in terms of the development of science.

   Today, the remnants of that great university have been excavated. Thirteen u-shaped auditoria, with an elevated seat in the center for a lecturer, and a theatre that has been repaired and is currently being used are available to visitors. The theater apparently held large groups of students. Perhaps someday lectures will again be held in the auditoria.

28. The style and tone of the passage could be called

    (A) historical
    (B) persuasive and historical
    (C) poetic
    (D) fictional
    (E) descriptive and historical

29. The first paragraph contains

    (A) compound sentences
    (B) compound/complex sentences
    (C) complex sentences
    (D) parallel structures
    (E) periodic sentences

30. The information included in the passage is important because

    (A) of its interest to tourists
    (B) of its archeological importance
    (C) of the historical and scientific importance of Alexandria
    (D) of the theater that is still used today
    (E) of the possibility of rebuilding the structures

GO ON TO THE NEXT PAGE

Questions 31–33

Prevention of some diseases may be more possible in the future as blood tests reveal antibodies of incipient diseases years before the diseases are diagnosed.

Researchers have found that patients in one study had antibodies for rheumatoid arthritis about four and a half years before they were diagnosed. Patients who had the antibodies experienced a more severe form of the disease than those who didn't. Antibodies seem to presage other diseases such as lupus, thyroid disease, and Type 1 diabetes. This discovery may lead to the development of treatments that can prevent a disease from becoming full blown. The difficulty at present is that not everyone who has the antibodies will definitely develop the disease.

Only the courageous will undertake blood testing to see what the future may hold and then, perhaps, take a risk to treat a disease that might not develop.

31. The word *incipient* means

   (A) made or cut clearly

   (B) an opening phase

   (C) beginning to exist or appear

   (D) to start up

   (E) an occurrence or event

32. The word *presage* means

   (A) soon

   (B) precondition

   (C) exclusive right

   (D) written direction by a physician

   (E) foreshadow

33. The reader might infer from this passage that

   (A) lupus and arthritis can be effectively treated

   (B) while medical science is making progress, it still has far to go

   (C) only the courageous will undertake testing

   (D) blood tests can predict illnesses before they happen

   (E) medical science will soon make our lives longer and better

Questions 34–36

How good are you at making decisions? Are you frozen with fear at choosing a household item? Do you put off getting a new car because deciding which car is the best one is more than you can deal with?

Many companies would rather have employees who are good at making decisions, even if some of their decisions turn out badly, than employees who put off making decisions and slow down the company's operations. Some people require so much time and information before making a decision that the company loses money, and sometimes it loses big!

So employees who are always looking for the best answer may end up with no answer at all and no job. Hone your decision-making skills, and you will be a more desirable employee.

34. The tone of this selection is

   (A) conversational

   (B) formal

   (C) didactic

   (D) inspirational

   (E) pedagogical

35. In the last two paragraphs, the writer

   (A) investigates options

   (B) draws a conclusion and gives a direction

   (C) supplies examples

   (D) offers advice

   (E) suggests a new idea

36. This selection is probably from

   (A) a periodical

   (B) a business journal article

   (C) a college business course

   (D) an employee development course

   (E) a self-help book

GO ON TO THE NEXT PAGE

Questions 37–39

The eradication of malaria around the world has been a goal of world health organizations for decades. Untold millions of dollars have been spent in the search for a solution to this most intractable of diseases, a major killer of the world's poor. Quinine derivatives, once the most popular treatment for malaria, and later drugs have lost their effectiveness as the disease has become resistant to them.

Now, out of an unlikely place, an herbal remedy that has emerged from China may finally solve the problem. Although the medicine used is from sweet wormwood, called ginghaosu in China, it was only developed in 1965 by Chinese military researchers. Its successful use since then has made it attractive to international health organizations. There are 300 million cases of malaria each year, 90 percent of them in Africa, and about 1 million people die as a result of the disease. One can only hope this new herbal remedy, called artemisinin, will provide the long-sought solution to this problem.

37. The word *intractable* means

   (A) occurring within the skull
   (B) not manageable
   (C) occurring within a muscle
   (D) hard to treat or cure
   (E) the existence of foreign matter

38. The percentage of people who die from malaria each year is

   (A) 33 percent
   (B) 30 percent
   (C) 10 percent
   (D) 3 percent
   (E) one third of 1 percent

39. To *eradicate* means

   (A) before long
   (B) destroy utterly
   (C) one that erases
   (D) equivalence
   (E) a disease of cereal grasses

Questions 40–42

The American Psychiatric Association's Diagnostic Statistical Manual lists 220 psychological disorders. Is that enough? Is there a category for normal? Or, are there guidelines for normal? What if you don't engage in *aberrant* behaviors? What if, overall, you enjoy your life, including watching football games, fishing, or reading a good book?

George had wondered all of these things and more over the last few years. Was there something wrong with him that he didn't take antidepressants or other medications to fine tune his psychological state? Why wasn't there a category for normal or even supernormal? That would be for people who held a job, were good at it, loved their wives and kids, didn't fight with their relatives or neighbors, in fact, people who could list a lot of good things in their lives.

These were the kind of questions he mused over as he drove to work each day on the road with thousands of other people.

40. The style of this selection suggests it is

   (A) nonfiction
   (B) autobiography
   (C) prose
   (D) essay
   (E) fiction

41. The word *aberrant* as used in this passage means

   (A) to shrink from in fear
   (B) turning away from what is right or true
   (C) deviating from what is normal or typical
   (D) mental derangement
   (E) to incite or sanction

42. The writer is suggesting that

   (A) George feels out of step with most people
   (B) there are too many drugs on the market
   (C) there are too many psychological diagnoses
   (D) George is unhappy
   (E) George wishes he had a psychological label

GO ON TO THE NEXT PAGE

Questions 43–45

In America, some of the northeastern mills that manufacture the most luxurious fabrics are moving to the South to new mills with computerized looms that can produce more yards of fabric in a day and where there are not strong labor unions, so workers earn about 40% less than they do in New York. It is an attempt to keep their businesses alive. As it is, some of the fabrics cost a thousand dollars a yard and are used only in the White House or in the homes of the very rich.

In Scotland, some of the cashmere sweater mills are closing as that sort of textile manufacturing can be done much more cheaply in China. The raw materials are in Inner Mongolia, and low cost labor is in China. The finest cashmere sweaters that sell for several hundred dollars apiece are nearly all that is left of Scottish manufacturing. China has taken over the lower end of the market. At that, because of trade agreements, China only controls about 17% of the market. In a few years it will control 50% or more of the cashmere market.

43. Based on this information, one might deduce that

    (A) American business is failing
    (B) China is taking over production
    (C) we will never have these goods again
    (D) goods will still be produced but at different locations
    (E) luxury goods will become scarce

44. According to the passage, China's manufacturing of cashmere products will

    (A) double in a few years
    (B) triple in a few years
    (C) grow exponentially
    (D) quadruple in a few years
    (E) eventually level out

45. Based on the information in the article

    (A) some workers will lose their jobs
    (B) some workers will work for reduced pay
    (C) some new workers will have jobs
    (D) all of the above
    (E) some of the above

Questions 46–48

Reading a map correctly is a special skill. It is not the same as reading a novel or even charts and graphs. Travelers in particular need to develop good map reading skills. Good map reading skills can help them get from one place to another in the most efficient way. Inveterate map readers will frequent map stores, spending hours going through laminated maps, foldout maps, historical maps, and topographic maps to find just the right map or maps for a trip they wish to take someday.

They say online maps are just not the same. Online maps will work in a pinch, but they don't offer the same wealth of information other paper maps offer. Automobile guidance systems are O.K., too, in a pinch.

People who love perusing maps are a special breed. They are not Columbus or Ponce de Leon, but they have a little of the explorer in them.

46. This selection distinguishes between

    (A) traditional maps and online maps
    (B) online maps and auto guidance systems
    (C) map readers and explorers
    (D) poor map readers and good map readers
    (E) Ponce de Leon and Columbus

47. The selection will probably go on to discuss

    (A) more famous explorers
    (B) the skills of good map reading
    (C) how maps developed historically
    (D) the pleasure of planning an exploration on a trip using maps
    (E) specific differences in maps

48. The selection does not

    (A) teach the reader how to read a map
    (B) list many different maps
    (C) compare traditional maps with electronic maps
    (D) compare map lovers to explorers
    (E) claim map reading is a special skill

49. The word *posit* as used here means

    (A) to place in safekeeping
    (B) top deliver an item
    (C) to assume a fact or principle
    (D) location
    (E) a formal statement

50. The word *cryptic* means

    (A) a recess or depression
    (B) mysterious in meaning, puzzling
    (C) a location for secret meetings
    (D) involving a code
    (E) an occult symbol

Questions 49–50

The concept of Core Knowledge was developed in America about twenty years ago and based on research in cognitive psychology. The concept *posits* that certain cultural and historical information must be incorporated into an individual in order for that person to understand otherwise *cryptic* references in movies, popular songs, literature, and even the daily newspaper.

When young people emerge from a movie theater and say about a film, "That was weird," it is often because the filmmaker knows more literature and history than the audience does and makes references they don't understand. That is one reason why "The Matrix" films have spawned books and websites to explain the symbolism and the references therein. Unless that knowledge becomes mainstreamed in society, the films will remain cult films.

The benefit of identifying core knowledge is that more people will be able to understand each other and, sometimes, share a good laugh. Sharing the same knowledge will also reduce misunderstanding and misinterpretations in our culture.

GO ON TO THE NEXT PAGE

Math Section

50 Questions

Directions: Each of the questions in this test is followed by five suggested answers. Select the one that is best in each case. Be sure to mark all of your answers in the Mathematics section of your answer sheet.

1. Which of the following numbers is (are) composite?

    I. 15
    II. 51
    III. 61
    IV. 91

   (A) I only

   (B) I, II, and IV only

   (C) II, III, and IV only

   (D) All of these numbers are composite.

   (E) None of these numbers is composite.

2. Find three consecutive whole numbers such that the product of the two smaller numbers is equal to two more than seven times the largest number.

   Which of the following equations may be used to solve the problem above?

   (A) $x(x + 2) = 7(x + 4) + 2$

   (B) $x(x + 1) + 2 = 7(x + 2)$

   (C) $x(x + 1) = 7(x + 2) - 2$

   (D) $x(x + 1) = 7(x + 2) + 2$

   (E) $(x + 1)(x + 2) = 7x + 2$

3. A line passes through $P(0, 4)$ and $Q(10, 0)$. What is the y-value of a point also on the line if the x-value is 3?

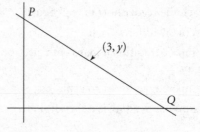

   (A) $\dfrac{14}{5}$

   (B) $\dfrac{40}{3}$

   (C) $\dfrac{6}{5}$

   (D) 2

   (E) None of these.

4. Which of the following numbers is between $\dfrac{1}{5}$ and $\dfrac{3}{10}$?

   (A) $\dfrac{1}{10}$

   (B) $\dfrac{2}{5}$

   (C) $\dfrac{3}{4}$

   (D) $\dfrac{1}{4}$

   (E) $\dfrac{1}{2}$

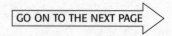

5. If x is an even number, which of the following expressions also represent even numbers?

       I. $2x + 1$
       II. $x + 5$
       III. $3x$

   (A) I only

   (B) II only

   (C) III only

   (D) II and III only

   (E) None of these are even.

6. Five ounces of pure citric acid is mixed with 45 ounces of a 20% solution of citric acid. What is the percent of citric acid in the final mixture?

   (A) 9%

   (B) 10%

   (C) 25%

   (D) 30%

   (E) 28%

7. Jon noticed that at 3:00 o'clock in the afternoon, a building that he knew to be 60 feet high casts a shadow that was 40 feet along the level ground. At the same time, another building casts a shadow 150 feet long. What is the height of the second building?

   (A) 225 feet

   (B) 170 feet

   (C) 100 feet

   (D) 16 feet

   (E) None of these.

8. Which of the following numbers is not equal to the others?

   (A) 80%

   (B) $2\frac{1}{2} \div 2$

   (C) $2 \div 2\frac{1}{2}$

   (D) $1 - 0.2$

   (E) $\frac{4}{5}$

9. Which of the following is a verbal interpretation of this algebraic expression?

   $$\frac{1}{3}(2n - 5)$$

   (A) One-third of the quantity twice a certain number less than five.

   (B) The quantity five less than twice a certain number divided by one-third.

   (C) One-third of the quantity five less than twice a certain number.

   (D) Five less than one-third of twice a certain number.

   (E) Two-thirds of a certain number minus five-thirds.

10. Perform the indicated operations.

    $$7 - [8 - 4(3 - 5)]$$

    (A) 15

    (B) 31

    (C) 9

    (D) −9

    (E) 7

11. A sheep is tied to a stake against the side of a large building, as shown in the figure below. If the rope that is used to secure the sheep is 25 feet long, what is the area over which the sheep may graze?

    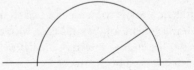

    (A) 25π square feet

    (B) $\dfrac{25\pi}{2}$ square feet

    (C) 625π square feet

    (D) $\dfrac{625\pi^2}{2}$ square feet

    (E) 312.5π square feet

GO ON TO THE NEXT PAGE

12. There is room on a bookshelf for four books, and a box of books contains six books. In how many different ways can the shelf be filled with books?

    (A) 720
    (B) 360
    (C) 24
    (D) 6
    (E) 4

13. Maria went on a diet, and her weight dropped from 125 pounds to 110 pounds. What is the percent decrease in her weight?

    (A) 12%
    (B) About 13.6%
    (C) 88%
    (D) About 114%
    (E) None of these.

14. Jenny drove 5 miles north; turned and drove 12 miles east. How far from her beginning point was she at the end of her trip?

    (A) 17 miles
    (B) $\sqrt{119}$ miles
    (C) 13 miles
    (D) $\sqrt{7}$ miles
    (E) $\sqrt{17}$ miles

15. An athletic track is composed of two straight parallel line segments of 75 yards each with two semicircles at the ends as shown in the figure. What is the area enclosed by the track?

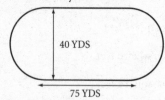

    (A) $(150 + 40\pi)$ square yards
    (B) $(3,000 + 400\pi)$ square yards
    (C) 3,000 square yards
    (D) $(4,600 + 400\pi)$ square yards
    (E) None of these.

16. Clarice took a standardized test with 60 questions. She received the following results of the test in the mail:

Raw score	56
Percent	93.3
Percentile	98
Stanine	9

    Which of the following statements is true regarding Clarice's test results?

    (A) One hundred people took the test.
    (B) Clarice's score is 9 standard deviations above the mean.
    (C) Clarice scored better than 93.3% of the people who took the test.
    (D) Clarice's friend, Eugene, scored lower than Clarice.
    (E) Ninety-eight percent of the people who took the test scored lower than Clarice.

17. The average age of the students at Pierce College is 24.8 years. The average age of the students at Valley College is 27.2 years. What additional information is needed in order to find the average age of the students at the two colleges together?

    (A) The oldest and youngest students at each college.
    (B) The graduation rates of the students at each college.
    (C) The average age of each class at each college.
    (D) The number of students at each college.
    (E) The needed information is given in the statement of the problem above.

GO ON TO THE NEXT PAGE

18. A small airplane leaves Van Nuys Airport and flies at a constant speed to San Diego Airport about 120 miles away. When the plane neared the airport in San Diego, the air controller informed the pilot that, because of heavy traffic, she should circle the airport three times before landing.

    Which of the following graphs represents this trip. The horizontal axis for each graph measures the time after leaving Van Nuys, and the vertical axis measures the distance from Van Nuys.

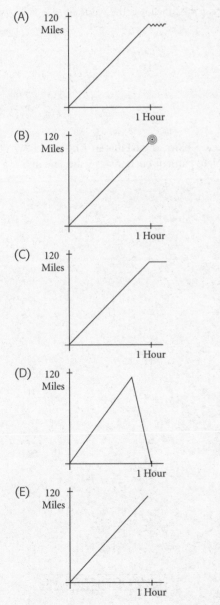

19. What is the solution set of the following equation?

    $5x - 2(x+1) = 7(x-2)$

    (A) {−3}

    (B) {4}

    (C) {3}

    (D) {0}

    (E) $\left\{\dfrac{3}{4}\right\}$

20. The diameter of a circle is equal to the length of a side of a square. If the perimeter of the square is 48, what is the area of the circle?

    (A) 9π

    (B) 12π

    (C) 18π

    (D) 36π

    (E) 144π

21. Two-fifths of Mrs. Sturm's fourth grade class read at least two books in January. One-sixth of those students read at least four books in January. If two of Mrs. Sturm's students read at least four books in January, how many students are there in her class?

    (A) 15

    (B) 24

    (C) 25

    (D) 30

    (E) 45

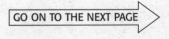

GO ON TO THE NEXT PAGE

22. If a positive number is subtracted from a negative number, which of the following will always be the result?

    (A) a positive number

    (B) a negative number

    (C) zero

    (D) a number that has the same sign as the original number with the larger absolute value

    (E) a number that has the same sign as the original number with the smaller absolute value

23. What is $\frac{1}{5}$ of 4%?

    (A) 0. 8

    (B) 0.08

    (C) 0.008

    (D) 0.0008

    (E) 0.00008

24. In a circle with center at O, the measure of arc AB is 120°. What is the measure of $\angle OBA$?

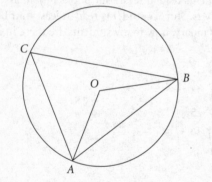

    (A) 120°

    (B) 60°

    (C) 30°

    (D) 15°

    (E) 10°

25. A men's suit is sold on sale for 15% off. What is the regular price of the suit if the sale price is $552.50?

    (A) $650.00

    (B) $82.88

    (C) $635.38

    (D) $3,683.33

    (E) None of these.

26. If $a = -3$ and $b = -5$, what is the value of $a^2 - b^2$?

    (A) −34

    (B) 34

    (C) 64

    (D) 16

    (E) −16

27. Grace can sew 5 pairs of curtains in 3 hours. How many complete pairs of curtains can she sew in 8 hours?

    (A) $13\frac{1}{3}$

    (B) 13

    (C) 14

    (D) 12

    (E) 11

GO ON TO THE NEXT PAGE

28. A poll among 38 members of a sorority showed that they were enrolled in the following classes:

    Enrolled in three classes
    3 students were enrolled in English, Math, and History.

    Enrolled in at least two classes
    5 students were enrolled in English and History.
    4 students were enrolled in English and Math.
    3 students were enrolled in History and Math.

    Enrolled in at least one class
    13 students were enrolled in English.
    15 students were enrolled in History.
    19 students were enrolled in Math.

    How many of the sorority members are enrolled in English but not in either Math or History?

    (A) 10
    (B) 6
    (C) 4
    (D) 7
    (E) 3

29. What is the probability of drawing either an ace or a club from a well-shuffled standard deck of cards?

    (A) $\frac{4}{13}$

    (B) $\frac{17}{52}$

    (C) $\frac{1}{4}$

    (D) 0

    (E) 1

30. The initial enrollment in an algebra class was 40 students. The enrollment dropped 10% during the first week of class and an additional 25% during the second week. What was the enrollment at the beginning of the third week?

    (A) 24
    (B) 25
    (C) 26
    (D) 27
    (E) 28

31. Which of the following sets of three numbers could represent the lengths of the sides of a right triangle?

    (A) $\{\sqrt{3}, 1, 3\}$
    (B) $\{\sqrt{2}, \sqrt{3}, 2\}$
    (C) $\{\sqrt{3}, 1, 2\}$
    (D) $\{\sqrt{5}, 2, 9\}$
    (E) $\{2, 2, \sqrt{3}\}$

32. Cheryl wants to carpet her living room that measures 10 feet by 15 feet and two bedrooms that measure 8 feet by 10 feet and 9 feet by 12 feet. If carpet must be bought in whole numbers of square yards, how many square yards of carpet must she purchase?

    (A) 338
    (B) 38
    (C) 37
    (D) 113
    (E) 13

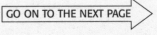

GO ON TO THE NEXT PAGE

KAPLAN

33. Which of the following statements means the same as the statement below?

    There is a real number solution to the equation $7x - 4 = x + 8$.

    (A) The number 2 is a real number.
    (B) There is only one number in the solution set of this equation.
    (C) Every linear equation has a real solution.
    (D) The number 0 is not in the solution set of this equation.
    (E) There is at least one number that, when substituted for x in the equation, makes the equation true.

34. If a and b are real numbers such that $0 < a \leq b < 1$, then which of the following must be false?

    (A) $a - b \geq 0$
    (B) $a^2 \leq b^2$
    (C) $\frac{a}{b} \leq 1$
    (D) $\frac{b}{a} \geq 1$
    (E) $ab < a$

35. Raymond won an election for school board. He beat David by 48 votes, and he beat Jack by 112 votes. If a total of 473 votes were cast in the election, how many votes did Raymond receive?

    (A) 262
    (B) 104
    (C) 158
    (D) 211
    (E) None of these.

36. What is the product of $(2x + 3)$ and $(x - 5)$?

    (A) $2x^2 - 15$
    (B) $2x^2 + 7x - 15$
    (C) $2x^2 - 7x - 15$
    (D) $2x^2 - 13x - 15$
    (E) $2x^2 + 13x - 15$

37. What is the result of performing these operations? *Divide three by one-half and then add one.*

    (A) $2\frac{1}{2}$
    (B) 7
    (C) $1\frac{2}{3}$
    (D) 2
    (E) None of these.

38. What is the sum of the interior angles of a hexagon?

    (A) $720°$
    (B) $360°$
    (C) $1,080°$
    (D) $540°$
    (E) $900°$

39. At Moneybags Bank, the number of personal accounts is 300 more than five times the number of business accounts. Which of the following equations expresses this relationship?

    (A) $b = 5p - 300$
    (B) $5p = b + 300$
    (C) $p = 5b + 300$
    (D) $5p + 300 = b$
    (E) $5(b - 300) = p$

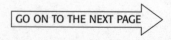

GO ON TO THE NEXT PAGE

40. A rectangular piece of cardboard is 5 feet long. A circle of greatest possible area is to be cut from this piece of cardboard. What additional information would allow calculation of the area of the circle?

    I. The width of the cardboard.
    II. The thickness of the cardboard.
    III. The area of the cardboard.

    (A) I only
    (B) II only
    (C) III only
    (D) I, II, or III
    (E) I or III only

41. Which of the following is greater than T for any positive value of T?

    (A) 80% of T
    (B) 20% of T
    (C) $\frac{2}{3}T$
    (D) $T \div \frac{2}{3}$
    (E) $T - \frac{1}{2}$

42. Five pizzas were ordered for a party. Each of the pizzas were divided into eight equal slices. Three-fourths of the pizza was eaten during the party. The next day for lunch, two-fifths of the remaining pizza was eaten. How many slices of pizza are left?

    (A) 6
    (B) 10
    (C) 8
    (D) 4
    (E) 30

43. In the accompanying diagram, $AB = BC$ and the measure of $\angle B$ is 70°. What is the measure of $\angle BCD$?

    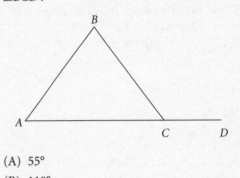

    (A) 55°
    (B) 110°
    (C) 70°
    (D) 35°
    (E) 125°

44. Roger rides his bike out into the country at a rate of 30 miles per hour. He eats lunch and rests for 2 hours. He then rides back at the rate of 20 miles per hour. If he was gone a total of five hours, how far did he ride out into the country?

    (A) 72 miles
    (B) 36 miles
    (C) 60 miles
    (D) 120 miles
    (E) 75 miles

45. A rectangular solid measures 8 inches by 5 inches by 2 inches. What is the total surface area of this object?

    (A) 80 square inches
    (B) 66 square inches
    (C) 132 square inches
    (D) 93 square inches
    (E) 160 square inches

GO ON TO THE NEXT PAGE

KAPLAN

46. Corey has taken four tests in his algebra class. He has kept the first three tests that have scores of 92, 86, and 90. He can't find the fourth test, but he knows that his average for all four tests is 90. What score did he have on his fourth test?

    (A) 89
    (B) 90
    (C) 91
    (D) 92
    (E) 93

47. Al is twice as old as Bobby, and Bobby is 9 years younger than Chuck. If Al is 14 years old, how old will Chuck be in 4 years?

    (A) 16 years old
    (B) 20 years old
    (C) 11 years old
    (D) 18 years old
    (E) 7 years old

48. What is the solution of the following inequality?

    $5 - 3(x - 2) > -1$

    (A) $x < 4$
    (B) $x > 4$
    (C) $x < \dfrac{4}{3}$
    (D) $x < 0$
    (E) $x > 0$

49. After a basketball game, the cleaning crew of 10 people can clean the Staples Center arena in 4 hours. On a day when there will be a hockey game in Staples Center 3 hours after the basketball game, how many cleaning crew people should be used?

    (A) 14
    (B) $13\dfrac{1}{3}$
    (C) 8
    (D) $7\dfrac{1}{2}$
    (E) 15

50. A box contains five identical slips of paper. On each slip of paper one of the following letters is written: a, b, c, d, and e. Three slips of paper are chosen one at a time and placed on a table in the order chosen. What is the probability that the slips of paper spell the word "bed" correctly?

    (A) $\dfrac{3}{5}$
    (B) $\dfrac{3}{5}$
    (C) $\dfrac{1}{5}$
    (D) $\dfrac{1}{30}$
    (E) $\dfrac{1}{60}$

GO ON TO THE NEXT PAGE

Writing Section

Directions: The Writing section contains two essay topics. Be sure you write about the given topics. Essays on topics of your choosing will not be acceptable. Your written responses must be your work, must be in your own words, and must not be plagiarized from some other work.

The topics are designed to give you an opportunity to demonstrate your skills in writing effectively. Spend some time considering the topics and organizing your ideas before you start. For the essays, be sure to address all parts of the topics, support generalizations with examples, and use multiple paragraphs.

You may use any space provided in the test booklet to write notes or to prepare an outline or rough draft. However, your score will be based solely on the versions written in the space provided in your answer document. Please write as neatly and legibly as possible. To ensure that you have enough space for your essays, do not skip lines, write in large print, or leave large margins.

TOPIC 1

Albert Einstein once wrote, "A hundred times every day I remind myself that my inner and outer life depends on the labors of other men, living and dead, and that I must exert myself in order to give in the measure as I have received and am still receiving." Do you agree or disagree with his view? Support your opinion with one or more specific examples.

_____

_____

_____

_____

_____

_____

_____

_____

_____

GO ON TO THE NEXT PAGE >

KAPLAN

GO ON TO THE NEXT PAGE

TOPIC 2

Many children show an early preference for either reading or math, and we have many memories of events early in life that shaped or defined our own attitudes toward those subjects. Write about one such event in your childhood. Identify the people involved and the effect each had on you. How did it affect your progress and choices in life?

GO ON TO THE NEXT PAGE ⟶

KAPLAN)

STOP

Practice Test Three: **Answer Key**

READING TEST		MATH TEST		WRITING TEST
1. B	26. B	1. B	26. E	See Sample Essay on page 337.
2. E	27. D	2. D	27. B	
3. D	28. E	3. A	28. D	
4. B	29. C	4. D	29. A	
5. A	30. C	5. C	30. D	
6. E	31. C	6. E	31. C	
7. E	32. E	7. A	32. B	
8. C	33. B	8. B	33. E	
9. B	34. A	9. C	34. A	
10. A	35. B	10. D	35. D	
11. B	36. D	11. E	36. C	
12. D	37. B	12. B	37. B	
13. C	38. E	13. A	38. A	
14. A	39. B	14. C	39. C	
15. B	40. E	15. B	40. E	
16. A	41. C	16. E	41. D	
17. D	42. A	17. D	42. A	
18. C	43. D	18. A	43. E	
19. D	44. B	19. C	44. B	
20. C	45. D	20. D	45. C	
21. B	46. A	21. D	46. D	
22. A	47. D	22. B	47. B	
23. B	48. A	23. C	48. A	
24. D	49. C	24. C	49. A	
25. C	50. B	25. A	50. E	

KAPLAN

Answers and Explanations

READING SECTION

1. B

(B) is the best because (D), which also looks like a possibility, assumes we already have a fixed body of knowledge. Choice (A) is too general a statement. There is no evidence for (C) or (E) in the paragraph.

2. E

The author gives two examples, but they are a little too brief to be called stories (B). (E) is a better choice than (A), which doesn't state the choice properly. Yes, there are details, but they are in the form of examples. (D) is not a suitable choice because this is an historical argument, so the use of historical information is a given.

3. D

This is the 5,000 coins found that included the Domitianus coin. (C) and (D) can also be difficult to choose between, but (D) is the better answer. Some pots are called "cache pots," but if you read the possible choices in place of *cache*, you will see that only (D) makes sense.

4. B

The last paragraph is the strongest persuasive part of the essay. The phrases "We need" and "We must" are signals of a persuasive tone. A *jeremiad* (A) has a very negative tone that is not applicable here. A *scientific report* (C) would have a very detached and straightforward tone. A *narrative* (D) tells a story so is set forth in some pattern of chronological development. A *review* (E) will summarize and evaluate.

5. A

Favorable statistics always strengthen arguments more than the other possible choices. The other choices are all less desirable. (B) is probably the next best choice if the examples were well chosen. (C), *testimony by celebrities*, would only be of value if the celebrities were experts in the field. *Comparison to historical conditions* (D) is too

vague an answer to know its effects. *Use of the passive voice* (E) will always be a weak choice because it is rarely forceful in tone.

6. E

(E) is the best choice. Here, the more general term is the best choice. *Document* (A) and *monograph* (B) are both unclear except that governments don't usually commission documents or monographs. They will commission studies and reports. Follow the general rule of trying to fit the word into the sentence to see whether or not it makes sense. (C) does not make sense at all.

7. E

Choices (A), (B), (C), and (D) are clearly stated in the passage. An implied statement is never clearly stated. A thoughtful reader will surmise (E) based on a reading of the whole passage.

8. C

The use of medical terminology should be a clue that more terminology may be expected in the remainder of the article. Look at the content of the article. (A) is too general, and (B) is not a satisfactory choice because the article does include explanations, but its topic is broader than simply medications (D) and the brain (E).

9. B

(B) is actually mentioned immediately before autoimmune disorders in the last sentence, and so the two are grouped in the passage as a joint idea. The other choices are symptoms of other disorders.

10. A

Reread carefully to understand this answer. If you are looking for an office number or name, it should be included in building abbreviations. (B) is not the best choice because it is between 149 and 151 (C), which have other designations. (D), the campus map, won't give a clear answer. (E), the telephone directory, won't provide the information you want.

KAPLAN

11. B

Department and program organization should list an office and phone number under individual titles. The other choices are inappropriate because of limitations inherent in their titles.

12. D

A map of the campus would probably be most helpful. It should show buildings and parking lots. The other choices are too narrow in their scope

13. C

The last paragraph states these plans that may or may not happen. Choice (A) does not follow logically from the prompt. (B) makes an assumption that is probably unwarranted. You might mistakenly choose (D), but a rereading of the middle paragraph says students recover from early frustration. Choice (E) does not follow logically from the prompt.

14. A

This is the most complete answer of the choices. Choices (B) and (D) are possible answers but not as comprehensive as choice (A). Choices (C) and (E) are not mentioned or implied.

15. B

This is deducible from reading the last sentence of the first paragraph. Choice (A) is stated, but not the best answer because it is not as broad a choice as (B). (C), (D), and (E) are not stated or implied. The passage says that parents believe it is important.

16. A

(A) is the most general of the choices, but it is the best. All of the examples show different sizes, ages, and goals of organizations with similar purposes. (B) goes beyond what is stated in the passage. (C) would be appropriate if this were a persuasive essay. (D) and (E) are poor choices because they state the opposite of what is claimed in the passage.

17. D

This choice that relies on evidence would be the most effective. Evidence is always a strong argument whether for or against a position. (A) is a poor choice because it represents a philosophy rather than evidence. (B), *a listing of costs*, would be interesting but is not relevant to the discussion. (C) is improper because opinions are not ever as strong as evidence. (E) is not a valid choice because experience in foreign projects cannot necessarily be equated to experience in American projects.

18. C

They think about leaving the world a better place. See the first sentence of the last paragraph to clarify this answer. Choice (B) does not follow logically, nor is it stated in the passage. (C), (D), and (E) are also not mentioned in the passage. In fact, *traditional ideas* is too vague to be meaningful.

19. D

Reread the two sentences in the last paragraph together to recognize the lack of logical connection. Choices (A), (C), and (E) reflect attitude and opinion. The tone of the piece doesn't support any of those choices. Choice (B) doesn't have any meaning in itself.

20. C

This is the correct denotative definition. Both (A) and (B) are negative definitions and do not fit if you substitute either of them in place of *prodigious*. Choices (D) and (E), although not so negative in tone, also do not make sense.

21. B

This also is the denotative definition. Can you figure it in the context? Read the choices into the sentence to see if they make sense. Choices (A), (C), (D), and (E) do not make sense.

22. A

(A) is the only answer justified by content. Choices (B) and (C) may be implied, but they are not specifically stated. (D) is neither implied nor stated, and (E) is something the reader may infer, but it is not stated.

23. B

(B) is the only possible answer based on an understanding of content. (A) is not supported by content. If anything, the author is in favor of these classes, so (C) is an improper choice, as is (D). He does mention AP and Honors classes separately but does not differentiate.

24. D

Only (D) is correct in terms of content. The question does not ask for your opinion (A) and (E). (B) and (C) are improper choices because the author states that students claim to be motivated, but he does not speculate about that, and he does not speculate about data and percentages.

25. C

(C) covers succulents and seed propagation. Choice (A) is not completely focused on plant propagation. (B) looks as if it may be a possible answer but only talks about seeds. Choice (D) refers to succulents and imported plants. (E) is completely focused on succulents.

26. B

Form and Mode of Life, page 11, may be helpful as well, but it is not a choice. (A), which refers to cultivation, is not relevant. (C) refers to *repotting*, (D) to *seed propagation*, and (E) *uses* and are also not suitable.

27. D

This section would be the most complete. The other choices all focus on selective topics, but a prospective gardener would want the most complete information.

28. E

Only this choice includes both correct options. The passage is not persuasive, and so (B) is not a proper choice. Choices (A), (C), and (D) only offer one choice each. None of them are appropriate meanings.

29. C

The passage contains *only* complex sentences. Complex sentences combine an independent and a dependent or subordinate clause. The alternative choices are not suitable.

30. C

This answer is the broadest in terms of who would be interested in this information. The other choices are much narrower in scope and therefore not as good as (C).

31. C

This is the denotative definition. Can you determine this from content? Use the method you have used before, reading the choices into the sentence. You will see that the sentence does not communicate meaning with any of the other choices.

32. E

(E) is another denotative definition. This answer should be determinable from the content of the sentence. Read the word choices into the sentence for meaning. (C) at first looks like a possibility, but is not as good a choice as (E). The others will not make sense.

33. B

This is an inference. All of the answers are not yet provided, as one can see by reading what is holding some cures back. (B) is not stated or even implied. (C) is directly stated, so the reader would not be inferring that information. (D) is not a good choice because the blood test predictors are not universally accurate. Some people get the disease without predictors having shown up on a blood test. (E) may be true, but it is not stated or suggested in the article.

34. A

The question and the phrases "loses big" and "and no job" all make the tone conversational. *Pedagogical* and *didactic* or instructive language, (C) and (E), are likely to be drier in tone. *Formal* language (B) would not include the above phrases, and *inspirational* language (D) would be more suitable to a different topic.

35. B

The author draws a conclusion in paragraph 3 and gives a direction in paragraph 4. The two choices in (B) make this a more complete answer than the other choices. The last two paragraphs are very brief, so none of the other choices are appropriate. Choices (A) and (C) would require longer paragraphs to be proper choices. Choice (D) is a possibility, but the structure of the sentence is directive. It does not make an offer. For the same reason, (E) is not a proper choice.

36. D

It is part of an attempt to develop effective skills in employees so they will have more success. Its informal tone suggests it is appropriate for instruction at the work place rather than choices (A), (B), or (C). (E) would also be possible but not as good because it would offer methods to hone decision-making skills if it were a self-help book.

37. B

Look at the context to help you answer this correctly. Read the word into the sentence for meaning. (A), (C), and (E) do not make sense. (B) and (D) could be difficult to choose between, but (B) is a better choice because of the prefix *in*, which means *not*.

38. E

First, estimate the relationship. One million is a small portion of 300 million. In fact, it's the smallest portion, even though a million is a very large number, particularly when you are speaking of disease. A third would be 100 million. Thirty percent would be slightly less than that. Ten percent would be 30 million, and 3% would be approximately 7 million.

39. B

Look at the grammatical form of the word. It is a verb; so nouns, such as (C) and (E), would not be appropriate substitutes. (A) and (D), if read into the sentence, don't make sense. (B) is also the denotative definition.

40. E

The second paragraph tells you this is fiction as George is introduced as someone who is ruminating as he drives to work. In other words, he is a character. (A) is not valid because this is obviously fiction. (B) is not appropriate because autobiography would be written in the first person, not the third person. (C) could be considered; however, although this is not poetry, fiction (E) is a more specific answer. (D) is an improper choice because this is clearly not an essay.

41. C

Aberrant is often used in psychological writing. This is the dictionary definition. A clue is in the first two letters of the word, similar to abnormal, but not the same because it

does not carry such a negative connotation. Another way to find the answer is to look at part of speech. In the sentence, *aberrant* is used as an adjective, modifying the noun *behaviors*. Choice (A) functions as a verb. (B) is similar. Neither (D) nor (E) would replace an adjective.

42. A

George's feeling different is evident through his thoughts in both paragraphs. There is no statement about too many drugs being on the market (B) or too many psychological diagnoses (C). George does not appear to be unhappy (D) or to be wishing for a psychological label (E). In fact, he seems to have a satisfying life.

43. D

There is no evidence the goods in question will not be produced. There is also no evidence in the passage of American business failing (A). Yes, China is taking over production in some cases, but not in all cases, (B). There is also no indication that we will never have these goods again (C). Also, it is clear from both paragraphs that luxury goods will continue to be produced (E).

44. B

Estimated growth increasing from 17% to 50% will nearly triple. If growth doubled, it would be at about 34% (A). Exponential growth is much faster than either of these choices (C). Quadrupling growth would mean an upward change of 84%. There is no indication in the passage that growth will level out (E).

45. D

All of the above will be true. The change in production locales will benefit some workers (C) and create problems for others (A) and (B). Since (A), (B), and (C) are each partially true, (E) is not a viable choice.

46. A

The contrast is between information given in the first and second paragraphs. Auto guidance maps are discussed similarly in the same paragraph, so there is no contrast between them (B). While explorers are mentioned (C), they are not specifically distinguished from modern map-readers. Choice (D) is not a good choice because that is not actually distinguished. Choice (E) is unsuitable because whereas de Leon and Columbus are mentioned, they are paired not contrasted.

47. D

The language (love) and the content suggest this will be the next topic. It will be a continuation of what has gone on before. The phrase about de Leon and Columbus is not significant enough to expect further discussion of explorers (A). (B) is poor because although it has been mentioned, it is not likely to be developed further following the last sentence. (C) and (E) are very specific and not likely to be continued in light of the general tone of the passage.

48. A

This is the only choice not included in the reading selection. The selection does mention different types of maps (B), and it does compare types of maps (C). It also includes choices (D) and (E).

49. C

This is the denotative definition, which should be obvious from the context of the sentence. Look at the grammatical identity of the word. It is used as a verb, but choices (A) and B, also possible to be used as verbs, do not make sense in the sentence. (C) and (D) are nouns, so they would not fit grammatically.

50. B

This is also a denotative meaning that should be clear from the paragraph. Here you must apply more than sentence usage to determine the correct meaning. (A) and (C) may look possible because of an association with the word *crypt*, but they don't make sense in the larger context. (D) and (E) also don't really make sense, although they could be erroneously associated with the something secret or unknown.

MATHEMATICS SECTION

1. B

Composite numbers have more than two factors.

    I. Composite

    II. Composite

    III. 61 is prime, not composite.

    IV. Composite

2. D

Let the consecutive whole numbers be x, $x + 1$, and $x + 2$. *The product of the two smaller numbers is* $x(x + 1)$, and *two more than seven times the largest is* $7(x + 2) + 2$. (A) If the problem had stated *consecutive even or odd whole numbers,* then this would have been the equation. (B) The "+ 2" is on the wrong side of the equation. (C) The problem states *two more than* not *two less than.* (E) In this equation, the two larger numbers are multiplied, not the two smaller.

3. A

By drawing a vertical segment at point P, similar triangles are formed. Set up a proportion to compare corresponding sides of the triangles:

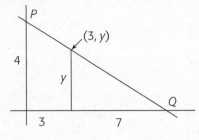

$\dfrac{4}{y} = \dfrac{10}{7}$ Cross multiply.

$10y = 28$ Divide both sides by 10.

$y = \dfrac{14}{5}$

(B) and (C) The 3 is not part of either of the similar triangles, so it shouldn't appear in the proportion. (D) is probably just a guess based on the diagram.

4. D

Write each number with the lowest common denominator 20.

$\dfrac{1}{5} = \dfrac{4}{20}$ and $\dfrac{3}{10} = \dfrac{6}{20}$, so $\dfrac{5}{20} = \dfrac{1}{4}$ is obviously between them. (A) $\dfrac{1}{10} = \dfrac{2}{20}$ Not between them.

(B) $\dfrac{2}{5} = \dfrac{8}{20}$ Not between them. (C) $\dfrac{3}{4} = \dfrac{15}{20}$ Not between them. (E) $\dfrac{1}{2} = \dfrac{10}{20}$ Not between them.

5. C

(A), (B), (D), and (E) Pick some representative even number, say 6. Then:

    I. $2x + 1 = 2 \times 6 + 1 = 13$ Odd

    II. $x + 5 = 6 + 5 = 11$ Odd

    III. $3x = 3 \times 6 = 18$ Even

So only $3x$ will be even for any even choice of x.

6. E

There are 9 ounces of pure citric acid in the original mixture.

20% of 45 is 9

By adding five ounces of pure citric acid to the mixture, there are now 14 ounces of pure citric acid in a total of 50 ounces of mixture. Then the question becomes:

14 is what percent of 50?

Set up a proportion: $\dfrac{14}{50} = \dfrac{P}{100}$ Cross multiply.

$50P = 1,400$ Divide both sides by 50.

$P = 28$ 28% of the final mixture is acid.

(A) No, there are 9 ounces of pure citric acid in the original mixture. (B) disregards the acid in the mixture to begin with. That is, 5 is 10% of 50. (C) and (D) appear to be guesses.

7. A

This is a direct proportion problem.

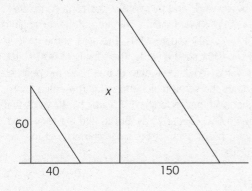

Set up a proportion:

$\dfrac{60}{x} = \dfrac{40}{150}$ Cross multiply.

$40x = 9{,}000$

$x = 225$

The second building is 225 feet high.

(B) Perhaps thinking that because the first building is 20 feet higher than its shadow is long, the second building will have the same relationship to its shadow. (C) is the solution to the incorrect proportion: $\dfrac{40}{x} = \dfrac{60}{150}$. (D) is the solution that would be the result of treating the problem as an indirect proportion problem.

8. B

The only one that's different is $2\dfrac{1}{2} \div 2$.

Write each number in simplest form.

(A) $80\% = \dfrac{80}{100} = \dfrac{4}{5}$

(B) $2\dfrac{1}{2} \div 2 = \dfrac{5}{2} \div 2 = \dfrac{5}{2} \times \dfrac{1}{2} = \dfrac{5}{4} = 1\dfrac{1}{4}$

(C) $2 \div 2\dfrac{1}{2} = 2 \div \dfrac{5}{2} = \dfrac{2}{1} \times \dfrac{2}{5} = \dfrac{4}{5}$

(D) $1 - 0.2 = 0.8 = \dfrac{8}{10} = \dfrac{4}{5}$

(E) $\dfrac{4}{5}$

9. C

(A) is the interpretation of this phrase: $\dfrac{1}{3}(5 - 2n)$. (B) is the interpretation of this phrase: $\dfrac{2n - 5}{\frac{1}{3}}$. (D) is the interpretation of this phrase: $\dfrac{1}{3}(2n - 5)$. (E) is the interpretation of this phrase: $\dfrac{2}{3}n - \dfrac{5}{3}$. Although this expression is equivalent to the original expression, it is not the direct interpretation of the given phrase.

10. D

$7 - [8 - 4(3 - 5)]$	Evaluate the innermost grouping symbol first.
$= 7 - [8 - 4(-2)]$	Perform multiplication before subtraction.
$= 7 - [8 - (-8)]$	
$= 7 - 16$	Apply the rule for subtraction.
$= 7 + (-16) = -9$	

(A) is the result of subtracting $8 - 4$ before multiplying—a violation of the order of operation rules. (B) is the result of misapplying the distributive property—there is a sign error. (C) is a sign error in the last step. (E) is probably the result of erroneously subtracting $8 - (-8)$ and getting 0.

11. E

The area is half a circle with radius 25. The formula for the area of half a circle is $A = \dfrac{1}{2}\pi r^2$. So this area is

$\dfrac{1}{2}\pi(25)^2 = \dfrac{1}{2}\pi(625) = 312.5\pi$ square feet. (A) and (B) are misinterpreting the formula. (C) Right formula but forgot the $\dfrac{1}{2}$. (D) The value of π is not squared in the formula.

12. B

For the four spaces on the shelf of books, the first space can be filled in 6 ways by picking any one of the 6 books from the box. The second space then can be filled in 5 ways, the third in 4 ways, and the fourth in 3 ways. So all four spaces can be filled in $6 \times 5 \times 4 \times 3 = 360$ ways. (A) For the answer, the 2 is not included because there are only 4 spaces. (C) Multiplying 6 times 4 is not the correct approach for this problem. (D) Six is just the number of ways of filling the first spot on the shelf. (E) The number of spots for books is not the same as the number of ways of filling the spots.

13. A

Maria's weight decreased 15 pounds, so the question is:

15 is what percent of 125?

Write a proportion: $\dfrac{15}{125} = \dfrac{P}{100}$ Cross multiply.

$125P = 1,500$ Divide both sides by 125.

$P = 12$ Maria lost 12% of her weight.

(B) is the answer to: *15 is what percent of 110.* (C) is the answer to: *110 is what percent of 125.* (D) is the answer to: *125 is what percent of 110.*

14. C

Use the Pythagorean theorem.

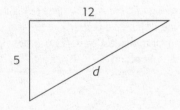

$d^2 = 5^2 + 12^2$

$d^2 = 25 + 144$

$d^2 = 169$

So $d = 13$.

(A) The addition must be done before the square root is done. (B) The Pythagorean theorem has a + sign in this form. (D) Square and add, not subtract. (E) Square and add.

15. B

The interior of the track consists of a rectangle that is 75 yards by 40 yards and two semicircles (one complete circle) with a 20-yard radius. The area of the rectangle is $75 \times 40 = 3,000$ square yards. The area of the circle is $\pi(20)^2 = 400\pi$ square yards. The total is $(3,000 + 400\pi)$ square yards. (A) is the length of the track—the perimeter. (C) ignores the semicircular ends. (D) The entire track is contained within a rectangle 115 yards by 40 yards that has area 4,600 square yards. But to find the requested area, you should subtract the small corners, not the semicircles.

16. E

This is exactly the interpretation of percentile. (A) There is no hint about the number of people who took the test. (B) The 9th stanine contains the top 14% of the scores. Nine standard deviations would be much farther out. (C) Clarice's percent on the test indicates that she got 93.3% of the questions correct. It has no relationship to others who took the test. (D) There is absolutely no information about Eugene's test results.

17. D

This is a weighted average, weighted by the number of students at each college. (A) The oldest and youngest students will not aid in finding the weighted average. (B) Graduation rates have nothing to do with age. (C) Some of the students will be counted more than once in this scheme, so the average would not be accurate. (E) You cannot find the average by averaging the averages.

18. A

The straight segment represents the constant speed, and the wavy section at the top indicates that the plane gets nearer and farther away from Van Nuys as the plane circles the airport. (B) This graph is not even continuous near the airport. The plane's trip is certainly continuous. (C) The short straight segment at the top indicates that the plane's distance from Van Nuys is not changing as it circles the airport, but the distance does change. (D) This graph indicates that the plane returns to Van Nuys. (E) This graph does not show the plane circling the airport.

19. C

$5x - 2(x + 1) = 7(x - 2)$ Simplify both sides.

$5x - 2x - 2 = 7x - 14$

$3x - 2 - 2 = 7x - 14$ Subtract $3x$ from both sides.

$-2 = 4x - 14$ Add 14 to both sides.

$12 = 4x$ Divide both sides by 4.

$3 = x$ The solution is {3}.

(A) There is a sign error probably near the end of the process. (B) Perhaps by adding 14 to both sides, you ended up with $16 = 4x$ in error. (D) is probably the result of incorrectly applying the distributive property on the right side of the equation: $7x - 2$. (E) is probably the result of incorrectly applying the distributive property on both sides of the equation: $5x - 2x + 1 = 7x - 2$.

20. D

The perimeter of a square is 4 times the length of a side. So the length of a side of a square is the perimeter divided by 4. The length of a side of the square in this question is $\frac{48}{4}$, which is 12. The diameter of this circle is equal to the length of a side of this square. So the diameter of this circle is 12. The diameter of a circle is twice the radius. So the radius of a circle is half the diameter. The radius of the circle in this question is $\frac{12}{2}$, or 6. The area of circle with a radius r is πr^2. The radius of this circle is 6, so the area of this circle is $\pi(6^2) = \pi(36) = 36\pi$.

21. D

Let x be the number of students in Mrs. Sturm's class. Then the equation is:

$\frac{1}{6}\left(\frac{2}{5}x\right) = 2$ Simplify the left side.

$\frac{1}{15}x = 2$ Multiply both sides by 15.

$x = 30$ There are 30 students in her class.

(A) Two-fifths of 15 is 6, and one-sixth of 6 is one student. (B) Two-fifths is not a whole number, so this could not be the answer. (C) Two-fifths of 25 is 10, and one-sixth of 10 is not a whole number. (E) Two-fifths of 45 is 18, and one-sixth of 18 is three students.

22. B

Use an example: $-4 - 7 = -4 + (-7) = -11$. For other choices of numbers, the result will always be negative. (A), (C), and (D) The example above serves as a counterexample for these choices. (E) The following is a counterexample: $-7 - 4 = -7 + (-4) = -11$.

23. C

A quick glance at the choices indicates that the problem should be done in decimal form. The fraction $\frac{1}{5}$ is equivalent to the decimal 0.2, and 4% is equivalent to the decimal 0.04. The word *of* is normally translated as multiplication, so: $\frac{1}{5} \times (0.04) = (0.2)(0.04) = 0.008$. (A), (B), (D), and (E) are each the result of some error in the explanation above.

24. C

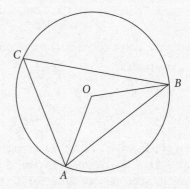

The central angle $\angle AOB$ has the same measure as the intercepted arc, 120°. In $\triangle AOB$, sides AO and BO have the same length because they are radii of the same circle. Angles OAB and OBA total 60°, and they have the same measure, so each angle measures 30°. (A) The central angle is 120°, not the requested angle. (B) The sum of the two base angles is 60°, so each is 30°. (D) and (E) are probably guesses based on the diagram.

25. A

If the suit is bought on sale for 15% off, then the buyer paid 85% of the original price. So, *552.50 is 85% of what price?* Write a proportion:

$\dfrac{552.50}{x} = \dfrac{85}{100}$ Cross multiply

$85x = 55{,}250$ Divide both sides by 85.

$x = 650$ The original price is $650.

(B) is approximately 15% of $552.50. (C) is the result of adding 15% of $552.50 to $552.50. This is not the proper approach to this problem. (D) is the answer to the question: *$552.50 is 15% of what number.*

26. E

Substitute the given values into the expression:

$(-3)^2 - (-5)^2$ Evaluate exponents first.

$= 9 - 25$ Apply the rule for subtraction.

$= 9 + (-25)$

$= -16$

(A) would have resulted from an incorrect sign on the first term. (B) would have resulted from an incorrect sign on the second term. (C) It appears that the values were added first and then squared. (D) is a sign error in the last step.

27. B

This is a direct proportion problem. Set up a proportion:

$\dfrac{5}{x} = \dfrac{3}{8}$ Cross multiply.

$3x = 40$ Divide both sides by 3.

$x = \dfrac{40}{3} = 13\dfrac{1}{3}$

Since fractions of pairs of curtains are not complete pairs, you must round down. She can make 13 pairs of curtains. (A) The answer must be rounded down. (C) The mixed number cannot be rounded up. (D) and (E) appear to be guesses.

28. D

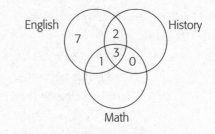

A Venn diagram will help answer this question. Three students were enrolled in all three classes. These three are in the center region. Five students are enrolled in English and History. But there are already 3 there, so there are 2 more in the region above the center. Four students are enrolled in English and Math, so there is one more in the region left of the center. Three students are enrolled in History and Math, so there are no more in the region right of center. Thirteen are enrolled in English, but there are already 6 in the English circle, so there will be 7 more in the remaining region in the English circle. There are 7 students enrolled in English but not in either Math or History. (You can fill in the remaining regions with the appropriate numbers.)

29. A

There are 52 cards in the deck and 4 aces and 13 clubs, but if you add 4 and 13, the ace of clubs is counted twice. So the probability is $\dfrac{4 + 13 - 1}{52} = \dfrac{16}{52} = \dfrac{4}{13}$

(B) The ace of clubs is counted twice. (C) is the probability of choosing clubs only. (D) A probability of 0 means that the event could not occur, but ace or club certainly can occur. (E) A probability of 1 means that the event is sure to happen, but a heart or other outcomes is also possible.

30. D

The enrollment dropped 10% (4 students) in the first week, leaving 36 students. In the second week, 25% dropped. Nine students (that's 25% of 36) dropped in the second week, so there are $36 - 9 = 27$ students left to begin the third week.

(A), (B), and (E) seem to be guesses. (C) If, in the second week, 25% of the *initial* enrollment had dropped, then this choice would be the result. But a percent change always refers to the beginning amount in that time period.

31. C

The lengths of the sides of a right triangle must satisfy the Pythagorean theorem, $a^2 + b^2 + c^2$, in which c is the longest side. $(\sqrt{3})^2 + 1^2 = 3 + 1 = 4 = 2^2 = 4$, so these lengths could be the sides of a right triangle.

(A) $(\sqrt{3})^2 + 1^2 = 3 + 1 = 4 \neq 3^2 = 9$ Not a right triangle.

(B) $(\sqrt{2})^2 + (\sqrt{3})^2 = 2 + 3 = 5 \neq 2^2 = 4$ Not a right triangle.

(D) $(\sqrt{5})^2 + (2)^2 = 5 + 4 = 9 \neq 9^2 = 81$ Not a right triangle.

(E) $2 + 2^2 = 4 + 4 = 8 \neq (\sqrt{3})^2 = 3$ Not a right triangle.

32. B

The total number of square feet of carpet is

$(10)(15) + (8)(10) + (9)(12) = 150 + 80 + 108 = 338$.

Because there are 9 square feet in a square yard, divide this total by 9, and because only whole numbers of square yards can be purchased, you must round up.

$338 \div 9 = 37.555\ldots$

Cheryl must buy 38 square yards of carpet.

(A) There are 338 square *feet*, not yards, of carpet. (C) The result of division must be rounded up, not down. (D) To convert square feet to square yards, divide by 9, not 3. (E) To convert square feet to square yards, divide by 9, not 27.

33. E

The phrase *there is…* means that there is at least one… .

(A) Even though 2 is the solution to the equation, this statement does not say that. (B) The phrase *there is…* means that there is at least one…, not that there is only one… . (C) refers only to this equation and no other. Not every linear equation has a real solution. (D) says nothing about any specific number.

34. A

Let $a = 0.2$ and $b = 0.5$, then $a - b = 0.2 - 0.5 = -0.3$, which is not greater than or equal to zero. (B) Since both a and b are positive, this will be true. Just square both sides of the inequality $a \leq b$. (C) Since both a and b are positive, divide both sides of the inequality $a \leq b$ by b. (D) Since both a and b are positive, divide both sides of the inequality $a \leq b$ by a and write it in reverse order.

$a \leq b$ \qquad Divide by a.

$$\frac{a}{a} \leq \frac{b}{a}$$

$1 \leq \dfrac{b}{a}$ \qquad This means the same as $\dfrac{b}{a} \geq 1$.

(E) Since both a and b are positive, multiply both sides of that portion of the inequality $b < 1$ by a: $ab < a$.

35. D

Let x equal the number of votes that Raymond received. Then, since he beat David and Jack, they must have received fewer votes than Raymond.

Raymond	x
David	$x - 48$
Jack	$x - 112$

The equation is therefore:

$x + (x - 48) + (x - 112) = 473$ \qquad Simplify the left side.

$3x - 160 = 473$ \quad Add 160 to both sides.

$3x = 633$ \quad Divide both sides by 3.

$x = 211$ \quad Raymond got 211 votes.

(A) His opponents received a total of 262 votes. (B) If you had subtracted 160 instead of adding it to both sides of the equation, this would have been an approximate answer. (C) is approximately one third of the total number of votes cast—a nonsense answer.

36. C

Use the procedure known by its acronym FOIL.

$(2x + 3)(x - 5)$

$= x^2 - 10x + 3x - 15$

$= x^2 - 7x - 15$

(A) Applying FOIL typically results in a polynomial with three terms, not two. (B) There is a sign error on the second term. (D) and (E) Since the Outer and Inner products have different signs, you must subtract, not add to get the middle term.

37. B

A literal translation of this sentence is:

$3 \div \dfrac{1}{2} + 1$ Do the division first.

$\dfrac{3}{1} \times \dfrac{2}{1} + 1$

$6 + 1 = 7$

(A) results from multiplying instead of dividing. (C) results from mistakenly multiplying instead of dividing and ending up with the answer inverted. (D) appears to be a guess.

38. A

Draw as many diagonals as possible from one vertex forming triangles. There are four triangles formed each with 180° as the sum of its angles. Therefore, the sum of the interior angles of a hexagon is 4(180) = 720 degrees. (B) The sum of the exterior angles of any polygon is 360°. (C), (D), and (E) The number of triangles is always two less than the number of sides of the polygon.

39. C

If p represents the number of personal accounts and b represents the number of business accounts, then the phrase *the number of personal accounts is 300 more than five times the number of business accounts* translates as:

$p = 5b + 300$

(A), (B), (D), and (E) None of these expresses the given relationship.

40. E

I. If the width is known, that dimension will be the diameter of the circle, and the area can be calculated.

II. The thickness of the cardboard has nothing to do with the area of the circle that can be cut from the cardboard.

III. Since the length of the rectangle is known, then knowing the area will allow calculation of the width, and the area of the circle can be calculated.

41. D

Pick some representative number for T, say 20.

$T \div \dfrac{2}{3} = 20 \div \dfrac{2}{3} = \dfrac{20}{1} \times \dfrac{3}{2} = 30$, which is greater than T.

(A) 80% of a positive number is less than that number. (B) Since 20% is equivalent to $\dfrac{1}{5}$, then 20% of $5T$ is equal to T. (C) Two-thirds of a positive number is less than the number. (E) Subtracting $\dfrac{1}{2}$ from any number will result in a number less than the number.

42. A

There were 40 pieces of pizza to begin with. After $\dfrac{3}{4}$ of the pizza was eaten, $\dfrac{1}{4}$ of it, 10 slices, was left. Then $\dfrac{2}{5}$ of the 10 remaining slices was eaten for lunch. Two-fifths of 10 is 4 slices. That means that 6 slices are left. (B) Ten is the number of slices left after the party. (C) Probably a guess. (D) Four slices were eaten for lunch. (E) Thirty slices were eaten at the party.

43. E

Since the triangle is isosceles, the two base angles are equal, and their sum is $180 - 70 = 110$. The measure of each base angle is half of $110°$ or $55°$. The requested angle is the supplement of $55°$: $180 - 55 = 125$.

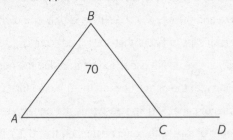

(A) Each base angle is $55°$, not the requested angle. (B) The sum of the two base angles is $110°$. (C) $\angle BCD$ is not equal to $\angle B$. (D) appears to be a guess that the answer is $\frac{1}{2}$ of $\angle B$.

44. B

Set up a chart using the formula $d = rt$.

	$d =$	r	t
Out	x	30	$\frac{x}{30}$
Back	x	20	$\frac{x}{20}$

Because the total time spent traveling is 3 hours, the equation is:

$\frac{x}{30} + \frac{x}{20} = 3$ Multiply both sides by 60.

$2x + 3x = 180$

$5x = 180$ Divide both sides by 5.

$x = 36$ He rode 36 miles into the country.

(A) is the total distance round trip.

(C) is the result of assuming that all 5 hours were spent traveling.

(D) is the distance round trip using the same mistake as in (C) above.

(E) is probably the result of assuming that the average of the rates, 25 miles per hour, can be used for the three hours traveling.

45. C

The rectangular solid has six faces, or 3 pairs of identical rectangles. The total surface area is:
$2(8 \times 5) + 2(8 \times 2) + 2(5 \times 2) = 2(40) + 2(16) + 2(10) = 80 + 32 + 20 = 132$ square inches.

(A) Eighty cubic inches is the volume of the object.
(B) means that the area of each face wasn't doubled.
(D) appears to be a guess. (E) is double the volume.

46. D

Let x be the score on the fourth test. Then the equation is:
$\frac{92 + 86 + 90 + x}{4} = 90$ Simplify the left side.

$\frac{268 + x}{4} = 90$ Multiply both sides by 4.

$268 + x = 360$ Subtract 268 from both sides.

$x = 92$ Corey got 92 on his fourth test.

(A), (B), (C), and (E) appear to be guesses or the result of making an error in the procedure above.

47. B

Let Bobby's age be x years. Then Al's age is $2x$. If Bobby is 9 years younger than Chuck, then Chuck is 9 years older than Bobby. Chuck's age is then $x + 9$. If Al's age is $2x$ equal to 14, then $x = 7$. Bobby is 7 years old. Chuck is 9 years older, or 16 years old. In 4 years, Chuck will be $16 + 4 = 20$ years old. (A) The question asked for the age in 4 years, not the current age. (C) is 4 years older than Bobby's age. (D) is four years older than Al's age. (E) is Bobby's age.

48. A

$5 - 3(x - 2) > -1$ Simplify the left side.

$5 - 3x + 6 > -1$

$-3x + 11 > -1$ Subtract 11 from both sides.

$-3x > -12$ Divide both sides by -3.

$x < 4$ Don't forget to reverse the inequality sign.

(B) The inequality sign was not reversed as required when you multiply or divide by a negative number. (C) is the result of a mistake in the distributive property. (D) is the result of a sign error in the distributive property. (E) The same mistake as in (D) above, but also, the inequality sign was not reversed.

KAPLAN

49. A

This is an indirect proportion problem because the time decreases as the number of workers increases. Set up an appropriate proportion. Remember to invert one of the ratios.

$\frac{10}{x} = \frac{3}{4}$ Cross multiply.

$3x = 40$ Divide both sides by 3.

$x = \frac{40}{3} = 13\frac{1}{3}$

Since fractions of workers are not possible, round up. Fourteen workers are needed. (B) The answer must be rounded up. (C) is the result of treating the problem as a direct proportion. (D) The same error as in (C) above but not rounded up. (E) is perhaps just a guess.

50. E

Because there are 5 slips of paper, the number of ways of choosing three slips in order is 60. The first position can be chosen in 5 ways, the second in 4 ways, and the third in 3 ways, and $60 = 5 \times 4 \times 3$. There is only one of these 60 orders of slips of paper that spell "bed" correctly, so the probability is $\frac{1}{60}$. (A) It is not correct to divide the number of slips with the right letters on them by the total number of slips of paper. (B) The answer is not one divided by the number of slips with correct letters on them. (C) The answer is not one divided by the total number of slips of paper. (D) Possibly a guess.

WRITING SECTION

Topic 1

4 Essay

Einstein was right that we accomplish most by building on the work of others. This includes the accumulated work of ordinary people, as well as the work of geniuses of the past.

W.B. Yeats was one of the greatest poets in the early 20th century. His unique language and imagery, as well as his tendency to bring fantasy into the real world, continues to influence poets today. What makes Yeats truly remarkable, though, is the inspiration he received from common Irish people, and the fight for national independence that he took up for them.

Despite his expensive, upper-class education, Yeats found his greatest inspiration from the Irish people. He traveled all over Ireland recording conversations he had. He often asked people to tell him folktales about the fairy people and ancient Irish heroes. Some of Yeats' most famous poetry is about the stories those people told and the lines of the poems echo the lyrical rhythm of an Irish accent.

Rather than focusing attention only on his own poems, Yeats wrote essays and gave lectures about the Irish farmer as natural poet. He insisted that the tales of old Ireland and the naturally musical way they were told were testaments to the greatness of the people. Presenting the Irish in a positive light was very different from the prevailing prejudices about the Irish as depressed, stupid, and drunk.

Yeats took his dedication and devotion to the Irish people even further when he began his fight for Ireland's freedom. Even though Yeats was a wealthy aristocrat who would gain nothing personally if Ireland were independent, he lobbied for decades because he believed freedom was a natural right. In the ultimate combination of art and politics, Yeats wrote many plays that presented the Irish as poetical, competent people who deserved to rule themselves. He based many of the characters in his plays on the people he met in his travels.

W.B. Yeats won the Nobel Prize and published volumes of poetry, plays, essays, and stories. Despite his tremendous talent and success, Yeats acknowledged the people as his greatest source of inspiration and material and he worked as tirelessly for their independence and betterment as he did on his poetry.

Grader's Comments

This is an strong essay. The writer displays a clear, somewhat unusual understanding of the prompt. He successfully presents and develops the topic throughout the essay without getting sidetracked. The argument is well developed with a single relevant example. The writer provides excellent, specific details to support the example further.

The organization of this essay is also excellent. Each paragraph addresses a new idea or issue, and the transition from one paragraph to the next is clear and logical. Each paragraph builds upon the others to create a strong and effective argument. For the most part spelling and diction are consistently correct.

The writer occasionally uses awkward phrasing (for example, "Some of Yeats' most famous poetry is about the stories those people told and the lines of the poems echo the lyrical rhythm of an Irish accent") and there's a run-on sentence. The errors are relatively minor, however, and they do not make the essay unclear.

1 Essay

I think it is very interesting that Albert Einstein said this quote. He clearly thought that it was very important to give back to the community if he felt so anxious about it like he says in the quote. In his case I think he succeeded because he contributed.

I am not sure about all this though. Is it really true to say that ever is indebting to someone? Perhaps, but not for certainly. What about self-made millionaires? They did it theirselves so why should they give to others when no one helped them. Also, if people are always contributing money, then their will be other people who don't work hard to make something of themselves because they know someone else will contribute it to them. Then their is no growth or change.

In conclusion, while I believe that Albert Einstein is a good example for his quote, it is not true all the time, so you have to take things as they come.

Grader's Comments

This essay is limited. The writer does not address the topic by using a relevant example, but rather, attempts to analyze the significance and truth of the quote itself. Because the writer did not write about the assigned topic, the highest grade he could receive is a 3, but other severe problems in the essay bring the grade down further. The writer doesn't seem to have a point, so there is nothing to support. The writer clearly mentioned Albert Einstein and self-made millionaires believing that they would function as examples in his essay, but neither Einstein nor the self-made millionaires were used in any way to support an argument, they were used as jumping off points for abstract ramblings.

There is no organization to this essay. The writer jumps from one topic to the next without any logical development. There are only two paragraphs. The writer presents everything he has to say in the first paragraph, and then concludes his jumbled thoughts in the second paragraph, but he ends that paragraph with an idea that is entirely unrelated to assigned topic.

The language is flawed, with several diction errors, such as "theirsevles" (which is not a word) or the sentence fragment, "Perhaps, but not for certainly," (which is also idiomatically incorrect). The writer regularly uses the possessive pronoun "their" when he should use "there." The sentence, "Also, if people are always contributing money, then their will be other people who don't' work hard to make something of themselves because they know someone else will contribute it to them" is a run-on.

Topic 2

4 Essay

A photograph that shows me sitting in a small rocking chair with a large book spread open on my lap evokes one of my favorite memories of childhood. The look on my face in that picture clearly reveals how excited I was by reading and how much I enjoyed that activity. Learning to read at a young age is certainly crucial for future success in school, since so many subjects, including history, science, and literature, rely on the ability to read. However, reading is not the only skill that students should learn when their young, since focusing too much on a single subject could be a disadvantage to kids when they encounter unfamiliar topics like math or language or art once they begin elementary school. I have seen proof of this from my experience and from my friends.

For example, although I could read above my grade level, my other skills weren't as strong, and I had to spend many hours learning the basic math skills that many of my peers had already mastered. In addition, I loved to read so much that I often neglected studying other topics, since I preferred to lose myself in a book rather than struggle with difficult math concepts. This made my first years of elementary school quite frustrating, since I excelled in verbal skills but not in math or science. Eventually, my knowledge and interest in other subjects caught up to my love of reading, but I still spent some tough moments trying to complete assignments and tests in other subjects.

My best friend had a very different experience when she was in grade school. Her parents taught her to read when she was really young, but they also taught her basic addition and subtraction and enrolled her in specialized science courses for young children. By the time she was in elementary school, she already had a basic knowledge foundation in several subjects. Although her reading skills were certainly not as strong as mine, they were sufficient for her to do all of her homework and to do well in all subjects. Thanks to her more well-rounded early education experiences, my friend struggled less in some of her classes than I did.

From these contrasting examples, I now believe its clear that no single skill should be the focus of a child's learning. Although reading is important to future learning and comprehension, other skills may be equally important. Learning how to calculate or think logically about problems is just as crucial for a child to achieve success in school.

Grader's Comments

This essay begins with a personal statement that shows the author's understanding of the prompt, and the essay remains consistently on topic from start to finish. The introductory paragraph contains the author's thesis and clearly indicates how she will develop it. In the next two paragraphs, the author provides two well-developed contrasting examples as strong support of her thesis. The essay concludes with a concise final paragraph that neatly summarizes the author's main point. The author uses several keywords and phrases ("However," "For example," "In addition," "Eventually," "but," "Although," "For these reasons") to organize her essay and provide clear transitions between each paragraph. This essay's strong support and coherent organization demonstrate that the author carefully planned her essay and then followed this plan while writing.

The author's language is varied and interesting, as is her sentence structure. The few grammatical errors in the essay ("their" instead of "they're" in the first paragraph; "its" instead of "it's" in the last paragraph) don't detract from the author's main point, but could have been avoided by saving time to proofread.

2 Essay

My sister taught me how to read when I was real young and I really enjoyed reading with her. I'm sure learning to read early helped me in school since I already knew how to read when I got to kindergarten and alot of other kids were just beginning. I could read books from a much higher grade level and could understand lots of vocabulary that other kids didn't know.

But I wasn't as good at math as some of my friends. They could do long division and knew their multiplication tables much faster than I did. So even though reading helped me for some parts of elementary school it wasn't enough to help me in every subject. I was definitely behind in math and had to catch up which was frustrating.

So reading isn't the only skill kids should learn young. They need to learn about math, too, and also maybe history and science. Since all students have to take different classes to graduate from high school, spending too much time on one subject like reading isn't going to do them any good when they have to pass other subjects to go on to the next grade.

Grader's Comments

This essay begins with a personal experience related to the topic, showing that the author has understood the prompt. What the introductory paragraph lacks, however, is a clear thesis statement, so the reader doesn't know what the author's opinion of the prompt is until the beginning of the second paragraph. The essay's weak organization continues through the second and third paragraphs since the author provides no clear transitions between ideas, making the essay difficult to follow.

Likewise, although the author includes a personal example in the second paragraph, she doesn't develop this example enough to fully support the thesis that finally appears in the first sentence of the third paragraph. The lack of support and structure in the essay detract from the author's main points, which are difficult to find. This author needs to spend more time brainstorming and planning her essay before writing to make sure she has a clear outline to follow, including a distinct introduction, at least one well-developed example, and a strong conclusion.

The language is acceptable but basic, with a few minor grammatical errors ("real" instead of "really" in the first sentence; "alot" instead of "a lot" in the second sentence). The weakest part of the author's language is her lack of punctuation in the majority of long sentences (commas after "and" if the conjunction joins another complete sentence; commas to separate dependent clauses and modifiers).

KAPLAN

CBEST Resources

Resource One: **Word Roots**

Knowing roots of words can help you in two ways. First, instead of learning one word at a time, you can learn a whole group of words that contain a certain root. They'll be related in meaning, so if you remember one, it will be easier for you to remember others. Second, roots can often help you decode an unknown Reading Comprehension word. If you recognize a familiar root, you can get a good enough idea of the word to answer the question.

A, AN—not, without
amoral, atrophy, asymmetrical, anarchy, anesthetic

AB, A—from, away, apart
abnormal, abdicate, ablution, abnegate, absolve, abstemious, abstruse, annul, avert

AC, ACR—sharp, sour
acid, acerbic, exacerbate, acute, acrimony

AD, A—to, towards
adhere, adjacent, adjunct, admonish, adroit, adumbrate, accretion, accertion, alleviate, aspire, assail, assonance, attest

ALI, ALTR—another
alias, alienate, inalienable, altruism

AM, AMI—love
amorous, amicable, amiable, amity

AMBI, AMPHI—both
ambiguous, ambivalent, ambidextrous, amphibious

AMBL, AMBUL—walk
amble, ambulatory, perambulator, somnambulist

ANIM—mind, spirit, breath
animal, animosity, unanimous, magnanimous

ANN, ENN—year
annual, annuity, biennial, perennial

ANTE, ANT—before
antecedent, antediluvian, antiquated, anticipate

ANTHROP—human
anthropology, philanthropy

ANTI, ANT—against, opposite
antidote, antithesis, antacid, antagonist, antonym

AUD—hear
audio, audience, audition

AUTO—self
autobiography, autocrat, autonomous

BELLI, BELL—war
belligerent, bellicose, antebellum, rebellion

BENE, BEN—good
benevolent, benefactor, beneficent, benign

BI—two
bicycle, bisect, bilateral, bilingual, biped

BIBLIO—book
Bible, bibliography, bibliophile

BIO—life
biography, biology, amphibious, symbiotic, macrobiotics

BURS—money, purse
reimburse, disburse, bursar

CAD, CAS, CID—happen, fall
accident, cadence, cascade, deciduous

CAP, CIP—head
captain, decapitate, precipitate, recapitulate

CARN—flesh
carnal, carnage, incarnate

CAP, CAPT, CEPT, CIP—take, hold, seize
capable, capacious, captivate, deception, intercept, inception, anticipate, emancipation

CED, CESS—yield, go
cease, cessation, incessant, cede, precede, accede

CHROM—color
chrome, chromatic, monochrome

CHRON—time
chronology, chronic, anachronism

CIDE—murder
suicide, homicide, regicide, patricide

CIRCUM—around
circumference, circumlocution, circumspect, circumvent

CLIN, CLIV—slope
incline, declivity, proclivity

CLUD, CLUS, CLAUS, CLOIS—shut, close, conclude, reclusive, claustrophobia, cloister, preclude, occlude

CO, COM, CON—with, together
coeducation, coagulate, coalesce, coerce, collateral, commodious, complaint, concord, congenial, congential

COGN, GNO—know
recognize, cognition, diagnosis, agnostic, prognosis

CONTRA—against
controversy, incontrovertible, contravene

CORP—body
corpse, corporeal, corpulence

COSMO, COSM—world
cosmopolitan, cosmos, microcosm, macrocosm

CRAC, CRAT—rule, power
democracy, bureaucracy, autocrat, aristocrat

CRED—trust, believe
incredible, credulous, credence

CRESC, CRET—grow
crescent, crescendo, accretion

CULP—blame, fault
culprit, culpable, inculpate, exculpate

CURR, CURS—run
current, concur, cursory, precursor, incursion

DE—down, out, apart
depart, debase, debilitate, defamatory, demur

DEC—ten, tenth
decade, decimal, decathlon, decimate

DEMO, DEM—people
democrat, demographics, demagogue, epidemic

DI, DIURN—day
diary, quotidian, diurnal

DIA—across
diagonal, diatribe, diaphanous

DIC, DICT—speak
abdicate, diction, indict, verdict

DIS, DIF, DI—not, apart, away
disaffected, disband, disbar, distend, differentiate, diffidence, diffuse, digress, divert

DOC, DOCT—teach
docile, doctrine, doctrinaire

DOL—pain
condolence, doleful, dolorous, indolent

DUC, DUCT—lead
seduce, induce, conduct, viaduct, induct

EGO—self
ego, egoist, egocentric

EN, EM—in, into
enter, entice, encumber, embroil, empathy

ERR—wander
erratic, aberration, errant

EU—well, good
eulogy, euphemism, eurythmics, euthanasia

EX, E—out, out of
exit, exacerbate, excerpt, excommunicate, elicit, egress, egregious

FAC, FIC, FECT, FY, FEA—make, do
factory, facility, benefactor, malefactor, fiction, fictive, rectify, vilify, feasible

FAL, FALS—deceive
infallible, fallacious, false

FERV—boil
fervent, fervid, effervescent

FID—faith, trust
confident, diffidence, perfidious, fidelity

FLU, FLUX—flow
fluent, affluent, superfluous, flux

FORE—before
forecast, foreboding, forestall

FRAG, FRAC—break
fragment, fracture, refract

FUS—pour
profuse, infusion, effusive, diffuse

GEN—birth, class, kin
generation, congenital, homogeneous, ingenious, engender

GRAD, GRESS—step
graduate, gradual, retrograde, ingress, egress

GRAPH, GRAM—writing
biography, bibliography, epigram

GRAT—pleasing
grateful, gratitude, gratuitous, gratuity

GRAV, GRIEV—heavy
grave, gravity, aggrieve, grievous

GREG—crowd, flock
segregate, gregarious, aggregate

HABIT, HIBIT—have, hold
habit, cohabit, habitat, inhibit

HAP—by chance
happen, haphazard, hapless, mishap

HELIO, HELI—sun
heliocentric, heliotrope, aphelion,
perihelion, helium

HETERO—other
heterosexual, heterogeneous,
heterodox

HOL—whole
holocaust, catholic, holistic

HOMO—same
homosexual, homogenize,
homogeneous, homonym

HOMO—man
homo sapiens, homicide, bonhomie

HYDR—water
hydrant, hydrate, dehydration

HYPER—too much, excess
hyperactive, hyperbole, hyperventilate

HYPO—too little, under
hypodermic, hypothermia,
hypochondria

IN, IG, IL, IM, IR—not
incorrigible, insomnia, interminable,
incessant, ignorant, ignominious,
ignoble, illicit, illimitable, immaculate,
immutable, impertinent, improvident,
irregular

IN, IL, IM, IR—in, on, into
invade, inaugurate, incandescent,
illustrate, imbue, immerse, implicate,
irrigate, irritate

INTER—between, among
intercede, intercept, interdiction,
interject

INTRA, INTR—within
intrastate, intravenous, intramural,
intrinsic

IT, ITER—between, among
transit, itinerant, transitory, reiterate

JECT, JET—throw
eject, interject, abject, trajectory, jettison

JOUR—day
journal, adjourn, sojourn

JUD—judge
judge, judicious, prejudice, adjudicate

JUNCT, JUG—join
junction, adjunct, injunction

JUR—swear, law
jury, abjure, perjure, jurisprudence

LAT—side
lateral, collateral, unilateral

LAV, LAU, LU—wash
lavatory, laundry, ablution, antediluvian

LEG, LEC, LEX—read, speak
legible, lecture, lexicon

LEV—light
elevate, levitate, levity, alleviate

LIBER—free
liberty, liberal, libertarian, libertine

LIG, LECT—choose, gather
eligible, elect, select

LIG, LI, LY—bind
ligament, oblige, religion, liable, liaison,
lien, ally

LING, LANG—tongue
lingo, language, linguistics, bilingual

LITER—letter
literate, alliteration, literal

LITH—stone
monolith, lithograph, megalith

LOQU, LOC, LOG—speech, thought
eloquent, loqucaious, colloquial,
circumlocution, monologue, dialogue

LUC, LUM—light
lucid, elucidate, pellucid, translucent,
illuminate

LUD, LUS—play
ludicrous, allude, delusion

MACRO—great
macrocosm, macrobiotics

MAG, MAJ, MAS, MAX—great
magnify, magnanimous, magnate,
magnitude, majesty, master, maximum

MAL—bad
malady, maladroit, malevolent,
malodorous

MAN—hand
manual, manuscript, manifest

MAR—sea
submarine, marine, maritime

MATER, MATR—mother
maternal, matron, matrilineal

MEDI—middle
intermediary, medieval, mediate

MEGA—great
megaphone, megalomania, megaton,
megalith

MEM, MEN—remember
memory, memento, memorabilia,
reminisce

METER, METR, MENS—measure
meter, thermometer, commensurate

MICRO—small
microscope, microorganism, microcosm, microbe

MIS—wrong, bad, hate
misunderstand, misapprehension, misconstrue, mishap

MIT, MISS—send
transmit, emit, missive

MOLL—soft
mollify, emollient, mollusk

MON, MONIT—warn
admonish, monitor, premonition

MONO—one
monologue, monotonous, monogamy

MOR—custom, manner
moral, mores, morose

MOR, MORT—dead
morbid, moribund, mortal, amortize

MORPH—shape
amorphous, anthropomorphic, morphology

MOV, MOT, MOB, MOM—move
remove, motion, mobile, momentum, momentous

MUT—change
mutate, mutability, immutable, commute

NAT, NASC—born
native, nativity, cognate, nascent, renascent, renaissance

NAU, NAV—ship, sailor
nautical, nauseous, navy, circumnavigate

NEG—not, deny
negative, abnegate, renege

NEO—new
neoclassical, neophyte, neologism, neonate

NIHIL—none, nothing
annihilation, nihilism

NOM, NYM—name
nominate, nomenclature, nominal, synonym, anonymity

NOX, NIC, NEC, NOC—harm
obnoxious, internecine, innocuous

NOV—new
novelty, innovation, novitiate

NUMER—number
numeral, numerous, innumerable, enumerate

OB—against
obstruct, obdurate, obsequious, obtrusive

OMNI—all
omnipresent, omnipotent, omniscient, omnivorous

ONER—burden
onerous, exonerate

OPER—work
operate, cooperate, inoperable

PAC—peace
pacify, pacifist, pacific

PALP—feel
palpable, palpitation

PAN—all
panorama, panacea, pandemic, panoply

PATER, PATR—father
paternal, paternity, patriot, compatriot, expatriate

PATH, PASS—feel, suffer
sympathy, antipathy, pathos, impassioned

PEC—money
pecuniary, impecunious, peculation

PED, POD—foot
pedestrian, pediment, quadruped, tripod

PEL, PULS—drive
compel, compelling, expel, propel, compulsion

PEN—almost
peninsula, penultimate, penumbra

PEND, PENS—hang
pendant, pendulous, suspense, propensity

PER—through, by, for, throughout
perambulator, percipient, perfunctory, pertinacious

PER—against, destruction
perfidious, pernicious, perjure

PERI—around
perimeter, periphery, perihelion, peripatetic

PET—seek, go towards
petition, impetus, impetuous, petulant, centripetal

PHIL—love
philosopher, philanderer, philanthropy, philology

PHOB—fear
phobia, claustrophobia, xenophobia

PHON—sound
phonograph, megaphone, phonics

PLAC—calm, please
placate, implacable, placid, complacent

PON, POS—put, place
postpone, proponent, juxtaposition, depose

PORT—carry
portable, deportment, rapport

POT—drink
potion, potable

POT—power
potential, potent, impotent, potentate, omnipotence

PRE—before
precede, precipitate, premonition, preposition

PRIM, PRI—first
prime, primary, primordial, pristine

PRO—ahead, forth
proceed, proclivity, protestation, provoke

PROTO—first
prototype, protagonist, protocol

PROX, PROP—near
approximate, propinquity, proximity

PSEUDO—false
pseudoscientific, pseudonym

PYR—fire
pyre, pyrotechnics, pyromania

QUAD, QUAR, QUAT—four
quadrilateral, quadrant, quarter, quarantine

QUES, QUER, QUIS, QUIR—question
quest, inquest, query, querulous, inquisitive, inquiry

QUIE—quiet
disquiet, acquiesce, quiescent, requiem

QUINT, QUIN—five
quintuplets, quintessence

RADI, RAMI—branch
radiate, radiant, eradicate, ramification

RECT, REG—straight, rule
rectangle, rectitude, rectify, regular

REG—king, rule
regal, regent, interregnum

RETRO—backward
retrospective, retroactive, retrograde

RID, RIS—laugh
ridiculous, deride, derision

ROG—ask
interrogate, derogatory, arrogant

RUD—rough, crude
rude, erudite, rudimentary

RUPT—break
disrupt, interrupt, rupture

SACR, SANCT—holy
sacred, sacrilege, sanction, sacrosanct

SCRIB, SCRIPT, SCRIV—write
scribe, ascribe, script, manuscript, scrivener

SE—apart, away
separate, segregate, secede, sedition

SEC, SECT, SEG—cut
sector, dissect, bisect, intersect, segment, secant

SED, SID—sit
sedate, sedentary, supersede, reside, residence

SEM—seed, sow
seminar, seminal, disseminate

SEN—old
senior, senile, senescent

SENT, SENS—feel, think
sentiment, nonsense, consensus, sensual

SEQU, SECU—follow
sequence, sequel, subsequent, consecutive

SIM, SEM—similar, same
similar, verisimilitude, semblance, dissemble

SIGN—mark, sign
signal, designation, assignation

SIN—curve
sine curve, sinuous, insinuate

SOL—sun
solar, parasol, solarium, solstice

SOL—alone
solo, solitude, soliloquy, solipsism

SOMN—sleep
insomnia, somnolent, somnambulist

SON—sound
sonic, consonance, sonorous, resonate

SOPH—wisdom
philosopher, sophistry, sophisticated, sophomoric

SPEC, SPIC—see, look
spectator, retrospective, perspective, perspicacious

SPER—hope
prosper, prosperous, despair, desperate

SPERS, SPAR—scatter
disperse, sparse, aspersion, disparate

SPIR—breathe
respire, inspire, spiritual, aspire, transpire

STRICT, STRING—bind
stricture, constrict, stringent, astringent

STRUCT, STRU—build
structure, obstruct, construe

SUB—under
subconscious, subjugate, subliminal, subpoena

SUMM—highest
summit, summary, consummate

SUPER, SUR—above
supervise, supercilious, superfluous,
insurmountable, surfeit

SURGE, SURRECT—rise
surge, resurgent, insurgent, insurrection

SYN, SYM—together
synthesis, sympathy, symposium,
symbiosis

TACIT, TIC—silent
tacit, taciturn, reticent

TACT, TAG, TANG—touch
tact, tactile, contagious, tangent,
tangential, tangible

TEN, TIN, TAIN—hold, twist
detention, tenable, pertinacious,
retinue, retain

TEND, TENS, TENT—stretch
intend, distend, tension, tensile,
ostensible, contentious

TERM—end
terminal, terminus, terminate,
interminable

TERR—earth, land
terrain, terrestrial, extraterrestrial,
subterranean

TEST—witness
testify, attest, testimonial, protestation

THE—god
atheist, theology, apotheosis, theocracy

THERM—heat
thermometer, thermal, thermonuclear,
hypothermia

TIM—fear, frightened
timid, intimidate, timorous

TOP—place
topic, topography, utopia

TORT—twist
distort, extort, tortuous

TORP—stiff, numb
torpedo, torpid, torpor

TOX—poison
toxic, toxin, intoxication

TRACT—draw
tractor, intractable, protract

TRANS—across, over, through, beyond
transport, transgress, transient,
transitory, translucent

TREM, TREP—shake
tremble, tremor, trepidation, intrepid

TURB—shake
disturb, turbulent, perturbation

UMBR—shadow
umbrella, umbrage, adumbrate,
penumbra

UNI, UN—one
unify, unilateral, unanimous

URB—city
urban, suburban, urbane

VAC—empty
vacant, evacuate, vacuous

VAL, VAIL—value, strength
valid, valor, ambivalent, convalescence,
avail

VEN, VENT—come
convene, intervene, venue, convention,
adventitious

VER—true
verify, verity, verisimilitude, verdict

VERB—word
verbal, verbose, verbiage, verbatim

VERT, VERS—turn
avert, convert, revert, incontrovertible,
divert, aversion

VICT, VINC—conquer
victory, conviction, evict, evince,
invincible

VID, VIS—see
evident, vision, visage, supervise

VIL—base, mean
vile, vilify, revile

VIV, VIT—life
vivid, vital, convivial, vivacious

VOC, VOK, VOW—call, voice
vocal, equivocate, invoke, avow

VOL—wish
voluntary, malevolent, benevolent,
volition

VOLV, VOLUT—turn, roll
revolve, evolve, convoluted

VOR—eat
devour, carnivore, omnivorous,
voracious

Resource Two: **Vocabulary Word List**

This Word List includes about 500 words. The more of these you know, the better.

MEMORIZING WORDS

In general, the very best way to improve your vocabulary is to read. Choose challenging, college-level material. If you encounter an unknown word, put it on a flashcard or in your vocabulary notebook. Here are some techniques for memorizing words.

1. Learn words in groups. You can group words by a common root they contain (see the word root list for some examples), or you can group words together if they are related in meaning (i.e., word families). Memorizing words this way may help you to remember them.

2. Use flashcards. Write down new words or word groups and run through them when you have a few minutes to spare. Put one new word or word group on one side of a 3 × 5 card and put a short definition or definitions on the back.

3. Make a vocabulary notebook. List words in one column and their definitions in another. Test yourself. Cover up the meanings, and see which words you can define from memory. Make a sample sentence using each word in context.

4. Think of hooks that lodge a new word in your mind—create visual images of words.

5. Use rhymes, pictures, songs, and any other devices that help you remember words.

To get the most out of your remaining study time, use the techniques that work for you, and stick with them.

This Word List includes about 500 words. The more of these you know, the better.

MEMORIZING WORDS

In general, the very best way to improve your vocabulary is to read. Choose challenging, college-level material. If you encounter an unknown word, put it on a flashcard or in your vocabulary notebook. Here are some techniques for memorizing words.

1. Learn words in groups. You can group words by a common root they contain (see the word root list for some examples), or you can group words together if they are related in meaning (i.e., word families). Memorizing words this way may help you to remember them.

2. Use flashcards. Write down new words or word groups and run through them when you have a few minutes to spare. Put one new word or word group on one side of a 3 × 5 card and put a short definition or definitions on the back.

3. Make a vocabulary notebook. List words in one column and their definitions in another. Test yourself. Cover up the meanings, and see which words you can define from memory. Make a sample sentence using each word in context.

4. Think of hooks that lodge a new word in your mind—create visual images of words.

5. Use rhymes, pictures, songs, and any other devices that help you remember words.

To get the most out of your remaining study time, use the techniques that work for you, and stick with them.

ABANDON

noun (uh <u>baan</u> duhn)

total lack of inhibition

With her strict parents out of town, Kelly danced all night with *abandon*.

ABATE

verb (uh <u>bayt</u>)

to decrease, to reduce

My hunger *abated* when I saw how filthy the chef's hands were.

ABET

verb (uh <u>beht</u>)

to aid; to act as an accomplice

While Derwin robbed the bank, Marvin *abetted* his friend by pulling up the getaway car.

ABJURE

verb (aab <u>joor</u>)

to renounce under oath; to abandon forever; to abstain from

After having been devout for most of his life, he suddenly *abjured* his beliefs, much to his family's disappointment.

ABNEGATE

verb (<u>aab</u> nih gayt)

to give up; to deny to oneself

After his retirement, the former police commissioner found it difficult to *abnegate* authority.

ABORTIVE

adj (uh <u>bohr</u> tihv)

ending without results

Her *abortive* attempt to swim the full five miles left her frustrated.

ABROGATE

verb (<u>aab</u> ruh gayt)

to annul; to abolish by authoritative action

The president's job is to *abrogate* any law that fosters inequality among citizens.

ABSCOND

verb (aab <u>skahnd</u>)

to leave quickly in secret

The criminal *absconded* during the night with all of his mother's money.

KAPLAN

ABSTEMIOUS

adj (aab <u>stee</u> mee uhs)

done sparingly; consuming in moderation

The spa served no sugar or wheat, but the clients found the retreat so calm that they didn't mind the *abstemious* rules.

ACCEDE

verb (aak <u>seed</u>)

to express approval, to agree to

Once the mayor heard the reasonable request, she happily *acceded* to the proposal.

ACCLIVITY

noun (uh <u>klihv</u> ih tee)

an incline or upward slope, the ascending side of a hill

We were so tired from hiking that by the time we reached the *acclivity*, it looked more like a mountain than a hill.

ACCRETION

noun (uh <u>kree</u> shuhn)

a growth in size, an increase in amount

The committee's strong fund-raising efforts resulted in an *accretion* in scholarship money.

ACME

noun (<u>aak</u> mee)

the highest level or degree attainable

Just when he reached the *acme* of his power, the dictator was overthrown.

ACTUATE

verb (<u>aak</u> choo ayt)

to put into motion, to activate; to motivate or influence to activity

The leaders rousing speech *actuated* the crowd into a peaceful protest.

ACUITY

noun (uh <u>kyoo</u> ih tee)

sharp vision or perception characterized by the ability to resolve fine detail

With unusual *acuity*, she was able to determine that the masterpiece was a fake.

ACUMEN

noun (<u>aak</u> yuh muhn) (uh <u>kyoo</u> muhn)

sharpness of insight, mind, and understanding; shrewd judgment

The investor's financial *acumen* helped him to select high-yield stocks.

ADAMANT
adj (<u>aad</u> uh muhnt) (<u>aad</u> uh mihnt)
stubbornly unyielding
She was *adamant* about leaving the restaurant after the waiter was rude.

ADEPT
adj (uh <u>dehpt</u>)
extremely skilled
She is *adept* at computing math problems in her head.

ADJUDICATE
verb (uh <u>jood</u> ih kayt)
to hear and settle a matter; to act as a judge
The principal *adjudicated* the disagreement between two students.

ADJURE
verb (uh <u>joor</u>)
to appeal to
The criminal *adjured* to the court for mercy.

ADMONISH
verb (aad <u>mahn</u> ihsh)
to caution or warn gently in order to correct something
My mother *admonished* me about my poor grades.

ADROIT
adj (uh <u>droyt</u>)
skillful; accomplished; highly competent
The *adroit* athlete completed even the most difficult obstacle course with ease.

ADULATION
noun (<u>aaj</u> juh lay shuhn)
excessive flattery or admiration
The *adulation* she showed her professor seemed insincere; I suspected she really wanted a better grade.

ADUMBRATE
verb (<u>aad</u> uhm brayt) (uh <u>duhm</u> brayt)
to give a hint or indication of something to come
Her constant complaining about the job *adumbrated* her intent to leave.

AERIE
noun (<u>ayr</u> ee) (<u>eer</u> ee)
a nest built high in the air; an elevated, often secluded, dwelling
Perched high among the trees, the eagle's *aerie* was filled with eggs.

AFFECTED

adj (uh <u>fehk</u> tihd)

phony, artificial

The *affected* hairdresser spouted French phrases, though she had never been to France.

AGGREGATE

noun (<u>aa</u> grih giht)

a collective mass, the sum total

An *aggregate* of panic-stricken customers mobbed the bank, demanding their life savings.

ALGORITHM

noun (<u>aal</u> guh rith uhm)

an established procedure for solving a problem or equation

The accountant uses a series of *algorithms* to determine the appropriate tax bracket.

ALIMENTARY

adj (aal uh <u>mehn</u> tuh ree) (aal uh <u>mehn</u> tree)

pertaining to food, nutrition, or digestion

After a particularly good meal, Sherlock turned to his companion and exclaimed, "I feel quite good, very well fed. It was *alimentary* my dear Watson."

ALLAY

verb (uh <u>lay</u>)

to lessen, ease, reduce in intensity

Trying to *allay* their fears, the nurse sat with them all night.

AMITY

noun (<u>aa</u> mih tee)

friendship, good will

Correspondence over the years contributed to a lasting *amity* between the women.

AMORPHOUS

adj (<u>ay mohr</u> fuhs)

having no definite form

The Blob featured an *amorphous* creature that was constantly changing shape.

ANIMUS

noun (<u>aan</u> uh muhs)

a feeling of animosity or ill will

Though her teacher had failed her, she displayed no *animus* toward him.

ANODYNE

noun (<u>aan</u> uh dyen)

a source of comfort; a medicine that relieves pain

The sound of classical music is usually just the *anodyne* I need after a tough day at work.

ANOMALY

noun (uh <u>nahm</u> uh lee)

a deviation from the common rule, something that is difficult to classify

Among the top-ten albums of the year was one *anomaly*—a compilation of polka classics.

ANTHROPOMORPHIC

adj (aan thruh poh <u>mohr</u> fihk)

suggesting human characteristics for animals and inanimate things

Many children's stories feature *anthropomorphic* animals such as talking wolves and pigs.

ANTIQUATED

adj (<u>aan</u> tih kway tihd)

too old to be fashionable or useful

Next to her coworker's brand-new model, Marisa's computer looked *antiquated*.

APHORISM

noun (<u>aa</u> fuhr ihz uhm)

a short statement of a principle

The country doctor was given to such *aphorisms* as "Still waters run deep."

APLOMB

noun (uh <u>plahm</u>) (uh <u>pluhm</u>)

self-confident assurance; poise

For such a young dancer, she had great *aplomb*, making her perfect to play the young princess.

APOSTATE

noun (uh <u>pahs</u> tayt)

one who renounces a religious faith

So that he could divorce his wife, the king scoffed at the church doctrines and declared himself an *apostate*.

APPOSITE

adj (<u>aap</u> puh ziht)

strikingly appropriate or well adapted

The lawyer presented an *apposite* argument upon cross-examining the star witness.

APPRISE

verb (uh <u>priez</u>)

to give notice to, inform

"Thanks for *apprising* me that the test time has been changed," said Emanuel.

APPROPRIATE

verb (uh <u>proh</u> pree ayt)

to assign to a particular purpose, allocate

The fund's manager *appropriated* funds for the clean-up effort.

ARABLE

adj (<u>aa</u> ruh buhl)

suitable for cultivation

The overpopulated country desperately needed more *arable* land.

ARCANE

adj (ahr <u>kayn</u>)

secret, obscure; known only to a few

The *arcane* rituals of the sect were passed down through many generations.

ARCHIPELAGO

noun (ahr kuh <u>pehl</u> uh goh)

a large group of islands

Between villages in the Stockholm *archipelago*, boat taxis are the only form of transportation.

ARREARS

noun (uh <u>reerz</u>)

unpaid, overdue debts or bills; neglected obligations

After the expensive lawsuit, Dominic's accounts were in *arrears*.

ARROGATE

verb (<u>aa</u> ruh gayt)

to claim without justification; to claim for oneself without right

Lynn watched in astonishment as her boss *arrogated* the credit for her brilliant work on the project.

ASKANCE

adv (uh <u>skaans</u>)

with disapproval; with a skeptical sideways glance

She looked *askance* at her son's failing report card as he mumbled that he had done all the schoolwork.

ASSENT

verb (uh sehnt)

to agree, as to a proposal

After careful deliberation, the CEO *assented* to the proposed merger.

ATAVISTIC

adj (aat uh vihs tik)

characteristic of a former era, ancient

After spending three weeks on a desert island, Roger became a survivalist with *atavistic* skills that helped him endure.

AUTOCRAT

noun (aw toh kraat)

a dictator

Mussolini has been described as an *autocrat* who tolerated no opposition.

AVER

verb (uh vuhr)

to declare to be true, to affirm

"Yes, he was wearing a mask," the witness *averred*.

AVUNCULAR

adj (ah vuhng kyuh luhr)

like an uncle in behavior, especially in kindness and warmth

The coach's *avuncular* style made him well-liked.

AWRY

adv (uh rie)

crooked, askew, amiss

Something must have gone *awry* in the computer system because some of my files are missing.

BALK

verb (bawk)

to stop short and refuse to go on

When the horse *balked* at jumping over the high fence, the rider was thrown off.

BALLAST

noun (baal uhst)

a structure that helps to stabilize or steady

Communication and honesty are the true *ballasts* of a good relationship.

KAPLAN

BEATIFIC

adj (bee uh tihf ihk)

displaying calmness and joy, relating to a state of celestial happiness

After spending three months in India, she had a *beatific* peace about her.

BECALM

verb (bih kahm)

to stop the progress of, to soothe

The warm air *becalmed* the choppy waves.

BECLOUD

verb (bih klowd)

to make less visible, to obscure, or blur

Her ambivalence about the long commute *beclouded* her enthusiasm about the job.

BEDRAGGLE

adj (bih draag uhl)

soiled, wet and limp; dilapidated

The child's *bedraggled* blanket needed a good cleaning.

BEGET

verb (bih geht)

to produce, especially as an effect or outgrowth; to bring about

The mayor believed that finding petty offenders would help reduce serious crime because, he argued, small crimes *beget* big crimes.

BEHEMOTH

noun (buh hee muhth)

something of monstrous size or power; huge creature

The budget became such a *behemoth* that observers believed the film would never make a profit.

BENEFICENT

adj (buh nehf ih sent)

pertaining to an act of kindness

The *beneficent* man donated the money anonymously.

BERATE

verb (bih rayt)

to scold harshly

When my manager found out I had handled the situation so insensitively, he *berated* me.

BILIOUS

adj (<u>bihl</u> yuhs)

ill-tempered, sickly, ailing

The party ended early when the *bilious* 5-year-old tried to run off with the birthday girl's presents.

BLASPHEMOUS

adj (<u>blaas</u> fuh muhs)

cursing, profane; extremely irreverent

The politician's offhanded comments seemed *blasphemous*, given the context of the orderly meeting.

BLATANT

adj (<u>blay</u> tnt)

completely obvious and conspicuous, especially in an offensive, crass manner

Such *blatant* advertising within the bounds of the school drew protest from parents.

BLITHELY

adv (<u>blieth</u> lee)

merrily, lightheartedly cheerful; without appropriate thought

Wanting to redecorate the office, she *blithely* assumed her co-workers wouldn't mind and moved the furniture in the space.

BOMBASTIC

adj (bahm <u>baast</u> ihk)

high-sounding but meaningless; ostentatiously lofty in style

The lawyer's speeches were mostly *bombastic*; his outrageous claims had no basis in fact.

BOVINE

adj (<u>boh</u> vien)

relating to cows; having qualities characteristic of a cow, such as sluggishness or dullness

His *bovine* demeanor did nothing to engage me.

BRAGGART

noun (<u>braag</u> uhrt)

a person who brags or boasts in a loud and empty manner

Usually the biggest *braggart* at the company party, Susan's boss was unusually quiet at this year's event.

BROACH

verb (brohch)

to mention or suggest for the first time

Sandy wanted to go to college away from home, but he didn't know how to *broach* the topic with his parents.

KAPLAN

BUCOLIC

adj (byoo <u>kah</u> lihk)

pastoral, rural

My aunt likes the hustle and bustle of the city, but my uncle prefers a more *bucolic* setting.

BURNISH

verb (<u>buhr</u> nihsh)

to polish; to make smooth and bright

Mr. Frumpkin loved to stand in the sun and *burnish* his luxury car.

BURSAR

noun (<u>buhr</u> suhr) (<u>buhr</u> sahr)

a treasurer or keeper of funds

The *bursar* of the school was in charge of allocating all scholarship funds.

CACHE

noun (caash)

a hiding place; stockpile

It's good to have a *cache* where you can stash your cash.

CACOPHONY

noun (kuh <u>kah</u> fuh nee)

a jarring, unpleasant noise

As I walked into the open-air market after my nap, a *cacophony* of sounds surrounded me.

CALUMNY

noun (<u>kaa</u> luhm nee)

a false and malicious accusation; misrepresentation

The unscrupulous politician used *calumny* to bring down his opponent in the senatorial race.

CANTANKEROUS

adj (kaan <u>taang</u> kuhr uhs)

having a difficult, uncooperative, or stubborn disposition

The most outwardly *cantankerous* man in the nursing home was surprisingly sweet and loving with his grandchildren.

CAPTIOUS

adj (<u>kaap</u> shuhs)

marked by the tendency to point out trivial faults; intended to confuse in an argument

I resent the way he asked that *captious* question.

CATACLYSMIC

adj (<u>kaat</u> uh <u>klihz</u> mihk)

severely destructive

By all appearances, the storm seemed *cataclysmic*, though it lasted only a short while.

CATALYST

noun (<u>kaat</u> uhl ihst)

something that provokes or speeds up significant change, especially without being affected by the consequences

Technology has been a *catalyst* for the expansion of alternative education, such as home schooling and online courses.

CAUCUS

noun (<u>kaw</u> kuhs)

a closed committee within a political party; a private committee meeting

The president met with the delegated *caucus* to discuss the national crisis.

CAUSTIC

adj (<u>kah</u> stihk)

biting, sarcastic

Writer Dorothy Parker gained her reputation for *caustic* wit, and her tombstone is inscribed with a fittingly clever "Excuse my dust."

CEDE

verb (seed)

to surrender possession of something

Argentina *ceded* the Falkland Islands to Britain after a brief war.

CELERITY

noun (seh <u>leh</u> rih tee)

speed, haste

The celebrity ran past his fans with great *celerity*.

CENSORIOUS

adj (sehn <u>sohr</u> ee uhs)

critical; tending to blame and condemn

Closed-minded people tend to be *censorious* of others.

CERTITUDE

noun (<u>suhr</u> tih tood)

assurance, freedom from doubt

The witness' *certitude* about the night in question had a big impact on the jury.

CESSATION

noun (seh <u>say</u> shuhn)

a temporary or complete halt

The cessation of hostilities ensured that soldiers were able to spend the holidays with their families.

CHARY

adj (<u>chahr</u> ee)

watchful, cautious; extremely shy

Mindful of the fate of the Titanic, the captain was *chary* of navigating the iceberg-filled sea.

CHIMERICAL

adj (kie <u>mehr</u> ih kuhl) (kie <u>meer</u> ih kuhl)

fanciful; imaginary, impossible

The inventor's plans seemed *chimerical* to the conservative businessman from whom he was asking for financial support.

CIRCUITOUS

adj (suhr <u>kyoo</u> ih tuhs)

indirect, roundabout

The venue was only a short walk from the train station, but a roadblock meant I had to take a *circuitous* route.

CIRCUMVENT

verb (suhr kuhm <u>vehnt</u>)

to go around; avoid

Laura was able to *circumvent* the hospital's regulations, slipping into her mother's room long after visiting hours were over.

CLOYING

adj (<u>kloy</u> ing)

sickly sweet; excessive

When Dave and Liz were together their *cloying* affection towards one another often made their friends ill.

COAGULATE

verb (koh <u>aag</u> yuh layt)

to clot; to cause to thicken

Hemophiliacs can bleed to death from a minor cut because their blood does not *coagulate*.

COGENT

adj (<u>koh</u> juhnt)

logically forceful; compelling, convincing

Swayed by the *cogent* argument of the defense, the jury had no choice but to acquit the defendant.

COLLOQUIAL

adj (kuh <u>loh</u> kwee uhl)

characteristic of informal speech

The book was written in a *colloquial* style so it would be user-friendlier.

COMMUTE
verb (kuh <u>myoot</u>)
to change a penalty to a less severe one
In exchange for cooperating with detectives on another case, the criminal had his charges *commuted*.

COMPLACENT
adj (kuhm <u>play</u> sihnt)
self-satisfied, smug
Alfred always shows a *complacent* smile whenever he wins the spelling bee.

COMPLIANT
adj (kuhm <u>plie</u> uhnt)
submissive, yielding
The boss was unused to an assistant who spoke her mind, but he grew to respect the fact that she wasn't *compliant*.

CONCOMITANT
adj (kuh <u>kahm</u> ih tuhnt)
existing concurrently
A double-major was going to be difficult to pull off, especially since Lucy would have to juggle two papers and two exams *concomitantly*.

CONCORD
noun (<u>kahn</u> kohrd)
agreement
The sisters are now in *concord* about the car they had to share.

CONDOLE
verb (kuhn <u>dohl</u>)
to grieve; to express sympathy
My hamster died when I was in third grade, and my friends *condoled* with me and helped bury him in the yard.

CONFLAGRATION
noun (kahn fluh <u>gray</u> shuhn)
big, destructive fire
After the *conflagration* had finally died down, the city center was nothing but a mass of blackened embers.

CONFLUENCE
noun (<u>kahn</u> floo uhns)
the act of two things flowing together; the junction or meeting place where two things meet
At the political meeting, while planning a demonstration, there was a moving *confluence* of ideas between members.

KAPLAN

CONSANGUINEOUS

adj (kahn saang <u>gwihn</u> ee uhs)

having the same lineage or ancestry; related by blood

After having a strange feeling about our relationship for years, I found out that my best friend and I are *consanguineous*.

CONSTERNATION

noun (kahn stuhr <u>nay</u> shuhn)

an intense state of fear or dismay

One would never think that a seasoned hunter would display such *consternation* when a grizzly bear lumbered too close to camp.

CONSTITUENT

noun (kuhn <u>stih</u> choo uhnt)

component, part; citizen, voter

A machine will not function properly if one of its *constituents* is defective.

CONSTRAINT

noun (kuhn <u>straynt</u>)

something that restricts or confines within prescribed bounds

Given the *constraints* of the budget, it was impossible to accomplish my goals.

CONTEMPTUOUS

adj (kuhn <u>tehmp</u> choo uhs)

scornful; expressing contempt

The diners were intimidated by the waiter's *contemptuous* manner.

CONTENTIOUS

adj (kuhn <u>tehn</u> shuhs)

quarrelsome, disagreeable, belligerent

The *contentious* gentleman ridiculed anything anyone said.

CONTIGUOUS

adj (kuhn <u>tihg</u> yoo uhs)

sharing a boundary; neighboring

The two houses had *contiguous* yards so the families shared the landscaping expenses.

CONTINENCE

noun (<u>kahn</u> tih nihns)

self-control, self-restraint

Lucy exhibited impressive *continence* in steering clear of fattening foods, and she lost 50 pounds.

CONVALESCE

verb (kahn vuhl <u>ehs</u>)

to recover gradually from an illness

After her bout with malaria, Tatiana needed to *convalesce* for a whole month.

CONVERGENCE
noun (kuhn vehr juhns)
the state of separate elements joining or coming together
A *convergence* of factors led to the tragic unfolding of World War I.

COQUETTE ·
noun (koh keht)
a flirtatious woman
The normally serious librarian could turn into a *coquette* just by letting her hair down.

COTERIE
noun (koh tuh ree)
an intimate group of persons with a similar purpose
Judith invited a *coterie* of fellow stamp enthusiasts to a stamp-trading party.

COUNTERVAIL
verb (kown tuhr vayl)
to act or react with equal force
In order to *countervail* the financial loss the school suffered after the embezzlement, the treasurer raised the price of room and board.

COVERT
adj (koh vuhrt)
secretive, not openly shown
The *covert* military operation wasn't disclosed until after it was determined to be a success.

CULL
verb (kuhl)
to select, weed out
You should *cull* the words you need to study from all the flash cards.

CUMULATIVE
adj (kyoom yuh luh tihv)
increasing, collective
The new employee didn't mind her job at first, but the daily, petty indignities had a *cumulative* demoralizing effect.

CURT
adj (kuhrt)
abrupt, short with words
The grouchy shop assistant was *curt* with one of her customers, which resulted in a reprimand from her manager.

DEARTH

noun (duhrth)

a lack, scarcity, insufficiency

The *dearth* of supplies in our city made it difficult to survive the blizzard.

DEBACLE

noun (dih baa kuhl)

a sudden, disastrous collapse or defeat; a total, ridiculous failure

It was hard for her to show her face in the office after the *debacle* of spilling coffee on her supervisor—three times.

DECLAIM

verb (dih klaym)

to speak loudly and vehemently

At Thanksgiving dinner, our grandfather always *declaims* his right, as the eldest, to sit at the head of the table.

DEFAMATORY

adj (dih faam uh tohr ee)

injurious to the reputation

The tabloid was sued for making *defamatory* statements about the celebrity.

DEMAGOGUE

noun (deh muh gahg) (deh muh gawg)

a leader, rabble-rouser, usually appealing to emotion or prejudice

The dictator began his political career as a *demagogue*, giving fiery speeches in town halls.

DENIZEN

noun (dehn ih zihn)

an inhabitant, a resident

The *denizens* of the state understandably wanted to select their own leaders.

DERIDE

verb (dih ried)

to laugh at contemptuously, to make fun of

As soon as Jorge heard the others *deriding* Anthony, he came to his defense.

DIFFUSE

verb (dih fyooz)

to spread out widely, to scatter freely, to disseminate

They turned on the fan, but all that did was *diffuse* the cigarette smoke throughout the room.

DIGRESS

verb (die grehs)

to turn aside, especially from the main point; to stray from the subject

The professor repeatedly *digressed* from the topic, boring his students.

DILAPIDATED
adj (dih <u>laap</u> ih dayt ihd)
in disrepair, run down
Rather than get discouraged, the architect saw great potential in the *dilapidated* house.

DILUVIAL
adj (dih <u>loo</u> vee uhl)
pertaining to a flood
After she left the water running in the house all day, it looked simply *diluvial*.

DISCOMFIT
verb (dihs <u>kuhm</u> fiht)
to disconcert, to make one lose one's composure
The class clown enjoyed *discomfiting* her classmates whenever possible.

DISCRETE
adj (dih <u>skreet</u>)
individually distinct, separate
What's nice about the CD is that each song functions as a *discrete* work and also as part of the whole compilation.

DISINGENUOUS
adj (<u>dihs</u> ihn <u>jehn</u> yoo uhs)
giving a false appearance of simple frankness; misleading
It was *disingenuous* of him to suggest that he had no idea of the requests made by his campaign contributors.

DISINTERESTED
adj (dihs <u>ihn</u> trih stihd) (dihs <u>ihn</u> tuh reh stihd)
fair-minded, unbiased
A fair trial is made possible by the selection of *disinterested* jurors.

DISPASSIONATE
adj (dihs <u>paash</u> ih niht)
unaffected by bias or strong emotions; not personally or emotionally involved in something
Ideally, photographers should be *dispassionate* observers of what goes on in the world.

DISSIDENT
adj (<u>dihs</u> ih duhnt)
disagreeing with an established religious or political system
The *dissident* had been living abroad and writing his criticism of the government from an undisclosed location.

DOCTRINAIRE
adj (dahk truh <u>nayr</u>)
rigidly devoted to theories without regard for practicality; dogmatic
The professor's manner of teaching was considered *doctrinaire* for such a liberal school.

DOGGED

adj (<u>daw</u> guhd)

stubbornly persevering

The police inspector's *dogged* determination helped him catch the thief.

DOLEFUL

adj (<u>dohl</u> fuhl)

sad, mournful

Looking into the *doleful* eyes of the lonely pony, the girl yearned to take him home.

DOUR

adj (<u>doo</u> uhr) (<u>dow</u> uhr)

sullen and gloomy; stern and severe

The *dour* hotel concierge demanded payment for the room in advance.

EFFLUVIA

noun (ih <u>floo</u> vee uh)

waste; odorous fumes given off by waste

He took out the garbage at 3 A.M. because the *effluvia* had begun wafting into the bedroom.

ELEGY

noun (<u>eh</u> luh jee)

a mournful poem, usually about the dead

A memorable *elegy* was read aloud for the spiritual leader.

ELUDE

verb (ee <u>lood</u>)

to avoid cleverly, to escape the perception of

Somehow, the runaway *eluded* detection for weeks.

EMOLLIENT

adj (ih <u>mohl</u> yuhnt)

soothing, especially to the skin

After being out in the sun for so long, the *emollient* cream was a welcome relief on my skin.

EMULATE

verb (<u>ehm</u> yuh layt)

to strive to equal or excel, to imitate

Children often *emulate* their parents.

ENCUMBER

verb (ehn <u>kuhm</u> buhr)

to weigh down, to burden

The distractions of the city *encumbered* her attempts at writing.

ENJOIN
verb (ehn <u>joyn</u>)
to direct or impose with urgent appeal, to order with emphasis; to forbid
Patel is *enjoined* by his culture from eating beef.

EPOCHAL
adj (<u>ehp</u> uh kuhl) (ehp <u>ahk</u> uhl)
momentous, highly significant
The Supreme Court's *epochal* decision will no doubt affect generations to come.

EPONYMOUS
adj (ih <u>pahn</u> uh muhs)
giving one's name to a place, book, restaurant
Macbeth was the *eponymous* protagonist of Shakespeare's play.

EQUIVOCATE
verb (ih <u>kwihv</u> uh kayt)
to avoid committing oneself in what one says, to be deliberately unclear
Not wanting to implicate himself in the crime, the suspect *equivocated* for hours.

ERSATZ
adj (uhr <u>sahtz</u>)
being an artificial and inferior substitute or imitation
The *ersatz* strawberry shortcake tasted more like plastic than like real cake.

ESCHEW
verb (ehs <u>choo</u>)
to shun; to avoid (as something wrong or distasteful)
The filmmaker *eschewed* artifical light for her actors, resulting in a stark movie style.

ESPOUSE
verb (ih <u>spowz</u>)
to take up and support as a cause; to marry
Because of his beliefs, he could not *espouse* the use of capital punishment.

ESPY
verb (ehs <u>peye</u>)
to catch sight of, glimpse
Amidst a crowd in black clothing, she *espied* the colorful dress that her friend was wearing.

EUPHEMISM
noun (<u>yoo</u> fuh mihz uhm)
an inoffensive and agreeable expression that is substituted for one that is considered offensive
The funeral director preferred to use the *euphemism* "passed away" instead of the word "dead."

KAPLAN

EUTHANASIA

noun (yoo thun <u>nay</u> zhuh)

the practice of ending the life of terminally ill individuals; assisted suicide

Euthanasia has always been the topic of much moral debate.

EXCORIATE

verb (ehk <u>skohr</u> ee ayt)

to censure scathingly; to express strong disapproval of

The three-page letter to the editor *excoriated* the publication for printing the rumor without verifying the source.

EXPONENT

noun (<u>ehk</u> spoh nuhnt)

one who champions or advocates

The vice president was an enthusiastic *exponent* of computer technology.

EXPOUND

verb (ihk <u>spownd</u>)

to explain or describe in detail

The teacher *expounded* on the theory of relativity for hours.

EXPUNGE

verb (ihk <u>spuhnj</u>)

to erase, eliminate completely

The parents' association *expunged* the questionable texts from the children's reading list.

EXTIRPATE

verb (<u>ehk</u> stuhr payt)

to root out, eradicate, literally or figuratively; to destroy wholly

The criminals were *extirpated* after many years of investigation.

EXTRAPOLATION

noun (ihk <u>strap</u> uh lay shuhn)

using known data and information to determine what will happen in the future, prediction

Through the process of *extrapolation*, we were able to determine which mutual funds to invest in.

EXTRINSIC

adj (ihk <u>strihn</u> sihk) (ihk <u>strihn</u> zihk)

external, unessential; originating from the outside

"Though they are interesting to note," the meeting manager claimed, "those facts are *extrinsic* to the matter under discussion."

EXTRUDE

verb (ihk <u>strood</u>)

to form or shape something by pushing it out, to force out, especially through a small opening

We watched in awe as the volcano *extruded* molten lava.

FACETIOUS

adj (fuh <u>see</u> shuhs)

witty, humorous

Her *facetious* remarks made the uninteresting meeting more lively.

FACILE

adj (<u>faa</u> suhl)

easily accomplished; seeming to lack sincerity or depth; arrived at without due effort

Given the complexity of the problem, it seemed a rather *facile* solution.

FALLACIOUS

adj (fuh <u>lay</u> shuhs)

tending to deceive or mislead; based on a fallacy

The *fallacious* statement "the Earth is flat" misled people for many years.

FEBRILE

adj (<u>fehb</u> ruhl) (<u>fee</u> bruhl)

feverish, marked by intense emotion or activity

Awaiting the mysterious announcement, there was a *febrile* excitement in the crowd.

FECKLESS

adj (<u>fehk</u> lihs)

ineffective, worthless

Anja took on the responsibility of caring for her aged mother, realizing that her *feckless* sister was not up to the task.

FEIGN

verb (fayn)

to pretend, to give a false appearance of

Though she had discovered they were planning a party, she *feigned* surprise so as not to spoil the festivities.

FERAL

adj (<u>fehr</u> uhl)

suggestive of a wild beast, not domesticated

Though the animal-rights activists did not want to see the *feral* dogs harmed, they offered no solution to the problem.

FICTIVE

adj (<u>fihk</u> tihv)

fictional, relating to imaginative creation

She found she was more productive when writing *fictive* stories rather than autobiographical stories.

FILIBUSTER

verb (<u>fihl</u> ih buhs tuhr)

to use obstructionist tactics, especially prolonged speech making, in order to delay something

The congressman read names from the phonebook in an attempt to *filibuster* a pending bill.

FITFUL

adj (<u>fiht</u> fuhl)

intermittent, lacking steadiness; characterized by irregular bursts of activity

Her *fitful* breathing became cause for concern, and eventually, she phoned the doctor.

FLIPPANT

adj (<u>flihp</u> uhnt)

marked by disrespectful lightheartedness or casualness

Her *flippant* response was unacceptable and she was asked again to explain herself.

FLOUT

verb (flowt)

to scorn, to disregard with contempt

The protestors *flouted* the committee's decision and hoped to sway public opinion.

FODDER

noun (<u>fohd</u> uhr)

raw material, as for artistic creation, readily abundant ideas or images

The governor's hilarious blunder was good *fodder* for the comedian.

FOREGO

verb (fohr <u>goh</u>)

to precede, to go ahead of

Because of the risks of the expedition, the team leader made sure to *forego* the climbers.

FORGO

verb (fohr <u>goh</u>)

to do without, to abstain from

As much as I wanted to *forgo* statistics, I knew it would serve me well in my field of study.

FORMIDABLE
adj (<u>fohr</u> mih duh buhl) (fohr <u>mih</u> duh buhl)
fearsome, daunting; tending to inspire awe or wonder
The wrestler was not very big, but his skill and speed made him a *formidable* opponent.

FORTITUDE
noun (<u>fohr</u> tih tood)
strength of mind that allows one to encounter adversity with courage
Months in the trenches exacted great *fortitude* of the soldiers.

FORTUITOUS
adj (fohr <u>too</u> ih tuhs)
by chance, especially by favorable chance
After a *fortuitous* run-in with an agent, Roxy won a recording contract.

FRENETIC
adj (freh <u>neht</u> ihk)
frantic, frenzied
The employee's *frenetic* schedule left him little time to socialize.

FULSOME
adj (<u>fool</u> suhm)
abundant; flattering in an insincere way
The king's servant showered him with *fulsome* compliments in hopes of currying favor.

FURLOUGH
noun (<u>fuhr</u> loh)
a leave of absence, especially granted to soldier or a prisoner
After seeing months of combat, the soldier received a much-deserved *furlough*.

FURTIVE
adj (<u>fuhr</u> tihv)
sly, with hidden motives
The *furtive* glances they exchanged made me suspect they were up to something.

GALVANIZE
verb (<u>gaal</u> vuh niez)
to shock; to arouse awareness
The closing down of another homeless shelter *galvanized* the activist group into taking political action.

GAMELY
adj (<u>gaym</u> lee)
spiritedly, bravely
The park ranger *gamely* navigated the trail up the steepest face of the mountain.

GAUCHE

adv (gohsh)

lacking social refinement

Snapping one's fingers to get a waiter's attention is considered *gauche*.

GRANDILOQUENCE

noun (graan <u>dihl</u> uh kwuhns)

pompous talk; fancy but meaningless language

The headmistress was notorious for her *grandiloquence* at the lectern and her ostentatious clothes.

GREGARIOUS

adj (greh <u>gaar</u> ee uhs)

outgoing, sociable

Unlike her introverted friends, Susan was very *gregarious*.

GROTTO

noun (<u>grah</u> toh)

a small cave

Alone on the island, Philoctetes sought shelter in a *grotto*.

HARANGUE

verb (huh <u>raang</u>)

to give a long speech

Maria's parents *harangued* her when she told them she'd spent her money on magic beans.

HEDONIST

noun (<u>hee</u> duhn ihst)

one who pursues pleasure as a goal

Michelle, an admitted *hedonist*, lays on the couch eating cookies every Saturday.

HEGEMONY

noun (hih <u>jeh</u> muh nee)

the domination of one state or group over its allies

When Germany claimed *hegemony* over Russia, Stalin was outraged.

HERETICAL

adj (huh <u>reh</u> tih kuhl)

departing from accepted beliefs or standards, oppositional

Considering the conservative audience, her comments seemed *heretical*.

HIATUS

noun (hie <u>ay</u> tuhs)

a gap or interruption in space, time, or continuity

After a long *hiatus* in Greece, the philosophy professor returned to the university.

HISTRIONICS
noun (hihs tree <u>ahn</u> ihks)
deliberate display of emotion for effect; exaggerated behavior calculated for effect
With such *histrionics*, she should really consider becoming an actress.

HUBRIS
noun (<u>hyoo</u> brihs)
excessive pride or self-confidence
Nathan's *hubris* spurred him to do things that many considered insensitive.

HUSBAND
verb (<u>huhz</u> buhnd)
to manage economically; to use sparingly
The cyclist paced herself at the start of the race, knowing that if she *husbanded* her resources she'd have the strength to break out of the pack later on.

HYPOCRITE
noun (<u>hih</u> puh kriht)
one who puts on a false appearance of virtue; one who criticizes a flaw he in fact possesses
What a *hypocrite*: He criticizes those who wear fur, but then he buys a leather shearling coat.

IGNOBLE
adj (ihg <u>noh</u> buhl)
having low moral standards, not noble in character; mean
The photographer was paid a princely sum for the picture of the self-proclaimed ethicist in the *ignoble* act of pick-pocketing.

ILLUSORY
adj (ih <u>loo</u> suhr ee) (ih <u>loos</u> ree)
producing illusion, deceptive
The desert explorer was devastated to discover that the lake he thought he had seen was in fact *illusory*.

IMBIBE
verb (ihm <u>bieb</u>)
to receive into the mind and take in, absorb
If I always attend class, I can *imbibe* as much knowledge as possible.

IMPASSIVE
adj (ihm <u>pahs</u> sihv)
absent of any external sign of emotion, expressionless
Given his *impassive* expression, it was hard to tell whether he approved of my plan.

IMPERIOUS

adj (ihm <u>pihr</u> ee uhs)

commanding, domineering; urgent

Though the king had been a kind leader, his daughter was *imperious* and demanding during her rule.

IMPERTURBABLE

adj (<u>ihm</u> puhr <u>tuhr</u> buh buhl)

unshakably calm and steady

No matter how disruptive the children became, the babysitter remained *imperturbable*.

IMPLACABLE

adj (ihm <u>play</u> kuh buhl) (ihm <u>plaa</u> kuh buhl)

inflexible; not capable of being changed or pacified

The *implacable* teasing was hard for the child to take.

IMPORTUNATE

adj (ihm <u>pohr</u> chuh niht)

troublesomely urgent; extremely persistent in request or demand

Her *importunate* appeal for a job caused me to grant her an interview.

IMPRECATION

noun (ihm prih <u>kay</u> shuhn)

a curse

Spouting violent *imprecations*, Hank searched for the person who had vandalized his truck.

IMPUDENT

adj (<u>ihm</u> pyuh duhnt)

marked by cocky boldness or disregard for others

Considering the judge had been lenient in her sentence, it was *impudent* of the defendant to refer to her by her first name.

IMPUGN

verb (ihm <u>pyoon</u>)

to call into question; to attack verbally

"How dare you *impugn* my motives?" protested the lawyer, on being accused of ambulance chasing.

IMPUTE

verb (ihm <u>pyoot</u>)

to lay the responsibility or blame for, often unjustly

It seemed unfair to *impute* the accident on me, especially since they were the ones who ran the red light.

INCANDESCENT
adj (ihn kahn <u>dehs</u> uhnt)
shining brightly
The *incandescent* glow of the moon made it a night I'll never forget.

INCARNADINE
adj (ihn <u>kaar</u> nuh dien) (ihn <u>kaar</u> nuh dihn)
red, especially blood red
The *incarnadine* lipstick she wore made her look much older than she was.

INCHOATE
adj (ihn <u>koh</u> iht)
being only partly in existence; imperfectly formed
For every page of the crisp writing that made it into the final book, Jessie has 10 pages of *inchoate* rambling that made up the first draft.

INCIPIENT
adj (ihn <u>sihp</u> ee uhnt)
beginning to exist or appear; in an initial stage
The *incipient* idea seemed brilliant, but they knew it needed much more development.

INCORRIGIBLE
adj (ihn <u>kohr</u> ih juh buhl)
incapable of being corrected or amended; difficult to control or manage
"You're *incorrigible*," yelled the frustrated mother to her son, in the middle of his third tantrum of the day.

INCREDULOUS
adj (ihn <u>krehj</u> uh luhs)
unwilling to accept what is true, skeptical
The Lasky children were *incredulous* when their parents told them they were moving to Alaska.

INDOMITABLE
adj (ihn <u>dahm</u> ih tuuh buhl)
incapable of being conquered
Climbing Mount Everest would seem an *indomitable* task, but it has been done many times.

INGRATIATE
verb (ihn <u>gray</u> shee ayt)
to gain favor with another by deliberate effort, to seek to please somebody so as to gain an advantage
The new intern tried to *ingratiate* herself with the managers so that they might consider her for a future job.

KAPLAN

INHERENT

adj (ihn <u>hehr</u> ehnt)

involving the essential character of something, built-in, inborn

The class was dazzled by the experiment and as a result more likely to remember the *inherent* scientific principle.

INQUEST

noun (<u>ihn</u> kwehst)

an investigation, an inquiry

The police chief ordered an *inquest* to determine what went wrong.

INSENSATE

adj (ihn <u>sehn</u> sayt) (ihn <u>sehn</u> siht)

lacking sensibility and understanding, foolish

The shock of the accident left him *insensate*, but after some time, the numbness subsided and he was able to tell the officer what had happened.

INSOLENT

adj (<u>ihn</u> suh luhnt)

insultingly arrogant, overbearing

After having spoken with three *insolent* customer service representatives, Shelly was relieved when the fourth one sympathized with her complaint.

INSULAR

adj (<u>ihn</u> suh luhr) (<u>ihn</u> syuh luhr)

characteristic of an isolated people, especially having a narrow viewpoint

It was a shock for Kendra to go from her small high school, with her *insular* group of friends, to a huge college with students from all over the country.

INSUPERABLE

adj (ihn <u>soo</u> puhr uh buhl)

incapable of being surmounted or overcome

Insuperable as our problems may seem, I'm confident we'll come out ahead.

INTER

verb (ihn <u>tuhr</u>)

to bury

After giving the masses one last chance to pay their respects, the leader's body was *interred*.

INTERLOCUTOR

noun (ihn tuhr <u>lahk</u> yuh tuhr)

ones who takes part in conversation

Though always the *interlocutor*, the professor actually preferred that his students guide the class discussion.

INTERNECINE

adj (ihn tuhr <u>nehs</u> een)

mutually destructive; equally devastating to both sides

Though it looked as though there was a victor, the *internecine* battle benefited no one.

INTERREGNUM

noun (ihn tuhr <u>rehg</u> nuhm)

a temporary halting of the usual operations of government or control

The new king began his reign by restoring order that the lawless *interregnum* had destroyed.

INTIMATION

noun (ihn tuh <u>may</u> shuhn)

a subtle and indirect hint

Abby chose to ignore Babu's *intimation* that she wasn't as good a swimmer as she claimed.

INTRACTABLE

adj (ihn <u>traak</u> tuh buhl)

not easily managed or manipulated

Intractable for hours, the wild horse eventually allowed the rider to mount.

INTRANSIGENT

adj (ihn <u>traan</u> suh juhnt) (ihn <u>traan</u> zuh juhnt)

uncompromising, refusing to abandon an extreme position

His *intransigent* positions on social issues cost him the election.

INTREPID

adj (ihn <u>trehp</u> ihd)

fearless, resolutely courageous

Despite freezing winds, the *intrepid* hiker completed his ascent.

INUNDATE

verb (<u>ihn</u> uhn dayt)

to cover with a flood; to overwhelm as if with a flood

The box office was *inundated* with requests for tickets to the award-winning play.

INVETERATE

adj (ihn <u>veht</u> uhr iht)

firmly established, especially with respect to a habit or attitude

An *inveterate* risk-taker, Lori tried her luck at bungee-jumping.

IRASCIBLE

adj (ih <u>raas</u> uh buhl)

easily angered, hot-tempered

One of the most *irascible* barbarians of all time, Attila the Hun ravaged much of Europe during his time.

IRONIC

adj (ie <u>rahn</u> ihk)

poignantly contrary or incongruous to what was expected

It was *ironic* to learn that shy Wendy from high school grew up to be the loud-mouth host of the daily talk show.

IRREVERENT

adj (ih <u>rehv</u> uhr uhnt)

disrespectful in a gentle or humorous way

Kevin's *irreverent* attitude toward the principal annoyed the teacher but amused the other children.

ITINERANT

adj (ie <u>tihn</u> uhr uhnt)

wandering from place to place; unsettled

The *itinerant* tomcat came back to the Johansson homestead every two months.

JETTISON

verb (<u>jeht</u> ih zuhn) (<u>jeht</u> ih suhn)

to discard, to get rid of as unnecessary or encumbering

The sinking ship *jettisoned* its cargo in a desperate attempt to reduce its weight.

JOCULAR

adj (<u>jahk</u> yuh luhr)

playful, humorous

The *jocular* old man entertained his grandchildren for hours.

JUNTA

noun (<u>hoon</u> tuh) (<u>juhn</u> tuh)

a small governing body, especially after a revolutionary seizure of power

Only one member of the *junta* was satisfactory enough to be elected once the new government was established.

KISMET

noun (<u>kihz</u> meht) (<u>kihz</u> miht)

destiny, fate

When Eve found out that Garret also played the harmonica, she knew their meeting was *kismet*.

LAMPOON

verb (laam <u>poon</u>)

to ridicule with satire

The mayor hated being *lampooned* by the press for his efforts to improve people's politeness.

LARGESS
noun (laar <u>jehs</u>)
generous giving (as of money) to others who may seem inferior
She'd always relied on her parent's *largess*, but after graduation, she had to get a job.

LAUDABLE
adj (<u>law</u> duh buhl)
deserving of praise
Kristin's dedication is *laudable*, but she doesn't have the necessary skills to be a good paralegal.

LAX
adj (laaks)
not rigid, loose; negligent
Because our delivery boy is *lax*, the newspaper often arrives sopping wet.

LEVITY
noun (<u>leh</u> vih tee)
an inappropriate lack of seriousness, overly casual
The joke added needed *levity* to the otherwise serious meeting.

LEXICON
noun (<u>lehk</u> sih kahn)
a dictionary; a stock of terms pertaining to a particular subject or vocabulary
The author coined the term Gen-X, which has since entered the *lexicon*.

LIBERTARIAN
noun (lih buhr <u>tehr</u> ee uhn)
one who advocates individual rights and free will
The *libertarian* was always at odds with the conservatives.

LIBERTINE
noun (<u>lihb</u> uhr teen)
a free thinker, usually used disparagingly; one without moral restraint
The *libertine* took pleasure in gambling away his family's money.

LICENTIOUS
adj (lih <u>sehn</u> shuhs)
immoral; unrestrained by society
Conservative citizens were outraged by the *licentious* exploits of the free-spirited artists living in town.

LILLIPUTIAN
adj (lihl ee <u>pyoo</u> shun)
very small
Next to her Amazonian roommate, the girl seemed *lilliputian*.

KAPLAN

LIMBER
adj (<u>lihm</u> buhr)
flexible, capable of being shaped
After years of doing yoga, the elderly man was remarkably *limber*.

LITHE
adj (lieth)
moving and bending with ease; marked by effortless grace
The dancer's *lithe* movements proved her to be a rising star in the ballet corps.

LOQUACIOUS
adj (loh <u>kway</u> shuhs)
talkative
She was naturally *loquacious*, which was always a challenge when she was in a library or movie theater.

MACABRE
adj (muh <u>kaa</u> bruh) (muh <u>kaa</u> buhr)
having death as a subject; dwelling on the gruesome
Martin enjoyed *macabre* tales about werewolves and vampires.

MACROCOSM
noun (<u>maak</u> roh cahz uhm)
the whole universe; a large-scale reflection of a part of the greater world
Some scientists focus on a particular aspect of space, while others study the entire *macrocosm* and how its parts relate to one another.

MALAISE
noun (maa <u>layz</u>)
a feeling of unease or depression
During his presidency, Jimmy Carter spoke of a "national *malaise*" and was subsequently criticized for being too negative.

MALAPROPISM
noun (<u>maal</u> uh prahp ihz uhm)
the accidental, often comical, use of a word which resembles the one intended, but has a different, often contradictory meaning
Everybody laughed at the *malapropism* when instead of saying "public broadcasting" the announcer said "public boredcasting."

MALEDICTION
noun (maal ih <u>dihk</u> shun)
a curse, a wish of evil upon another
The frog prince looked for a princess to kiss him and put an end to the witch's *malediction*.

MALEVOLENT
adj (muh <u>lehv</u> uh luhnt)
exhibiting ill will; wishing harm to others
The *malevolent* gossiper spread false rumors with frequency.

MALFEASANCE
noun (maal <u>fee</u> zuhns)
wrongdoing or misconduct, especially by a public official
Not only was the deputy's *malfeasance* humiliating, it also spelled the end of his career.

MALLEABLE
adj (<u>maal</u> ee uh buhl)
easily influenced or shaped, capable of being altered by outside forces
The welder heated the metal before shaping it because the heat made it *malleable*.

MANNERED
adj (<u>maan</u> uhrd)
artificial or stilted in character
The portrait is an example of the *mannered* style that was favored in that era.

MAVERICK
noun (<u>maav</u> rihk) (<u>maav</u> uh rihk)
an independent individual who does not go along with a group
The senator was a *maverick* who was willing to vote against his own party's position.

MAWKISH
adj (<u>maw</u> kihsh)
sickeningly sentimental
The poet hoped to charm his girlfriend with his flowery poem, but its *mawkish* tone sickened her instead.

MEGALOMANIA
noun (<u>mehg</u> uh loh <u>may</u> nee uh)
obsession with great or grandiose performance
Many of the Roman emperors suffered from severe *megalomania*.

MELLIFLUOUS
adj (muh <u>lihf</u> loo uhs)
having a smooth, rich flow
She was so talented that her *mellifluous* flute playing transported me to another world.

MICROCOSM
noun (<u>mie</u> kruh kahz uhm)
a small scale representation of a larger system
This department is in fact a *microcosm* of the entire corporation.

KAPLAN

MILIEU

noun (mihl yoo)

the physical or social setting in which something occurs or develops, environment

The *milieu* at the club wasn't one I was comfortable with, so I left right away.

MISANTHROPE

noun (mihs ahn throhp)

a person who hates or distrusts mankind

Scrooge was such a *misanthrope* that even the sight of children singing made him angry.

MISNOMER

noun (mihs noh muhr)

an error in naming a person or place

Iceland is a *misnomer* since it isn't really icy; the name means "island."

MISSIVE

noun (mihs ihv)

a written note or letter

Priscilla spent hours composing a romantic *missive* for Elvis.

MITIGATE

verb (miht ih gayt)

to make less severe, make milder

A judge may *mitigate* a sentence if it's decided that the crime was committed out of necessity.

MODICUM

noun (mahd ih kuhm)

a small portion, limited quantity

I expect at least a *modicum* of assistance from you on the day of the party.

MOLLIFY

verb (mahl uh fie)

to soothe in temper or disposition

A small raise and increased break time *mollified* the unhappy staff, at least for the moment.

MORDANT

adj (mohr dnt)

biting and caustic in manner and style

Roald Dahl's stories are *mordant* alternatives to bland stories intended for kids.

MORES

noun (mawr ayz)

fixed customs or manners; moral attitudes

In keeping with the *mores* of ancient Roman society, Nero held a celebration every weekend.

MOROSE

adj (muh <u>rohs</u>) (maw <u>rohs</u>)

gloomy, sullen

After hearing that the internship had been given to someone else, Lenny was *morose* for days.

MOTE

noun (moht)

a small particle, speck

Monica's eye watered, irritated by a *mote* of dust.

MUTABILITY

noun (myoo tuh <u>bihl</u> uh tee)

the quality of being capable of change, in form or character; susceptibility of change

The actress lacked the *mutability* needed to perform in the improvisational play.

MYOPIC

adj (mie <u>ahp</u> ihk) (mie <u>oh</u> pihk)

lacking foresight, having a narrow view or long-range perspective

Not wanting to spend a lot of money up front, the *myopic* business owner would likely suffer the consequences later.

NEBULOUS

adj (<u>neh</u> <u>byoo</u> luhs)

vague, undefined

The candidate's *nebulous* plans to fight crime made many voters skeptical.

NECROMANCY

noun (<u>nehk</u> ruh maan see)

the practice of communicating with the dead in order to predict the future

The practice of *necromancy* supposes belief in survival of the soul after death.

NEFARIOUS

adj (nih <u>fahr</u> ee uhs)

intensely wicked or vicous

Nefarious deeds are never far from an evil-doer's mind.

NEONATE

noun (<u>nee</u> uh nayt)

a newborn child

The *neonate* was born prematurely so she's still in the hospital.

NIHILISM

noun (<u>nie</u> hihl iz uhm)

the belief that traditional values and beliefs are unfounded and that existence is useless; the belief that conditions in the social organization are so bad as to make destruction desirable

Robert's *nihilism* expressed itself in his lack of concern with the norms of moral society.

NOMENCLATURE

noun (<u>noh</u> muhn klay chuhr)

a system of scientific names

In botany class, we learned the *nomenclature* used to identify different species of roses.

NON SEQUITUR

noun (nahn <u>sehk</u> wih tuhr)

a statement that does not follow logically from anything previously said

After the heated political debate, her comment about cake was a real *non sequitur*.

NOVEL

adj (<u>nah</u> vuhl)

new and not resembling anything formerly known

Piercing any part of the body other than the earlobes was *novel* in the 1950s, but now it is quite common.

OBDURATE

adj (<u>ahb</u> duhr uht)

stubbornly persistent, resistant to persuasion

The president was *obdurate* on the matter, and no amount of public protest could change his mind.

OBFUSCATE

verb (<u>ahb</u> fyoo skayt)

to confuse, make obscure

Benny always *obfuscates* the discussion by bringing in irrelevant facts.

OBSTINATE

adj (<u>ahb</u> stih nuht)

unreasonably persistent

The *obstinate* journalist would not reveal his source, and thus, was jailed for 30 days.

OLFACTORY

adj (ohl <u>faak</u> tuh ree)

relating to the sense of smell

Whenever she entered a candle store, her *olfactory* sense was awakened.

OLIGARCHY
noun (<u>oh</u> lih gaar kee)
a government in which a small group exercises supreme control
In an *oligarchy*, the few who rule are generally wealthier and have more status than the others.

ONUS
noun (<u>oh</u> nuhs)
a burden, an obligation
Antonia was beginning to feel the *onus* of having to feed her friend's cat for the month.

OPINE
verb (oh <u>pien</u>)
to express an opinion
At the "Let's Chat Talk Show," the audience member *opined* that the guest was in the wrong.

OPPORTUNIST
noun (aap ore <u>too</u> nist)
one who takes advantage of any opportunity to achieve an end, with little regard for principles
The *opportunist* wasted no time in stealing the idea and presenting it as his own.

OPPROBRIOUS
adj (uh <u>proh</u> bree uhs)
disgraceful, shameful
She wrote an *opprobrious* editorial in the newspaper about the critic who tore her new play to shreds.

ORNERY
adj (<u>ohr</u> nuh ree)
having an irritable disposition, cantankerous
My first impression of the taxi driver was that he was *ornery*, but then he explained that he'd just had a bad day.

OSCILLATE
verb (<u>ah</u> sihl ayt)
to swing back and forth like a pendulum; to vary between opposing beliefs or feelings
The move meant a new house in a lovely neighborhood, but she missed her friends, so she *oscillated* between joy and sadness.

OSSIFY
verb (<u>ah</u> sih fie)
to change into bone; to become hardened or set in a rigidly conventional pattern
The forensics expert ascertained the body's age based on the degree to which the facial structure had *ossified*.

OSTRACIZE

verb (<u>ahs</u> truh size)

to exclude from a group by common consent

Despite the fact that Tabatha had done nothing wrong, her friends *ostracized* her.

OUST

verb (owst)

to remove from position by force; eject

After President Nixon so offensively lied to the country during Watergate, he was *ousted* from office.

PAEAN

noun (<u>pee</u> uhn)

a tribute, a song or expression of praise

He considered his newest painting a *paean* to his late wife.

PALATIAL

adj (puh <u>lay</u> shuhl)

relating to a palace; magnificent

After living in a cramped studio apartment for years, Alicia thought the modest one bedroom looked downright *palatial*.

PALIMPSEST

noun (<u>pahl</u> ihmp sehst)

an object or place having diverse layers or aspects beneath the surface

Years ago, paper was very expensive, so the practice was to write over previous words, creating a *palimpsest* of writing.

PALPABLE

adj (<u>pahlp</u> uh buhl)

capable of being touched or felt; easily perceived

The tension was *palpable* as I walked into the room.

PALTRY

adj (<u>pawl</u> tree)

pitifully small or worthless

Bernardo paid the ragged boy the *paltry* sum of 25 cents to carry his luggage all the way to the hotel.

PANACHE

noun (puh <u>nahsh</u>)

flamboyance or dash in style and action

Leah has such *panache* when planning parties, even when they're last-minute affairs.

PANDEMIC

adj (paan <u>deh</u> mihk)

occurring over a wide geographic area and affecting a large portion of the population

Pandemic alarm spread throughout Colombia after the devastating earthquake.

PANEGYRIC

noun (paan uh <u>geer</u> ihk)

elaborate praise; formal hymn of praise

The director's *panegyric* for the donor who kept his charity going was heart-warming.

PARADIGM

noun (<u>paar</u> uh diem)

an outstandingly clear or typical example

The new restaurant owner used the fast-food giant as a *paradigm* for expansion into new locales.

PARAGON

noun (<u>paar</u> uh gon)

a model of excellence or perfection

She's the *paragon* of what a judge should be: honest, intelligent, and just.

PARAMOUNT

adj (<u>paar</u> uh mownt)

supreme, of chief importance

It's of *paramount* importance that we make it back to camp before the storm hits.

PARE

verb (payr)

to trim off excess, reduce

The cook's hands were sore after she *pared* hundreds of potatoes for the banquet.

PARIAH

noun (puh <u>rie</u> ah)

an outcast

Once he betrayed those in his community, he was banished and lived the life of a *pariah*.

PATENT

adj (<u>paa</u> tehnt)

obvious, evident

Moe could no longer stand Frank's *patent* fawning over the boss and so confronted him.

PATHOGENIC

adj (paa thoh jehn ihk)

causing disease

Bina's research on the origins of *pathogenic* microorganisms should help stop the spread of disease.

PATRICIAN

adj (puh trih shuhn)

aristocratic

Though he really couldn't afford an expensive lifestyle, Claudius had *patrician* tastes.

PATRONIZE

verb (pay troh niez)

to act as patron of, to adopt an air of condescension toward; to buy from

LuAnn *patronized* the students, treating them like simpletons, which they deeply resented.

PECULATE

verb (pehk yuh layt)

to embezzle

These days in the news, we read more and more about workers *peculating* the system.

PECUNIARY

adj (pih kyoon nee ehr ee)

relating to money

Michelle's official title was office manager, but she ended up taking on a lot of *pecuniary* responsibilities such as payroll duties.

PELLUCID

adj (peh loo sihd)

transparently clear in style or meaning, easy to understand

Though she thought she could hide her ulterior motives, they were *pellucid* to everyone else.

PENCHANT

noun (pehn chehnt)

an inclination, a definite liking

After Daniel visited the Grand Canyon, he developed a *penchant* for travel.

PENITENT

adj (peh nih tehnt)

expressing sorrow for sins or offenses, repentant

Claiming the criminal did not feel *penitent*, the victim's family felt his pardon should be denied.

PENURY

noun (<u>pehn</u> yuh ree)

an oppressive lack of resources (as money), severe poverty

Once a famous actor, he eventually died in *penury* and anonymity.

PEREGRINATE

verb (<u>pehr</u> ih gruh nayt)

to travel on foot

It has always been a dream of mine to *peregrinate* from one side of Europe to the other with nothing but a backpack.

PHALANX

noun (<u>fay</u> laanks)

a compact or close-knit body of people, animals, or things

A *phalanx* of guards stood outside the prime minister's home day and night.

PHILISTINE

noun (<u>fihl</u> uh steen)

a person who is guided by materialism and is disdainful of intellectual or artistic values

The *philistine* never even glanced at the rare violin in his collection but instead kept an eye on its value and sold it at a profit.

PHILOLOGY

noun (fih <u>lahl</u> uh jee)

the study of ancient texts and languages

Philology was the predecessor to modern-day linguistics.

PHLEGMATIC

adj (flehg <u>maa</u> tihk)

having a sluggish, unemotional temperament

His writing was energetic but his *phlegmatic* personality wasn't suited for television, so he turned down the interview.

PIQUE

verb (peek)

to arouse anger or resentment in; provoke

His continual insensitivity *piqued* my anger.

PLAINTIVE

adj (<u>playn</u> tihv)

expressive of suffering or woe, melancholy

The *plaintive* cries from the girl trapped in the tree were heard by all.

PLATITUDE

noun (<u>plaa</u> tuh tood)

overused and trite remark

Instead of the usual *platitudes*, the comedian gave a memorable and inspiring speech to the graduating class.

PLEBEIAN

adj (plee <u>bee</u> uhn)

crude or coarse; characteristic of commoners

After five weeks of rigorous studying, the graduate settled in for a weekend of *plebeian* socializing and television watching.

PLUCKY

adj (<u>pluh</u> kee)

courageous; spunky

The *plucky* young nurse dove into the foxhole, determined to help the wounded soldier.

POLITIC

adj (<u>pah</u> luh tihk)

shrewd and crafty in managing or dealing with things

She was wise to curb her tongue and was able to explain her problem to the judge in a respectful and *politic* manner.

POLYGLOT

noun (<u>pah</u> lee glaht)

a speaker of many languages

Ling's extensive travels have helped her to become a true *polyglot*.

PORE

verb (pohr)

to read studiously or attentively

I've *pored* over this text, yet I still can't understand it.

PORTENTOUS

adj (pohr <u>tehn</u> tuhs)

foreshadowing, ominous; eliciting amazement and wonder

Everyone thought the rays of light were *portentous* until they realized a nine-year-old was playing a joke on them.

POSIT

verb (<u>pohz</u> iht)

to assume as real or conceded; propose as an explanation

Before proving the math formula, we needed to *posit* that x and y were real numbers.

POTABLE

adj (<u>poh</u> tuh buhl)

suitable for drinking

Though the water was *potable*, it tasted terrible.

POTENTATE

noun (<u>poh</u> tehn tayt)

a ruler; one who wields great power

Alex was much kinder before he assumed the role of *potentate*.

PRECARIOUS

adj (prih <u>caa</u> ree uhs)

lacking in security or stability; dependent on chance or uncertain conditions

Given the *precarious* circumstances, I chose to opt out of the deal completely.

PRECIPITOUS

adj (pree <u>sih</u> puh tuhs)

steep

The *precipitous* cave was daunting for the first-time climber.

PRESAGE

noun (<u>preh</u> sihj)

something that foreshadows; a feeling of what will happen in the future

The demolition of the Berlin Wall was a *presage* to the fall of the Soviet Union.

PRESTIDIGITATION

noun (<u>prehs</u> tih <u>dihj</u> ih <u>tay</u> shuhn)

a cleverly executed trick or deception; sleight of hand

My hunch was that he won the contest not so much as a result of real talent, but rather through *prestidigitation*.

PRETERNATURAL

adj (pree tuhr <u>naach</u> uhr uhl)

existing outside of nature; extraordinary; supernatural

We were all amazed at her *preternatural* ability to recall smells from her early childhood.

PRIMEVAL

adj (priem <u>ee</u> vuhl)

ancient, primitive

The archaeologist claimed that the skeleton was of *primeval* origin, though in fact it was the remains of a modern-day monkey.

PRODIGAL

adj (<u>prah</u> dih guhl)

recklessly extravagant, wasteful

The *prodigal* expenditures on the military budget during a time of peace created a stir in the cabinet.

PROFFER

verb (<u>prahf</u> uhr)

to offer for acceptance

The deal *proffered* by the committee satisfied all those at the meeting, ending a month-long discussion.

PROGENITOR

noun (proh <u>jehn</u> uh tuhr)

an ancestor in the direct line, forefather; founder

Though he had been born here, his *progenitors* were from India.

PROLIFERATE

verb (proh <u>lih</u> fuhr ayt)

to grow by rapid production of new parts; increase in number

The bacteria *proliferated* so quickly that even the doctor was surprised.

PROMULGATE

verb (<u>prah</u> muhl gayt)

to make known by open declaration, proclaim

The publicist *promulgated* the idea that the celebrity had indeed gotten married.

PROPENSITY

noun (proh <u>pehn</u> suh tee)

a natural inclination or preference

She has a *propensity* for lashing out at others when stressed, so we leave her alone when she's had a rough day.

PROSAIC

adj (proh <u>say</u> ihk)

relating to prose (as opposed to poetry); dull, ordinary

Simon's *prosaic* style bored his writing teacher to tears, though he thought he had an artistic flair.

PROSCRIBE

verb (proh <u>skrieb</u>)

to condemn or forbid as harmful or unlawful

Consumption of alcohol was *proscribed* in the country's constitution, but the ban was eventually lifted.

PROSTRATE

adj (<u>prah</u> strayt)

lying face downward in adoration or submission

My friends teased me for lying *prostrate* when I met my favorite musician.

PROVINCIAL

adj (pruh <u>vihn</u> shuhl)

limited in outlook, narrow, unsophisticated

Having grown up in the city, Anita sneered at the *provincial* attitudes of her country cousins.

PROXY

noun (<u>prahk</u> see)

a person authorized to act for someone else

In the event the shareholder can't attend the meeting, he'll send a *proxy*.

PSEUDONYM

noun (<u>soo</u> duh nihm)

a fictitious name, used particularly by writers to conceal identity

Though George Eliot sounds as though it's a male name, it was the *pseudonym* that Marian Evans used when she published her classic novel *Middlemarch*.

PUGILISM

noun (<u>pyoo</u> juhl ih suhm)

boxing

Pugilism has been defended as a positive outlet for aggressive impulses.

PUISSANT

adj (<u>pwih</u> sihnt) (<u>pyoo</u> sihnt)

powerful

His memoir was full of descriptions of *puissant* military heroics, but most were exaggerations or outright lies.

PUNCTILIOUS

adj (puhngk <u>tihl</u> ee uhs)

concerned with precise details about codes or conventions

The *punctilious* student never made spelling errors on her essays.

PUNDIT

noun (<u>puhn</u> diht)

one who gives opinions in an authoritative manner

The *pundits* on television are often more entertaining than the sitcoms.

PURLOIN

verb (<u>puhr</u> loyn)

to steal

His goal was to *purloin* the documents he felt belonged to him.

PURPORT

verb (puhr <u>pohrt</u>)

to profess, suppose, claim

Brad *purported* to be an opera lover, but he fell asleep at every performance he attended.

RANCOR

noun (<u>raan</u> kuhr)

bitter hatred

Having been teased mercilessly for years, Herb became filled with *rancor* toward those who had humiliated him.

RANKLE

verb (<u>raang</u> kuhl)

to cause anger and irritation

At first the kid's singing was adorable, but after 40 minutes it began to *rankle*.

RAPACIOUS

adj (ruh <u>pay</u> shuhs)

taking by force; driven by greed

Sea otters are so *rapacious* that they consumer 10 times their body weight in food every day.

RAPT

adj (raapt)

deeply absorbed

The story was so well performed that the usually rowdy children were *rapt* until the final word.

RAREFY

verb (<u>rayr</u> uh fie)

to make rare, thin, or less dense

The atmosphere *rarefies* as altitude increases, so the air atop a mountain is too thin to breathe.

RAZE

verb (rayz)

to tear down, demolish

The house had been *razed*; where it once stood, there was nothing but splinters and bricks.

REACTIONARY

adj (ree aak shuhn ayr ee)

marked by extreme conservatism, especially in politics

Her *reactionary* beliefs were misunderstood by her friends.

RECAPITULATE

verb (ree kuh pihch yoo layt)

to review by a brief summary

After the long-winded president had finished his speech, his assistant *recapitulated* for the press the points he had made.

RECIDIVISM

noun (rih sihd uh vih zihm)

a tendency to relapse into a previous behavior, especially criminal behavior

According to statistics, the *recidivism* rate for criminals is quite high.

REFRACT

verb (rih fraakt)

to deflect sound or light

The crystal *refracted* the rays of sunlight so they formed a beautiful pattern on the wall.

REFUTE

verb (rih fyoot)

to contradict, discredit

She made such a persuasive argument that nobody could *refute* it.

RELEGATE

verb (reh luh gayt)

to send into exile, banish; assign

Because he hadn't scored any goals during the season, Abe was *relegated* to the bench for the championship game.

REMISSION

noun (rih mih shuhn)

a lessening of intensity or degree

The doctor told me that the disease had gone into *remission*.

REMUNERATION

noun (rih myoo nuh ray shuhn)

payment for goods or services or to recompense for losses

You can't expect people to do this kind of boring work without some form of *remuneration*.

REPLETE

adj (rih <u>pleet</u>)

abundantly supplied, complete

The gigantic supermarket was *replete* with consumer products of every kind.

REPOSE

noun (rih <u>pohz</u>)

relaxation, leisure

After working hard every day in the busy city, Mike finds his *repose* on weekends playing golf with friends.

REPREHENSIBLE

adj (rehp ree <u>hehn</u> suh buhl)

blameworthy, disreputable

Lowell was thrown out of the restaurant because of his *reprehensible* behavior toward the other patrons.

REPROVE

verb (rih <u>proov</u>)

to criticize or correct, usually in a gentle manner

Mrs. Hernandez *reproved* her daughter for staying out late and not calling.

REQUITE

verb (rih <u>kwiet</u>)

to return or repay

Thanks for offering to lend me $1,000, but I know I'll never be able to *requite* your generosity.

RESCIND

verb (rih <u>sihnd</u>)

to repeal, cancel

After the celebrity was involved in a scandal, the car company *rescinded* its offer of an endorsement contract.

RESILIENT

adj (rih <u>sihl</u> yuhnt)

able to recover quickly after illness or bad luck; able to bounce back to shape

Psychologists say that being *resilient* in life is one of the keys to success and happiness.

RESOLUTE

adj (<u>reh</u> suh <u>loot</u>)

marked by firm determination

Louise was *resolute*: She would get into medical school no matter what.

RESPLENDENT

adj (rih splehn dihnt)

splendid, brilliant

The bride looked *resplendent* in her gown and sparkling tiara.

REVILE

verb (rih veye uhl)

to criticize with harsh language, verbally abuse

The artist's new installation was *reviled* by critics who weren't used to the departure from his usual work.

RHETORIC

noun (reh tuhr ihk)

the art of speaking or writing effectively; skill in the effective use of speech

Lincoln's talent for *rhetoric* was evident in his beautifully expressed Gettysburg Address.

RIFE

adj (rief)

abundant prevalent especially to an increasing degree; filled with

The essay was so *rife* with grammatical errors that it had to be rewritten.

ROSTRUM

noun (rahs truhm)

an elevated platform for public speaking

Though she was terrified, the new member of the debate club approached the *rostrum* with poise.

SACCHARINE

adj (saa kuh ruhn)

excessively sweet or sentimental

Geoffrey's *saccharine* poems nauseated Lucy, and she wished he'd stop sending them.

SACRILEGIOUS

adj (saak rih lihj uhs)

impious, irreverent toward what is held to be sacred or holy

It's considered *sacrilegious* for one to enter a mosque wearing shoes.

SALIENT

adj (say lee uhnt)

prominent, of notable significance

His most *salient* characteristic is his tendency to dominate every conversation.

SANCTIMONIOUS

adj (saangk tih moh nee uhs)

hypocritically devout; acting morally superior to another

The *sanctimonious* columnist turned out to have been hiding a gambling problem that cost his family everything.

SATIATE

verb (say shee ayt)

to satisfy (as a need or desire) fully or to excess

After years of journeying around the world with nothing but backpacks, the friends had finally *satiated* their desire to travel.

SATURNINE

adj (saat uhr nien)

cold and steady in mood, gloomy; slow to act

Her *saturnine* expression made her hard to be around.

SAVANT

noun (suh vahnt)

a person of learning; especially one with knowledge in a special field

The *savant* so impressed us with his knowledge that we asked him to come speak at our school.

SCRUPULOUS

adj (skroop yuh luhs)

acting in strict regard for what is considered proper; punctiliously exact

After the storm had destroyed their antique lamp, the Millers worked to repair it with *scrupulous* care.

SEAMY

adj (see mee)

morally degraded, unpleasant

The tour guide avoided the *seamy* parts of town.

SECULAR

adj (seh kyoo luhr)

not specifically pertaining to religion, relating to the world

Although his favorite books were religious, Ben also read *secular* works such as mysteries.

SEDITION

noun (seh dih shuhn)

behavior that promotes rebellion or civil disorder against the state

Li was arrested for *sedition* after he gave a fiery speech in the main square.

SEMINAL
adj (<u>seh</u> muhn uhl)
influential in an original way, providing a basis for further development; creative
The scientist's discovery proved to be *seminal* in the area of quantum physics.

SEQUESTER
verb (suh <u>kweh</u> stuhr)
to set apart, seclude
When juries are *sequestered*, it can take days, even weeks, to come up with a verdict.

SERAPHIC
adj (seh <u>rah</u> fihk)
angelic, sweet
Selena's *seraphic* appearance belied her nasty, bitter personality.

SIMIAN
adj (<u>sih</u> mee uhn)
apelike; relating to apes
Early man was more *simian* in appearance than is modern man.

SINECURE
noun (<u>sien</u> ih kyoor)
a well-paying job or office that requires little or no work
The corrupt mayor made sure to set up all his relatives in *sinecures* within the administration.

SOBRIQUET
noun (<u>soh</u> brih <u>kay</u>) (<u>soh</u> brih <u>keht</u>)
a nickname
One of former president Ronald Reagan's *sobriquets* was "The Gipper."

SOJOURN
noun (<u>soh</u> juhrn)
a temporary stay, visit
After graduating from college, Iliani embarked on a *sojourn* to China.

SOLICITOUS
adj (suh <u>lih</u> sih tuhs)
anxious, concerned; full of desire, eager
Overjoyed to see the pop idol in her presence, the *solicitous* store owner stood ready to serve.

SOPHOMORIC

adj (sahf <u>mohr</u> ihk)

exhibiting great immaturity and lack of judgment

After Sean's *sophomoric* behavior, he was grounded for weeks.

SPARTAN

adj (<u>spahr</u> tihn)

highly self-disciplined; frugal, austere

When he was in training, the athlete preferred to live in a *spartan* room so he could shut
out all distractions.

SPECIOUS

adj (<u>spee</u> shuhs)

having the ring of truth but actually being untrue; deceptively attractive

After I followed up with some research on the matter, I realized that the charismatic
politician's argument had been *specious*.

SPORTIVE

adj (<u>spohr</u> tihv)

frolicsome, playful

The lakeside vacation meant more *sportive* opportunities for the kids than the culinary
tour through France.

SQUALID

adj (<u>skwa</u> lihd)

filthy and degraded as the result of neglect or poverty

The *squalid* living conditions in the building outraged the new tenants.

STALWART

adj (<u>stahl</u> wuhrt)

marked by outstanding strength and vigor of body, mind, or spirit

The 85-year old went to the market every day, impressing her neighbors with her *stalwart*
routine.

STASIS

noun (<u>stay</u> sihs)

a state of static balance or equilibrium; stagnation

The rusty, ivy-covered World War II tank had obviously been in *stasis* for years.

STINT

verb (stihnt)

to be sparing or frugal; to restrict with respect to a share or allowance

Don't *stint* on the mayonnaise, because I don't like my sandwich too dry.

STIPULATE

verb (<u>stihp</u> yuh <u>layt</u>)

to specify as a condition or requirement of an agreement or offer

The contract *stipulated* that if the movie was never filmed, the actress got paid anyway.

STRATIFY

verb (<u>straa</u> tuh fie)

to arrange or divide into layers

Schliemann *stratified* the numerous layers of Troy, an archeological dig that remains legendary.

STRIDENT

adj (<u>strie</u> dehnt)

loud, harsh, unpleasantly noisy

The traveler's *strident* manner annoyed the flight attendant, but she managed to keep her cool.

STRINGENT

adj (<u>strihn</u> guhnt)

imposing severe, rigorous standards

Many employees found it difficult to live up to the *stringent* standards imposed by the company.

STYMIE

verb (<u>stie</u> mee)

to block or thwart

The police effort to capture the bank robber was *stymied* when he escaped through a rear window.

SUBTERRANEAN

adj (<u>suhb</u> tuh <u>ray</u> nee uhn)

hidden, secret; underground

Subterranean tracks were created for the trains after it was decided they had run out of room above ground.

SULLY

verb (<u>suh</u> lee)

to tarnish, taint

His outrageous gaffe *sullied* his public image.

SUPERFLUOUS

adj (soo <u>puhr</u> floo <u>uhs</u>)

extra, more than necessary

The extra recommendations Jake included in his application were *superfluous*, as only one was required.

SUPERSEDE

verb (<u>soo</u> puhr <u>seed</u>)

to cause to be set aside; to force out of use as inferior, replace

Her computer was still running version 2.0 of the software, which had been *superseded* by at least three more versions.

SUPPLANT

verb (suh <u>plaant</u>)

to replace (another) by force, to take the place of

The overthrow of the government meant a new leader would *supplant* the former one.

SURMOUNT

verb (suhr <u>mownt</u>)

to conquer, overcome

The blind woman *surmounted* great obstacles to become a well-known trial lawyer.

SYBARITE

noun (<u>sih</u> buh riet)

a person devoted to pleasure and luxury

A confirmed *sybarite*, the nobleman fainted at the thought of having to leave his palace and live in a small cottage.

TACTILE

adj (<u>taak</u> tihl)

producing a sensation of touch

The Museum of Natural History displays objects for people to touch so that they have a *tactile* understanding of how different peoples and animals lived.

TANTAMOUNT

adj (<u>taan</u> tuh mownt)

equal in value or effect

If she didn't get concert tickets to see her favorite band, it would be *tantamount* to a tragedy.

TAUTOLOGICAL

adj (<u>tawt</u> uh <u>lah</u> jih kuhl)

having to do with needless repetition, redundancy

I know he was only trying to clarify things, but his *tautological* statements confused me even more.

TAWDRY

adj (<u>taw</u> dree)

gaudy, cheap, showy

The performer changed into her *tawdry* costume and stepped onto the stage.

TEMERITY

noun (teh mehr ih tee)

unreasonable or foolhardy disregard for danger, recklessness

I offered her a ride since it was late at night, but she had the *temerity* to say she'd rather walk.

TEMPESTUOUS

adj (tehm pehs choo uhs)

stormy, turbulent

Our camping trip was cut short when the mild shower we were expecting turned into a *tempestuous* downpour.

TEMPORAL

adj (tehmp ore uhl)

having to do with time

The story lacked a *temporal* sense, so we couldn't figure out if the events took place in one evening or over the course of a year.

TENACIOUS

adj (teh nay shuhs)

tending to persist or cling; persistent in adhering to something valued or habitual

Securing women's right to vote required a *tenacious* fight.

TENET

noun (teh niht)

a principle, belief, or doctrine accepted by members of a group

One of the *tenets* of the school is that it is not acceptable to cheat.

TENUOUS

adj (tehn yoo uhs)

having little substance or strength; flimsy, weak

Francine's already *tenuous* connection to her cousins was broken when they moved away and left no forwarding address.

TERSE

adj (tuhrs)

concise, brief, free of extra words

Her *terse* style of writing was widely praised by the editors, who had been used to seeing long-winded material.

THWART

verb (thwahrt)

to block or prevent from happening; frustrate, defeat the hopes or aspirations of

The heavy lock *thwarted* his attempt to enter the building.

TITULAR

adj (<u>tihch</u> yoo luhr)

existing in title only; having a title without the functions or responsibilities

Carla was thrilled to be voted Homecoming Queen until somebody explained that the *titular* honor didn't mean she could boss anybody around.

TOADY

noun (<u>toh</u> dee)

one who flatters in the hope of gaining favors

The king was surrounded by *toadies* who rushed to agree with whatever outrageous thing he said.

TORTUOUS

adj (<u>tohr</u> choo uhs)

having many twists and turns; highly complex

To reach the remote inn, the travelers had to negotiate a *tortuous* path.

TOUT

verb (towt)

to praise or publicize loudly or extravagantly

She *touted* her skills as superior to ours, though in fact, we were all at the same level.

TRAJECTORY

noun (truh <u>jehk</u> tuh ree)

the path followed by a moving object, whether through space or otherwise; flight

The *trajectory* of the pitched ball was interrupted by an unexpected bird.

TRANSIENT

adj (<u>traan</u> see uhnt)

passing with time, temporary, short-lived

The reporter lived a *transient* life, staying in one place only long enough to cover the current story.

TRANSITORY

adj (<u>traan</u> sih <u>tohr</u> ee)

short-lived, existing only briefly

The actress's popularity proved *transitory* when her play folded within the month.

TREMULOUS

adj (<u>treh</u> myoo luhs)

trembling, timid; easily shaken

The *tremulous* kitten had been separated from her mother.

TROUNCE

verb (trowns)

to beat severely, defeat

The inexperienced young boxer was *trounced* in a matter of minutes.

TRUCULENT

adj (truhk yuh lehnt)

disposed to fight, belligerent

The bully was initially *truculent,* but eventually stopped picking fights at the least provocation.

TURGID

adj (tuhr jihd)

swollen as from a fluid, bloated

In the process of osmosis, water passes through the walls of *turgid* cells, ensuring that they never contain too much water.

TUTELAGE

noun (toot uh lihj)

guardianship, guidance

Under the *tutelage* of her older sister, the young orphan was able to persevere.

UNCANNY

adj (uhn kaa nee)

so keen and perceptive as to seem supernatural, peculiarly unsettling

Though they weren't related, their resemblance was *uncanny*.

UNCONSCIONABLE

adj (uhn kahn shuhn uh buhl)

unscrupulous; shockingly unfair or unjust

After she promised me the project, the fact that she gave it to someone else is *unconscionable*.

UNTOWARD

adj (uhn tō rd)

difficult to handle or work with

Charli's negative comments at work were a bit untoward.

USURY

noun (yoo zuh ree)

the practice of lending money at exorbitant rates

The moneylender was convicted of *usury* when it was discovered that he charged 50 percent interest on all his loans.

VARIEGATED

adj (<u>vaar</u> ee uh <u>gayt</u> ehd)

varied; marked with different colors

The *variegated* foliage of the jungle allows it to support thousands of animal species.

VEHEMENTLY

adv (<u>vee</u> ih mehnt lee)

marked by extreme intensity of emotions or convictions

She *vehemently* opposed the closing of the neighborhood garden, and was even arrested for protesting when the bulldozers came.

VERACITY

noun (vuhr <u>aa</u> sih tee)

accuracy, truth

She had a reputation for *veracity*, so everyone believed her version of the story.

VERBOSE

adj (vuhr <u>bohs</u>)

wordy

The DNA analyst's answer was so *verbose* that the jury had trouble grasping his point.

VERITABLE

adj (<u>vehr</u> iht uh buhl)

being without question, often used figuratively

My neighbor was a *veritable* goldmine of information when I was writing my term paper on the Civil Rights era because she had been a student organizer and protester.

VERNACULAR

noun (vuhr <u>naa</u> kyoo luhr)

everyday language used by ordinary people; specialized language of a profession

Preeti could not understand the *vernacular* of the South, where she had recently moved.

VERNAL

adj (<u>vuhr</u> nuhl)

related to spring; fresh

Bea basked in the balmy *vernal* breezes, happy that winter was coming to an end.

VICARIOUSLY

adv (vie <u>kaar</u> ee uhs lee)

felt or undergone as if one were taking part in the experience or feelings of another

She lived *vicariously* through the characters in the adventure books she was always reading.

VILIFY
verb (<u>vih</u> lih fie)
to slander, defame
As gossip columnists often *vilify* celebrities, they're usually held in low regard.

VIM
noun (vihm)
vitality and energy
The *vim* with which she worked so early in the day explained why she was so productive.

VINDICATE
verb (<u>vihn</u> dih kayt)
to clear of blame; support a claim
Tess was *vindicated* when her prediction about the impending tornado came true.

VIRULENT
adj (<u>veer</u> yuh luhnt)
extremely poisonous; malignant; hateful
Alarmed at the *virulent* press he was receiving, the militant activist decided to go underground.

VISCERAL
adj (<u>vihs</u> uhr uhl)
instinctive, not intellectual; deep, emotional
When my twin was wounded many miles away, I had a *visceral* reaction.

VITUPERATE
verb (vih <u>too</u> puhr ayt)
to abuse verbally, berate
Vituperating someone is never a constructive way to effect change.

VOCIFEROUS
adj (voh <u>sih</u> fuhr uhs)
loud, noisy
Amid the *vociferous* protests of the members of parliament, the prime minister continued his speech.

VOLLEY
noun (<u>vah</u> lee)
a flight of missiles; round of gunshots
The troops fired a *volley* of bullets at the enemy, but they couldn't be sure how many hit their target.

VOLUBLE

adj (<u>vahl</u> yuh buhl)

talkative, speaking easily, glib

The *voluble* man and his reserved wife proved the old saying that opposites attract.

WAN

adj (wahn)

sickly pale

The sick child had a *wan* face, in contrast to her rosy-cheeked sister.

WANTON

adj (<u>wahn</u> tuhn)

undisciplined, unrestrained; reckless

The townspeople were outraged by the *wanton* display of disrespect when they discovered the statue of the town founder covered in graffiti.

WAX

verb (waaks)

to increase gradually; to begin to be

The moon was *waxing*, and would soon be full.

WIELD

verb (weeld)

to exercise authority or influence effectively

For such a young congressman, he *wielded* a lot of power.

WILY

adj (<u>wie</u> lee)

clever; deceptive

Yet again, the *wily* coyote managed to elude the ranchers who wanted it dead.

WINSOME

adj (<u>wihn</u> suhm)

charming, happily engaging

Dawn gave the customs officers a *winsome* smile, and they let her pass without searching her bags.

WORST

verb (wuhrst)

to gain the advantage over; to defeat

The North *worsted* the South in America's Civil War.

WRY

adj (rie)

bent or twisted in shape or condition; dryly humorous

Every time she teased him, she shot her friends a *wry* smile.

YEN

noun (yehn)

a strong desire, craving

Pregnant women commonly have a *yen* for pickles.

ZENITH

noun (<u>zee</u> nihth)

the point of culmination; peak

The diva considered her appearance at the Metropolitan Opera to be the *zenith* of her career.

ZEPHYR

noun (<u>zeh</u> fuhr)

a gentle breeze; something airy or unsubstantial

The *zephyr* from the ocean made the intense heat on the beach bearable for the sunbathers

Resource Three: **Getting Started: Advice for New Teachers**

So you've passed the CBEST with flying colors and fulfilled all the requirements for becoming a teacher in California or Oregon. Now it's time to put all your learning into practice!

FINDING THE RIGHT POSITION

It is common knowledge that more good teachers are needed across the country. According to the National Center for Education Statistics, approximately two million new teachers will be needed in the United States by 2008–2009 (**nces.ed.gov**). But finding the right job for you can be a daunting process.

1. Do Your Research

First, determine the grade levels and/or subjects that you are most interested in teaching. Make sure you have fulfilled all the qualifications for teaching in your state.

Becoming a Certified Teacher in California

The basic credential requirements for a five-year preliminary credential are as follows:

- Bachelor's degree or higher from an accredited university
- Teacher preparation program
- Passing score on the CBEST
- "Developing English Language Skills"—a reading instruction course
- U.S. Constitution course
- Demonstration of subject competency through a subject matter exam (CSET) and/or subject matter program
- Computer technology course

To teach elementary school, you need the Multiple Subject Teaching Credential, which will allow you to teach preschool, kindergarten, grades 1–12, and adult education. In addition to the requirements above, you must take the:

- Reading Instruction Competence Assessment (RICA)
- CSET

KAPLAN

To teach middle or secondary school, you need a Single Subject Teaching Credential, which will allow you to teach specific subjects in a departmentalized classroom. You may be authorized for preschool, kindergarten, grades 1–5, and adult classes. For your preliminary credential, you must meet the basic requirements above, along with:

- Demonstrating subject matter competency by passing the appropriate CSET exams
- Completing an approved single subject program

For all of the above, you will receive a Professional Clear Credential after fulfilling the basic requirements and the five-year preliminary credential by completing one of two options: the Professional Teacher Induction Program or National Board Certification.

Requirements for teaching special education or vocational education are more complicated. Information on these credentials, along with all the basics, can be found at **teachcalifornia.org**. You may also visit the California Commission on Teacher Credentialing at **ctc.ca.gov**.

Becoming a Certified Teacher in Oregon

For an initial teaching license in Oregon, you need the following.

To teach early childhood/elementary school:

- PRAXIS I Pre-professional Skills Tests (PPST) or CBEST
- ORELA: Multiple Subjects Examination (MSE) Subtests I & II

To teach middle/high school:

- PRAXIS I or CBEST
- ORELA: Multiple Subjects Examination (MSE) Subtests I & II
- PRAXIS II: Subject Assessments

2. Identify Where You Would Like to Work

Make a list of the districts and/or schools where you would most like to work. Many school districts have websites on which they post job openings. In addition, you should call the district office to find out if there are any positions open and what their application procedures are. The California Department of Education website has a directory of school districts at **cde.ca.gov/re/sd/**. An Academic Performance Index for California schools can be found at **api.cde.ca.gov**. Go to **teachcalifornia.org** for a general overview of teaching in California and choosing a school district.

In Oregon, you can find a list of schools and districts at **www.ode.state.or.us/search/results/?id=227**. School report cards are listed at **www.ode.state.or.us/search/results/?id=116**.

Use the Internet as a resource. In addition to the many general websites for job hunters, there are websites devoted solely to teaching jobs. A few websites will ask you for a subscription fee, but there are many others with free listings. A list of some of these sites, including those specific to California and Oregon, can be found at the end of this chapter.

Attend Job Fairs

Job fairs are a good way to learn about openings and to network with other education professionals. Many schools within the California State University and University of California host teaching job fairs. In addition, use resources such as the California Association for Employment in Education, **caeelink.org/fairs.htm**, or the Oregon Professional Educator Fair website, **teachoregon.com/ospa/opef/**, to find a job fair near you. Several of the websites for job seekers listed at the end of this chapter also have job fair listings by state.

Remember that you are assessing potential employers as much as they are assessing you. Consider asking the following:

- What is the first professional development opportunity offered to new teachers?
- What additional duties outside the classroom are expected of teachers?
- When can I expect to meet my mentor?
- What is the top school-wide priority this year?
- What kinds of materials or resources would be available in my classroom? (if applicable)
- What is your policy on lesson planning?

You may also want to ask about the demographics of the student population and what kinds of unique challenges they present.

Sign Up for Substitute Teaching

Substitute teaching can be another good strategy for getting your foot in the door in a particular school or district, even if there are no permanent jobs available. Think of this as an opportunity to impress principals and to learn from other teachers about possible openings. You can even submit your resume to the principals in the schools where you are substitute teaching and give them the chance to observe you in the classroom.

STARTING IN THE CLASSROOM

Don't get disillusioned if you're not immediately comfortable in your role as a teacher. Give yourself time to adjust, and don't hesitate to ask for advice from others. Be persistent about finding a mentor who can provide support during your first year and beyond. Try to find one in your subject area and determine how much experience you would like that person to have. For the sake of convenience, it's a good idea to find someone who has a similar class schedule or daily routine.

Teach Rules and Respect

With students, be friendly but firm. Establish clear routines and consistent disciplinary measures early on. This way, the students have a firm understanding of what is expected of them and when certain behaviors are appropriate. Have the principal review your disciplinary plan to make certain that he or she will support it and that there aren't any potential legal issues. Be aware of how cliques and social hierarchies impact classroom dynamics, and don't underestimate the power of your own advice.

Although disciplinary issues vary according to grade level, there are some general tips you may find helpful in setting rules in the classroom:

- Often, troublesome students misbehave merely to get your attention. Reduce this negative behavior by paying the least amount of attention when a student is acting out and giving that child your full attention when he or she is behaving.
- When it comes to establishing classroom rules, allow your students to have some input. This will increase their sense of empowerment and respect for the rules.
- Convince *all* of your students that they are worthwhile and capable. It is easy to assume that struggling students are lazy or beyond help—do not allow yourself to fall into this trap.
- When disciplining students, absolutely avoid embarrassing them in any way, especially in front of their peers.
- Double standards and favoritism will lose you the respect of all your students—always be firm, fair, and consistent. Never talk down to your students.
- Avoid becoming too chummy with your students. Young teachers often feel that they must make "friends" with students, particularly in the older grades. However, it's important to maintain some professional distance and to establish yourself as an authority figure.
- Admit your mistakes. If you wrongly accuse a student of doing something she did not do, make an inappropriate joke, or reprimand a student more harshly than necessary, be sure to apologize and explain. If a parent or administrator criticizes you for your mistake, calmly explain how you felt at that moment and why. Also, explain how you plan on handling that kind of situation in the future.

Do Your Homework

Any veteran teacher will tell you that you will spend almost as many hours working outside the classroom as you do with your students. Preparing lessons and grading homework and tests can take an enormous amount of time, so it's a good idea to be as organized as possible.

Also consider what your expectations will be:

- Will you grade every homework assignment or just some of them?
- Will you give students an opportunity to earn extra credit?
- What kind of system will you use for grading tests?

Design Lesson Plans Early

Before you start planning, be aware of holidays off, assemblies, and other interruptions. Design your lessons accordingly. Similarly, be sure you know your content, your state's standards, your school's expectations, and the ins and outs of child development. Be prepared with multiple learning styles and differentiated teaching strategies.

Try to develop time-saving strategies. Saving your lesson plan outline as a template on the computer can be very helpful—instead of rewriting the whole plan every day, you can just fill in the blanks.

Establish Rules for Grading Homework

Along with establishing a consistent disciplinary policy early on, it's important to develop grading guidelines. Some teachers set the bar high at the beginning of the year by grading a little tougher than they normally would. Just as many students will underachieve if they think you are a soft grader, they will work hard to meet your expectations if your standards are high. However, it's important to assess your students' abilities and set realistic standards.

Grading every single assignment can get overwhelming; sometimes verbally assessing comprehension is enough. Rubrics are another useful tool for outlining expectations and scoring, as well as making sure you cater to the needs of all your students. They are also effective when students grade each other.

Returning graded assignments as soon as possible sets a good example, keeps your workload manageable, and prevents students' interest from waning. However, you should never use a student's work as an example of what not to do.

Consider sending grades home on a regular basis and getting them signed by a parent in order to keep everyone aware of students' progress. This prevents students and parents from being blindsided by poor grades at report card time.

Don't mistake quietness for comprehension. Check in with all students, because some may be afraid to admit that they don't understand what's going on. If you feel there is a problem, don't wait to address a student's needs. If you believe that a student may have an undiagnosed disability, let your principal know and follow your school's procedure.

Finding tangible rewards for students' achievements is a great way to keep them motivated, particularly if you focus their efforts around gradually earning the rewards. These types of incentive systems work particularly well in the elementary grades.

Deal with Parents Early On

Establish a relationship with parents from the beginning—frequent, positive communication is essential to helping the children attain the best education possible. Here are a few tips for keeping in touch with parents:

- Make phone calls, even if you're just going to leave a message. Doing so will allow you to share good news and help guardians become more familiar with you.
- Give students homework folders that frequently travel between school and home.
- Be ready to deal with breakdowns in communication: it may be necessary to send multiple messages home.
- Send home a short newsletter of things to come.

Set Up Parent-Teacher Conferences

Meeting with parents can often be intimidating for new teachers, particularly if a student is not performing well. It's a good idea to seek guidance from experienced teachers, and communicate with administrators if you encounter problems. In addition, try to follow these general guidelines when talking with parents:

- Remain professional. Choose your words carefully, have good things to say about the student, don't take heated words personally, keep examples of the student's work on hand, and document what is said during the meeting.
- Allow parents to ask the first question. This will help you understand their tone and their concerns.
- Be as thick-skinned as possible when dealing with problems: some parents want to vent a little before getting to the crux of the issue. Let them vent, try to put them at ease, and then look for a solution or compromise.
- If a parent becomes excessively confrontational, inform an administrator.
- Be confident. Listen to what the parents suggest, but also stand up for what you believe is the best course of action.

Build Strong Relationships with Colleagues

Meet as many teachers in the building as you can: not only will you gain valuable insights about the inner workings of the school, but you'll also make new friends. Don't be afraid to step up and ask questions when information isn't offered. Veteran teachers are a tremendous resource for all kinds of information, from labor contracts to strategies for staying sane under pressure. Also, get to know the other new teachers. These people will be valuable sounding boards and will help you feel less alone.

Earn the respect of your colleagues by stepping up to committee work, and by proving yourself to be a reliable, competent teacher. You should also be polite and friendly with the staff and custodians: you'll need their help for all sorts of reasons.

Finally, be professional, timely, and unafraid to calmly share your opinions or disagree with administrators. Your professionalism and enthusiasm will earn you their respect and ensure that your needs are met.

Dealing with Paperwork

Be aware of what kinds of paperwork you need to fill out and file, including the school Improvement Plan, special education forms relating to Individualized Education Plans, budget requests, reading and math benchmarks, and permanent record cards. Try to sit with fellow teachers when filling out forms. Their companionship will make these tedious tasks more fun.

Understanding Unions

Depending on your school district, you may be part of a teacher's union. It is important to gain a clear understanding of union requirements. You'll want to know:

- How much money will be deducted from your paycheck for union dues
- How you can obtain a copy of the most recent union contract

For more information about teachers' unions in California, visit **cta.org/CTA.htm**, the California Teacher's Association, or **cft.org**, the California Federation of Teachers.

For information about unions in Oregon, go to the Oregon Education Association, **www.oregoned.org**.

Allow Yourself "Down Time"

Finally, always give yourself time to wind down and distance yourself from the classroom. This is essential to prevent burnout or resentment over a lack of free time, and will allow you to pursue other interests and personal relationships.

ADDITIONAL RESOURCES

Books

Capel, Susan, Marilyn Leask, and Terry Turner. *Learning to Teach in the Secondary School: A Companion to School Experience*. Oxford: Taylor & Francis, 2005.

Dillon, Justin. *Becoming a Teacher*. Berkshire, England: Open University Press, 2001.

Goodnough, Abby. *Ms. Moffett's First Year: Becoming a Teacher in America*. New York: Public Affairs, 2004.

Howe, Randy. *Training Wheels for Teachers: What I Wish I Had Known My First 100 Days on the Job: Wisdom, Tips, and Warnings from Experienced Teachers*. New York: Kaplan, 2004.

Maloy, Robert W., and Irving Seidman. *The Essential Career Guide to Becoming a Middle and High School Teacher*. Westport, CT: Bergin & Garvey, 1999.

Parkay, Forrest W., and Beverly Hardcastle Stanford. *Becoming a Teacher, 6th edition*. Boston: Allyn & Bacon, 2003.

Shalaway, Linda, and Linda Beech (Editor). *Learning to Teach…Not Just For Beginners*. Jefferson City, MO: Scholastic, 1999.

Staff of U.S.News and World Report. *U.S. News Ultimate Guide to Becoming a Teacher*. Naperville, IL: Sourcebooks, 2004.

Wong, Harry K., and Rosemary T. Wong. *The First Days of School: How to be an Effective Teacher*. Mountain View, CA: Harry K. Wong Publications, 2001.

Magazines and Journals

American Educator

Harvard Educational Review

The New York Times Education Life

Phi Delta Kappan

Internet Resources

teachernet.com/htm/becomingateacher.htm
Community for K–8 educators

pbs.org/firstyear/beaTeacher/
PBS: How to become a teacher

newsweekshowcase.com/teacher-training/
Teacher education and recruitment; teaching as a second career

eric.ed.gov/: Education Resources Information Center
Large teaching and education database

aft.org
American Federation of Teachers

proudtoserveagain.com/index.html
Troops to Teachers program—gives former members of the U.S. military the opportunity to become public school teachers, providing help with certification, job searching, and more

ed.gov
U.S. Department of Education

teach-nology.com
Free and easy-to-use resources for teachers

teachingtips.com
Tips from an experienced teacher

atozteacherstuff.com
A teacher-created site listing online resources and tips

theteachersguide.com

behavioradvisor.com/

kidsource.com

Lesson Plan Sites
www.education-world.com

theteacherscorner.net

lessonplansearch.com

moteachingjobs.com/lessons/mainsearch.cfm

teachnet.com

General Teaching Job Sites
www.jobs2teach.doded.mil/
Part of the Troops to Teachers website

wanttoteach.com/newsite/jobfairs.html
National teaching job fair website

schoolspring.com

teachers-teachers.com

job-hunt.com/academia.shtml

educationjobs.com

abcteachingjobs.com

k12jobs.com

California Resources
cde.ca.gov
California Department of Education

teachcalifornia.org
Info for teachers and those considering it; gives you an opportunity to "try being a teacher" by doing sample teacher's work online; also lists median salaries

teachcalifornia.org/job/index.html
Job listings

cta.org/CTA.htm California Teachers Association
Includes news, workshops, teaching tips, and information on grants and awards; explains the benefits of membership in the CTA, including insurance

www.ctc.ca.gov
California Commission on Teacher Credentialing

california.teachers.net
Includes jobs and chat boards for teachers

edjoin.org
Over 10,000 California job postings for grades K–12

caeelink.org
California Association for Employment in Education

cft.org
California Federation of Teachers

Oregon Resources
ode.state.or.us
Oregon Department of Education

teachoregon.com
Oregon School Personnel Association

teachoregon.com/ospa/opef/
Oregon Professional Educator Fair

cosa.k12.or.us
(Pull down "Member Services" and click on "Job Search")
Confederation of Oregon School Administrators' job listings

www.oregoned.org
Oregon Education Association—teacher's union